SYNTACTIC ANCHORS

One of the major arenas for debate within generative grammar is the nature of paradigmatic relations among words. Intervening in key debates at the interface between syntax and semantics, this book examines the relation between structure and meaning, and analyses how it affects the internal properties of words and corresponding syntactic manifestations. Adapting notions from the Evo-Devo project in biology (the idea of 'co-linearity' between structural units and behavioural manifestations), Juan Uriagereka addresses a major puzzle: how words can be both decomposable so as to be acquired by children, and atomic, so that they do not manifest themselves as modular to adults.

JUAN URIAGEREKA is Professor in the Linguistics Department at the University of Maryland at College Park, USA. His previous publications include *A Course in Minimalist Syntax* (2005, with H. Lasnik) and *Derivations* (2002).

In this series

Series list continued on page after index

CAMBRIDGE STUDIES IN LINGUISTICS

General editors: P. AUSTIN, J. BRESNAN, B. COMRIE, S. CRAIN, W. DRESSLER, C. J. EWEN, R. LASS, D. LIGHTFOOT, K. RICE, I. ROBERTS, S. ROMAINE, N. V. SMITH

Syntactic Anchors: On Semantic Structuring

SYNTACTIC ANCHORS

ON SEMANTIC STRUCTURING

JUAN URIAGEREKA

University of Maryland, College Park

CAMBRIDGE
UNIVERSITY PRESS

CAMBRIDGE UNIVERSITY PRESS
Cambridge, New York, Melbourne, Madrid, Cape Town, Singapore, São Paulo, Delhi

Cambridge University Press
The Edinburgh Building, Cambridge CB2 8RU, UK

Published in the United States of America by Cambridge University Press, New York

www.cambridge.org
Information on this title: www.cambridge.org/9780521865326

First published 2008

Printed in the United Kingdom at the University Press, Cambridge

A catalogue record for this publication is available from the British Library

Library of Congress Cataloging in Publication Data

Uriagereka, Juan.
  Syntactic anchors : on semantic structuring / Juan Uriagereka.
    p. cm. – (Cambridge studies in linguistics ; no 118)
  Includes bibliographical references and index.
  ISBN 978-0-521-86532-6 (hardback : alk. paper)
  1. Grammar, Comparative and general–Syntax. 2. Semantics. 3. Generative
grammar. I. Title. II. Series.
P295.U75 2008
415–dc22
2008004203

ISBN 978-0-521-86532-6 hardback

'Dad, why are other people's words okay, but when I make them up they sound funny?'
(Isabel Uriagereka Herburger, after discussing with her sister Sofia the meaning of their Spanish neologism *desalrevesar*, lit. 'unturnaround'.)

To my life insurance

Contents

Tables

Figures

Acronyms

ACD	antecedent-contained deletion
BPS	bare phrase structure
CCU	condition on chain uniformity
CED	condition on extraction domains
CFC	Case freezing condition
CH	Chomsky Hierarchy
CLT	co-linearity thesis
CT	cue thesis
CU	command unit
DIT	distributed interpretation thesis
DTC	derivational theory of complexity
EC	erasure convention
ECM	exceptional case marking
ECP	empty category principle
EM	external Merge
EPP	extended projection principle
ERP	event-related potential
FI	condition on full interpretation
FSA	finite-state automata
IM	internal Merge
LBA	linear bounded automaton
LCA	linear correspondence axiom
LCT	linear correspondence theorem
LF	Logic Form
LI	lexical item
LIG	linear indexed grammars
LPT	lexical projection thesis
LRC	last resort condition
MAC	minimal array condition
MLC	minimal link condition

MP	Minimalist Program
MSO	multiple spell-out
P&P	principles & parameters
P/W^2	part/whole-to-part/whole thesis
PDA	pushdown automata
PF	Phonetic Form
PIC	phase impenetrability condition
PSC	principle of strong compositionality
SCT	strong compositionality thesis
SMT	strong minimalist thesis
UG	Universal Grammar

Introduction

Generative grammar is a divided field, one of the major arenas for argumentation being the nature of paradigmatic relations among words. The first attempt to address this topic was made by generative semanticists in the 1960s. Their proposal was that such relations are governed by standard syntactic principles which directly manipulate units smaller than words, with words themselves relegated to a surface phenomenon.

This 'decompositionalist' proposal met a reaction from the 'lexicalist' camp, on the basis not of the new theory's elegance, but of its factual support. Paradigmatic relations among words are in fact drastically less systematic, productive and transparent than would result from corresponding syntagmatic relations simply building up phrases. In the heat of battle, unfortunately, the important question being discussed was left unresolved, and each camp continued to pursue their line of reasoning, but the issue has become all the more significant within the current Minimalist Program.

This book makes a new stab at that question, from the perspective of the Evo-Devo project in biology, itself arguably part of an emergent field of complex-dynamic systems – to which minimalism can be seen as making a contribution. The line to be explored here is that both decompositionalists and atomists were right, albeit about two different developmental stages in the language faculty. To put this graphically, it was once common for natural philosophers to treat as members of different species creatures which were simply at different development stages. The argument here will be that a similar phase transition takes human beings from a decompositionalist/generative stage to a lexicalist/atomist one.

In effect the human brain undergoes a metamorphosis of a probably endocrinal origin, roughly around the so-called critical age beyond which new languages are hard to acquire. In the end, it is hard to see how children could literally *latch onto* ten words a day, in the early stages of acquisition, without throwing a fully syntactic net of relations over incoming stuff-to-be-acquired; but it is equally hard to see how that system could ever stabilize into anything if it couldn't bottom out, more or less arbitrarily, into words that – at that new point of stability – are truly atomic.

That general argument, though easy to present in the abstract, is hard to make concrete. This is not surprising. Even atoms are only stable up to a point. In extraordinary conditions they can be destabilized, and features that are otherwise almost impossible to isolate suddenly become 'manipulable', to some extent. There are no fully worked-out theories of how the entire array of those features, in the physical case, happen to yield or not yield stable atoms, and it would be irrational to expect a worked-out theory of these matters in the linguistic instance, where many such theoretical musings are still metaphorical.

Therefore, this book will have nothing to say about why syntactic processes largely do not manipulate features on their own, but work with fully assembled words (feature matrices) instead. Nor will it attempt to explain why, in the rare instances when features do seem manipulable, they are so only in truly local conditions, for which purpose the system is often forced into elaborate processes involving words. Understanding such interactions remains a quest for the future, the present purpose being to focus the matter in terms of the classical battle, to turn it into a research avenue.

Language is both features and words (*is* used in its essential meaning). There wouldn't be a human language without both features and words: no features, no latching into the words that carry them; no words, no fixing concepts as manipulable objects. No attempt will be made here to understand why this is, because even the more modest focus of establishing this solution to an old conundrum carries with it a significant amount of work. The prospect of applying regular syntactic operations to sub-lexical features doesn't work. So what *does* work for those necessary features? Is whatever does the job entirely different or somehow part of syntax in a more or less customary way? And in the end how does all of this relate to the thought it manipulates? Does thought get literally built this way? Or are these sorts of syntactic constructs supposed to correspond to independently formed semantic entities? A more or less linear correspondence? Something else? And so on.

Below those central foundational concerns, the guiding thesis in this book is that semantics is opportunistic, in that it takes all sorts of cues from the syntax *as the derivation unfolds*. This idea will be called the distributed interpretation thesis, or DIT. The DIT is very much akin to what Distributed Morphology does with the mapping to Phonetic Form (PF), except on the 'meaning' side of things. In such radically 'cyclic' systems there are no levels of representation proper; that is, *unified* formal objects with characteristic substantive properties. There can, however, be relevant *components* with similar formal and substantive properties, although we must worry about why the emergent system has the 'points of stability' it does, where interpreted notions can be identified. Intuitively, we cannot blame this on D-structure, S-structure, Logical Form (LF) and the like, since there are literally no such 'cuts' in the ensuing system.

To address that question, the present project relies on an auxiliary conceptual hypothesis, which (taking the notion from Evo-Devo studies) will be called the co-linearity thesis, or CLT. It is based on the idea that syntax and semantics turn out to be narrowly matched, perhaps trivially so. To ground the notion 'syntax', aside from some updated version of the strong minimalist thesis (SMT), it is suggested that we must update, also, the Chomsky Hierarchy (CH). Originally this hierarchy was observed in the study of formal languages, which makes its relevance to the study of natural language questionable to some, starting with Chomsky. There are, however, reasonable ways of recasting the old intuition in terms that remain pertinent to the study of *the generative procedure* underlying natural language. In particular, the relevant levels in the hierarchy can be shown to emerge as a consequence of the systemic memory accessed in each instance by the automaton implementing the grammar: none, some or all of the symbols in a derivation combined with its memory regime (whether symbols are stacked and only the top is accessed, or more possibilities are granted). The updated hierarchy is meaningful within computational systems, and thus can be understood as a primitive for the purposes of the SMT.

From the outset, a familiar taboo must be addressed: the belief that memory conditions only have to do with a system's resources or performance. There are certainly vague resource issues that memory (attention span, physical state, age) poses, which may even vary across individuals and their particular skills. But it is also the case that memory considerations play a key role in linguistic competence. For instance, for a system to allow a word grouping as being *of type X* it must have a built-in way of determining words as belonging to a type. That essentially distinguishes finite-state systems (lacking any such systemic memory) from more complex ones. Among the latter, too, there are differences. A system may allow the manipulation of a symbol X *if symbol Y has already been processed*. That requires a record of a given derivation itself (technically called a *context*). This distinguishes context-free from context-sensitive systems. Within parameters along such lines individual, 'performative', variations are possible; but the considerations themselves are systemic, thus squarely part of competence.

With all of that in mind, semantics can be (ultimately projected as) *a network over maximally stable syntactic objects of the various types within the CH*. That can be interpreted in two ways, one more radical than the other. In the more traditional interpretation, one can argue for the presence of a 'Numeration' component corresponding to maximally analysable *finite-state* CH objects, a 'D-structure' component corresponding to maximally analysable *context-free* CH objects, and an 'LF' component corresponding to maximally analysable *context-sensitive* CH objects. (To insist: in none of these instances are we dealing with levels of representation; we involve, instead, weaker formal objects that simply have the substantive properties of a Numeration, a D-structure, or an LF.) In the radical, in effect eliminative, interpretation there is no such 'correspondence' with interfaces. The (finite-state, context-free, context-sensitive) chunks of structure themselves *are* all that is systemic about the relevant semantic objects. In the first instance we involve three – not one – semantic interfaces; in the second we construct three – again, not one – semantic structures. Then, regardless of whether the idea is interpreted in its eliminative guise or not, 'semantics' is not a unique entity.

One should also address the matter of why the system obeys the distributed interpretation thesis, and does so in terms of the co-linearity thesis. In so doing, this book will conceptualize the CLT as specifically involving the *mapping of an nth order syntax to an nth order semantics*. This is no logical necessity, but it will be argued to make good 'minimalistic' sense. In any case, it will force us to say that the articulation of something as simple as a VP demands various orders of syntactic complexity – characterized through mechanisms that must go beyond first order logic – which correspond to equally multi-dimensional orders of semantic complexity. This turns out to be a fruitful way to understand syntactic arrangements of the Thematic hierarchy sort, and why they correspond to semantic Aktionsart hierarchies.

Reflecting on the present system, Chomsky (2006, p.10) calls it a 'more radical' conception than the one he has maintained in recent years of the interface between the faculty of language and 'semantics', in that (some) properties of 'thought contents' derive from the structures generated by the syntax. Quoting passages from Hinzen (2006) to that effect, he notes that optimally designed faculty of language:

> 'provides forms that a possible human structured meaning may have, leaving a residue of non-structured meanings (concepts), a substantive amount of which we share with other animals that lack syntax [. . .].' These forms are natural objects 'that we can study as such, even though we see them, somewhat miraculously, systematically condition properties of linguistic meaning that we can empirically attest'.

Strictly speaking, all of this is true about what was called above the 'eliminative' interpretation, which Hinzen (2006, 2007) sets out. The 'traditional' interpretation, however, is more directly consistent with Chomsky's own views, particularly his recent 'cyclic' (phase-based) approach. The system may be naturally seen as *cyclic to the limit*, thereby simply distributing the semantic interface(s) all along the derivational flow. At the same time, it should be emphasized that 'cycles' are non-trivial in this approach. That is, the 'cyclic limit' will not be the mere association involved in Merge, in a standard interpretation of the derivational process as obeying a one-at-a-time condition on rule application. Indeed, derivations will be argued to be more parallel in some instances, several (even evaluative) processes occurring at the same time, precisely within cyclic domains. Part of the task ahead is understanding how such cycles emerge.

This book is divided into three parts: a conceptual section (chapters 1 and 2); two empirically-driven sections, one exploring the syntax of argument-taking (chapters 3 through 5) and another going beyond 'core syntax' (chapter 6); and a concluding section (chapters 7 and 8) devoted to a detailed presentation of the overall architecture of the system from a wider perspective.

Chapter 1 starts by reviewing the idea that a mapping exists from context-free D-structures to context-sensitive LFs. The empirical reasons are examined to eliminate the level of representation of D-structure; as it turns out, none of those affect a weaker, more dynamic notion of a substantive *component* of the system. It is then shown how Chomsky effectively assumes all the defining characteristics of a component (though not a level) of D-structure in his recent works. That being the case, the next questions pertain to what are the natural interactions and design mechanisms in the system that make it coalesce into a whole.

Chapter 2 reviews the 'generative semantics' proposal for lexical decomposition and how, despite fatal problems with that approach, the question it addressed is still unresolved. Taking seriously the uniformity and universality in syntax and semantics, and especially their mapping, ways are then considered in which the relevant anchoring relation can be naturally constrained. This leads us to raising the question of whether a multidimensional theory of syntactic representation, which semantic nuances are cued to, is plausible. In the process of examining these matters, it can be shown how much of what has been said in favor of lexical decomposition in the end largely begs the underlying question.

An original take on these questions starts to be developed in chapter 3, to ground mapping processes along the lines of what will be referred to as the part/whole-to-part/whole (P/W^2) thesis. Mechanisms of this sort should, first, be as transparent as possible, on learnability and minimalistic grounds. In addition, for such a co-linearity between syntax and semantics to hold (the CLT) we have to understand what is meant by the specifics of relevant structures that get mapped on both, the syntactic and the semantic sides. This leads us to study part/whole relations, in the guise of 'possessive' dependencies. In the present approach, a proper understanding of possession requires both context-free relations of the conceptual sort and context-sensitive relations of the intentional sort. This duality is central in signaling in the emerging complex syntactic object the dimensional shifts that, it is argued, are required to understand corresponding semantic nuances, both of the 'relational' sort but also, by extension, of the more standard 'thematic' sort. The approach pursued here leads to a relativistic intentional semantics (whereby elements *become* referential – contextually confined if quantificational – if in the appropriate syntactic structure) and ultimately the need for a very dynamic Case theory.

Chapter 4 is aimed at empirically grounding the model called for by the previous chapters; it addresses otherwise puzzling phenomena that can be naturally stated as conditions on derivational stages exploiting a substantive connection with semantic interfaces. Crucially, these interactions are not *output* ones for the derivation: they must be formulated in terms of domains of lexico-conceptual dependency and so-called *surface syntax*, respectively – interface demands that happen *prior* to the derivational output at LF. Pragmatic cues, which are neither lexico-conceptual (predicate/argument) matters nor logico-intentional (scopal) specifications, affect syntactic derivations in some languages, curiously correlating with the personal axis in discourse and a variety of informational specificity nuances. The fact that it is so only in some languages demands a parameterization, hopefully related to the mechanisms under study.

Chapter 5 focuses on how Case conditions affect transformational syntax and corresponding semantic structuring. By analysing Case puzzles in a novel way, an account of the Case Hierarchy is provided, which can be observed in the distribution of Case values within derivational phases. This again relies on a careful distinction between context-free and context-sensitive conditions, and a dynamic interplay between structures obeying both. Case features are uninterpretable. The fact, then, that a hierarchy holds for them is not something that can be summarily dismissed on 'interface demands'. In the present approach Case values themselves can exist only because derivations exist, given cyclic properties that define both (context-free) command units and (context-sensitive) phases – a central argument for the DIT approach. Chapter 5 develops a dynamic system of feature release that distinguishes nominal and verbal combinations, the basis for what will be called 'complement assumption'. This is the mechanism that allows us to relate the 'integral' structures (which articulate theta-structures) argued for in chapter 3 to representations of the head-complement sort – and doing so while keeping internal hierarchical layers of the lexical-implication sort. This, it will be suggested, allows us to use minimalistic components of the system (Case/agreement and conditions on transformations) in substantiating a natural correspondence between syntax and semantics in natural language.

Chapter 6 is devoted to showing that syntax can manifest itself in even simpler guises – anchoring interestingly trivial semantic correlates. We start with the problem posed by iterative expressions, which surprisingly mean very similar things in all languages. This is puzzling for any theory assuming the essential arbitrariness of the syntax/semantics interface. The present solution to this puzzle implies treating the relevant expressions in finite-state fashion: there is not much to interpret in these instances, given such an impoverished support machinery to anchor the relevant semantic structuring, so different languages come up with similar (impoverished) results. This possibility arises only if *all* levels of the CH presupposed by the language faculty are relevant to semantic interpretation(s). Rather than being the locus of merely exotic expressions, it is then argued that 'finite-state syntax' is central to understanding the small clauses we need to get thematic structure off the ground, as well as adjunctal dependencies.

After examining the (formal) nuances of the CH, chapter 7 shows its continued significance within linguistics, albeit admitting that it must be reformulated in terms that are more sensitive to present concerns and machinery. Some interesting experimental cases are also discussed here, which substantiate the relevance of complexity measures of the sort emerging if the CH holds in some form, suggesting that there is room for reconsidering the old derivational theory of complexity in current terms. The chapter then explicitly formulates the distributed interpretation thesis and proposes a way to go into how paradigmatic notions may relate to complexity in syntax. To that effect, a useful concept is introduced from topology, the notion of a *manifold*, and it is then shown how that can help us rationalize Aktionsart arrays.

Finally, in chapter 8 various (standardly assumed) semantic conditions, now sketched within the topological assumptions, are made to more or less naturally correspond to progressively more complex finite-state, context-free and context-sensitive syntactic structures – this constituting the desired co-linearity. The chapter argues that syntactic complexity emerges because of a crucial mismatch between features and categories (sets of features). While the latter allow for context-free relations – as they constitute typed sets – the former do not, and must remain finite-state dependencies. But this has an interesting consequence. When features needing to relate happen to fall in distant areas of a phrase-marker mounted in categorial terms, the system literally warps relevant phrasal objects, so that appropriate features match up in relevantly adjacent terms. This entails a variety of structural adjustments sketched in the chapter, which give us both a rationale for the DIT and for why the stable lexicon is ultimately so different from the dynamic syntax.

Ideas introduced in chapter 8 are meant as a prologue to a more involved project, of the bio-linguistic sort, as mentioned in the epilogue. Readers familiar with the Evo-Devo program will find several echoes of that enterprise, which Uriagereka (1998) made a preliminary attempt to relate to linguistics. Although this book doesn't touch on the biochemical support of the language faculty, linguistic research as characterized here seeks to present Minimalism in a light that makes language searchable within brains, genomes and proteomes.

Readers not interested in the details of the Minimalist Program may wish to skip chapter 1, while those who can live without an analysis of the conceptual underpinnings behind the theses in this book can also skip chapter 2. In other words, one could go directly into the empirical presentation in chapters 3 through 6, where most specifically linguistic phenomena are examined. Regardless of whether one agrees with the goals and solutions presented here, those chapters will introduce data to deal with in any framework. Chapters 7 and, especially, 8 are the most personal. Because of that they are also bound to appear the most controversial. At any rate the most far-reaching, if open-ended, ideas are sketched there.

Chomsky (2006) has described the present program as 'a novel approach to what has been called "naturalization of meaning",' summarizing it with the idea that it is as if syntax carved the path that interpretation must blindly follow. That can be true in two ways, which a transportation metaphor may clarify.

Nature provides the geological backdrop against which – negotiating existing peaks, valleys or faults – a hauling system can be determined. However, that system itself may be more or less controlling. A canal is different from a road in that regard. Relatively little is manufactured in a canal system, other than getting a water source to the relevant topological landscape – as a consequence, also, the system has severe limitations and can be controlled only to some extent and in some circumstances. In contrast, in the road instance an entire infrastructure has to be built upon the natural array – and the result is more controllable. A third way is even more aggressive: a highway is built according to its own demands, ignoring (through tunnels and viaducts) the original topology. The canal and road approaches are both compatible with assigning the underlying syntax as much importance as it's given here; the highway approach is actually the popular one in contemporary semantics, where meaning is not seen as needing naturalization – much less through syntax. At any rate, in both meaning naturalizing scenarios the primacy of the Conceptual/Intentional interface(s) is reduced.

The 'canal' and 'road' scenarios can be distinguished in terms of whether resources are given to purely semantic notions to exploit the properties of the structures generated by the syntax. What was called above the 'eliminative' view implies that satisfaction of Conceptual/Intentional conditions is eliminated; the syntactic anchor is the semantic boat as well, co-linearity between syntax and semantics then reducing to transparency. In contrast the 'traditional' approach allows for a range of semantic resources to exploit the properties of syntactically generated expressions, along with whatever is involved in the use of language to refer, communicate perspicuously and so on; that would still be a genuinely semantic boat, albeit one that only the syntactic anchor can secure. This book will not choose between those compatible interpretations, although, if either one succeeds, as Chomsky puts it, 'SMT and the concept of principled explanation would be correspondingly simplified.'

Acknowledgements

Materials leading to the present text have been presented in venues too numerous to mention, but I want to highlight courses where the issues were discussed in detail and audience participation was particularly helpful. Apart from seminars at Maryland, these include mini-courses at the universities of the Basque Country, Comahue, Illinois, Kanda, Constance, Leiden, Indiana, Potsdam, Seville, and Tsukuba, as well as the Instituto Ortega y Gasset. The bio-linguistics project is impossible without the cross-pollination that happens in some of these open-minded institutions. I have been blessed with my co-authors, cited throughout the book; their expertise beyond narrow syntax is the main reason for whatever originality may hide inside these pages – though they should not be held responsible for any errors springing from my own interpretations of their contributions. In addition I am indebted, for helpful detailed comments on earlier versions of various fragments of this book, to Ángel Gallego, Elena Herburger, Atakan Ince, Terje Lohndal, Roger Martin, Rebecca McKeown, Irene Moyna, Chizuru Nakao, Juan Romero, Usama Soltan, and Asad Sayeed, as well as for the very valuable and fair reviews that this book received. Young-mi Jeong and Ivan Ortega-Santos deserve separate credit for their enormous and much-needed editorial assistance. I am very thankful, also, to Andrew Winnard at Cambridge University Press for his interest in this text, and his advice on various related matters as well as to Lois Sparling who did the final copy-editing, and to Jo Bottrill, who supervised the production process.

1 *In defence of D-structure*

1.1 Introduction

While the relation between expression and meaning is fixed and arbitrary in words, in sentences it is mediated through syntax, a complex system. This then poses the question of how exactly that mediation takes place, whether it too is arbitrary despite the fact of being unfixed, or it is somehow sensitive to the particular derivational dynamics that result in phonetically expressible semantic concepts. Let's call this the Mapping Problem.

Successive stages of the generative enterprise have addressed the Mapping Problem differently. In the Standard Model, syntactic derivations were thought to start in a semantically articulated logical form, which after various adjustments reaches its phonetic form. In contrast, in the current Minimalist Program (MP), those two 'levels of representation' are situated as end-points of a forked derivation, which starts in a purely syntactic object constructed from a list of token words. The latter is the residue of yet a third conception, within the principles & parameters model, for which the starting point of the derivation was a full-fledged level of representation called D(eep)-structure. This level was taken to code lexico-conceptual relations, distinct from the scopal relations achieved through the derivation itself.

A priori, none of these answers to the Mapping Problem seem better or worse: it is an interesting empirical matter to determine which one wins – including possible alternatives. Minimalism, moreover, adds a further twist to the discussion: whichever answer works ought to be demonstrated as *an ideal* one, in some non-trivial sense, if the language faculty is to be seen in this conception as an optimal relation between meaning and its expression (sound or sign).

Wouldn't it be nice if optimality considerations alone could chose between alternative answers to the Mapping Problem? Unfortunately, we face a 'blackbox' sort of puzzle. Whereas it is reasonably clear what we find in the expression side of things, what goes on in the Conceptual/Intentional domain(s) is harder to ascertain. Perhaps if we had as clear a picture on that side as we

1

have on the other, it would be easier to let sheer elegance decide on what the best possible mapping is between the two. But we have what we have, and part of our job is to deepen our understanding of the semantic side by sharpening our judgements about the syntax that carries us there – which we understand reasonably well.

This book can be seen as an exercise of this sort, which wagers for a particular answer: *semantics is 'opportunistic'*, a bit like a needy child. It won't drive the syntactic derivation (as in the Aspects Model) and it won't wait for it to finish either; rather, in a more dynamic fashion, it will take what it can literally as it can, for better and also for worse. This empirical thesis is actually not too far, at least reconstructing history a bit, from either Chomsky's original (1955) proposal – prior to the Aspects Model – or more accurately the cyclic systems that various researchers explored in the 1970s (Bresnan 1971; Jackendoff 1972; Lasnik 1972). In particular, this book will attempt to show that not only is what we can think of as 'higher-order' syntax (arising in context-sensitive terms as the derivation unfolds) subject to interpretation; simpler, 'lower-order' phrasal configurations are, too.[1]

In order to establish that 'dynamic' thesis, the book will start by analysing, in the present chapter, why the idea that there is a directional mapping from context-free D-structures to context-sensitive LFs was given up, or to what extent it really was. In section 2 of the chapter, the empirical reason for eliminating D-structure is presented, and next the technical notion of a 'level of representation' is analysed, and how that differs from a weaker notion of what may be thought of as a 'component' of grammar. Section 3 is devoted to providing arguments that the empirical discovery in point, while surely arguing against the notion of D-structure as a level of representation, has *no bearing on D-structure as a component of grammar*. In section 4 we can see how, despite his rhetoric within the MP, Chomsky himself effectively assumes all the defining characteristics of a component of D-structure. Section 5 examines the question of whether relevant arguments for complex derivations involving conditions on their input remain solid within the program. Section 6 considers different possible ways of coding D-structure information: in LF, in the lexicon, in a separate component of D-structure. Conclusions are presented in section 7, where it is suggested that either we should eliminate D-structure residues within the MP, or else explore ways of rationally incorporating them.

---

1 By 'context' we mean, here, the derivational history of a given phrase-marker. Context-free relations pay no attention to such nuances, while context-sensitive ones (for instance transformations) must.

The rest of the book can be seen as a long argument for that second position. The alternative one is certainly coherent, and equally minimalist,[2] but it should provide ways to explain away the evidence adduced here in favor of the more dynamic view. At any rate, these issues must be raised because, if semantic interpretation is to be dynamic and opportunistic, it won't wait until the end of the derivation. But then we must show that it is profitable for semantics to start interpreting stuff early on, and moreover that, if the system is minimalist, it does so for good reason.

1.2   Why D-structure was eliminated

Let's start with a bit of history, to put things in perspective.

1.2.1   Kearney's example and Lasnik's argument

An unpublished example by Kevin Kearney dramatically questioned the level of D-structure, as understood in the principles and parameters (P&P) system. The context for the argument was Chomsky's (1981, p. 309ff.) discussion of 'Tough'-movement:

(1)   John is easy (for anyone) to please.
       (cf. It is easy (for anyone) to please John.)

Chomsky reasons that:

> the matrix [*John*] is not inserted at D-structure, but is also not moved to the matrix subject position. The only resolution to this paradox . . . is to assume that lexical insertion of the matrix subject is at S-structure in this case . . . We are therefore led to the conclusion that lexical insertion can take place freely. [p. 313]

This is correctly considered a way to 'simplify the theory of lexical insertion'. That said, however, observe Kearney's example:

(2)   A man who is easy (for anyone) to please is easy (for anyone) to convince.

One might be persuaded to insert *John* anywhere in the derivation, but it is harder to accept the *lexical* insertion of *a man who is easy (for anyone) to please*, in the very same context where *John* creates a problem in (1). Howard Lasnik raised this difficulty with Chomsky through personal communication, and they both realized the need for traditional *generalized transformations*, of the sort postulated in Chomsky (1955), to handle the difficulty. If the latter

---

2 See in particular Hornstein *et al.* (2005), and its references.

are part of the grammar, we can (in current terms) merge not just *John*, but also a phrase of arbitrary complexity, such as the (previously assembled) *a man who is easy (for anyone) to please*. But conceding that point undermines D-structure, for the whole purpose of that level of representation was to create a *unified* object to express configurational relations – crucially prior to the occurrence of transformations.

D-structure's troubles started much earlier, however, when generative semanticists proposed getting rid of it.[3] Their classic argument went as follows. Assume syntactic principle P (it does not matter which). Show how assuming P explains why an unattested word *glarf* – whose meaning appears to be composed of X plus Y – may actually *not* arise by relating X to Y, as this would violate P (concrete arguments on this are reviewed in section 2.2.2). Therefore objects like *glarf* – that is, words – do not matter for the linguistic system as much as *the component elements* X and Y, moreover as related through principles like P in relevantly viable conditions. If so D-structure (a collection of grammatical counterparts to *glarf* arranged in terms of principles like P) is a spurious generalization. The linguist must, rather, study X, Y and other similar 'thoughts', and how they arrange themselves to compose surface language.

The fate of that proposal is well-known (see chapter 2), although it is not often admitted that much of the aftermath gave way to assumptions and conditions that are, on the surface at least, not unlike the rejected ones.[4] Differences, of course, exist; for instance, meaning is nowadays typically read off output syntax (LF), whereas in those days it was coded in the input – and that, we will see shortly, makes a significant difference. That said, this book will try to show that the overall problem that led to generative semantics is far from resolved.

1.2.2   *Levels and components*

The fact that we cannot maintain a level of D-structure, for empirical reasons, does not entail that we should get rid of D-structure *information*. That issue would arise anywhere else in the grammar, too. Suppose some crucial empirical argument A questions LF as a level of representation. That in itself does not argue for the need to eliminate an LF *component*, mapping (say) S-structure (or

---

3 See for instance McCawley (1968), Lakoff (1971) or Postal (1972), and also Newmeyer (1980, 1996), Harris (1993), Huck and Goldsmith (1995), and Barsky (1997) for related discussion.

4 This point is critically raised in Seuren (2004); for a more sympathetic view of minimalism, though still admitting connections to generative semantics, see Lasnik and Uriagereka (2005).

any other input component) to the semantic interface. It is entirely possible that A may have nothing to say about the LF component proper, and instead it only affects LF strictly as a unified level of representation.

To see this in detail, let us remind ourselves of what a *level of representation* is, technically, and compare it to a less strict component of the grammar. That way we may be able to decide whether Lasnik's point with Kearney's example does argue, specifically, against the level of D-structure, or it has instead a more radical, and eliminative, consequence on D-structure information at large within the system.

The way Chomsky speaks of those notions is currently tentative: 'A standard assumption,' he observes, 'is that UG [Universal Grammar] specifies certain *linguistic levels*, each a symbolic system ... Each linguistic level provides the means for presenting certain systematic information about linguistic expressions. [UG] must specify the interface levels ... the elements that constitute these levels, and the computations by which they are constructed' (Chomsky 1995, p. 167ff.). Two things are noteworthy here. First, that Chomsky speaks of a 'standard assumption', thus something that may or may not be acceptable as the MP unfolds – with its emphasis in questioning, precisely, traditional, often unmotivated, assumptions. Second, the paragraph just mentioned would read very similarly if we substituted the word 'component' where it uses 'level'. That is, if all we are talking about is the *systematicity* of a given sort of information in a linguistic expression, and how it is organized as it relates to other systems, then we are not really speaking of the technical notion *level of representation*. The more unassuming notion *component* would do.

In *Aspects of the theory of syntax* (1965, chapter 3, fn. 2), Chomsky sums up what we commit to when we seriously speak of levels of representation:

> Linguistic theory provides a (universal) system of *levels of representation*. Each level L is a system based on [1] a set of primes (minimal elements – i.e., an alphabet); [2] the operation of concatenation, which forms strings of primes of arbitrary finite length (the terms and notions all being borrowed from the theory of concatenation algebras – cf. e.g., Rosenbloom [1950]); [3] various relations; [4] a designated class of strings (or sets of strings) of primes called L-markers; [5] a mapping of L-markers onto L′-markers, where L′ is the next 'lower' level (thus levels are arranged in a hierarchy). In particular, on the level P of phrase structure and the level T of transformations we have P-markers and T-markers ... A hierarchy of linguistic levels (phonetic, phonological, word, morphological, phrase structure, transformational structure) can be developed within a uniform framework in this way. For details, see Chomsky (1955). [*Numbers added.*]

Note, first of all, that all of that talk is within *concatenation* algebras. Strictly, none of these notions survive untouched as we move towards what may be called 'merge algebras', which haven't been systematically formalized yet (see chapter 7 for more detailed discussion). Being generous with the formalism, though, we can translate the relevant notions, and much of the paragraph above – specifically an adapted notion 'level of representation' – will survive. Concretely, [2] is where adjustments need to be made, given Minimalist 'bare phrase-structures', which do not involve concatenation (in fact the system takes linear order to obtain only in the PF string); nonetheless, one could relax the definition so as not to demand a linearly organized set of categories to operate on, resulting from Merge.[5] That qualification made, [1] and [3] are straightforward – for levels or for more unassuming components. All that [1] and [3] say is that these are substantive parts of the system, in the primitives they use (symbols from some alphabet) and the relations they allow (e.g. phrases). Whether [5] obtains *trivially* (with no mapping) is an architectural decision; standard minimalism insists on the idea that substantive parts of the model must interface with *language external* systems, and if so the ultimate need for [5] depends on the empirical details of those. If the model is organized as in Chomsky (1995), [5] is irrelevant; but even if [5] did hold, it could be expressed equally well for levels or for less articulated components (e.g. a chain, by definition, is structured from a phrase, whether or not either one of those – phrase or chain – is integrated into a level of representation). Finally we are left with [4]. This is really it: what distinguishes a level from a mere component is whether we can justify *a designated class* of (sets of) strings. There is a *unification* implied in the characterization of that designated class of objects; D-structure is a designated class of phrases; LF is a designated class of chains; PF is a designated class of speech objects and so on. There is no meaningfully unified class of D-structures (P-markers) or S-structures (T-markers) in the derivation of any given sentence. Those *collections* of classes can be regarded as a (weaker) *component* of the system, but not one of its levels of representation.

---

5 Concatenation is normally meant to correspond to mere 'derivational activation' in a one-step-at-a-time (Markovian) derivation, yielding sets of strings. The relevant ensuing linearity need not translate into PF linearity, although it can (and if so it would arguably run in the opposite direction to Kayne's (1994) Linear Correspondence Axiom; see chapter 6 on this, which can actually be used to address a puzzle that arises with adjunct linearization). In the revised minimalist system, derivational activation should, instead, correspond to merged set-theoretic objects.

Although a formal definition is probably unnecessary at this point, for concreteness we may understand a component of the system, in effect, as any kind of information that is syntactically analysable *as a coherent unit*. A level of representation is, of course, that and more, as we have seen: essentially the idea that all such components in a given derivation constitute a unified whole of some sort, from which further operations may be defined. Apart from asking which is a more empirically adequate tool to model the workings of the language faculty – a level or a component – the minimalist must also ask which, if any, is a priori more desirable. If simplicity is relevant, then surely the component trumps the level: its characterization makes fewer commitments and the resulting objects are less complex, in computational terms (a component does not have to involve a collection of objects of *in-principle-arbitrary complexity*).[6] Therefore, one must find strong empirical arguments in favor of the notion of a level of representation if it is to be preferred over that of a corresponding system component.

1.3 Rethinking the case against D-structure

The Kearney/Lasnik argument against D-structure is very serious: 'Tough'-movement shows that we cannot have a 'unified' notion of D-structure. However, as we have just seen, that is in fact the central difference between a level and a component. That said, we must ask a related question.

1.3.1 Is Kearney's an argument against a D-structure component?

Note that each of the sub-parts one has to construct in order to undergo the generalized transformation that Lasnik proposed as a solution to Kearney's puzzle was, in itself, a sort of 'micro-D-structure', prior to the application of transformations. To put it differently, in that pristine derivational moment when only Merge has occurred, *whatever we have* is arguably a D-structure analogue. Granted, that is not a D-structure *level*, but it may perfectly well be a D-structure 'chunk' of the system – part of a D-structure component.

Whether that conclusion ought to be maintained depends on whether, *in the input to derivations*, there is reason to believe that a part of the language faculty is responsible for coding a system based on [1] a set of primes and organized in terms of [2] some associative operation that forms collections of primes of

---

6 An immediate issue arises in what may be thought of as an 'address' problem: how the various chunks of structure that arguably spell-out separately are 'put together' into a coherent unit. See chapter 4 on this.

arbitrary finite length such that [3] non-trivial relations among them can be established. The answer to all these questions is empirical. Yet Chomsky has maintained, in his minimalist works, that there is a *conceptual* reason to answer them prior to investigation. By assumption the language faculty arises only as an optimal device connecting points of interface with extra-linguistic systems. If there is *no point of interface* between the syntactic engine and an outside system that would code information relevant to D-structure, then there should be no such component. On the other hand, we could challenge the major premise. Could there be an interface that is relevant to our purposes? If the answer were Yes, it would be legitimate to postulate a D-structure to represent that juncture.

That option is occasionally forgotten. As noted above, minimalism explores the optimal connection between sound and meaning. Of course 'sound' and 'meaning' interfaces are *empirically* established. In that sense, if it turned out that, in fact, the system also interfaces, say, a visual, tactile, or musical capacity, for all the linguist should care, then so long as the interface and what drives the system there are both optimal, the minimalist should be satisfied. In other words, the key is not in relevant interfaces being 'sound' and 'meaning', specifically; rather, *whatever the interfaces happen to be*, the minimalist issue is accessing them in an optimal way. The empirical task, needless to say, is then to determine what the actual interfaces are.

1.3.2   What are the linguistic interfaces?

In short, nobody knows. That is already important, since although the question is perfectly empirical, the answer should not be a truism, when so much is at stake. These matters are familiar on the 'sound' side of the grammar. When we say that there is a *single* level of PF that interfaces with both the perception and articulation of phonetic sound, what we are subscribing to, in essence, is the Analysis by Synthesis theory (see Poeppel *et al.* [in press] for a recent perspective and references). This is an important empirical finding, which researchers naturally argue for and against. Note in this respect that much important work on signed languages, whose communicative modality is – at least on the surface – quite different, hasn't immediately entailed a crisis on the 'externalization' side of grammar. The relevant interface is or is not of the same sort, depending on whether it targets speech or manual signs; the matter is interesting regardless of what the answer is, and totally consistent with the MP if the relevant mapping is optimal in some appropriate sense. And if it turned out that language could also be externalized on a tactile system, say, so long as we are still within optimality parameters, absolutely nothing changes in the overall reasoning.

Curiously, on the 'meaning' side of the grammar we often do not even pose these questions. Of course, nobody has a complete enough picture of what is implicated in meaning to seriously entertain the possibility that it is coded in terms of one, two, or seven components, alternative or universal. There is, no doubt, a vague intuition that meaning deals with 'intentional' information (of the sort involved in reference, the calculation of truth, and so on), and 'conceptual' information (which distinguishes predicates from arguments, and, among those, sorts of either, and so forth). Surely there are very elaborate formal systems that pack these notions into mathematical artifacts. Whether that does have much, little, or nothing to do with the way human beings actually 'mean' things is anybody's guess. To jump from that to the conclusion that 'there is a *single level of representation* that the system has to optimally interface' seems hasty.

In part the hastiness may come from a traditional philosophical perspective that was never central to the program of structural linguistics, and becomes even less so within the MP. This is the idea that knowledge of language may have something to do with linguistic representation. Philosophically, a representation can be seen as a relation between a subject and a theory of a (formal) language; in that sense, representation is *by definition* intentional, the sort of relation existing between a 'symbol' and 'what it stands for'. But there are two reasons why all of this may not be relevant to the minimalist characterization of the language faculty. First, not even purely linguistic notions ('feature', 'category', 'phrase', 'c-command', and so on) stand in any 'symbolic' relation with regards to what their import is within the grammar; there is no obvious, useful, linguistic gain in saying that 'the feature [+consonantal] represents such-and-such'. Surely an important naturalistic issue arises as to what [+consonantal] (or any such notion) ultimately *is*, but calling its nature representational (in the philosophical sense) hasn't had any consequences. Second, when it comes to more familiar 'reference'-bearing elements, or more generally elements with a denotation (*John*, *book*, *sing*, and the like) not a single theory exists that clarifies what sort of relation takes place between such words and what they denote. This may seem too harsh a comment to make, but the truth is all familiar theories – all of them, really – *presuppose* the relation, in statements of the sort of *'snow' refers to snow*. Indeed, contemporary semantics prides itself in being able to operate without detailed knowledge of that intentional dependency, solely on the basis of the algebraic combinations that work above those relations, which are deemed either irrelevant – where the theory bottoms out – or something that psychologists ought to work out the details of. But the details themselves are not forthcoming.

At any rate, one can call *those details* representational too, and in that sense assume their intentionality again by definition; this however will not tell us even the most basic properties of how the referential process is achieved. For instance, it is customarily assumed that *book* merely denotes the set of books, and in that sense denotation is in large part presupposed as a lexical process, to be turned into genuine reference the moment some determiner is compositionally added to one such predicate. Thus *a book* is supposed to be able to refer to whatever is in the reader's hands, in essence quite independently of whether the reader is actually using that expression in any given derivation and any given situation.

That may, in the end, be the way human intentionality works; then again it may not. It could actually be the case, for instance, that a variety of semantic cues are built into the, as it were, 'ultimate reference' of an expression: not just purely conceptual issues like its being a book, but also more contextual ones, like its being conceptualized in a given speech act qua its physical characteristics (as opposed to intellectual ones); or even duller ones, like whether the speaker has decided to place the phrase intending to refer to the book in a prominent grammatical region, like the clausal left-periphery. If all of that does contribute to the phenomenon, intentionality may well be a *process*, rather than a pre-established (lexical) category. As is customary in science, this has to be established empirically, not assumed as dogma handed down by tradition, venerable as it may be.

It will take us some time to get to the level of certainty with which questions like these are asked on the sound – or more accurately 'externalization' – side of grammar, if only because the answer is (probably) buried deeper inside our mind/brains, and at any rate linguists have been focussing on it for less time. Nonetheless, there are some obvious considerations one can already raise. As mentioned above, generative studies once suggested a model that usefully separates broadly semantic notions in terms of, on the one hand, purely conceptual information (D-structure) from, on the other, the ultimate intentional information that it leads to (LF), and in fact specifically maps the latter from the former (from the Extended Standard Theory on). That conception is either right or wrong, but certainly not senseless.

Suppose we had reason to believe that a system we are studying – say, vision – has components to differentiate the perception of color, depth, outline, and so on. Then surely two possible, extreme, ways to proceed suggest themselves. A 'modular' approach would try to relate *each* of the observed components, through some 'deep' array of relations; a 'holistic' approach, in contrast, would try to pack all the information together. Neither of these is better or worse a priori, one just has to see how things turn out to be, and it may well be that the result is mixed. In our case, the modular approach separates (at least) conceptual and intentional components, and the holistic alternative assumes a single place for all that. These are, simply, two minimalist alternatives – which cannot both be true at the same time. That's when things get interesting – deciding which one trumps the other.

1.3.3 Is there a mapping between conceptual and intentional information?

The P&P system assumes that intentional information is mapped *from* conceptual information. That is, the way in which different truth conditions come out depends on what got 'plugged in' as a subject or an object; similarly, different scopal relations depend on c-command hierarchies established by thematic relations. Importantly, the *converse* mapping does not hold, although it is very easy to imagine: a language could have been such that its conceptual relations depended on its intentional associations. For instance, it could have been that the meaning '$\forall$x, $\exists$y, x loves y' is pronounced *x pfunk y*, whereas '$\exists$y, $\forall$x, x loves y' is pronounced *x smurk y* (*pfunk* and *smurk* being two *entirely different* lexical predicates). That is not a human language, but there is nothing logically wrong with it. The conclusion is then quite reasonable: in fact *conceptual structure is not mapped from intentional structure*, whereas the converse may well be the case. If this is true it suggests, at the very least, that the two types of information are real enough that a mapping between them is definable, indeed with a given directionality.[7]

1.3.4 Do conceptual and intentional structures have unique properties?

The answer to that question for intentional structures seems obvious: to the extent that such notions as 'referentiality', 'truth', 'contextual grounding' within quantifiers, even 'judgment', are at least to some extent linguistic, their uniqueness within the system is warranted. It is worth asking what the best ways are to understand these notions within the human language faculty,

---

7 In effect, this is a modified version of the observation in Chomsky (1981) that no idioms emerge solely after transformations have applied – which remains a forceful argument for a D-structure component. In current models mapping LF from internal Merge (Move), external Merge is stipulated to apply before, and moreover be subject to, the No-tampering Condition (called the ban against 'overwriting' in Uriagereka [1998]); under those conditions the bizarre predicates in the text cannot be mapped, but then the questions are (a) why there should be an ordering between the types of merge, and (b) why 'overwriting' should be an issue.

but probably not *whether* they exist. It may turn out to be the case, for instance, that the syntactic engine itself has much to say with regards to how all of this turns out to be; but that doesn't deny the relevant notions. In any case, a worked out system is unfortunately still missing where the relevant notions are given a non-trivial, independent, characterization, or are shown to follow from systems that are entirely independent from language.[8]

This book is also concerned with whether there are conceptual properties peculiar to language, and which furthermore we want to capture *in the linguistic system*, rather than elsewhere. Some seem obvious. For example, if thematic hierarchies and thematic alignment seriously obtain in grammars,[9] that must be purely conceptual, since any intentional theory would be consistent with it. Intentionality *per se* certainly doesn't get affected by, say, whether agents are mapped lower or higher than themes.[10]

Other properties are less obvious, and take us into a current and lively debate: whether the lexical atom is decomposable (see chapter 2). For example, whether *John melted the ice* logically entails that *the ice melted* is surely not a necessary condition an intentional system should have. Suppose it is indeed the case that the entailment holds, and furthermore that it mirrors syntactic structure (à la Hale and Keyser [1993, 2002]); then trivially there must be some conceptual structure here, precisely that through which we code the entailment in question.[11] Then again, if the entailment does not hold, of course, all bets are off.

A third set of properties are still less clear, although they are very suggestive. Human predicates and arguments have limitations to them that are not logically necessary. For instance, logic does not dictate that the space we use to conceptualize countable objects should have a characteristic contiguity (e.g., one does not designate the four, attached, legs of a cow, as a separate notion). This is very simply seen in the sorts of games children play with notions in story telling. My three-year-old daughter Sofia had no problems with the Lady of the Lake turning into a butterfly, or even a storm; but she strongly resisted her turning into *two* (or more) butterflies or storms. 'You'd

---

8 For example, the notion 'truth' is relevant to proof theory, but it is highly unlikely that, cognitively speaking, the foundations of the underlying system in that instance are different from those of the language faculty.

9 Works too numerous to mention raise this simple point. For a recent presentation and references see Mori (2005), and Newmeyer (2002) for a critical assessment.

10 A version of this point is raised by Dowty *et al.* (1981), who observe that their model-theoretic system could have started composing the subject to the verb before the object.

11 Basically, the intransitive *melt* is a proper sub-part of the transitive version. In chapter 2 this is referred to as the part/whole-to-part/whole thesis.

have to cut her in two,' she insisted. If whatever systematicity is implied here is part of language, one cannot deny the existence of a component that, strictly, is different from the intentional one(s), and responsible for all this,[12] unless this sort of thing is not part of language at all, and different, broader, cognitive domains are involved.[13]

These are difficult, if empirical, questions. Implicitly, many minimalists appear to have answered them. Those who believe there should be a single intentional interface system must be denying them all, or hoping they all rest on extra-linguistic conditions that do not affect the linguistic objects. More curious is the position of those who believe that, say, the system of Hale and Keyser is necessary for whatever reason, and yet are not willing to accept the presence of a conceptual component in the grammar. The first of these two positions is immediately coherent, but to justify the second, one has to do a lot of work. In order to demonstrate this, and since it has been Chomsky's position over the years, we need to delve into some technical details.

1.4   Chomsky's assumptions

Although Chomsky's assumptions in the MP seem generally clear, on this issue they are more difficult to pin down. Here we should concentrate on the role of the conditions that define the *input to derivations*.

1.4.1   *The lexical array*
One such element is the lexical array (LA). If there are separate meaning elements (at least a conceptual (C) and an intentional (I) one), one could naturally serve as input to the other; on the other hand, if there is only a single I/C interface, then it would be best if the input to that system is unarticulated, a random collection of symbols (e.g. the lexicon). Chomsky admits this much, but then proposes a more articulated input, initially for empirical reasons.

The *lexical array* was conceived in Chomsky (1995) as a way of addressing *compatibility* and *optimality* questions. The first issue is to make sure that, say, *John loves Mary* does not end up meaning '*Peter says that* John loves

---

12 Admittedly, ultimately these nuances do bear on how human beings refer, and thus have intentional consequences. But many things do, including pronunciation; for instance, the phrase *a martini* may actually denote different things if pronounced with an Italian or a New York accent. This doesn't make pronunciation immediately intentional.

13 The notion of a 'manifold', discussed in chapter 7, is very consistent with the strong contiguity just observed in lexico-conceptual mental spaces. But is that notion linguistic or broader?

Mary', in a derivational system. The optimality question arises when deciding whether the derivation of *John loves Mary* should compete with that of *Mary loves John* (see below for more examples). Such questions were trivially answered in a system with D-structure, since all those examples obviously had different initial inputs.

The lexical array was then, originally, a way of having something more articulated than the lexicon so that not just 'anything goes' – then came justifying it. A minimalist who is restricted to postulating only interface representational conditions cannot blame something like the lexical array on what D-structure meant in the P&P system; it must follow from *virtual conceptual necessity*. Chomsky's argument (2000, pp. 100–101) is based on the following steps:

(3)   (i)   Select [F] from the universal feature set {F}.
        (ii) Select LEX, assembling features from [F].
        (iii) Select LA from LEX.
        (iv) Map LA to EXP, with no recourse to [F] for narrow syntax.

Human beings come equipped with an innate set of features {F}, and they select a subset [F] for the language they are acquiring.[14] This is what Chomsky has to say about step (i): 'Operative complexity is reduced if [the language faculty] makes a one-time selection of a subset [F] of {F}, dispensing with further access to {F}' [p. 100]. Here we must pause for a moment.

First, it is unclear what sort of complexity this is. *Operational* complexity is generally considered with regards to comparable derivations; but here what we are considering is *sets of derivations* that are possible from an unarticulated set of primitive features, as opposed to sets possible from a more articulated subset of that set. That kind of complexity is not standardly computational (Chomsky's computational system *starts* operating at level (3iv) above, perhaps (3iii), but not before). Second, it is unclear how the simplicity argument for step (3i) to (3iii), even if granted, can be maintained when we see the argument given for the transition from (3ii) to (3iii): '[Operational complexity] is reduced further if L includes a one-time operation that assembles elements of [F] into a lexicon LEX, with no new assembly as computation proceeds' [p. 100]. Two difficulties emerge with this.

The claim just discussed is arguing for the lexicalist hypothesis *on simplicity grounds*. The argument, in the limit, should deny the need for

---

14 Chomsky is implicitly opposing atomists; see chapter 2 on this general topic.

anything other than the lexicon, again on 'simplicity' grounds. For why not code *any* relevant combination of elements in [F] as a separate word, thereby not having any need for combinations? *John loves Mary* would be *BAH*, *Mary loves John* would be *BUH*, *everyone loves someone* would be *BEH* and so on (all separate words). Of course, that does not give us a recursive system, but why should it? Recursiveness holds, no doubt, of the language faculty, but it is hard to blame on just either natural *interactions* or the internal *coherence* of the system. So apart from 'simplicity', a further assumption has to be made to give us a lexicon *of the right sort*.[15] A second difficulty with Chomsky's claim arises in seeing how the lexicon can be justified as an *optimal* way of accessing [F]; why not have a (universal) LEX that accesses {F} directly instead? Why waste system resources in the intermediate step [F]? In fact, while we are at it, observe what Chomsky says next: 'Is it also possible to reduce access to LEX ... ? The obvious proposal is that derivations make a one-time selection of a *lexical array* LA from LEX, then map LA to expressions, dispensing with further access to LEX. That simplifies computation far more than the preceding steps' [p. 100]. That is true; but why do we have LEX then, if we can get away with LA, a subset, and simplify computation *far more* than in the preceding steps? Why not have LA tap directly into {F}? That would be generative semantics – and it is hard to see why that's not the most elegant solution.[16]

Chomsky's memory motivation for LA is interesting, but hard to evaluate until we establish some basic points about systemic memory, which will be discussed in chapter 7. At any rate, he seems to favor the idea that LA is there because '[i]f the derivation accesses the lexicon at every point, it must carry along this huge beast' (Chomsky 2000, p. 100). Granting that in some form,[17] we would accept that LA is real, a subset of LEX, and more – but the actual arguments given are far from clear. This would not be all that important if, in the end, LA were a mere formal object that can be abstracted from LF, so that its properties are in the end not essential to computation. But this does not seem to be what Chomsky has in mind, as we discuss next.

---

15 That assumption might have something to do with 'expressiveness' or some such thing, which doesn't follow from the customary minimalist premises. See section 8.4.
16 This doesn't entail that it is the right theory – see chapter 2. In any case, Postal's (1972) was not accidentally entitled 'The Best Theory'. In large part this book is about why what arguably the best theory did not survive.
17 Drury (2005) develops this idea, which we return to in chapter 8.

1.4.2   The numeration

The LA is emphatically not a subset of LEX, but an object *constructed* from LEX, according to Chomsky (2000). This is because he wants LA to be not a set of lexical types, but rather a set of tokens. In fact, he goes as far as to point out, in fn. 41, that: 'chain properties can be reduced in significant part to identity if lexical arrays are enriched to numerations'. In other words, Chomsky wants to identify chains at LF as equivalence relations over the objects in the numeration, but for that he needs lexical tokens, not types. In a sentence like *John's mother loves John* we want each *John* in the numeration to correspond to different chains headed by *John*.

Chomsky (1995, 2000) takes the numeration even more seriously than as a set of lexical tokens. This is because of his analysis of paradigm (4):

(4)   a. *There was believed [a man to be t here].
       b.   There was believed [t to be a man here].

In Chomsky's terms, (4b) outranks (4a) because Move can be argued to be more complex than Merge,[18] and the examples in (4) share the step in (5b) and the partial numeration in (5a):

(5)   a. {there, was, believed, ... }
       b. [to be a man here]

While both derivations end up involving one instance of movement (in (4a) *a man*, and *there* in (4b)), *at the stage of the derivation we witness in (5)* the system could get away with merging *there* (as in (4b)), instead of moving *a man* (as in (4a)), and thus (4b) is preferred.[19] But now consider examples as in (6) and (7), of the sort discovered by Alec Marantz and Juan Romero:

(6)   a. [And the fact is [that there is a monk in the cloister]]
       b. [And there is the fact [that a monk is t in the cloister]]

(7)   a. [A ball-room was [where there was a monk arrested]]
       b. [There was a ball-room [where a monk was t arrested]]

The derivations in these paradigms come from the same numerations. However, the embedded clauses show that the (b) examples involve a local

---

18 In recent papers Chomsky does not make much of this interesting machinery, involving (local) derivational comparisons. That said, the derivational phases that were used to justify it are still very much alive. And, regardless of the current or some future state of MP, we are analysing matters here in broad ontological terms, thus including reasonable minimalistic ideas regardless of whether they may have been (temporarily?) abandoned.

19 This is an argument for the derivational system, which gets strengthened shortly by introducing cyclic considerations, also natural in that sort of system.

movement of *a monk*, where the option of inserting *there* exists, which the (a) examples take. If so, by the reasoning just given, the (a) examples should outrank the (b) examples – but in fact both are grammatical.

To solve this puzzle we must split the derivations of the examples in (6) and (7). Basically, we want two separate cycles (derivational *phases* in Chomsky's terminology) each taking stock from a separate access to the numeration. If this is granted, the embedded clauses in each pair simply do not compete (crucially, *there* falls in each of the two separate cycles). Although before we go any further we must also prevent the sort of analysis just sketched for (4) above. Again, (4b) outranks (4a). But if we allow (4a) to be the result of two derivational phases, as in (8), then there is no way (4b) can outrank (4a), just as (6b) and (7b) do not outrank (6a) and (7a):[20]

(8)   there was believed ...
        [a man to be here]

The way Chomsky prevents (8) is perplexing, given the rest of his explicit assumptions. He does not want a TP to count as a derivational phase (short of running into troubles with (8)), although he does want CP to count (or he would not have accounted for (6) and (7)). He asserts that a phase is, in some sense, propositional. Suppose we grant that point, accepting some technical definition of 'proposition'. How far is the object we have created, built around a proposition of sorts, and crucially coding all the lexical tokens that are justified within a proposition, from what we have called above *a D-structure component*? In fairness, such a D-structure component would be more articulated than the mere collection of its tokens. Nonetheless, in the next section we discuss how, in Chomsky's system, the collection does turns out to be articulated.

1.4.3   The theta criterion

Keep in mind the argument we have just examined, and consider now (9):

(9)   a.   {I, believed ... } [to be a man here]
        b. * [I believed   [t [to be a man here]]]
        c.   [I believed   [a man [to be t here]]]

If the derivation proceeds to the point in (9a), how come movement of *a man* is this time preferred (yielding (9c)) over merge of *I* (as in (9b))? There

20 An alternative approach to these facts emerges in terms of denying the EPP altogether, at least in non-finite T (Castillo *et al.* 1999; Boskovic 2002). See however Lasnik and Uriagereka (2005, chapter 1) for a review of an argument by Lasnik that the EPP is, to date, irreducible.

are various answers one can give to this question, but the one Chomsky (1995, pp. 311–316) chooses is interesting: the reason (9b) is impossible is that it would not converge. This is because the chain (I, t) receives its subject theta-role in the 'wrong' position. Why? Because we only allow the assignment of roles in positions with a 'base property'. Chomsky hastens to add that the use of the notion 'base' is expository, but it is hard to find an alternative one. In Chomsky's system roles are assigned in the *initial* phrase-marker, in the *base* or, one could say in plain English, *the D-structure component*.

In fact, when Chomsky introduces this idea he takes much of this to be a self-evident consequence of assuming a theory of the sort Hale and Keyser (1993) advocated, where theta-roles are not features but, quite literally, configurations. To speak of a role assigned to a *collection* of configurations (explicitly, the result of movement) in these terms is just a category mistake, like marrying a country. But the point of Hale and Keyser's theory was to argue for a *non-trivial* level of theta-structure. The moment one assumes this system, packed together with the notion of lexical array just discussed (which is limited to a cyclic access to the relevant symbols-to-combine), one is speaking of a bona fide component of D-structure.

To avoid a terminological nightmare, it is worth emphasizing that as recently as 2006 Chomsky still speaks of D-structure, in his current formulations, as literally 'unformulable'. To insist, this has been known for a quarter century if we are talking about D-structure as a level of representation, for the reasons already mentioned. But the comment would be incoherent about D-structure understood as a mere component, just as it would be incoherent to say that the notion of an intermediate S-structure component – at the point where the system spells-out structures – is unformulable. A unified S-structure level is surely unformulable in systems of a 'dynamically split' sort – there is no single point of S-structure – but that doesn't mean one cannot formulate an S-structure component as a collection of indefinitely many objects of the appropriate format (with no covert characteristics). In turn, whether these formulable notions can resist a minimalist scrutiny will depend solely on whether there is a bona fide interface that can be attached to them. This is dubious for an S-structure component, but less so for a D-structure one.

1.4.4   Conservation of phrases
Importantly, the traditional model had a sort of *conservation law* enforcing the preservation of structure from D-structure to S-structure to LF; this was

the Projection Principle.[21] Indirectly, such a principle argued for D-structure, whose points of structural stability (phrases) could be traced down a derivation, simply running it backwards. This is not a necessary assumption. One could have had a non-conservative mapping, of the sort possibly existing in the way to PF. That is, transformations could have been such that they erased structure, literally destroying the context of rule application as the derivation unfolds; such an information-losing system could not be run backwards. Importantly, thus, the Projection Principle in the P&P model was *an empirical property* of the computational system, one which argued for harmony among successive components in a derivation, and thus for the components themselves. If the present system has a Projection Principle analogue, that very analogue will argue for the hidden components.[22]

Observe the following comments by Chomsky (2000):

> Sisterhood relations presumably remain if LI [a lexical item] is modified to MLI [a lexical item involved in a transformation]: if VP is sister of T, for example, it should remain so even if uninterpretable features are deleted from T. More generally, LI and its modifications [after transformations] are not distinguished with regard to the fundamental relations defined in terms of Merge. [p. 117]

That seems rather explicit. Configurational relations established upon Merge are kept after transformations apply. The obvious question is why Merge relations should persist that way. A phrasal 'conservation law' is clearly implied (see fn. 29), and the issue is how to state it. If a D-structure component exists, the answer is direct: it goes from it to LF.

1.5   Where have all those arguments gone?

The conclusions above do not change in present incarnations of MP, despite Chomsky's unification of, say, Merge and Move by treating the latter as internal Merge (IM), while keeping the former as external Merge (EM). Importantly, EM involves no derivational search, and so is clearly a context-free process; in contrast, IM (formerly Move) is parasitic on the

---

21 Lasnik and Uriagereka (2005) cast a variety of conditions (e.g. 'inclusiveness', 'recoverability', 'uniformity' and so on) as 'conservation of patterns' laws in mind, likening them to 'conservation of quantity' situations in physics. Such regularities are interesting in that they point to deep hidden causes.

22 This 'conservation' argument was made already, in some form, in Chomsky (1965, p. 132).

application of an Agree process that crucially involves a search mechanism, matching a Probe to a Goal in category features – this being a quintessential context-sensitive mechanism.[23] The matter may have been anecdotal if Chomsky didn't also insist on restricting EM to thematic relations, while associating intentional dependency (scope, binding, control) to IM or its precondition, Agree. This is a division of labor that Chomsky has not abandoned since he proposed it: configurational (context-free) relations are of a lexico-conceptual sort while chain-like (context-senstive) relations are logico-intentional. The names may have changed, but not the conception.

1.5.1   Reconstruction effects

That conclusion is important, also, for the validity of the argument given in section 1.4.2, for numerations as the basis for comparing derivations. One may be tempted to dismiss all that as new treatments emerge for the phenomena mentioned there that do not imply comparing derivations. Suppose one does, however, buy such an alternative analysis of the data: does this eliminate the need for comparing derivations and thus some reference set thereof? As it turns out, analyses of different data sets are routinely assumed that still presuppose such comparisons.

For instance, so-called reconstruction effects involve copies of displaced categories:

(10)   a. Which picture of himself does John like ~~which picture of himself~~?
        b. Which picture of John does he like ~~which picture of John~~?

The examples in (10) represent relevant structures as they make it to PF (with the crossed-out material unpronounced). Corresponding LF forms, as in (11) below, do not involve the same strike-through (now representing sites that remain uninterpreted). Semantics dictates relevant 'points of access' to interpretation, with the operator *which* in its scope position and the corresponding variable corresponding to the thematic site. Since the restrictive predicate *picture of* ... can appear anywhere (as this does not affect the corresponding semantics), the possibility in (11a) results in the anaphor *himself* being in the c-command domain of the antecedent *John*, and the possibility in (11b) in the same fate for the name *John*. This entails that

---

23 In particular, the Probe is called that because it has to seek a relevant feature, via a matching procedure, within its complement domain, in particular within an active derivational phase.

anaphor licensing obtains for the (a) examples and obviation for the (b) examples, which disallow co-reference between *he* and *John*:

(11)   a. Which ~~picture of himself~~ does John like ~~which~~ picture of himself? [LF]
       b. Which ~~picture of John~~ does he like ~~which~~ picture of John? [LF]
       c. Which picture of John does he like ~~which picture of John~~? [LF]

One can then ask, if *picture of ...* can indeed reach LF in *any* of the sites it moves through, why doesn't one of the relevant representations of (10b), namely (11c), result in a perfect co-referent interpretation for this surface form? To avoid this problem, Chomsky (1995, chapter 3) proposes a 'Preference Principle', which requires that, all other things being equal, restrictive predicates like *picture of* must, in the end, be interpreted in their thematic position – for syntactic reasons.

The matter has to be appropriately qualified, though, or the predicate in question wouldn't ever be able to appear in positions other than the thematic ones. This is problematic in (12):

(12)   a. Which picture of himself did John say ~~which picture of himself~~ Mary
          likes ~~which picture of himself~~?
       b. Which ~~picture of himself~~ did John say ~~which~~ picture of himself Mary
          likes ~~which picture of himself~~? [LF]
       c. Which picture of John did Mary say ~~which picture of John~~ he likes
          ~~which picture of John~~?
       d. Which ~~picture of John~~ did Mary say ~~which picture of John~~ he likes
          ~~which~~ picture of John? [LF]
       e. Which ~~picture of John~~ did Mary say ~~which~~ picture of John he likes
          ~~which picture of John~~? [LF]

To make the surface form in (12a) grammatical, the anaphor *himself* has to be local to its antecedent *John*. The only way this will happen is if *picture of himself* is interpreted precisely in the intermediate c domain that the phrase displaces through, as in (12b). The lower position is not local and the higher position is not c-commanded by *John*. But if such freedom existed for all restrictive predicates (regardless of whether they contain an anaphor or a name), then nothing would prevent a representation as in (12e) for the grammatical (12c), as opposed to (12d). The bit that allows the extra leeway for (12a) is that it involves, precisely, the anaphor *himself*, which by its very nature requires an antecedent, and thus by hypothesis an extra licensing relation, vis-à-vis (12c), which involves a name, instead, associated to *picture*.

Now let's think of the nature of the Preference Principle. Apparently, it compares two derivations with different deletion procedures, for instance (11b) and (11c), and picks one (the one where the restrictive predicate is in its theta position) over the other. This comparison does not happen over the entire lexicon or the grammar as a whole: it does, instead, over derivations with the precise lexical tokens we examined. In the absence of a D-structure level that fixes this comparison prior to the derivation, it is hard to see exactly how the comparison works. For example, relevant LFs cannot be compared, as those obtain only *after* the appropriate deletions have been executed (a comparison at that time would be pointless). Then again, perhaps this particular data set can be analysed without resorting to derivational comparisons, by tagging the property of interpreting a restriction out of a thematic position to the presence within it of a given anaphor. From that perspective, if no such anaphor is present, the interpretation would automatically be assigned to the site where the restriction was first merged; if, in contrast, an anaphor is detected, perhaps it can be stored in some derivational memory until it can resolve its anaphoricity in whichever domain this happens. Then (11b) and (11c), say, would never be compared. But this gambit can be controlled for by complicating the paradigm as follows.

Chomsky (1995, chapter 3) also observes that the idiomatic reading of *take a picture* is lost as in (13a), when the anaphor forces an intermediate reconstruction as in (13b) – which breaks the integrity of the idiom. This reasoning falls apart if the reconstruction in (13c) is possible:

(13)   a. Which picture of himself did John say ~~which picture of himself~~ Mary
            took ~~which picture of himself~~?
        b. Which ~~picture of himself~~ did John say ~~which picture of himself~~ Mary
            took ~~which~~ picture of himself? [LF]
        c. Which ~~picture of himself~~ did John say ~~which picture~~ of himself Mary
            took ~~which~~ picture ~~of himself~~? [LF]

This is an instance of a 'scattered deletion' of the restrictor, which nothing semantic prevents (remember, the restrictive material makes its contribution to meaning on *any* of the sites it displaces through). How can we prevent (13c)? We could say that it involves four deletion operations, as opposed to (13b), which only involves three.[24] But that clearly presupposes comparing (13b) to (13c), with all the sorts of implications raised above. This time it doesn't help to give the derivation the power to hold an anaphor in some interpretive limbo: in both (13b) and (13c) such a storage would have to obtain, but we still need to compare these two and decide against the derivation with massive scattered deletion – because a simpler alternative exists. Note also that in rigor *all* reconstruction involves *some* scattered deletion: the

24 See Nunes (2004) for related ideas on the PF side, and much relevant discussion.

operator is interpreted up and the variable down, at least (and occasionally the restriction somewhere in the middle). So scattered deletion as such cannot be prevented; only a complex version of this process, where a simpler one is possible. That is clearly a derivational comparison.

There is no worked-out alternative analysis to the facts just discussed; in fact they are routinely described that way in introductory minimalist classes. So the issue of comparing derivations is quite real for examples of this sort, which raises the question of what the comparison set is. Alternatives to numerations have been suggested (e.g. by Boskovic [1997]; Fox [2000] or Hornstein [2001]), but they pose intricate questions that we cannot afford to discuss now, and certainly appear to be as elaborate as the sort of mechanism discussed here. At the very least, then, numerations (i.e. sets of token words from which relevant derivations are constructed) seem like reasonable constructs, if derivational comparisons are real.

1.5.2 How complex should the derivation be?

Chomsky's (1955) system assumed a 'Traffic Convention', whereby no two grammatical rules apply at once. This is customarily referred to as the grammar 'being Markovian' (see section 7.3.1 on this and related notions). As Baltin (2005) puts it, 'for a computational device to be Markovian, it can only make reference to the current state that the device is in, when deciding what the next state of the device can be'. Naturally, there cannot be a comparison among derivations without *evaluating alternative derivational states*. And as Baltin observes, at least the following sorts of analyses have been proposed that violate the Traffic Convention:

(14)   a. There seems [t to be [a man here]] vs. a'. *There seems [a man to be [t here]

        b. [A man [who everyone likes]] arrived vs. b'. [[A man] arrived who everyone likes]]

        c. [C-Q [I said [John likes what]]] vs. c'. [C-Q [who said [John likes what]]]

        d. I believe [him to be smart] vs. d' *I believe [that [him to be smart]]

(14a') was argued above to be ruled out by comparing it to the simpler derivation involved in (14a). The next set of examples presents an apparently optional process, in this instance relative clause extraposition. Baltin claims that a desire to minimize derivations rules out optional transformations. That, however, depends on the ultimate cost of each derivational alternative, and whether by inhibiting, say, extraposition, the grammar doesn't incur in other costs – a subtle matter. It may not be accidental, in this regard, that so-called stylistic processes like extraposition are subject to Ross's (1968) Right Roof Constraint, basically preventing any such operation beyond the cycle it originates in. This may be rationalized in terms of relevant such adjustments in the end not being transformational at all, alternative derivations all having the same grammatical cost.[25] The examples in (14c) vs. (14c′) show how only by having access to the higher cycle can the derivation of *John likes what* proceed forward: the semantically active matrix C requires a Wh-element, and there is no way, until reaching the upper clause, of determining whether it will be the upper *who* or the lower *what* that meets this requirement (Lasnik and Uriagereka 2005, chapter 7). One can introduce an artificial 'successive-cyclic' feature just to distinguish each example, but from the point of view of grammatical design that is not the solution – it is the problem to address. (14d) vs. (14d′) constitutes one of many contrasts that have been argued to involve the desire to minimize representational apparatus. In this instance the issue is what used to be called 'S-bar deletion': the fact that, in its exceptional case marking (ECM) guise, predicates like *believe* select only the necessary TP, and not an extra CP without any apparent grammatical function in this instance, indicates that no superfluous representation is invoked if simpler alternatives exist and can be evaluated (Boskovic 1997). In all these instances the grammar is not acting in Markovian fashion. Evidently, if all of this can be successfully explained away, then perhaps Chomsky's original Traffic Convention still holds. There is reason to doubt, however, that alternative sound explanations are forthcoming for all these paradigms.

Examine also familiar *parallelism* conditions on ellipsis:

(15)   Daisy kicked the bucket and so did farmer Smith, who was milking her.

Unless both Daisy and Smith died in their interaction, (15) can only be meant as a joke. The impossible (though plausible) interpretation that Daisy kicked the bucket which Smith was milking her on, and as a result the farmer died, is generally unavailable. As is well-known, for ellipsis conditions to obtain, *the elided material has to be 'parallel' to its antecedent*. A device making use of this sort of parallelism simply cannot be Markovian, which is one of the reasons a variety of analyses attempt to place this sort of condition outside sentence grammar. However, much recent work summarized in Lasnik and Merchant

---

25 This can be executed in various ways. Hoffman (1996) assumes that the relevant sub-components do not even Merge until the LF component. For Nunes (2004), sub-parts of a complex object (copies) are in principle linearizable in higher or lower sites (see also Ortega-Santos [2006]). Chomsky (2001) allows such phonetic realizations at various sites, even for simpler phrasal objects, to deal precisely with theme/rheme extraposition.

(in progress) directly argues for the core grammatical nature of ellipsis. Pervasive facts of the relevant sort have been used, for instance, by Fox (2000) to reach important conclusions about grammatical architecture. Consider (16):

(16)   a. Some boy read [books by every author]; some girl did too ~~read books by every author~~.
        b. Johnny read [books by every author]; some girl did too ~~read books by every author~~.

In (16a) we observe the parallel effect, this time limited to fixed scopal conditions on each side of the ellipsis (i.e. if *every* takes wide scope in the antecedent clause, it must also in the elided one). Importantly, *every* cannot take wide scope in (16b) even when this would determine, in parallel conditions, a universal wide-scope reading for the elided material, yielding a distributed interpretation there. Fox reasons that this is the case because the putative raising of *every author* over *Johnny* has no scopal effect on the antecedent clause in (16b), names being scope rigid. In other words: the grammar has to know that this step, which has no interpretational consequences, is not justified. This is a non-Markovian calculation.

Several matters that will not be treated here (involving binding and control, for example, particularly as analysed by Hornstein [2001]) have been analysed in non-Markovian terms as well. For reasons of space only one last example, originally discussed by Lakoff (1974), will be given to show that grammatical constructions require non-Markovian generative procedures, given our present understanding. These are 'syntactic amalgams' of the sort analysed in Guimaraes (2004) (see also van Riemsdijk [2006]):

(17)   a. Jack went to I wonder what sort of a party.
        b. Guess who went to I wonder what sort of a party in I cannot even imagine whose car at God knows just what time in the a.m. hours after having met you can surmise who.

Guimaraes demonstrates that examples of this kind are not just 'mere performance': they involve clear limitations that cannot be left open to speakers' whims or particular states. Next, Guimaraes shows how constructions of this sort, even though universal, involve parametric differences (e.g. in terms of whether preposition-stranding is allowed by the underlying grammar). Moreover he evaluates in detail how any attempt to solve an example like (17a) by way of a single-rooted phrase-marker, with cleverly triggered displacements and remnant adjustments, is hopeless, particularly in instances where multiple qualifying intrusions as in (17b) are possible. Finally, Guimaraes provides a minimalist analysis of these constructions, involving the possibility of *a single derivation taking stock from different numerations*, a non-Markovian process if there is one. No alternative proposal exists in the literature to address these data (van Riemsdijk's is a variant of comparable complexity).

Discussions on whether the grammar is Markovian were heated in the mid-1970s, particularly because, as Baltin (2005) notes, it was assumed that languages differ in terms of which particular 'trans-derivational' conditions they deploy. From the point of view of learnability this makes little sense, as such differences would be unlearnable. But all of the non-Markovian processes just reviewed are assumed to be universal, nothing that a learner has to be concerned with; moreover relevant parameters, where they obtain, are assumed to come from their usual (lexicon-related) source. In recent times the debate around these matters became once again intense – particularly after the polemic of Lappin *et al.* (2000). This is in terms of the computational tractability of comparing alternative derivations and representations.

The criticism in Lapin *et al.* pertains to the putative computational blow-up of a system that no minimalist ever seriously contemplated: one without derivational cycles. The moment alternative rankings are limited to definable and (very) limited phases in the system, the putative blow-up dissipates. So the only issue left is whether it is more appropriate, in terms of grammatical design, for the grammar to be Markovian or not. It is hard to imagine how this can be addressed, given how little is known about complex systems in nature. Some exhibit a Markovian character, others don't, while others involve nuanced levels of complexity (e.g. nucleic acid dependencies, perhaps relevantly for cognitive systems).[26] At any rate, the most adequate analysis to date of the linguistic data reviewed above is in non-Markovian terms, entailing that the grammar responsible for the workings of the various analyses outlined does not make reference exclusively to the current state the device is in.[27]

In recent papers, Chomsky has definitely assumed derivational procedures that take place in parallel (see for instance Chomsky [2001, 2006], and chapter 5 will present one such sort of argument in detail, involving Case valuation. In fact, Chomsky has kept the Numeration very much alive to define those domains in a derivation where parallel conditions obtain, via a 'cyclic access to the Numeration'. It is ultimately an empirical matter whether such parallel computations do obtain, or whether the derivation ever

---

26 See Searls (2002) on modeling as context-sensitive dependencies different structures that appear in biological domains (e.g. RNA secondary structures or folded proteins).

27 This still presupposes the notion 'current state', taken from classical computation. We do not even know whether the human brain acts as that sort of computer, or is instead capable of engaging in multiple current computational states, much as quantum computers theoretically can.

backtracks or comes up, instead, with the right representation on first pass. The ensuing grammar would be equally minimalist in both instances. All that matters at this point, however, is that, if the facts take us where they seem to be taking us, we need a way to define derivational domains for non-Markovian computation: whether it is through massive derivational comparison and ranking, or more modest processes of simultaneity in rule application. And it is hard to see exactly how these derivational domains are to be defined, if it is not through some variant of Numeration or some similar 'input' condition.

1.6   Is there still a way to eliminate D-structure?

One could deny the theta criterion, cyclic access to the Numeration, conservation of phrases, and so forth. Some current proposals can be read in that light. But consider other alternatives.

1.6.1   Coding D-structure at LF

Suppose we stick to Chomsky's assumptions: some genuine Hale/Keyser-type information must be coded somewhere, together with notions about lexical tokens and cyclic access to a lexical array in some form. Can we still *not* talk about D-structure? One possible strategy would be to get all the 'base' properties we want in the system, and distribute them throughout.

First, the lexical array would have to be either eliminated or blamed on complexity arguments, refining them beyond the obvious.[28] Second, that the array should be coding lexical tokens as opposed to types (so be constructed, not merely *selected*, from the lexicon) would perhaps have to follow from some kind of conservation law designed to capture the interpretive uniqueness of various chains; that is, given that different chains are interpreted as satisfying different roles, a proviso may be added to the effect that roles correspond to lexical tokens and nothing else (perhaps tokens could be identified by the system in terms of their occurrence in the phrase-marker).[29] Finally, it would have to be argued that something in the interpretation of a set of configurations needs to recover *purely configurational* information. That it can is indeed the case, since a set of configurations is mapped *from* a configuration. That it needs

---

28 There are many ways to cut complexity. The substantive issue is why the language faculty chose the option it did, assuming it is *for that purpose*. See Drury (2005) for much relevant conceptual discussion.

29 This is far from obvious, since the system must have room for (chain) occurrences too, identified precisely in terms of phrasal context (that is, the history of the derivation).

to, though, would seem to concede the point that theta structure exists; after all, why would the system otherwise worry about what specific configurations went *into* the formation of the chains?

The resulting system would work, but unnaturally. The definition of 'level of representation' was built around various relations of a certain sort; when facing *different* sorts of relations, one assumed *different* levels (the rationale behind having levels of representation to start with, and of defining point [5] in section 1.2.2 above, involving a mapping between them). If one admits the existence of (context-free) theta structure together with the existence of (formally different, context-sensitive) intentional relations, and one insists on packing theta structure *together* with intentional stuff in the same level, one is mangling the internal elegance of both these systems. One then wonders: is it so costly to admit that they each correspond to a separate interface?

1.6.2   Coding D-structure in the lexicon

Some current works propose the coding of a D-structure component in the lexicon, thus yielding some kind of generative lexicon (in the sense to be discussed in chapter 2).[30] Quite aside from the issue of whether there should be a generative procedure to build the relevant information (and if so, whether it is the standard syntactic one), this view partially clouds the picture too: surely aside from the productive part of that would-be lexicon, we would also need this entity to be a 'repository of idiosyncrasies', in Bloomfield's famous (1933) formulation – those plainly exist. If so, instead of having a messy lexicon *and* a pretty one, we may as well have one lexicon – and a D-structure. At any rate, one should not then continue the argument, since we would be talking about the same object with different names.

There are non-trivial properties even to the messy lexicon. For example, we may want to code the notion 'paradigm' there, which allows us to predict regularities based on the Elsewhere Condition and 'canonicity' restrictions (see section 2.2.1 for some details). Those are reasonable properties a lexicon-list should have, relating to whatever goes on in the organization of information for the purposes of long-term storage, perhaps touching on matters of lexical acquisition (see chapter 8). All that is, it seems, rather different from the fundamental properties that Hale and Keyser associated to the component

---

30 The idea that there is a syntactic component in the lexicon is explicitly defended even in Hale and Keyser (2002), although for them it doesn't have the full-blown capacities of standard syntax. The issue is what sort of 'syntax' that special one is. We won't be delving into this matter until chapter 8.3.

of the system that is responsible for studying possible conceptual arrays: whether this kind of verbal unit may compose with that one, the sort of notional structure that results from the process and predicts certain implicational relations, and ultimately the machinery that powers this kind of system. If all that is syntactically real, it seems appropriate that it should build a D-structure, as it did for Hale and Keyser in (1993).

1.6.3   Coding D-structure in D-structure

If there happens to be a unique interface with information of a conceptual sort, then we *must* have a D-structure component. It's that simple, given minimalist assumptions: the system is characterized as an optimal mechanism to access interfaces, whether these are one, two, or many. If so, then, the emphasis should be on determining *whether* there is such an interface. A minimalist should probably not care one way or the other, as it wouldn't alter the essence of the program – it would just be an interesting fact.

It would have some advantages, too. To start with, one would not have to go into *complexity arguments* to justify D-structure: it would be there by the mere fact that it interfaces conceptual structure (C), whatever that turns out to be in detail (see chapter 7, and keep in mind that the computational simplification would still obtain, albeit not as a *justification* for the component). Similarly, one would arguably not have to wonder how to justify the system's reliance on tokens. The tokenization of a lexical type in some phrasal object like D-structure is doable through phrasal context. A noun-phrase sister to a verb, for instance, is obviously different from a noun-phrase sister to *v* (another matter is how the mechanics of that work precisely, which is examined in chapters 4 and 5).[31] Finally, one would not have to justify the system's input combinatorial apparatus – whatever it turns out to be – in 'virtually conceptually necessary' terms: that apparatus would be there in order to *build the representations that the C interface demands*. For example, say for concreteness that the interface has to give us predicate calculus; the syntax would have to build representations that can be mapped into that, no more, no less.[32]

Suppose we were trying to derive any of the examples seen above. For (4), we would have, in the D-structure component, [to be a man here] – built

---

31 It may seem as if this poses the same issue raised on fn. 29, but it does not precisely if the system has separate context-free and context-sensitive components. See chapter 7 on this.

32 More radically, in what was called in the Introduction the 'eliminativist' interpretation of the present approach, one would argue that predicate calculus – or whatever is relevant – literally *emerges* as a semantics at D-structure.

through Merge. Then the next phase would come in, treating [to be a man here] as a unit of Spell-out, a giant compound of sorts, and merging that in a larger D-structure component: [there T [to be a man here]]. That is more economical than moving *a man*, as before. Then again, if *there* is not selected, *a man* would be forced to move to satisfy demands on subjects, as usual (yielding *a man was believed to be t here*). Notice: the reasoning still implies a lexical array, as pleonastic *there* may (or may not) be selected to build D-structure. We return in section 8.4 to whether this array is, still, a set of tokens, and if so what is the nature of this – in effect, *pre*-D-structure – kind of formal object.

Similar observations obtain for (6) and (7), assuming that D-structure components are accessed cyclically. If *there* is selected for the lower cycle, (6a) and (7a) are preferred; if not, the (b) examples are possible. Then the issue of what counts as the *size* of the cycle arises again, but now Chomsky's answer is straightforward. Do we want it to be CP (or *v*P) and not TP (or any such substantive claim)? We say that *D-structure conditions require that*, and take it as a substantive characteristic of the interface. What is great about having an interface is precisely the freedom it gives us to make such claims, so long as they are consistent with others holding for the same interface. All of this is business as usual – a profitable one, judging from past experience.

Finally, the fact that (9b) does not converge also follows trivially: its D-structure component is ill-formed, since thematic relations cannot involve the head of a chain, by definition of D-structure. We do not need to appeal to a derivational requirement or any such move, which is dubious on merely formal grounds, but acceptable as a substantive demand about a given representational component: it says, reasonably, that *D-structure is about configurations*. Of course a different issue is *why* it should be, a matter we start discussing at the end of chapter 2.

1.7   Conclusions

We started this chapter examining the syntax/semantics interface, by way of the Mapping Problem, or how forms expressed in the phonetics relate to interpretation. The basic line this book is pursuing is that the mapping in question is intricate, involving several derivational points of access to interpretation, not just the output one, as is customarily assumed within the MP. That presupposes showing that input representations too have an interpretive effect, and thus are bona fide interfaces (or in the more radical interpretation of this project, create such interfaces). As seen here, (a) nothing in the logic of the MP prevents us from having, in particular, a D-structure component (as opposed to an undesirable level of representation of that sort); (b) some minimalist analyses tacitly assume much of what goes into D-structure; and (c) it seems both empirically and technically advantageous to do that, in any case. This naturally entails that various theories could implement the minimalist logic; but isn't the MP a *program*? Certainly Chomsky has always maintained that attitude – in every piece he wrote on the topic.

That said two issues remain open to investigation. What are, in the end, the natural interactions of the system – its interfaces? What design mechanisms make the system coalesce into an elegant whole, with internal coherence in meeting the demands *of those* interfaces, whatever they may be? (In the radical interpretation of the project: What sorts of natural properties do such stability points have that result in the creation of interfaces of the right sort?) Alternatively, if one seriously wants to eliminate D-structure, one should explore a system with absolutely *no* D-structure residues, and see whether it works. The remainder of this book can be seen as both providing empirical support for the idea that a D-structure component would be useful, and a minimalist analysis of why it would make sense for the language faculty to be organized that way.

2 So what's in a word?

2.1 Introduction

Issues with the 'base' component of D-structure, not unlike those already posed in chapter 1 for the current MP, led to a deep rift within generative linguistics, whose consequences are still felt. In this chapter we examine what fueled the so-called 'Linguistic Wars': where and how syntax should bottom out. Prima facie syntax involves combinations *of words* – a common-sense intuition defended by atomist philosophers. However, linguistically it is not always clear what a word is, a matter we must put in perspective. In section 2 some background is provided, separating inflectional and derivational morphology, and describing the 'generative semantics' proposal for lexical decomposition. In section 3 we see how the problem that led to generative semantics is still unresolved, if matters of uniformity and universality are taken earnestly in syntax and semantics. Section 4 is devoted to the mapping in between, and to what extent the assumption that it is entirely arbitrary can lead to feasibility in language acquisition and naturalness in linguistic design. A multi-dimensional theory of syntactic representation is then sketched, which semantic nuances (to be developed in further chapters) can be cued to.

2.2 The source of the issue

Let's start by considering why it ever occurred to linguists to decompose words.

2.2.1 Derivational vs. inflectional morphology
As is well-known, derivational morphology occupies a layer in the word that is internal to the inflectional one. Thus we have [[[[imagin]at]ion]s] and not *[[[[imagin]s]at]ion], or [[[privat]ize]d] but not *[[[privat]ed]ize]. We could surely conceive of a meaning for those impossible words – for instance, *[[[privat]ed]ize] may have turned out to be the state of having past privacy – but no language has a word like this.

There are many other significant differences between inflectional and derivational processes. Some have to do with their sound properties (cf. *preVAIL* vs. *PREvalent*). Others involve apparent semantic properties: typically, derivational processes change categorial distinctions; in contrast, inflectional morphemes either do not have semantic consequences (e.g. a structural Case marker), or if they do only minor features are affected, not the general category of the relevant stem. More importantly for us, while inflectional processes are productive, transparent and systematic, corresponding derivational processes do not seem to be.[1]

To review some basic facts, one can *hospitalize* someone but not **clinicize* them, *enlighten* but not **endarken* an audience, or be a great admirer of *electricity* but not **eclecticity*. This lack of systematicity, apparent language after language, entails that speakers have to learn lexical exceptions. Likewise, lexical meanings are highly idiosyncratic. A *decent* something (sort of) contrasts with an *indecent* one; but a *flammable* object doesn't contrast with an *inflammable* one. Our biological fathers have *fathered* us, but our mother may not have *mothered* us, and one doesn't generally get **grandmothered*. All of this must be learned.

Prima facie, the idiosyncrasy and unsystematicity of 'derivational' morphology constitute arguments against predicting it derivationally, via a standard syntactic computation. Fodor (1970) provides a third kind of argument, based on semantic transparency. Consider (1):

(1) a. I have caused to become normal the entire data set.
     b. I have normalized the entire data set.

Although there are different shades of meaning in these examples, the two are reasonable paraphrases: if we normalize data we cause that data to become normal (in some appropriate sense). Now consider (2), where we have added adverbial modifications:

(2) a. ? Today in my office I have caused to become normal tomorrow the entire data set.
     b. *Today in my office I have normalized tomorrow the entire data set.

The meaning in (2a) is entirely unattainable as in (2b).[2] The word boundary around #normal-ize# seems opaque enough not to allow modification into the

---

1 See Chomsky (1970), Fodor (1970), Jackendoff (1972), and Newmeyer (1980) for perspective.
2 The meaning in question is easier to obtain in the bi-clausal expression in (i)

(i)   Today in my office I have caused that, tomorrow, the data set will become normal.

This interpretation is absent in (2b), and rather marginal in (2a), though not impossible.

word's parts. But why should it be if *normal* has merely incorporated into *-ize*? Surely we can *modify into* syntactic structures, as (2a) shows. So whoever wants to equate *normalize* with *cause to become normal* owes us an explanation as to why the modification patterns in each instance differ. Alternatively – Fodor's conclusion – *normalize* is not derived from anything like *cause to become normal*.

Word-internal processes present their own interesting regularities. Take for instance the notion 'paradigm', in the sense of Williams (1994). For example, alongside *possible* and *necessary* we can say *impossible* (not possible), but not **innecessary* (not necessary). Horn (1989) observes that, rather generally, the extant negative form is an antonym to the less specific element in a pair of (in some sense) lexically related items, such as those involving possibility and necessity. Necessity entails possibility, but not conversely. Why does this situation arise? Consider again the hypothetical **innecessary*. It could have held where something is not necessary, but possible. Except when something is not even possible, which we call *impossible*. So *possible, impossible*, and *necessary* cover all three situations that need to be designated. However, one can indeed say *unnecessary*, involving a different prefix (*un-* as opposed to *in-*), which is part of a different lexical paradigm. It is enough to vary the paradigms slightly for the regularity we've just seen to fall apart. This is a hallmark of lexical relations, not syntactic ones.

Paradigms make sense from a language acquisition perspective.[3] While learning Language L, imagine someone saying that such-and-such is *blah*. Suppose the situation and our knowledge of L (the part already acquired) allow us to conclude that *blah* means either 'necessary' or 'possible'. Which should we guess? Say we go with 'possible'. If in fact *blah* means possible, we're in business. Suppose otherwise. How would we eventually learn that *blah* actually means necessary? Every time speakers utter *blah* in front of a necessary state of affairs, since all that is necessary is also possible, we will be confirming our wrong guess. The only way we could 'unlearn' it is if someone corrected our mistake. Suppose instead that we went with 'necessary'. If *blah* means that, we're trivially right. But even if we let it mean 'possible', there can be a time when someone utters *blah* in front of a possible state of affairs that is not necessary; then we find for ourselves that our guess

---

3 This view is criticized by Bobaljik (2001). The facts discussed above correspond to the expression's 'paradigmatic meaning'. Words like 'possible' involve extra connotations beyond the obvious 'logical possibility'. Horn's point, however, still stands about this core meaning, from which extensions are possible.

was wrong. The information is learnable with positive data. It is to the learner's advantage to always guess the more specific form within those the paradigm offers, since this guess is easiest to unlearn in case of error. Plausibly, the fact that the *least* specific form is the one which systematically has a negative expression in the paradigm is a consequence of this learnability sequence: the learner does not come up with a negative of her own until the entire paradigm is learned – before this, the learner cannot be certain to have converged on the right meaning.[4] Once the paradigm is in place, the need for the second negative expression disappears, since more specific expressions are already known to the learner.

But paradigms have no obvious use within syntax. In part this must be because paradigms are worthless if their size is in principle boundless – the situation with syntactic structures. So there is much room to study lexical relations and how they affect the overall form of the grammar, even if (because of that) lexical relations are simply not identical to syntactic ones.

2.2.2 *Generative semantics*

The main reason that a different view exists is empirical, and it has a serious philosophical consequence. Let Principle P predict some possible and impossible sentences. Next suppose we find out some possible and impossible words, and to our surprise we discover P predicting the distribution of those words too, if we assume that their parts are regular syntactic objects that enter the computation where P obtains. That's a powerful sort of argument to make.[5] We can illustrate its logic with causatives. Why is it that, alongside the possible (1a), repeated now as (3a), and corresponding to (3b), we do not find the impossible (4a) corresponding to (4b)?

(3)   a. I have caused to become normal the entire data set.
       b. I have caused [that the entire data set become normal].

(4)   a. *The entire data set caused to become normal quite a stir.
       b. [That the entire data set has become normal] has caused quite a stir.

---

4 These cases are common for polar-opposite adjectives in a gradual scale, like *sad* and *happy*, from which we obtain *unhappy* but not **unsad*. For Horn's argument to hold here too we need to think of *sad* as marked, vis-à-vis *happy*. There may be cognitive reasons for this, as the paradigm is common across languages. The issue may relate to why scalar implicatures easily go up but not down, as scalarity for 'positive' notions is open-ended, while it must hit a limit for 'negative' notions (sadness could diminish 'only' to a zero point of 'total misery').

5 For various forms of the argument in its classical formulation see Newmeyer (1980, chapter 4).

This fact has a modern explanation given by Baker (1988) in terms of the empty category principle (ECP). In (3) *cause* c-commands and is in some sense close to (i.e. 'governs') the incorporating predicate *become normal*, while this is not the case in (4) (where *become normal* is included in a phrase that c-commands *cause*, not the other way around). If the trace of incorporating predicates must associate to whatever they incorporate to in terms of government (assuming traces must be governed), we have an explanation for why the causative formation in (3) is fine, unlike the one in (4). In chapters 3, 4, and 5 we will be making much use of a modern version of this Head Movement Constraint (a sub-case of the ECP for Baker).

Now let's move to the important contrasts, first pointed out by Ray Jackendoff in Chomsky's 1987 Fall Seminar at MIT, at the time Chomsky was reviewing Baker's account:

(5)   a.   I have normalized the entire data set.
       b.   *The entire data set has normalized quite a stir.

Just as (4a) is impossible, its *lexical version* as in (5b) is also ungrammatical. One could say that the verb *normalize* just doesn't happen to have that meaning in English; but such a verb doesn't exist in language after language. Generative semanticists had an explanation: if we assume that *normalize* is to be decomposed along the lines of CAUSE to BECOME NORMAL, whatever we say about the contrasts in (3) and (4) can extend to those in (5). The abstract CAUSE and BECOME and so on are, in this view, words just as the very concrete *cause* or *become* are. One could complain that *cause* is pronounced [koz] whereas CAUSE is pronounced [aiz] (for *-ize*) and BECOME is not even pronounced. Generative semanticists had an answer to that criticism: *lexical insertion does not take place until what we now call Spell-out*. The derivation proceeds with abstract syntactic units, and after putting words together – e.g., [CAUSE [BECOME [NORMAL]]] – we pronounce that in different ways.[6]

Generative semanticists were reacting against the notion of D-structure. This component imposes a clear boundary between language and thought – particularly in systems of the sort assumed in the 1960s. Traditionally, D-structure was seen as the first syntactic level, which bleeds the semantic components and translates semantic relations into syntactic expressions built around arbitrary words from the lexicon. What generative semanticists did

---

6 This point, with roughly these sorts of examples, is raised in Lakoff and Ross (1976).

when questioning the need for D-structure is question also the need for a boundary between semantics and syntax. Generative semanticists are called thus because their generative engine works with semantic primitives and presumably semantic principles. Once we show that Principle P above (whatever it is) tells us what possible relations exist among abstract concepts like CAUSE, BECOME, and so on, we have in effect discovered a principle of semantics – even a principle of thought.[7]

This is a bold claim, and many linguists think, also, the wrong one. To start with, the general architectural argument about semantics and thought is much diffused the moment one conceives thought (as we do now) as being rather more elaborate than we once imagined. For example, it is difficult to think of semantics as something *deeper* in the model than, say, phonetics. Those are just different mental interfaces that the system needs. Indeed, in the case of semantics possibly more than one kind of information is at stake, if the ideas in this book are remotely on track. And if semantics are read off of the customary LF (output) component of the grammar, then there is virtually nothing we can conclude about the grand nature of thought from whether Principle P operates on words or on more abstract units.[8]

2.3   The problem remains

The architecture that generative semanticists attempted met with difficulties of the sort outlined above. There just seems to be an interesting boundary between the realm of words and the realm of syntax. At the same time, certain impossible words *would* be explained if we treated them as syntactic units. The real question then is whether these two apparently irreconcilable tenets can be made compatible. A group of researchers led by Ken Hale and Jay Keyser have attempted just that. Let's next evaluate their project, which has been challenged by atomist philosophers.

---

7 The fact that the principles that generative semanticists used for their arguments were first proposed as syntactic conditions need not be decisive. Constraints of that sort may have *seemed* syntactic to researchers only because they hadn't gone deep enough. See e.g. Lakoff (1986), where it is argued that the Coordinate Structure Constraint follows from semantic limitations on the 'natural course of events'. It is not clear, however, whether all generative semanticists agreed on this point.

8 Jackendoff (1972) and Chomsky (1972, 1977) paved the way for the prevalent idea that meaning is read off derived structure, not input (e.g. D-structure) representations.

We can present the general debate around four basic theses:

1.   The lexicon is productive.
2.   A simple, typically first-order, formal language is enough to capture the subtleties of natural language semantics.
3.   In fundamental respects, all languages are (not virtually, but) literally the same.
4.   Analyticity is an achievable goal.

2.3.1   *The lexicon project*

There are two different ways to approach the issue of whether the lexicon is productive (Thesis 1). One is empirical. Jackendoff (1990) assumes that the lexicon is productive in the Cartesian sense, thus posing the familiar 'poverty of the stimulus' difficulty already alluded to above.

To ground that interesting claim, it won't do to say that 'we have as many words as we need'; that could be many, but the key here is *infinite*. One could worry about how a child could acquire an even 'just very large' lexicon; however, the lexicon is obviously acquired throughout life, even if at different rates at different stages. This is obviously not true for functional or grammatical items (a handful of them, all acquired very rapidly), but is demonstrable for lexical items. So that can't be a serious issue.

If what we are worried about is an *infinitude* of words, then the concern should not just be learnability, but also the boundedness of human knowledge in a larger, indeed Cartesian, way: How can we know something infinite with merely finite means? The only known take on the problem is recursion. A priori, recursion relevant to concept-formation could be found in two places. Perhaps the world happens to have a recursive structure, which concepts, expressed as words, somehow passively reflect. Or perhaps the linguistic system has a recursive structure, which serves meaningfully to characterize some aspects of the world, recursive or not.

But there's an even more fundamental question we must ask: how do we *know* that we are dealing with an infinite number of words? When asked about this in syntactic terms, we answer that we have an (in principle) infinite number of sentences because we can keep embedding them – so there is no longest sentence. Is there such an obvious proof in lexical terms? The only one who bothers even to attempt to construct a proof is Pinker (1994, p. 129). He takes the Guinness record holder for 'longest word in English', *floccinauchinihilipilification* (which is defined as 'the categorizing of something as worthless or trivial') and turns it into *floccinaucinihipilificational*, *floccinaucinihipilificationalize*, and so on. He appends a meaning to these new words, which predictably involves 'pertaining to . . . '

for the one involving *-al* and 'cause to . . . ' for the one involving *-ize*. But this won't do as a proof of infinity. Suppose Jones causes the floccinauchinihilipilifacation of our theory by calling an editor to urge Smith to write a nasty review. Has Jones floccinauchinihilipilificationized our theory? Even if one has intuitions about such words, the answer is arguably no; Jones would have to *do it himself* (not just cause someone to charge Smith with the unpleasant task). Well, then, *floccinauchinihilipilificationizing* must mean *CAUSE something to floccinauchinihilipilificate PLUS X* (X being whatever guarantees the relevant additional nuance). Call this 'the X problem'. Syntax doesn't pose the X problem; the lexicon does. Let's see why this is important.

The X problem undermines a proof that the lexicon is productive. An atomist philosopher (wanting to argue against decomposing words) will complain that, unless we say what X is, we may as well have told them that *floccinau . . . ize* is an entirely different word from *floccinau . . . (period)*, as they just mean different things. And if so, all we have shown is *another* word, not that words could systematically go on forever. To show that numbers are infinitely many it won't do to show just *another* number: we have to show one related to a previous one (the base of the proof), and furthermore show that the relation cannot be stopped (the proof's induction). As we see shortly, researchers haven't been successful in characterizing X.

There is a more sophisticated version of the argument that basically takes *floccinau . . . (period)* in, say, Japanese (where it can be easily decomposed into separate morphemes) and runs some syntax-like devices over it. We return to this argument. But keep in mind that the more syntax-like our argument becomes, the less impressed atomist philosophers are going to be about it; surely they admit to the recursivity (hence the associated unboundedness) of syntax – the *lexical* one is what's at stake.

It should be emphasized that the point being made is quite modest: nobody is asserting that the lexicon is finite. We are just observing that *we don't know* how to prove that it might be infinite. There's a second way of evaluating the lexicon's productivity: a priori, would it make sense for the lexicon to be fixed? Most reasonable scientists make the assumption that systems bottom out. This is not a necessary assumption, but the alternative is too obscure a notion to get into. So if we do have to bottom out, the question is where.

In that respect atomists take a sound approach. We have intuitions about sentences and words, but does anybody really have *intuitions about the alleged components of words*? One could ask one's grandmother about the meaning of *food*, but good luck asking her about such notions as SUBSTANCE. That, of course, doesn't mean we can't do scientific inquiry about these notions – grandma doesn't normally have intuitions about protons either – but it does mean we'd better have a really good theory about them (the same holds for protons). Now, there's the rub. Suppose we claim the impossible word **pfzrrt* doesn't exist because it's derived from *CAUSE x to do something*, which violates principle P. An atomist accepting this much will ask why *pfzrrt* couldn't mean what it means *as a primitive*, just as CAUSE does. We complain: '*Pfzrrt* cannot be a primitive!' Their punchline: 'Why? Do you have intuitions about primitives?' So either we have a really good theory of those primitives or we lose.

The argument makes sense. We think we must bottom out somewhere; we don't have (at any rate robust) intuitions below words; so why not bottom out *with* words? This is important. Atomists aren't just saying *concepts* are atomic – everyone has to say that about at least some concepts. They are saying, also, that *the relevant atoms pretty much correspond to natural language words*. Of course, even stringent atomists would give or take a detail here, for they know words might involve systematic inflectional morphemes, which might mean we actually bottom out *within* those morphemes, about which we (arguably) do have direct intuitions. That said, it's pretty much observable stuff all the way down. And we must grant atomists this much: they may not have 'the best theory' – but they surely have the null hypothesis.

In sum, avoiding bizarre territory, we need a limited set of primitives. Atomists invite us to think that the lexicon as such is, more or less, that very set; that might be large, but nobody said the primitives have to be few, so long as they are finite. Insisting on the implausibility of that view shouldn't move anyone, given that other aspects of the biological universe (e.g. our immune system) also seem to work with a huge, pre-determined class of primitives.[9] A serious, sophisticated theory of a (small?) number of primitives will fare better, but we have to produce that theory; atomists don't have to produce the lexicon, because it's there.

2.3.2   Lexical semantics
Consider again the X problem, illustrated with a case of the sort Fodor and Lepore (1998, p. 272ff.) present. Suppose we define *cat*, decomposing it into *feline plus X*. For X to be definitional, it must be a necessary condition of *cat*. Is there any characteristic X of cats which isn't already felinity? Those feline implies already (say, mammal) are irrelevant, since we've already defined *cat* as

---

9 As Piattelli-Palmarini (1989) observes, the atomistic view of a huge number of primitive concepts is consistent with what is found in the adaptive immune system, where classes of antibodies are equally numerous.

feline. But the only more specific X we can really say a cat has that is not covered by feline is, precisely, cattishness. So we've defined cats as being cattish...

Suppose with Pustejovsky (1995, p. 296) that, say, *food* is understood a *substance plus X*. In the classical view he argues against, X turns out to be *edible*. All (should) agree that this approach is hopeless. Of course, that's not what Pustejovsky is saying. For him, X should instead be a 'qualia' – a dimension of some sort that structures a semantic type, rather than it 'inheriting properties... in a homogeneous property structure' [p. 297]. In other words, Pustejovsky goes *into a higher order* descriptive apparatus in order to avoid the X problem. This actually denies the second general thesis presented in section 2.3 above: according to Pustejovsky, a simple, typically first-order, formal language is *not* enough to capture the subtleties of lexical semantics. That does avoid the pitfall. All *first-order* characteristics of *cat* one may think of are either implied by feline or meant by cattish. But *any* higher order property (e.g. for expository purposes, *IS SELECTED BY MEOW-TYPE VERBS*) is neither implied by feline nor meant by cattish.

The issue is whether we're willing to let our system go in the direction of higher order representations (Thesis 2 above). Pustejovsky takes '[t]he semantic potential of language... [as] the result of an appropriately expressive and adequately constrained generative system, devised essentially to this end' [p. 291]. A question then emerges concerning the very status of a semantic theory. The field of linguistics remains divided on this. On one hand, some assume a semantic theory corresponding to bona fide semantic facts; this is the view, in particular, that model-theoretic semanticists advocate.[10] On the other hand, there are those for whom semantics is restricted to intentionality (ultimately referentiality), the rest being dependent on syntax; the neo-Davidsonian rhetoric is often of that sort (e.g. Higginbotham [2000a]). Neo-Davidsonians cannot, at least trivially, admit higher order semantic devices to solve the X problem, as the driving syntactic engine determines the order and combinatorial devices in the system.[11]

2.3.3 Semantic uniformity

A different consideration should be brought to bear on these matters – Thesis 3 above. Chomsky has argued over the years that all languages are uniform at

---

10 Jackendoff's view in (2002) is also consistent with this approach, although for Jackendoff there are *also* unique syntactic (for that matter phonological) principles to reckon with, each equally robust.

11 The possibility is discussed below, and especially in chapter 7, that *the syntax itself* is of a higher order.

LF, so that if *such-and-such* means 'so-and-so plus X' in Japanese, then we know that 'so-and-so plus X' must more or less be the representation of the corresponding English word, regardless of pronunciation. This is the view defended by Hale and Keyser in 1993 and 2002. That line of reasoning should be making two separate points. One is semantic, the other syntactic (and addressed in section 2.3.4).

Suppose it is true that if Jones squares the circle, the circle squares. If we do want our formalism to capture this, we would try what, for instance, Pietroski (2000) shows. A neo-Davidsonian semantic analysis of the first statement would be something like (6):[12]

(6)   *There is an event e of Xing* (whatever X means in Japanese),
        QUANTIFICATIONAL EXPRESSION #1

        for an event e' of squaring, such that
        QUANTIFICATIONAL EXPRESSION #2

        Jones is the subject at e, and e' is the object at e,
        PROPOSITION #1 WITH BASIC ROLES

        and
        NEO-DAVIDSONIAN CONJUNCTION

        the circle is the subject at e'.
        PROPOSITION #2 WITH BASIC ROLES

The conjunction in (6) is the key in capturing the key entailment here.[13] This conjunction is not a word of English, but it is assumed to be the semantic connective between proposition #1 and proposition #2, which result from decomposing *square* into something with the import of 'cause to square' (or the Japanese equivalent). If the neo-Davidsonian representation of *the circle squares* is (7), the first proposition entails the second, *regardless of what X means*.

(7)   *There is an event e'' of squaring*, such that
        QUANTIFICATIONAL EXPRESSION #2

        the circle is the subject at e'.
        PROPOSTION #2 WITH BASIC ROLES

---

12 Here is a more formal version of the structure (see section 2.4.2 for the notion 'Terminater'):

$\exists e$ [X(e) & Subject(e, *Jones*) & $\exists e'$ & *Square*(e') [Terminater (e, e') & Subject (e', *the circle*)]]

13 That is, if (i) is true (note the boldfaced conjunct), then (ii) must be true also.

(i) $\exists e$ [X(e) & Subject(e, *Jones*) & $\exists e'$ **[*Square*(e')** [Terminater (e, e') & **Subject (e',**
        ***the circle*)]]]]

(ii) $\exists e'$ [*Square*(e') & Subject (e', *the circle*)]

If propositions #1 *AND* #2 are true, proposition #2 has to be true. So if we capture the entailment relations through Neo-Davidsonian decomposition, the X problem doesn't arise. Whatever X means in Japanese, it does in English; the entailment holds regardless.

Actually, do we know that X in Japanese must mean *something*? Formatives like *there* and *do* don't. Certainly, attaching X to a Japanese intransitive verb 'causitivizes' it. But it could (merely) be that X *marks* the 'transitivity' of the 'causative' verb, which is neither causitivized nor, in any serious sense, caused.[14] That would be bad, for it wouldn't then sanction the important mapping to the neo-Davidsonian logical form, which given the assumed 'and' connective yields the proper analysis of the entailment relations. That is, we might be allowed to translate X as something or other to fill in the slot of the main predicate in the main event above if, and indeed only if, X is more than an uninterpretable grammatical marker. It then matters what X means. Here just insisting on what it *intuitively* means in Japanese poses two problems: whether the intuitions are reliable in sub-lexical units, and whether they are translatable.[15] Which leaves us with one familiar kind of solution: (good) theory demands that X mean something.

We should say, also, that essential to Pietroski's conjunction argument is the cleverness of the phrasal axioms. Mapping is cheap, and we are allowed to axiomatically relate our formal language to anything we want, as a first-order formalism like the one (context-free) syntax employs doesn't fix its own interpretation.[16] Now Pietroski's argument is based on the mapping to the neo-Davidsonian semantics involving the useful 'and' operator in (6), which he associates to binary branching. Although he assumes what everybody else does in the Neo-Davidsonian literature, an equally transparent mapping, on merely formal grounds, would relate the syntactic parts in terms of, say, 'or'

14 In many languages (e.g. Tagalog or Indonesian) explicit 'transitivity markers' associate to transitive constructions. As such morphemes are specific to the relevant constructions, it is not easy to determine what they mean.
15 This is an instance of Quine's famous (1960) 'Indeterminacy of Translation' problem. See chapter 7 on this.
16 The Lowenheim/Skolem Theorem, underlying this claim, is the expression of an intuitive fact for formal systems: even if we know a statement to be true, we don't know what it is true of – unless we have a translation code at our disposal (see chapter 7 for more on this). The Lowenheim/Skolem result shows, for any formal system that has a corresponding interpretation, that there are no formal constraints imposed *by the system* that can determine its interpretation. Putnam (1970) extends this result to systems that include empirical representations, thus proving that even an entire (first-order) linguistic system cannot determinately refer, in and of itself.

operators. That would destroy the argument. Even if it is true that proposition #1 OR proposition #2, it obviously doesn't follow that proposition #2. One could then take that to mean that we *have to* assume the mapping from the syntax to the semantics in terms of an (abstract) 'and' operator, instead of the unwanted 'or' operator. The question is *why* that should be; there doesn't seem to be anything more primitive about 'and' than about 'or'.[17]

So we need *another interpretive assumption*, call it XTRA, to make sense of the most basic reason for lexical decomposition. For the example discussed, different syntactic arguments *map to conjuncts* of a neo-Davidsonian logical form. XTRA is not just a mere part of intentional involvement (at the level, say, of the disquotational *'Jones' refers to Jones*).

2.3.4   *Syntactic uniformity*

The other general consideration behind the decompositional approach we're now considering is strictly syntactic. If our parameters are going to be rationally simple, then we want more or less to say that 'English is (like) Japanese', or 'Japanese (like) English'.[18] However, it is not easy to make that argument run smoothly. In this respect, there is a criticism that one could raise against Hale and Keyser's approach from the perspective of Fodor and Lepore, although they themselves did not raise it in their otherwise exhaustive critique (1997).

The present concern has two parts, one of which is partly directed not to Hale and Keyser, but actually to Fodor and Lepore. As Hale and Keyser (2002) observe, Fodor and Lepore seem to think Hale and Keyser have a common source for the 'denominal' verbs *saddle* and *shelve*, roughly (8), which also underlies locative constructions involving prepositions *in* or *on*.

(8)
```
        V'
        Λ
       V  VP
          Λ
         x  V'
            Λ
           V  PP
         PUT Λ
             P y
            ON
```

---

17 The opposite is usually taken to be the case: given 'not' and 'or', 'and' can be defined – although see Pietroski (2005) for an alternative approach where 'and' is more primitive.
18 See section 2.4.1 for a more detailed presentation of the implicit reason for this move, and some consequences.

Intuitively, *saddle* is formed by incorporating a type x element (as in 'put-saddle on y', after PUT moves to the higher V), while *shelve* is formed by incorporating a type y element (as in 'put-on-shelve x', again after PUT moves up). But this is not what Hale and Keyser say. Their analysis of *shelve* is indeed along the lines suggested; but their analysis of *saddle* is, rather, as in (9). Note: the source structure is not as in the locative (8), where *saddle* would occupy the x site. Rather, the underlying representation is supposed to be akin to *provide the horse with a saddle*.

(9)

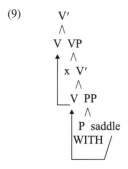

Fodor and Lepore were right that Hale and Keyser *should have* stuck to (8). We have few intuitions about sub-lexical stuff. So if something is promising about the story implicit in (8), it is the fact that we have two arguments x and y, and by incorporating one or the other we get two different words. If we have to start playing with words whose meaning is reasonably related (put x on shelf vs. put saddle on y), but involve *totally different primitives*, we open a whole new set of problems. Why can't the primitives themselves be as complex as the examples examined? What is the contribution of WITH to the meaning, as opposed to ON, or PROVIDE vs. PUT? Why is it that if we place men on shuttles we can both be manning the shuttles or shuttling the men, *at the same time*? What about *man* makes it involve the PROVIDE notion, if when we shuttle the men we also are providing the shuttle with men; or conversely, what is it about *shuttle* that makes it invoke the PUT notion, if when we man the shuttles we are also putting the men on the shuttles? Some clarification is necessary – and has never been provided.

Why is it that Hale and Keyser did not follow Fodor and Lepore's 'advice'? This is more interesting, since Hale and Keyser seem to think that incorporating x in (8) would be an ECP violation. But that's surely not the ECP! All the ECP demands is that a movement trace be properly governed. The trace of x in (8) or (9) seems to be properly governed, since that's a standard configuration, for instance, of ECM. That might seem inconsequential but it is not. If we say that principle P, a standard syntactic principle like the ECP, predicts why we can't say *pfzrrt*, that's impressive – the generative semanticists' argument seen in section 2.2.2. But if we say that the absence of *pfzrrt* follows if we grant the existence of a principle P' which *reminds* us of the ECP... we are just doing reminiscence.

Interestingly syntactic uniformity can be seen to argue against Fodor and Lepore, on their conceptual criticism of Hale and Keyser if we look at things at a different level of abstraction. To anticipate, the matter has nothing to do with the proper analysis of denominal constructions (a topic we return to in chapter 5, section 5.5.4). One version of the argument is based on Burzio's generalization (Burzio 1986) – the idea that when a verb doesn't assign a theta role to its subject, it doesn't check the abstract Case of the corresponding object. True as this appears to be, it is not a principle, and in fact it follows from nothing obvious. Now suppose the structure of sentences is the way Hale and Keyser want it to be, interpreted along the lines of Chomsky (1995, chapter 4):

(10)

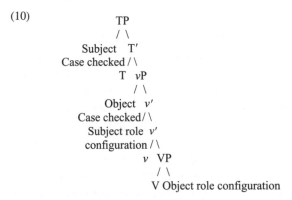

The key here is *v*, which is responsible both for Object Case checking (in its higher specifier) and determining a Subject role configuration (in its lower specifier). We cannot have one of these tasks performed without the other; Burzio's generalization, then, follows.

One can be accused of having turned the generalization into a bruteforce principle. But here is where the 'English is Japanese' line becomes reasonable. The deduction of Burzio's generalization has nothing to do with the 'grand schema of things'. Quite simply, if English mimics Japanese (or any relevant language) to the degree that (10) assumes, then we solve an English (or Japanese) mystery. That's sound reasoning, which turns the present line into a *syntactic argument for decomposing a transitive verb* into V and *v*, and so for decomposition of morphemic elements which are presumably not merely inflectional (assuming that *v* isn't).

Needless to say, that sort of argument is based on a robust syntactic observation, which if eventually shown to be wrong would undermine its validity. But the point of principle remains, and can be reproduced with other such robust observations. Consider, for instance, a more elaborate version of the argument, due to Higginbotham (2000b), based on the ambiguity in (11).

(11)   The ship floated under the bridge.

This can mean either that the ship was statically floating under the bridge at an unspecified time, or that at a particular stretch of time the ship moved through a space under the bridge. Compare:

(12)   The ship floated its way under the bridge.

(12) is synonymous to the second reading of (11). Importantly, in the Romance languages neither the second reading of (11) nor the paraphrase in (12) is possible. Witness Spanish.[19]

(13)   a. El barco flotó   (de)bajo   (d)el puente.
            the ship floated (of-)under (of-)the bridge
         b.*El barco flotó   su camino (de)bajo   (d)el puente.
            the ship floated its way   of- under of-the bridge

Higginbotham (2000b) predicts the difference between 'static' and 'dynamic' readings of (11).

Higginbotham's insight is that in the dynamic reading the 'semantic head' of the construction is the preposition *under*, whereas in the static reading the 'semantic head' is the verb *float*. In a sense, for the dynamic reading we're invoking a hypothetical *'underfloat'* (analogous with *undergo*), for which the preposition *under* contributes something crucial to the compositional meaning 'going-under-through-floating', whereas *under* does not contribute much in the static reading and is instead a circumstantial (the floating could have been *over* the bridge, say). Thematic relations are roughly as in (14) (simplifying complexities inside the PP).[20]

---

19 Remarkable linguistic variation exists for this structure. Snyder (1995) studies two relevant variants, associating the structures in point to various others. A comprehensive cross-linguistic study of these matters is still missing.
20 Note that *under* expresses a relation for an object *x*, between a given space and a process with an end-point.

(14)   PP: *under* <x, *the bridge*, (e′, e″)>; V: *float* <y, e>

In turn, a more articulated syntactic structure (prior to movement) comes out as (15).[21]

(15)   [*float* <y, e> [*under* <x, *the bridge*, (e′, e″)>]]

When the semantic head of the construction is P, for some reason we identify *e* with *e′* (*e″* being the *telos* of process *e′*) and *y* with *x* (and notice also the translation, again through XTRA, of the relevant brackets in (15), or equivalently a *v*, into the conjunction &).[22]

(16)   *float* (x, e′) & *under* (x, *the bridge*, (e′, e″))

That's the dynamic, 'underfloat', reading. In contrast, when the semantic head of the construction is V instead, the events are not identified (floating *e* and being under the bridge *e′*), and instead only *y* and *x* (ultimately corresponding to *the boat*) are identified.[23]

(17)   *float* (x, e) & *under* (x, *the bridge*, e′)

If a language permits that sort of 'agglutination' of a semantic and syntactic head (a 'head split' in Higginbotham's terminology) it will allow the dynamic, 'underfloat' reading. This is in fact the gist of the syntactic decomposition argument. Languages of the appropriate sort will also allow (12), which can be understood on analogy with (18).

(18)   The ship made its way under the bridge by floating.

---

21 Here we have added syntactic representations, so we must go from the realm of lexical axioms (as needed to interpret the representations in (14)) to whatever phrasal axioms are required by the system to factor in syntax.

22 Our phrasal axioms must allow for the following correspondence, the lower structure somehow being obtained in the course of the derivation (in what follows a syntactic base is suggested for this correspondence):

$$[\textit{float} <y, e> [\textit{under} <x, \textit{the bridge}, (e', e'')>]]$$
$$|\ |$$
$$\textit{float} (x, e') \ \& \ \textit{under} (x, \textit{the bridge}, (e', e''))$$

23 To go on with the observation in the previous footnote, this time only the correspondence below must obtain – and note that in the static reading there is no end-point to the process of 'being under', now a state e′:

$$[\textit{float} <y, e> [\textit{under} (x, \textit{the bridge}, e')]]$$
$$|$$
$$\textit{float} (x, e) \ \& \ \textit{under} (x, \textit{the bridge}, e')$$

The latter structure, incidentally, is fine in Romance – for instance Spanish.

(19)   El barco hizo/abrió   su camino bajo el puente flotando.
         the ship made/opened its way under the bridge floating

Thus the issue must depend on the relation between structures of the sort in (18) and (19) and their more compact version in (12), only possible in 'agglutinative' languages – so (12) itself ought to be, in some form, the source of the even more compact structure in (11), in the relevant dynamic reading. Of course all of this is 'decompositional' talk.

From the perspective being entertained, the ungrammaticality of the dynamic reading in Romance, vis-à-vis in particular (12), may stem from the specific derivation in (20).[24]

(20)   a. [V+ed [[[the ship 's way] under the bridge] (by) float]]
         ↑_____/

         b. [float+ed [[[the ship 's way] under the bridge] t]]]

         c. [the ship [float+ed [[[t's way] under the bridge] t]]]
            ↑_____/

Note that *ship* starts the derivation in (20a) as possessor of *way* (arguably a lexicalization of process e'), and *float* incorporates to a null V head (20b). It is via incorporation (to V) that e identifies to the e' associated to *way*, this element introducing the 'semantic head' *under* (the correspondence alluded to in fn. 22).

(21)   [[[V+ed [[under <x's, the bridge, (e', e'')>]] (by) float <y, e>]

(21) is meant as a structure for both (11) in the dynamic reading and (12), with overt lexicalization of *its way*.[25] Inasmuch as these two are synonymous, it cannot be a necessary condition – in order to obtain the *'underfloat'* reading – that the process e' that *way* lexicalizes should have to overtly incorporate to the V complex: in (12) it doesn't. But we may assume that even in (12) incorporation does take place, albeit covertly, ultimately the intuition behind the *'underfloat'* suggestion.[26] After all, *way* is mere lexical support for the event position that *under* introduces in this reading; incorporating *under* to *float* would have the consequence of carrying *way* as a 'free-rider', as the

---

24 If things are as suggested below, the assumed parameter may well be syntactic (which is less obvious in Higginbotham's specific formulation).

25 In one structure process e' lexicalizes as *way*, while in the other it is left implicit.

26 The idea of incorporation in the LF component is first discussed in Baker (1988), for causative constructions in languages (like English) where it typically does not manifest itself lexically (as in Japanese).

latter clearly has no meaning in isolation of the preposition. Note in this respect that a ship can be said to float its way *under a bridge* (for instance) but not float its way, period. In other words, *x way* idioms require a locative expression, which is expected if *way* lexicalizes the event position associated to the relevant preposition (*under, out of, over*, and so on).

Observe also how the possessor *the ship* undergoes 'possessor raising' (see chapter 3 on this notion), thus being promoted to subject position, in the process identifying the variable *y* of *float*, in the incorporated site V+*ed*, with the variable *x* of the semantic head *under*.[27]

(22)   [[[*float*+*ed* <x, e'> [[*under* <x's, the bridge, (e', e'')>]]]

Now (22) can translate as (17). This process of identifying the variables for *float* and for *under* must also take place in the static reading, so must be a possibility in Romance as well. The latter reading, however, won't involve anything as complex as (18) or (19), where the event introduced by *under* lexicalizes as *way*.[28] (See section 3.4.3 for a more refined analysis.)

To put it in Higginbotham's own words (personal communication): 'English "under" can mean both "be under" and "go under", though in the latter avatar it requires the support of a V (perhaps empty, like "go"). That Italian 'sotto' [in our examples the Spanish "bajo"] . . . can't be ambiguous in this way must be a principled fact . . . [This] provides a clear and explicit semantics and isn't just some metaphor about "encoding the path of motion." ' Indeed one may also add that: (a) Higginbotham is able to predict the meaning of *float* in the dynamic reading using standard syntactic devices (in the present rendering, incorporation, and some form of possessor raising) and (b) he is able to relate the meaning of *float* in the dynamic reading to that of the *x way* construction. All of that has little to do with Fodor and Lepore's ultimately philosophical objections to lexical decompositon, and is just good theory.

But now examine the sequence of representations (20), (21), and (22). Higginbotham's phrasal axioms produce the intended results in direct ways, by mapping things compositionally in correspondence with sisterhood relations, and introducing neo-Davidsonian *and* operators as the need emerges. That's within minimalist expectations. However the assumption about split heads, coded here by way of incorporation (and possessor raising) to get the

---

27 Just as we saw an incorporation process responsible for one of the variable identifications in fn. 22, this incorporation process is responsible for the other variable identification in fn. 22, and the one in fn. 23. We return in section 3.4.3, and chapter 6 more generally, to further discussion of identification processes.

28 In this reading there will not be a process (implicit or not) of 'underfloating'.

relevant, identified, heads together, is just another instance of XTRA. For why should incorporation result *precisely in the variable identification we need* (see chapter 3 on this)?

The semanticist might complain: just why is XTRA so worrisome? It is because we don't have independent and simple direct evidence for it. For the existence of v in Japanese, whatever it means, we have serious syntactic evidence, as we do for Burzio's generalization, or for the sheer fact of the cross-linguistic paradigm just presented. But XTRA (here, that different syntactic dependents *map as conjuncts*, and also the *identification gambits* needed for Higginbotham's elegant analysis) can only be justified by the need to obtain the appropriate semantics. Surely that's serious, but it either implies a domain of knowledge that imposes that substantive phrasal axiom, or else has it follow formally from something else. The latter is not obvious. The former is troubling on conceptual grounds: the language that would result from *not* assuming XTRA (from using 'or' instead of 'and' in neo-Davidsonian dependencies; from *not* identifying the variables of incorporated elements, for Higginbotham's analysis, or similar such alternates) is logically coherent and perfectly communicable.[29]

2.4   Analyticity redux

To conclude, we must return to the question of analyticity (Thesis 4 above), not so much philosophically – a matter left for philosophers – as from the perspective of: (a) what it may say about language in a naturalistic environment and (b) how we can deal with analyticity without assigning it the standard hallmarks of syntax, which leads to generative semantics. The second issue will only be outlined now, as we return to it at the end of the book. In the background is the idea, alluded to in the Introduction, of what it might mean to 'naturalize meaning'. Readers that find such conceptual matters uninteresting may wish to skip directly to chapter 3.

2.4.1   How arbitrary is the syntax/semantics mapping?

To raise the following point we must make certain abstract generalizations. The gist of the idea was already alluded to in Lakoff and Johnson (1980): to some extent, and in some sense, *semantic complexity tracks syntactic*

---

29 In that language we couldn't infer, from saying that Jack boiled the soup, that the soup indeed boiled. Moreover, such a language wouldn't allow the identificational gambits that result in the 'x-way' construction, so in order to express such thoughts one would have to proceed as in the Romance languages.

complexity. This, of course, is a point that cognitive grammarians, such as Langacker (1997), have often emphasized though their ultimate take on why such a correlation should hold is quite different from the one advocated in this book. Although we cannot focus on arguing the matter in any detail yet – and the rest of the book can be seen as a particular substantiation of the claim – we can attempt to ponder it fairly.

Being deliberately naïve about the suggestion, an abstract noun like *beauty* denotes a kind of *gestalt* space that seems intuitively simpler than the 'space' denoted by a concrete noun like *beer*.[30] This is not because the denotations in each instance, *beauty* and *beer*, have whatever complexity they may have 'out there', in the denoted reality. Rather, such a proposition may hold because, as it turns out, the grammatical expression *beauty* typically appears in simpler grammatical guise than the expression *beer*. For instance, *beauty* (in its abstract sense) cannot be determined by such articles as *this*, which are of course fine with *beer*.[31] In turn, *beer* denotes a kind of space which is again simpler than the objectual space denoted by a noun like *mug*. For example, we don't directly classify or quantify *beer* beyond rough estimates of the sort of 'much' or 'little',[32] whereas when it comes to *mugs* we do get the whole array of classificatory (e.g. number and gender markers, but also other such devices in languages with overt repertoires for the purpose) and quantificational expressions (not just 'many' or 'few' beers, but also specific numbers of mugs or proportionate quantities, to name the obvious). And the same can be said about objectual expressions vis-à-vis more complex animate nouns, like *man*: the latter has all the objectual properties mentioned for mugs, plus the possibility of appearing in so-called specificity contexts associated to various sorts of grammatical marking ('personal' markers, overt topical displacement and so on).[33] In short, a familiar hierarchical arrangement of nominal spaces

---

30 Here the notion 'space' is used metaphorically. However see chapter 7 for a more technical view.
31 When we say *this beauty* we refer to either a *kind* of beauty, or (uninterestingly here) an entity we denote with a count use of *beauty* (e.g. when a cow is described as 'a beauty'). The purely abstract, bare, *beauty* clearly denotes a less complex notion. See Borer (2004) for a different, though related view.
32 We can say *most beers*, but similarly to what was noted in the previous note, expressions of this sort denote either *kinds* of beer or (again uninterestingly now) entities referred to in count-guise, as in *a beer*. These are non-canonical uses of the mass expression, which involve intriguing 'type-lifting' mechanisms that appear to be covert in English. Such expressions are generally unavailable in languages with rich classifier systems.
33 'Animacy' has little to do with sentience or similar characteristics of the denotation. At issue is conceiving an entity, via its denotatum, as capable of undergoing characteristic shifts (in shape, function, perceived intention, and so on).

suggests itself – abstract < mass < objectual < animate – which is not based on corresponding denotations, but relates to them (see Muromatsu [1998] for discussion).

Verbal expression can also be modeled in abstractly similar ways, given grammatical arguments that we need not review now. This yields a hierarchy along the lines discussed in Vendler (1967), to organize states, activities, achievements and accomplishments. The emerging hierarchy is not based, again, on the complexity of corresponding denotations, but on grammatical facts: more syntactic phenomena obtain in, say, accomplishments than for states.[34]

As Mourelatos (1978) attributes Leech to have first observed, many formal characteristics of the nominal and verbal expressions coincide. Just as abstract or mass terms are boundless, so too are states and activities endless; in contrast, countable and animate nouns are bounded in ways that recall the telicity of achievements and accomplishments. The correspondence seems to be formal in some *gestalt* sense, again not denotationally, particularly since, in terms of their respective denotations, it is not obvious how the boundedness of objects has much to do with that of events. It is not simple to show formally how boundedness makes sense for each kind of abstract notion (a matter we return to in section 7.4). The project, however, makes sense, if only because, in languages with classifiers, it is both countable nominal expressions and telic verbs that receive (often identical)[35] classifiers, and typically the same sort of quantifiers are used in both instances, even if different grammatical categories (determiners vs. adverbs of quantification) are used for each purpose: *A lot of beer* goes with *Capone run a lot*, just as *two mugs of beer* goes with *Capone reached his hideout twice*.

These observations, in themselves, are straightforward. If they can be maintained, they pose an a priori puzzle for the atomist. Ontologies are common, and these look Aristotelian. As claims about the universe and its physics, they are nowadays unacceptable, given what we've learned about this matter in the last millennium.[36] Yet the fact stubbornly remains that our linguistic systems insist on categorizing the world they are used to denote in

---

34 Mori (2005) states it as *state < achievement < activity < accomplishment*, based on arguments that refine the thesis presented below. We return to this in section 7.4.4.

35 For instance Zhang (2002) shows Chinese classifiers on eventualities expressed on verbal constructions, roughly corresponding to adverbs of quantification in a language like English.

36 Although they were once meant ontologically, in the tradition of natural philosophy (see Moravcsik [1995] on this general matter, and Prasada [2003, 2005], for relevant discussion).

pretty much these terms. Moreover, this network of relations exhibits obvious patterns that cut across grammatical expression into nouns and verbs. The serious atomist, smart enough not to blame these facts on the structure of 'outside' reality that somehow penetrates the mind through the senses,[37] can only do two things: either deny the facts, or blame them not on the world in general as the expressions' denotations, but rather *on the world that serves as denotatum* – that is, thought itself. But there's a catch: the relevant 'cuts' appear to *correspond to structural devices that we find in grammatical guise* across the world's languages – classifiers, quantifiers, animacy markers, and more. So either the pertinent thoughts for some reason determine the syntactic manifestation, or else syntax manages to carve some basic aspects of those thoughts.

To see how difficult it is to tease apart these alternative approaches, consider the strong compositionality thesis, specifically in the form given in Larson and Segal (1995, p. 78):

(23)   Strong Compositionality Thesis (SCT)
        A possible semantic rule for natural language is strictly local and purely interpretive.

By 'strictly local' it is meant that a rule R cannot look down any deeper than the immediate constituents of a given category X. By 'purely interpretive', it is meant that R cannot create structure of its own – it only interprets structure given by the syntax. Larson and Segal also assert that by making a semantic theory 'highly sensitive' to the syntactic configurations over which it is stated, the learner must consider less potential interpretive theories. What learning is this, though?

We take children equipped with UG to acquire a language by fixing open parameters on the basis of input data – positive, readily available, data. So what sorts of interpretive theories must children postulate? Surely we cannot be implying that learners of language L postulate interpretive theory I, while languages of language L′ might postulate interpretive theory I′.[38] Few researchers imagine that there are purely semantic parameters (not indirectly set on the basis of morpho-syntactic information), as it is hard to see what sort

---

37 Contrary to much current practice of the connectionist sort, Piattelli-Palmarini (1989) offers some reason to be skeptical about this general approach to cognition, if it is based on anything biological. There we know of no instance where a complex structure (multi-cellular being) simply 'subsumes' a different, external complex structure.

38 The problem was rationalized this way a generation ago, when learners were taken to be hypothesis testers (see in particular Chomsky [1965, chapter 1] and Fodor [1976]). This theory was given up because of its implausibility.

of *semantic* evidence a child could use to set such putative areas of variation.[39] But if in effect human semantics is universal (Chomsky's assumption that 'from LF onwards' English *is* Japanese), there cannot be an issue of learning anything about it.

However, children do have to acquire the entirely arbitrary relations among word forms and word meanings, the so-called bootstrapping problem. This is a phenomenally complex task: how a human child relates some parsed noise within the speech signal to some unit (for instance, 'agent' or 'theme') in her 'language of thought', even if the latter is granted a priori. To illustrate with a concrete example, take (24a), with the logical form in (24b).

(24)   a. Vesuvius exploded Saturday
        b. ∃e [exploded (e) & Theme (e, Vesuvius) & Saturday (e)]

Suppose children can have (rough) thoughts in pretty much the form in (24b). The bootstrapping problem is that with thoughts like (24b) and tokens like (24a) – or rather *the phonetic form* of (24a) – the child has to acquire the arbitrary lexicon of her language. In other words, the 'easy' part is acquiring the syntax, since that is either universal or something one can deduce from the morpho-phonemic facts. The complex task is acquiring the lexicon *from syntactically and semantically organized tokens presented in phonetic guise*.[40] At this point the Larson/Segal take on the SCT makes some sense: if the set of notions one can hypothesize from seeing how symbols combine is reduced by syntax, bootstrapping is not impossibly difficult.

In this instance, if the reasoning above obtains, a fact about language acquisition dictates the need for a particularly restrictive mapping between syntax and semantics. But one could deny this justification of strong compositionality entirely, arguing that it is actually a primitive of thought that the syntax passively reflects. (Evidently, then, we are owed an explanation of what aspect of organized thought has something like (23) as a consequence.) Once again the direction of explanation becomes an issue: is syntax prior to semantics or vice versa? or do they 'run in parallel'?

---

39 Chierchia (1998) postulates parameters in the way syntax is projected to distinguishable semantics. If it is meant in its purest form (without a directly observable percept of a morpho-syntactic sort), this view owes us an explanation as to how the system can be acquired. Hornstein (1995) observes how, in principle, parameters could be set in terms of intentional or conventional information, but relevant learnability models have never been developed and tested.

40 It is tempting to think that the task is simplified by contextual salience, but, as Lasnik (1990) or Gleitman (1990) show, salience of anything linguistic that is not a concrete, pointable, noun is a hopeless prospect.

2.4.2   *Lost in translation*

The questions just posed affect the problem outlined before: if, given a feasible (learnable) human syntax, some aspects of interpretation followed, then perhaps what was called XTRA above ought to also emerge from the very structure of the syntactic object. We can examine the matter in this light if we analyse attempts to motivate XTRA from its syntax. For example, Pietroski and Uriagereka (2001) assume a condition expressible as in (25).

(25)   Part/Whole-to-Part/Whole (P/W^2) Thesis
        If X is a proper part of Y in the syntactic object, and only then, the denotation [|X|] of X is a proper part of the denotation [|Y|] of Y assigned by interpretive axioms in the system.

To see, first, the need for the P/W^2 thesis, recall an idea mentioned already in section 2.2.1: the fact that I may cause the data to become normal is not enough for me to *normalize* them. Intuitively, the causing and the caused event have to be *directly linked*. One must then be concerned with how to express this, and moreover with why it obtains.

There is a certain sense in which theta roles come in two varieties, which we may call 'articulating' and 'participating'. Intuitively, when we say that *Jack drank a beer on his pals*, the theme *beer* plays a part in the 'event play' that is central in calculating the action, so much so that without it there wouldn't be liquid consumption; in contrast, Jack's or his pals' roles are merely participatory, to various degrees – the liquid consumption would still be presupposed even if this extra participation were absent or not specified (see Kratzer [in press] on this sort of distinction). This difference between role types becomes even more interesting when considering a more complex sequence of events e_1, e_2, ... e_i ..., e_{n-1}, e_n expressed as interrelated, through some verbal predicate or a collection thereof – henceforth an 'event matrix'.[41] These add a further twist to the distinction among roles, as they show that the very first theta it is not only role discharged in a verbal projection (i.e. the theme associated to the lowest predicate) that is articulating in the intended sense. Light verbal expressions denoting sub-events whose composition to the event matrix comes in later also introduce role nuances in an event matrix, and they can do so either

---

41 The notion 'event matrix' was introduced in Uriagereka (1988) to refer to the sorts of event dependencies that arise in processes of reanalysis (e.g. causatives) and restructuring (e.g. obligatory control), where clitic climbing obtains. The notion is now being used even more tightly to refer to the sub-events that a given verb decomposes as. The distinction is not clear-cut, because some languages express as reanalysis or restructuring (through 'main verbs' associated to separate morphemes) what others express as single lexical units.

in articulating or participating terms. Quite generally, the complement to a light verb will be presenting an articulating argument of the expression, while its specifier presents, instead, a merely participating argument. In a complex event matrix, this makes a significant difference to the overall contribution of each role to the verbal denotation. All articulating arguments set up the basic 'event space', either from scratch (the Theme) or adding some extension to it (the other articulating roles). In contrast, the participating arguments only carve up that basic event space, qualifying its characteristics in ways that are not important for us now.

With those distinctions in mind, consider Pietroski and Uriagereka's (26).[42]

(26) $\exists$e {Agent (e, Pat) & $\exists$x [Terminater (e, x) & normal (x)] & Theme (e, the data)}

'Terminater' makes reference to a kind of *articulating* thematic role in the sense just discussed. *If event x plays the role of Terminater of event e, then x relates to e by virtue of being e's final part* (Assumption 1). In addition, Pietroski and Uriagereka must make an Assumption 2: *given an event matrix e_i, the Theme of e_i serves an articulating role of any Terminater-of-e*. In other words, within an event matrix we cannot have the Theme and the Terminater only weakly related; they must both be articulating roles.[43] Now recall the implicational hierarchies discussed in section 2.3.1, the relevant part of which can be roughly expressed as in (27) (in this instance for a contrast of the sort existing between (a gun) *being shot* and someone *shooting* (it)).[44]

(27)   a. $\exists$s<Shot(s) & [Theme (s, x)]>
           (e.g. 'the gun was shot.') STATE
       b. $\exists$f [$\exists$s<Change(f, s) & Shot(s) & [Theme (s, x)]>
           (e.g. 'the gun shot.') EVENT
       c. $\exists$e{Agent (e, y) & $\exists$f [Terminater(e, f) & $\exists$s<Change (f, s) & Shot(s) & [Theme (s, x)]>]}
           (e.g. 'Pat shot the gun.') PROCESS

---

42 This is omitting irrelevant details. (26) expresses a causative event which Pat is the agent of, and whose Terminater is the state of the data being normal.

43 This is plausible if, as Tenny (1994) argued, Themes are used to 'measure out' events with duration by somehow establishing their *telos*. The prominent status of themes is seen in other works as well, as outlined in Mori (2005).

44 These logical forms are given for expository purposes only, its nuances being immaterial to the present discussion. Roughly, (27a) expresses a state of being shot; (27b) refers to a shooting event (i.e. a change of state, resulting in the previous); finally (27c) refers to a process whereby some agent makes the shooting event come about.

The intuition behind those two assumptions acting together is that an eventuality expressed through an event matrix is built around a 'lower' Theme, x in (27), the Theme of s. If, for an event matrix $[e, f, s]$, we 'extend' an event f involving s and its Theme (as in (27b)) into a process e (as in (27c)), by making f e's Terminater, then the Theme x of e must be an articulating role of f. That only follows through some version of XTRA. For why couldn't it have been, for instance, that if we extended f into e then the Theme of e would be an *entirely separate* entity?

A bizarre scenario can be constructed to show how, without an assumption along the lines of the P/W^2 thesis, a logical form as in (27c) can describe a situation for which native speakers either have no intuitions or actually have the wrong ones. Consider a sub-atomic particle decaying with a certain probability, an event connected to an observer whose very observation precipitates the event in either direction (decay or not decay). In turn, consider another a priori connected event: the fact that, say, Schroedinger describes the theory behind such a state of affairs in terms of a gun that, at the end of a lever connected to one such radioactive particle, will fire depending on the fate of the particle – hence, by hypothesis, the connected act of the experiencer. At last, consider a final connected event: a physicist-cum-cognitive-psychologist, Dick Bierman, actually tests the most radical interpretation of the theory by using a real particle, a real lever, a real observer, and a real gun. This situation, incidentally, happens to obtain in the real world, and it presents events whose connection is crucial, certainly to Bierman's project (see Bierman 2003). If the physicist hadn't concocted his theory (and others hadn't interpreted it radically) Bierman wouldn't have imagined his experiment, and so the relevant gun would have never shot.[45] At the same time, as we see immediately, the causal relations between the various events, or more importantly our *interpretation* of relevant relations as being causal, is far from obvious. To make this point clear, following Schroedinger's suggestion, suppose that shooting the gun in the event sequence happens to kill a cat. No court of law, no matter how stringent, would hold *Schroedinger* responsible for this turn of events – even if the court is (unintuitively) so much against free speech that they hold a poor theorist responsible for the fact that a separate experimentalist runs a questionable experiment. The stochastic character of the particle decay makes such a prospect hopeless. Just as the gun may have shot as a result of the experiment, it may have (say with equal probability) remained still.

---

45 Bierman does not use guns in his experiments, or otherwise mistreats animals – the point is purely expository.

Consider the expression in (28a). This is patently false for the scenario described. However, it is not clear what makes it false, given the logical form in (27c), for 'the physicist' binding the agent variable *y* and 'the gun' binding the theme variable *x*, and where event matrix [*e*, *f*, *s*] has the event *f* of causing something or other (in particular a theoretical edifice) as its Terminater (a 'structuring' role) and the gun *x* as its theme (*another* 'structuring' role).

(28)   a. The physicist shot the gun.
         b. The physicist made Bierman shoot the gun through the experiencer.
         c. The physicist made the experiencer shoot the gun for Bierman.

Note: in a rather non-trivial sense the relevant events are significantly connected. Someone could complain that in (28a) we have left Bierman or the experiencer out of the picture. However, bringing them in doesn't make relevant sentences truer, as (28b) or (28c) show. Quite simply, for some reason the physicist is taken to be 'too removed' from what happened to the gun in the experiment. This is what the assumptions that Pietroski and Uriagereka introduce ensure: the Theme associated to the gun's shooting within this would-be event matrix does not have an 'articulating' role in just *any* Terminater of the event matrix. In particular, if the Terminater *f* associated to the physicist's agency is supposed to relate to the event matrix as its *final part*,[46] then it is not the case that the Theme *gun* has any 'articulating' role in this event matrix.[47]

Assumption 2, coupled with the more basic Assumption 1, follows if we insist on three non-obvious requirements: (i) mapping the direct object of a verb into a Theme in the semantics, (ii) making the resulting verb phrase a syntactic part of a larger expression properly containing it and expressing the Terminater role in the semantics, and (iii) preventing any further putative syntactic dependent of the larger event thus obtained from becoming a new Theme for that event in the semantics. In other words, the lower verb phrase, which is *a proper syntactic part* of the larger verb phrase constructed from the lower materials, must be made to correspond to a denotation which also has to be *a proper semantic part* of the corresponding denotation for the containing expression. This is the P/W^2 thesis, which is compatible with, but stronger

---

46 For concreteness, do take this to be the conclusion of the theoretical presentation regarding quantum physics.
47 It is not easy to test the predictions of the P/W^2 thesis with simpler scenarios. In essence, there are various ways of making either relevant sub-events 'significantly connected' or the manifested syntax irrelevant to thematic structure.

than, the SCT. In addition to demanding purely interpretive and strictly local semantic processes (the formal requirements involved in strong compositionality), the narrower thesis imposes something substantive: the structural nuances of the syntactic composition, in particular with regards to what is a proper part of what, must be 'preserved' in the interpretive correlate.[48] Aside from requiring a justification beyond the empirical, there is a twist to the issue just posed: if semantic processes are to be reduced to intentional mechanisms of the disquotational sort ('snow' refers to snow), how does the semantics even know that *something is a proper syntactic part of something else*?

This is a form of the translation problem.[49] It may be tempting to think that mere syntactic brackets do the job, but this is not true, for two reasons. A standard syntax of bracketing produces trivial set-theoretic objects that may contain arbitrarily many other set-theoretic objects. Lewis (1991) famously suggested a possible *interpretation* of Set Theory in Part/Whole or *integral* terms, whereby a set can be interpreted as having its members as parts.[50] However, this is not a necessary property of sets and their members, and if it is a merely possible interpretation, the translation difficulty remains: a *necessary* interpretation of something in the syntax is what's at stake, as involving parts and wholes, to then map that into some neat corresponding semantics. The first reason not simply to rely on (standard) set-theoretic notions to determine what's a part of what, then, is that those are too weak for the task.

A second reason why mere brackets won't do for the mapping we are seeking is that many syntactic associations are not as central as the one we are implying for Themes. Take adjuncts, and more concretely recall our discussion around *under the bridge* in section 2.3.4. In the dynamic reading coding the intuition of 'underfloating', *under the bridge* contributes to the compositional semantics of the derived verb; in the static reading it merely gives us a context for the floating event, it doesn't introduce a process or a *telos* for this process through the

---

48 The words 'preserved' are in quotes because, as becomes clear shortly, we have a translation problem here: in one instance we are talking about Part/Whole relations in the syntax, and in the other about Part/Whole relations in the corresponding semantics. There is no necessity in this mapping, and therefore the 'preservation' is only metaphorical, if the matter is not qualified in much detail. This is what we are about to embark on next.

49 Although strictly this is a denotational version of the problem, the issue here is more the indeterminacy *of reference* than that of translation. See fn. 16 and Bostrom (2005) for clarification, as well as chapters 7 and 8.

50 Lewis argues that the Part/Whole relation, rather than sets, should be taken as the foundation of math and abstract reasoning. That is ultimately not very different from what will be assumed here for language too. If this thesis could be shown to have necessary validity then the argument now being entertained would be weakened.

nuances of syntactic incorporation. But brackets are taken to introduce *under the bridge* as an adjunct as much as they introduce it as an argument (in both instances one can determine constituency relations). So brackets cannot have a Part/Whole interpretation in syntax, or we would be mapping adjuncts in the wrong way to the semantics, assuming the P/W^2 thesis.[51]

2.4.3 Towards a dimensional theory of syntactic representation

It seems as if we have then reached an impasse: the syntax provides us with bracketed expressions, yet in some instances we need more. But we don't want to beg the mapping question by forcing an interpretive mechanism onto the syntactic object. So something's got to give. To see the seriousness of our problem, imagine we have to code a message in a space craft, hoping to reach a civilization which shares our logic, although not our language. Suppose our message is 'humans created this', which we hope to characterize with a logical form along the lines in (29), for something with the import of 'humans made this become existent':

(29) $\exists e \{ Agent(e, Humans) \& \exists f [Terminater(e, f) \& \exists s < Change(f, s) \& Exist(s) \& [Theme (s, this)] >]\}$

To make the problem remotely solvable, suppose we take *this* to point to itself (the craft), and *humans* to involve an iconic depiction. The issue is how to code the transitivity of the expression in the terms that we use by way of the P/W^2 thesis, which we may hope the aliens share. The question being posed, then, is: what do we write in order to reflect the fact that we want whatever structure corresponds to the denotation of, roughly, 'become existent' to be *a proper part* of whatever structure corresponds to the denotation of the entire expression?

To address that seriously, we must discuss several other ideas in this book. Most will be standardly linguistic; for instance, in chapter 3 we will go into the syntax of Part/Whole or more generally integral relations, as they seem so central to comprehending the important P/W^2 thesis. Once we do that, and examine some related questions and consequences in chapter 4, we will need to make technical adjustments on the model, a task undertaken in chapter 5. In chapter 6 things will be examined from a broader perspective, all of it working in the direction of making a new proposal in chapter 7. In a nutshell, the idea that will be explored has two roots: (i) human syntax has various

---

51 Adjuncts might actually exist in very different formal terms, not involving brackets proper (a matter touched upon in section 6.5, and see Lasnik and Uriagereka [2005, chapter 7]). That would reopen the possibility that only arguments involve brackets. If so, the argument in the text would be weakened.

'orders of complexity' to it and (ii) the differences in complexity that syntax presents correspond naturally to different semantic arrays, in particular one of the D-structure sort (thematic relations) and one of the LF sort (scopal relations). That way we can have our cake and eat it too: (i) arguing that there was something right to the P&P distinction between D-structure and LF (once we clarify our claims from levels of representation to less stipulative *components* of the system – see chapter 1) and, at the same time, (ii) suggesting, both, that there are at least two different interfaces with semantic components of the system, and also that this makes sense – each interface corresponds to an order of syntactic complexity.

We may remind ourselves that a given logic is defined as *first order* if it allows quantification over one type of variable; in contrast, a logic is *second order* if it allows quantification over two types of variables: objects of interest in the system and also functions on those objects.[52] These notions apply to the formal system we conceive of as 'syntax', and the sorts of laws we take to hold of it. The first explicit discussion of matters of this sort comes from Chomsky (1965), where the question is posed whether transformations should include quantificational statements. On learnability grounds it was argued that such a possibility was unwelcome. As a consequence, an issue emerged for a variety of transformational analyses that presuppose quantification over transformations. Lasnik (2000, p. 107ff.) discusses in detail one such instance, and recalls a solution of the sort first systematically explored in Chomsky and Lasnik (1977): a filter preventing a class of representations, in particular those involving stranded affixes. Such a move addresses the learnability concern, if filters are universal (or obey markedness restrictions). At the same time, the solution presupposes enriching our system to allow for both the sorts of objects that the theory has to introduce statements about (e.g. affixes in Lasnik), and for quantifications over such objects.[53]

---

52 For these and related notions see for instance Mendelson (1997).

53 In some instances a formal trick could be performed not to go into a higher-order logic for the system, if one thinks such a move is undesirable. For example, one can recode, say, an affix about which something-or-other must hold (e.g. that it can be born as a separate lexical entry, but nonetheless must finish its morphological life attached) as a first-order predicate (on a par with objects-of-interest in the system, i.e. entries from the lexicon). In fact, in essence that is the generative semantics program, which we have seen is problematic, but certainly not incoherent. Supposing one had no scruples with a move that entails treating 'x is an affix' on a par with 'x is *a dog*', one could then restate the generalization about stranded affixes as the mere fact that the relevant predicate holds under certain conditions – no quantification over when that is, then, being necessary. But many of the tools explored in the literature over the last four decades do not allow for such a way out, a matter we return to in chapter 7.

In the history of transformational grammar there have been a variety of proposals like Lasnik's, involving postulates that require irreducible quantificational statements. There's no learnability issue with them, if they are part of universal machinery. The fact that the logic we use to describe them is of a higher order shouldn't be reason to dismiss them.[54] But it is an interesting formal fact, which we may take advantage of here. Perhaps the greatest insight of Noam Chomsky's has been that human syntax must have a context-free 'layer' and a context-sensitive 'layer' defined on the basis of the previous. If we take phrases to be our objects of interest in our formal syntax, even if we allow quantification over the predicational ones among them in stating our principles, the logic deployed need not be more complicated than first order. But note that, in particular, chains are defined as *sets* constructed over phrases (through customary transformations, or any equivalent method). Inasmuch as we also want to have (non-trivial) quantification over these elements in stating contextually-defined relevant principles (of locality, last resort, uniformity), our theory will need to be able to quantify, also, *over functions on the elementary objects*. The most straightforward logic behind this syntax will be second order.

This is not a necessary conclusion. One could ignore the definitional fact that a chain is a set of phrases, and take a chain to be a different sort of object in the system, still an object *of the same type* as a phrase from that perspective. One could furthermore (possibly) recode all contextually defined conditions on sets of phrase-markers and generalize them in such a way that they become predicates of some cumbersome sort, whose generality is a fact of mere satisfaction (see fn. 53). In that instance quantification would be over a single type, and thus first order. Indeed, much recent minimalist work takes essentially this approach, conceiving Move (the usual chain-formation operation) as a mere sub-case of Merge (the usual phrase-forming mechanism).[55] In this book, instead, it is proposed that taking the opposite view is profitable, inasmuch as a division of labor between a D-structure and an LF component (at least) is both sound and in fact tacitly assumed in many works that rhetorically deny it – see chapter 1. Moreover, a further overall assumption will be central: the ensuing higher-order syntax constitutes a clean formal system to map into the semantics of natural language. This is not a necessary

---

54 A reviewer observes, correctly, that higher-order logics have no known model theory. Far from being an a priori problem, this may be seen as an indication that the correct semantics for natural language are in fact not model-theoretic. See Tomalin (2006) for much relevant discussion.

55 Though see sections 1.5 and 7.2.2 for indications that the reduction in this instance is far from complete.

assumption either: one could have had an nth order syntax and arbitrarily mapped it to any semantics of one's choice. But a key point raised in this book is that, in effect, *mapping a more or less entangled syntax specifically to a semantics of comparable complexity* is realistic, both from a developmental (learnability) and, ultimately, an evolutionary (minimalistic) perspective.[56]

The subsequent pages attempt to show that, aside from addressing an issue on the syntax/semantic interface(s), the present approach provides us with a 'dimensional' syntax, where in a deep sense there are parts and wholes, which observed lexical entailments (e.g. of the Aktionsart sort) can be naturally built on. This dimensional theory will be reminiscent of various details of both Pustejovsky's and Hale and Keyser's proposals (these being used as model representatives of different approaches). However, the line of research deployed here will also differ in crucial respects. Although Pustejovsky's system, too, has various dimensions of complexity, these are semantic for him, whereas in the model sketched here the dimensions are purely syntactic. In turn, for Hale and Keyser the various configurations they study arbitrarily *correspond* to notional constructs; the dimensional model can obviously inherit that. But that poses the XTRA problem, quite generally. In the dimensional model, instead, *the syntactic model itself* provides crucial clues as to what turns out to be a natural mapping to corresponding semantic representation. This is what is meant, in this context, by 'naturalizing meaning'.

Returning to the specific issue of analyticity, Fodor and Lepore have good and not-so-good reasons to worry about all of this. The latter relates to a philosophical program that is skeptical about analyticity (since Quine 1960). One can be even *pessimistic* about that enterprise without finding evidence, one way or the other, in the empirical details of how the linguistic system works. The good reason to worry about decomposing is what was called above the X problem. From the perspective of the dimensional theory one would basically need to take a Higginbotham-style approach to the matter, where X is merely 'whatever it is in Japanese'; of course, that faces the XTRA objection, but this issue doesn't obviously arise once the syntax is higher order, assuming a natural mapping to the semantics (one constrained by learnability, naturalistic or similar considerations). This hasn't been shown, but it will be discussed in chapter 8. More importantly, as will also be seen at the end of the book, the dimensional theory need not face Fodor and Lepore's toughest question: why is the system not transparent, productive or systematic,

---

56 In the radical, eliminativist interpretation of this project, there is not so much a correspondence, as a total deduction of semantic structuring from the underlying syntax.

after all? This is because the dimensional layers provide the machinery for mere *paradigmatic cuts* in the system, and there is no a priori reason to take these to have the transparency, productivity or systematicity associated to *syntagmatic cuts* (the standard syntactic ones). That, though, still leaves the unanswered, and very tough, question of how paradigms relate to syntagms.

2.5   Conclusions

The plot of the Linguistic Wars aftermath reviewed above can be summarized as follows. Fodor and Lepore don't want to open again Pandora's box; Pustejovsky dares to, going into higher-order semantic tools. Pustejovsky is then told by Fodor and Lepore that much of what he seeks to explain is either not explainable or needs no explanation. Hale and Keyser do want to open Pandora's box, somewhat – enough to cover the fact that 'English is Japanese', and vice versa, which has an interesting semantic consequence. One need not embrace Pustejovsky's program to do what Hale and Keyser attempt; for example, one can extract semantic consequences staying within first-order semantics. But that raises an architectural difficulty – which was called XTRA. One reason to 'stay first order' relates to not assuming an elaborate semantic theory, and sticking instead to 'mere intentional involvement' ('such-and-such' refers to such-and-such). However, that's not easy, if one wants to have one's lexical implications right, while enjoying a trivial semantics at the same time. Only one syntactic twist was added to that plot. In agreement with Fodor and Lepore's contention that much of what has been said in favor of decomposition is too fast, one syntactic argument was raised in its defence: some decomposition is necessary to yield, for instance, Burzio's generalization as a corollary. To emphasize the point, another version of that sort of argument, from Higginbotham (2000b), was also presented, adding a few syntactic details. In turn, the dimensional theory exercise poses the question of what would happen if we take seriously the formal moves we need to assume in order to make our syntax work. In particular, could we get some of Pustejovsky's tools, but without his architectural commitments? Attempting to address that question will take us to the next chapter.

3 *Relational nouns, reference and grammatical relations*

3.1 Introduction

The previous chapter sketched some of the issues that arise in clarifying what may be a natural mapping of semantics from syntax. We studied lexical semantics and its component elements, specifically an ordering mechanism that was referred to as the part/whole-to-part/whole (P/W^2) thesis. There are two sides to a mechanism of this sort. On one hand is the mapping itself, which this book argues ought to be as minimalistic as possible. On the other, for the presupposed co-linearity to obtain we have to understand what is meant by relevant structures mapped on each side – in this instance, Part/ Whole (P/W) relations. Many researchers have devoted much thought to this concrete matter, especially because P/W relations manifest themselves in the guise of the interesting 'possessive' syntax (as in *this whole has parts*). Being concrete in characterizing such 'possessive relations' will help us ground the (multi-)dimensional syntax briefly alluded to in the previous chapter. More-over, these relations are curious in that they provide a snapshot of the main thesis here: understanding the subtleties of possession requires both context-free relations of the conceptual sort and context-sensitive relations of the intentional sort. Indeed, the book will end up arguing that it is *because* of this dual nature of possession that we obtain dimensional shifts in the underlying syntax. Section 3.2 presents the basic problem posed by possessive expres-sions, and especially logically possible combinations that do not actually exist. In the course of this presentation inalienability is distinguished from context confinement, and relevant relations are extended beyond the usually discussed ones, into combinations of a sort that will be called 'integral'. A syntactic analysis is proposed in section 3.3, and section 3.4 explores some semantic consequences, and discusses a puzzle that the syntax in point raises, which is that relational expressions as analysed here should allow more internal quantifications than they appear to. In order to solve this, a syntax/ semantics for identification is considered in section 3.5, and a general syntactic solution to the puzzle is proposed in section 3.6, assuming a Case theory which will be more fully developed in chapter 5. Section 3.7 extends relational syntax to thematic structures more generally and general conclusions are presented in section 3.8.

3.2   Possession

Traditional analyses (e.g. Keenan 1987) postulate that a 'relational term' like *sister* carries two variable positions. Different elements saturate each variable: if the *referent* of *sister* is 'promoted' to the subject of the sentence, we obtain *Jill is a sister (of Jack's)*; if the *possessor* is so promoted, we get *Jack has a sister (, Jill)*. In what follows, this general approach is shown to be problematic, and the consequences of remedying that quite appealing.

3.2.1   *Possession without a verb to express it*
As is well-known, *have* does not systematically mark a possessive relation, particularly in languages that lack this lexical item altogether.[1] Even in English, parallel to the expression in (1a), we also find all of the other 'possessions' in (1) – with no *have*.

(1)   a. Jack has a house, only one arm, very bad temper, and a nice sister: Jill.
      b. (I never knew) Jack with(out) a house.
      c. (I never saw) Jack's only arm.
      d. (I never met) a sister of Jack's.
      e. Jack is bad tempered.

To code 'possession' as opposed to 'mere predication' in lexical terms does not seem very illuminating, if we take the lexicon to be a mere repository of idiosyncrasies. Even if we allowed ourselves a generative lexicon (of the sort argued against in chapter 2), we'd have to account for the surprising fact, reviewed for instance in Uriagereka (2002: chapter 10), that the things that can be 'haved' are much the same cross-linguistically: objects, body parts, mental states, relatives ... This is a surprisingly disparate repertoire. To see this, consider the ambiguous verb *carry*. You can carry your nice lover in your arms, and you can also carry a broad smile on your face. But it is odd to say that you are carrying a broad smile on your face *and* your

---

1 Benveniste (1971) illustrates the point with examples from Vai, Turkish, Mongol, Ewe, and other languages. For perspective on this general matter of possession, and references, see den Dikken (1997).

nice lover in your arms. This is as expected: carrying a person is an action, while carrying a smile is an attribute. Factoring out the verb produces an effect that is technically referred to as *zeugma*.[2] In contrast, it is acceptable to say, upon describing you, that you normally have a broad smile on your face and your nice lover in your arms. There is no zeugma effect in this instance, much as there isn't one when conjoining attributes associated to copula *be*, disparate as they may be: you are lucky to be broad-smiled and blessed with such a nice lover. This suggests that the looseness of *have* relates to the looseness of *be*, both being, in some sense, predicative. What causes zeugma has to do with words that, although having identical PF representations, present diverse lexico-semantic dependencies, which get ignored when conjoining the disparate dependents.[3] If *be* or *have* presents no theta structure, it follows that neither should exhibit zeugma either, no matter how disparate the dependents they take may be. The good news is that this tells us something about possession: it is different from a standard theta relation; the bad news is that it doesn't distinguish standard essential predications from possessive ones.

One often finds claims in the literature to the effect that essential possessions are all inalienable – and that this would distinguish them from other forms of predication. That can be shown to be wrong. First of all, there is great cross-linguistic consensus on things that can *not* be 'haved', even when relevant relations are mathematically necessary. For instance, fractions relate to natural numbers, in as 'inalienable' a way as can be defined: involving logical necessity. Yet 2 isn't normally assumed to *have*, say, 3/4. In addition, as is shown next, inalienability can be syntactically distinguished from any reasonable notion of possession.

3.2.2   Inalienability and possession
Consider first some facts in a language, Spanish, where relevant nuances are apparent.

(2)   a. Vi el   cordón de Isabel.
            saw.I the cord   of Isabel
            'I saw Isabel's cord.'

---

2 A classic zeugma from Dickens is: "Mr. Pickwick took his hat and his leave".
3 Carrying something like a smile on your face is arguably a state, while carrying someone like a lover in your arms is clearly an activity. If so, these differences in Aktionsart may be behind the zeugma effect.

b. Le vi   el   cordón a Isabel.
   her saw.I the cord   to Isabel
   'I saw Isabel's cord.'
c. Vi su   cordón de la niña.
   saw.I her cord   of the girl
   'I saw that cord of the girl's.'

These data are taken from Uriagereka (2001, 2005). The neutral way of saying in Spanish that I saw my daughter's umbilical cord is (2a). That sentence comes out true if the cord is inalienably hers, or actually also if it is a cord that she happens to be using, let's say, for a science experiment. The alienable reading disappears when clitic doubling is involved (2b). Here the possessor comes out in dative guise, resembling a 'raised possessor'. However, what codes 'inalienable possession' cannot be the presence of the clitic, in itself, for (2c) exhibits an inalienable interpretation *without clitic placement.*[4]

There is an important difference between the 'merely inalienably possessive' (2c) and the expression in clitic guise (2b): (2c) involves no presupposition about the attachment of the cord to the child (it may hold true without the child having the cord *on*). Inalienably possessed items can abandon their host – an umbilical cord typically does, but it does not cease to be inalienably possessed.[5] In contrast, for (2b) to hold true what matters is that the cord *be attached* to the child.

One can construct situations of the sort in (2b) where what is had is not inalienable, yet it must be in some sense attached. Imagine that the discarded liver of a transplant patient is placed in a location which happens to be the target of a missile attack. A terrorist activates the missile ten minutes before the liver is removed from the patient. The missile travels for twenty minutes, and strikes the target as the old liver is being discarded. Thus the terrorist destroyed the patient's (old) liver (with the missile). Observe then the Spanish data in (3).

(3)   a. El terrorista destrozó el   hígado del paciente.
          the terrorist destroyed-he the liver of-the patient
          'The terrorist destroyed the patient's liver.'

---

4 This sort of archaic expression is restricted to inalienable expressions. Thus even Castilian speakers who normally wouldn't use (2c) find (i) more acceptable with kinship terms:

(i)   Ya nos presentaron a su sobrina/*enfermera de usted, abuelo.
          Already to us introduced to your niece nurse of yours grandfather
          'That niece/nurse of yours has already been introduced to us, grandfather.'

5 The rationale behind blood banks is to keep cords for the specific use of their inalienable, DNA-specified, owner.

b. El terrorista le   destrozó el hígado al   paciente.
the terrorist him destroyed the liver to-the patient
'The terrorist destroyed the liver in the patient.'

(3a) is true and proper, but not (3b): the statement works only if the liver the missile destroys is attached to the patient.[6] If the <clitic, double> pair were somehow related to the entire event being denoted, (3b) should come out true, for at the time of the missile's launching the liver which ends up being hit *was* still attached to the patient's body. But speakers interpret (3b) as true only if a newly attached liver – unattached *at the launching time* – is destroyed. Inalienability has little to do with this; indeed, the inalienable expression in (4) (involving no clitic) is true under the circumstances just assumed (speaking of the old, inalienable liver).

(4)   El terrorista destrozó su   hígado del paciente.
the terrorist destroyed POSS liver of-the patient
'The terrorist destroyed that liver of the patient's.'

In sum, we must distinguish '(in)alienability' from 'attachment'. To put things graphically, one could be cutting a patient's liver by either performing a (small) incision on that part of the patient's anatomy, or by severing the liver from the body. The liver continues to be inalienably the patient's in both instances, but only in the first event does it remain attached, in its normal context.[7] Both of these nuances can be expressed in Spanish, and although they are not easy to tease apart, they can be, as in the terrorist example. So '(in)alienability' – at least in the form of what we may call 'integrality' to explore further – is ultimately a basic lexico-conceptual notion. In contrast 'attachment' and similar contextual specifications are logico-intentional notions (see fn. 6), cued to a rather more complex transformational syntax.

3.2.3   *Reversibility of possessive relations*

Another puzzling aspect of possessive relations is their (partial) 'reversability', something apparent in the punch line of a notorious commercial: *I*

---

6 To be accurate, speakers can also force other contextual dependencies – attachment being only the most natural. For example, if the speaker takes the unattached liver to be important to the patient, its being destroyed on him could also be expressed with clitic doubling. The treatment of context confinement below is consistent with this result.

7 'Proper' or ontological attachment is irrelevant. A surgeon can stitch, say, an ear lost in an accident on a patient's area where blood supply is more plentiful than in the skull skin, for example the abdomen, so that a successful grafting develops. When the time comes that the newly attached organ is ready for transplant to its proper place, that would still count as cutting the man's ear (from his abdomen), and could be expressed in Spanish in dative clitic-doubling guise (and see fn. 6). All of this is true, also, if the attached ear happens to be donated by someone else.

want the soldier that belongs to this beer to step forward! This situation is far
from anecdotal. Observe these Spanish contrasts.[8]

(5)   a. El oro tenía forma de anillo.
          the gold had form of ring
          'The gold had the form of a ring.'
       b. El anillo tenía (9g. de) oro.
          the ring   had   9g. of gold
          'The ring had (9g.) of gold.'

(6)   a. La ciudad tenía (estructura de) barrios.
          the city   had structure of neighborhoods
          'The city had a neighborhood structure.'
       b. Los barrios   tenían lo peor y lo mejor de la ciudad.
          the neighborhoods had the worst and the best of the city
          'The neighborhoods had the worst and the best in the city.'

These instances manifest a possession in some direction (say, from a whole
to a part) *and its inverse*, with very similar syntax; in fact in (7) to (10),
apparently *identical* syntax.[9]

(7)   a. El peso   de un kg.
          the weight of one kg.
       b. Un kg. de peso
          one kg. of weight

(8)   a. Una concentración de 70 grados
          a   concentration of 70 degrees
       b. 70 grados de concentración
          70 degrees of concentration

(9)   a. Una organización de subgrupos
          an   organization of subgroups
       b. Subgrupos de organización
          subgroups of organization

---

8 These reversals are more felicitous in some languages than others, for obscure reasons.
9 Of course there are differences in the 'definiteness' of the determiners in each instance. Thus
  compare:
  (i)   a. ?Un peso de un kg.
                a weight of one kg.
             b. ?*El kg. de peso
                the kg. of weight

  While this must be important, it is not evidence as to whether *the conceptual part* of these
  expressions is the same. In the view to be defended here these effects must depend on the
  'surface semantics' issues studied in section 4.3.

(10)   a. Un ensamblaje de partes
            an assembly of   parts
        b. Partes de ensamblaje
            parts   of assembly

While the expression referents differ in all these pairs, 'integrality' is preserved in all of them. That is, for instance, the P/W relation in (6) obtains whether we are referring to the whole or the part. The same is true about the Form/Substance relation in (5), the Unit/Measure relations in (7) and (8), or the constitutive notions in (9) and (10), all of which obtain directly, it being immaterial exactly which term of the lexico-conceptual relation (the part or the whole, the unit or the measure, and so on) is being referred to in each instance.

Reversibility is not an obvious notion. As Higgins (1979) observes, it happens with some, typically identificational, predications: *he is 007* vs. *007 is him*. But it is impossible in attributive predications: *007 is a secret agent* does not swing in tandem with **A secret agent is 007*. And as we see in the next section, possessive reversibility is not complete in some intriguing paradigms.

3.2.4   *Extending 'relational' notions*

To complicate things, we cannot confine these subtle possessive notions to 'relational terms' like *sister*. Hornstein *et al.* (1994) show that the kind of structures that Kayne (1994) proposes for inalienable possession, building on insights from Szabolcsi (1983), are apparent in all sorts of P/W relations as well. But if we extend coverage to P/W possessions, just what isn't a part of something? Surely all count nouns have parts and are themselves parts of wholes. In turn mass nouns cannot be said to have parts, but that doesn't prevent them from entering into constitutive and measure relations of the sort seen previously. If we want to express this richness in purely lexical terms, our lexicon will grow geometrically. This is partially so inasmuch as, given a relation R between, say, a *city* and its *neighborhoods*, we can generate an expression that refers to the neighborhoods (*the poor neighborhoods of the city*) or to the city (*a city of poor neighborhoods*). If we demand that those two, because of having different referents, should involve different lexical properties, the implied lexicon is going to be even less elegant. Every time we have one integral relation we will need two *different* relational terms: say, *neighborhoods* and *city*, for each of these can project its own structure *and* be related. In other words, not only do we need to say that virtually all nominal terms in the lexicon are relational, but we furthermore have to sortalize relation R. The way a city relates, *as a whole*, to a neighborhood is different from how it relates, *as a part*, to a state. And in fact a city is normally part of other structures (an urban infrastructure, a city network, a consortium of cities) and is whole to structures other than neighborhoods (its citizens, its parks, its public ways and monuments). So the implied lexical growth may well be exponential.

Consider also the intriguing facts in (11) and (12):

(11)   a. The poor neighborhoods of the city
         b. The city's poor neighborhoods
         c. The city has poor neighborhoods.

(12)   a. A city of poor neighborhoods
         b. *The/a poor neighborhoods' city
         c. The poor neighborhoods are the city's.

The P/W relation (city, neighborhood) is deliberately kept constant in all these instances. In (11) and (12) we see *the city* and *the neighborhoods* each promoted to subject position (or associated to *of*). This is all as expected. What is not expected is that (12b) should be out.[10]

Observe also the Spanish facts in (13) and (14).[11]

(13)   a. Los brazos largos de un calamar
            the arms long   of a squid
            'The long arms of a squid.'
         b. Sus brazos largos (los del calamar)
            its arms   long   those of-the squid
            'Its long arms (the squid's).'

---

10 Some informants can assign a marginal contrastive reading to expressions like (12b). It is unclear what role that extra focalization is playing or how it affects the overall syntactic expression being studied. Such a focal reading is drastically limited if the genitive phrase is presented in pronominal guise:

(i)   a. Its poor neighborhoods (I mean the city's)
        b. *Its city (I mean the neighborhoods')

11 Asad Sayeed provides the following scenario. There is only one squid on the plate. I eat the squid, but leave one tentacle behind. My melancholy friend says, 'I've been thinking about the tentacle on your plate. Its squid swam free in the Atlantic.' Under these circumstances, one can be persuaded to accept the relevant example, but it arguably changes the 'figure/ground' relations – the basic conceptual space. In this convoluted instance the arm is the mental space, and the situation begs a reading whereby the body of that arm is used as a representation for it. We will see shortly that these 'radical reversals' are natural with 'relational' nouns. This poses the important question of how to ground the various possibilities, a very complex matter raised in sections 7.4.3 and 8.3.

c. El calamar tiene brazos largos.
    the squid   has   arms long
    The squid has long arms.

(14)   a. Un calamar de brazos largos
            a   squid of   arms long
            'A long-armed squid.'
        b. *Su calamar (el de los brazos largos)
            their squid   that of the arms long
        c. Los brazos largos son del calamar.
            the arms   long are of-the squid
            'The long arms are the squid's.'

Aside from showing that we are not dealing here with a quirk of English, these examples demonstrate that the phenomenon cannot be confined, say, to inanimate possession or some such notion. Differences of detail exist between the present and the previous paradigm,[12] but neither language allows *the long arms' squid* or *their squid* (14b), meaning the one with long arms.

3.3   Towards a syntactic analysis

Assuming the Kayne/Szabolcsi syntax alluded to above,[13] that surprising gap can be predicted. Let's take (15) to be common to both sorts of structures, although suppose a feature [+r] is used to distinguish each: in one the element marked [+r] is *city* while in the other it is *neighborhoods*.

---

12 Spanish disallows non-pronominal elements in pre-nominal position, unlike English. English uses *a long-armed squid*, with noun incorporation, for the corresponding Spanish 'a squid of long arms' (14a).

13 Here it is presented in the shape argued for by Hornstein *et al.* (1994), which involves a basic small-clause for independent reasons that we return to shortly. In that piece the need for this move was empirical, since expressions like (ia) were analysed in terms of the Kayne/Szabolcsi syntax, by analogy with (ib).

(i)   a. There is a Ford engine in my car.
        b. My car has a Ford engine.

In most proposals in the literature that involve the relevant syntax, *engine* starts the derivation as the mere complement of some possessive element in (ib), with *car* as the possessive specifier of said element. This works for (ib), but not obviously for (ia) (see below for the relevant assumptions on such displacements), where the possessed element (not the possessor) must displace to the specifier of *in*. These issues are discussed further in section 5.3.2.

(15)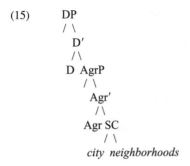

That sort of feature could have the syntactic effect of allowing displacements involving its checking to satisfy the last resort condition.

(16)   Last Resort Condition (LRC)
          Movement of α to β is sanctioned only if β c-commands α and some crucial feature F in β is checked as a result.

Suppose in particular that the [+r] element moves to the checking domain (here, specifier) of Agr, where it checks some referential feature, as in (17), yielding *(a) city of (poor) neighborhoods* and *(the) neighborhoods of the city*:[14]

(17)   a. DP   b. DP

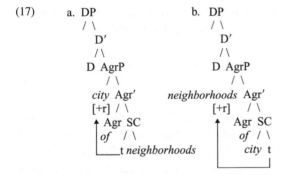

Observe next the further movements in (18), involving the D projection. Suppose also that a feature [+c], for context, triggers that movement, again in satisfaction of the LRC if we assume that some appropriate contextual specification gets checked in the D-checking domain:[15]

---

14 We return in much detail to the lexical realization of Agr as *of*, and also to the issue of whether a dummy Agr, or some other (more substantive) category, should be the relevant projection in these instances.
15 Several corners are being cut here, for ease of presentation. The most important simplification involves the movement of the small-clause predicate to a specifier, which as is shown in 3.6.2 is not obviously a grammatical option. At that point this analysis will be corrected to a more

(18)

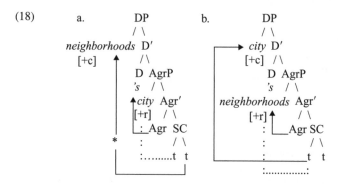

Genitive's is taken to materialize as a D head when its specifier is occupied (Abney 1986), and following Kayne, Agr won't be lexicalized when not supporting lexical material. (See section 3.6 for a refinement and corresponding operations.) The important point now is the shape of the movement paths: the ones in (18b) cross, while those in (18a) are nested. This situation can be accounted for in terms of the Minimal Link Condition in Chomsky (1995).

(19)   Minimal Link Condition (MLC)
        Movement of α to β is sanctioned only if there is no γ of the same type as α closer to β than α is, where γ is closer to β than α is if β c-commands γ and γ c-commands α.

Given the MLC, the head D cannot attract *neighborhoods* in (17a), since *city* is closer.

But regardless of the implementation details, the real point is that, whereas the movements as in (18) are meaningfully different, we cannot say much about the relevant lexical correspondences, which would all seem to be licit. What is *lexically* wrong with (12b) if (12a) is fine, especially when both (11a) and (11b) are grammatical? Why is it that whereas the part can take the whole in the two canonical forms of genitive (prepositionally and in 'morphological case' form), the whole can only take the part in prepositional guise? It is not even clear how one would stipulate that lexically, if the notions involved are syntactic. But if the explanation is to be syntactic, then what advantage is there in *also* coding the relevant relations in lexical terms?

As Armin Mester points out (personal communication) the paradigms in (20) and (21) would seem to contradict the central observation above.

---

accurate one, which nonetheless poses the same basic point: syntax can account for this sort of contrast, unlike lexical semantics.

(20)   a. (Oedipus is) the/a husband of his mother.
       b. (Oedipus is) his mother's husband.

(21)   a. (Jocasta is) the/#a mother of her husband.
       b. (Jocasta) is her husband's mother.

In this instance, all the possibilities appear to emerge, and the question is how (21b) is grammatical if it involves a structure of the sort in (18a). Note, however, that there is no definiteness effect in (20a) or (21a).[16] This is unlike what happens in examples of the sort discussed thus far; thus observe how (12a) degrades with a definite article (and see fn. 9): ?? *the city of poor neighborhoods.* Regardless of its explanation, we can take this effect as diagnosing that some integral relation is being expressed where the 'whole' (more generally, what will be called the mental 'space') is assuming the reference of the expression.

(22)   *Definiteness generalization in integral expressions*
       Given a mental space (e.g. a whole) and a presentation of that space (e.g. a part) conceptually expressed as an integral predication, intentional reference to the mental space can only be assumed if the entire expression is indefinite.

Given (22), it is reasonable to expect, say, *the mother* in (21a) *not* to be expressing a mental space, but rather a presentation of the *husband* space. This is true reversibility at the level of lexico-conceptual dependencies, vis-à-vis (20a) in the definite instance involving *the husband* – thus a shift in perspective holding of what one may think of as *intrinsically* relational expressions. Oedipus cannot be Jocasta's son without her being his mother, and the same goes for their spousal relation. There is no sense in which one of two intrinsically relational expressions can be privileged over the other to constitute a presentation for it, the way, for instance, a measure unit can be said to necessarily present a mass, or a constitutive notion like a part presents the whole it is the part of (though see fn. 11). Differently put, one can have wholes without parts or masses without measure, but not vice versa. However, one can't have relatives without also being one, so in kinship expressions it is possible for either term in a relation to be seen as presenting the other. As Juan Carlos Castillo observes (personal communication), this may relate to why it is not very felicitous to express intrinsically relational terms in bare referential guise.

---

16 If anything, (21b) at least is worse with an indefinite, although this oddity may be merely pragmatic (see fn. 9).

(23)   ?? The brother knocked on the door and a sister opened.

That said, given the definiteness generalization in (22), the appropriate analysis of the definite examples in (20) and (21a) is with *mother* and *husband*, respectively, as small-clause *subjects*. If so ensuing movements in the (b) examples satisfy the MLC, as relevant paths overlap.

That gives credence to the traditional intuition regarding relational terms. The objection raised to that idea is that these terms should provide a *general* approach to possession. For that we need a syntax that is complex enough to predict the paradigm gaps we are encountering. Nothing in it, however, has anything to say about the order in which lexical expressions enter the derivation. This appears to be a purely lexico-conceptual matter, ultimately relying on a characterization of what is a mental space in these terms and how relevant spaces can be presented in different grammatical guises. An intrinsically relational term is thus one whose lexico-conceptual dependencies with some other term can be reversed, so that no specification determines which is the mental space and which the presentation (unlike what happens with wholes and parts, masses and units, and so on). This means there *is* a way of generating an ungrammatical expression involving a purely relational term and an MLC violation; the resulting phonetic string, however, is homophonous with a legitimate one, as just discussed.

3.4   A relativistic intentional semantics

Concrete import can be provided to the features deployed in (17) and (18), starting with [+r]. Obviously, this one has to be referential, since whatever moves to the Agr domain determines the reference of the expression, which is different in each type of example. In turn, the contents of the small clause in these constructs remain identical, which can be interpreted if the lexico-conceptual (thematic) parts differ structurally from their intentional import. That makes sense in any system where conceptual relations are captured in some variant of the Hale and Keyser (1993) system, while intentional ones are expressed in terms of chains in the LF component. The present exercise is merely extending these notions to relational nominals, in a fairly direct way.

3.4.1   *Retained integrality under different referentiality – plus a direct consequence*

Consider next the evident semantic differences between *Q cities of neighborhoods* and *Q neighborhoods of cities* (the roles WHOLE and PART are used to set aside the issue of precisely what the relevant lexico-conceptual relations are):[17]

(24)   a. [Qx: *city* (x)] WHOLE(*city*, x) & PART(*neighborhood*, x)
       b. [Qx: *neighborhood* (x)] WHOLE(*city*, x) & PART(*neighborhood*, x)

While (24a) quantifies over cities, (24b) does over neighborhoods; yet the 'thematic' dependencies are identical in each instance: the cities are neighborhood-endowed cities, and the neighborhoods are city-building neighborhoods. It doesn't matter, to make this point, what the relevant shared roles ultimately are, so long as they stay the same.

This is important in understanding the bizarre entailments that often ensue when involving integral relations. As Castillo (2001) emphasizes, if one cuts a chicken's head (or as it is expressed in Romance, one 'cuts the head to a chicken') it is not just a given relation that is affected: the chicken itself is then cut. In the terms presented here, the relationship between the chicken and the head is of the integral sort, corresponding to the roles in (24). But in addition intentionality for the entire expression is obtained transformationally, as in (18). This dual process (conceptual specifications prior to the transformations and intentional specifications thereafter) make it possible for the system to capture *two sorts of semantic nuances* in the course of the very same derivation, indeed within the same object. First the system handles the presupposed relation between the chicken and its head; later on – as the relevant element (here *chicken*) is promoted to the referential site – the system deals with the referential support. Thus one can both cut an entity and moreover the relationship between that entity and one of its parts, indeed *because* the latter relation has been fatefully affected. In an arguably similar way, if one folds a hat out of a newspaper, and one tears the paper apart, both that 'formal support' for the hat will go away and, in that drastic move, so will the hat thus created. As we will see in chapter 7, this origami allusion is, in its topological implications, more than a convenient metaphor.

But the examples in (24) pose a problem. *City* in (24b) is a predicate associated to x in the quantifier restriction, and an argument associated to x, via the WHOLE theta role. Similarly for *neighborhood* in (24b): it is the restriction of the quantification and an argument associated to the PART theta role. A single expression is not supposed to act semantically in this dual way: its type is of *either* an argument *or* a predicate, not both. What follows is devoted to addressing this puzzle, but before we do that we need to consider a direct consequence of the present approach.

Observe the kind of examples in (25), which are left unjudged on purpose.

(25)   a. *A container of itself* is the only way to describe certain 4-dimensional topologies.
        b. *A measure of itself* was shown by Wittgenstein to pose Russell's paradox.
        c. *A picture of itself* in an art gallery was Escher's most troubling etching.
        d. *A critic of himself* who is also a liar may run into performance problems.

The notions in (25) raise familiar 'i-within-i' issues.[18] Nevertheless, if there is something weird about these examples, it hardly seems to be in their syntactic properties. Moreover, compare:

(26)   a. [A critic of the president] shot himself/him last night.
        b. [A critic of himself/him] shot the president last night.

(26a) exhibits a standard binding configuration. Here the anaphor *himself* is bound, and so licensed, by the antecedent *a critic of the president*, and for the very same reason the pronoun *him* must be obviative with regards to that expression. Factually, the same binding conditions arise for (26b): *himself* is licensed and *him* is obviative. But they are licensed and obviative with respect to what? They can't be bound by the entire expression *a critic of himself/him* because they are contained within the large expression, and binding presupposes c-command – which in turn presupposes *absence* of containment. Pre-theoretically, it would seem as if it is 'just' *critic* that performs the binding job in this instance, and at the very least *critic* does c-command *himself* or *him*. The problem is that in the standard view *critic* is a mere predicate – not the sort of thing that enters into referential dependencies that result in binding or obviation. In contrast, the syntax proposed in (18), which explicitly displaces elements like *part, container, measure, picture* or *critic* to a referential site, has as a consequence that these particular elements should be valid antecedents for *himself* or *him*, with the intended binding consequences.

---

18 Contrary to what is now being assumed, Chomsky (1981, p. 212) judges the sorts of examples in the text ungrammatical, and proposes his 'i-within-i' condition to rule them out:

(i)   *[α ... β ...], where α and β bear the same index.

3.4.2   Integral identification

To start addressing the puzzle posed above by type conflict, let's assume the non-committal semantics in (27). There the question mark signals *some* predicate which needs to be specified, and we involve three quantifiers: Qx for the main quantification, Q'y for whatever referent holds of the 'whole', and Q"z for whatever is the 'part' (as roles, WHOLE and PART involve two variables, being mutually dependent – hence the proliferation of variables).

(27)   (Qx: ?(x)) {(Q'y: *city*(y)) [(Q"z: *neighborhoods*(z)) <WHOLE(x, y) & PART(x, z)>]}

So far this just quantifies over (nominal event) x's that are something-or-other (the question mark), for a different quantification Q' over cities that are taken to be the 'wholes' at x, and yet a third quantification Q" over neighborhoods taken to be the 'parts' at x. The key is to determine how the question mark gets settled. Given everything said so far, for the syntax in (18a), we want Q to quantify over cities (28a), while for the syntax in (18b) we want Q to quantify over neighborhoods (28b). We are not making any commitments yet as to *how* a syntax as in (18a) or (18b) reaches the corresponding semantics. The type puzzle does not arise yet, because at no point are the expressions *city* or *neighborhoods* arguments;[19] rather, they are always *restrictions* of relevant quantifications. The issue here, however, is that in (28a) and (28b) we can't guarantee that the cities referred to are *the same ones* as those that constitute wholes to the neighborhoods, or the neighborhoods referred to as those that constitute parts to the cities.

(28)   a. (Qx: city(x)) {(Q'y: *city*(y)) [(Q"z: *neighborhoods*(z)) <WHOLE(x, y) & PART(x, z)>]}

    b. (Qx: neighborhoods(x)) {(Q'y: *city*(y)) [(Q"z: *neighborhoods*(z)) <WHOLE(x, y) & PART(x, z)>]}

In other words, (28a) could be denoting some city or other such that a *different*, somehow relevant, city is whole to its parts, and (28b) could be denoting some neighborhoods such that *different*, again somehow relevant, neighborhoods are parts to the city that comprises them.

To give an intuitive idea about the (as it turns out, logically possible but grammatically impossible) concept we're after, consider the ungrammatical expression *my wife of yours*, to be compared to *that wife of yours* and *my*

---

19 This is not to say that the *quantified* expressions that take *neighborhoods* or *city* as restriction are not arguments; in fact they are, centrally, as we saw for a formula along the lines in (27).

wife. Why can't these be combined, even if obviously the resulting amalgam could denote an individual married to the speaker but being the significant other of a third party. The same could be said, perhaps even more reasonably, of the expression **my daughter of yours*, to denote the offspring of someone who has had daughters of two different partners. These are reasonable, yet ungrammatical combinations.[20]

That oddity is not peculiar to 'pure' relational terms. Take for instance New York City (NYC), and imagine referring to the set formed by all its non-insular boroughs (Brooklyn, Queens, and the Bronx). That set is such that Manhattan and Brooklyn are parts to a city, NYC, which has the referred to, non-insular, entities as parts. In turn, consider a divided city like Jerusalem, that referring to the Jewish part of this city, with Al-Quds denoting its Muslim counterpart. Let's concentrate on the disputed Temple Mount. Now consider referring, from the Arab perspective, to a city of Al-Quds that in some sense has a crucially important neighborhood, Temple Mount, which is part to a whole that is in most respects (legally, culturally, politically, geographically) different from Al-Quds – namely, Jerusalem. Sensible though these notions are, human language can't seem to make reference to them. We just can't say **the non-insular neighborhoods of NYC (comprising) Manhattan and Staten Island* to refer to Brooklyn, Queens and the Bronx, or **a city of a highly religious neighborhood (integrated in) Jerusalem* to refer to Al-Quds.[21] But as they stand (28a) and (28b) *should* allow reference to such entities, since nothing forces the 'unification' implied in the usual instances, where if we refer to a certain whole, that must be the whole *assumed of the parts denoted*, and if to a certain part, that must be the part *assumed in the whole denoted*. What we need is, first, some process of identification in integral expressions;[22] moreover, we must gain some understanding of why the semantically legitimate structures just mentioned cannot survive, hopefully because of some syntactic reason. To understand these topics we must take a detour.

---

20 A Google search indicates that relevant strings (or similar combinations) are not attested.
21 For that matter, we can't say the grammatical *NYC's non-insular neighborhoods of Manhattan and Staten Island* referring to Brooklyn, Queens, and the Bronx, as neighborhoods such that Manhattan and Staten Island constitute their complement in NYC. Or take the ungrammatical **Jerusalem's city/entity of (among others) a highly religious neighborhood called Temple Mount*; this cannot be referring to Al-Quds, even if there is nothing wrong with the paraphrase 'zone in Jerusalem/Al-Quds constituting its own neighborhood within the occupied territory'.
22 We need a process for the whole denoted by the entire expression and the whole that determines the integral relation or, *mutatis mutandis*, the part denoted by the entire expression and the part that determines the integral relation.

3.4.3 Identification in the 'x way' construction

In the section 2.3.4 we discussed Higginbotham's (2000b) analysis of the ambiguous English expression *the ship floated under the bridge*. For a semantics as in (29), the syntax in either (30) or (31) was proposed, which relates the availability of a 'dynamic' reading with processes like *float* in English (31) to the availability of the 'x way' construction in this language (30).

(29) $[[[V+ed\ [[under\ [<x's,\ the\ bridge,\ (e',\ e'')>]]]\ (by)\ float\ <y,\ e>]$

(30)   a. [V+ed [[[the ship's way] under the bridge] (by) float]]
         b. [float+ed [[[the ship 's way] under the bridge] t]]]
         c. [the ship [float+ed [[[t's way] under the bridge] t]]]

(31)   a. [V+ed [[[the ship's way] under the bridge] (by) float]]

         b. [float+'way'+ed [[[the ship t] under the bridge]t]]]

         c. [the ship [float+ed [[[t t] under the bridge]t]]]

Preposition *under*, whose terminated-at-e'' event position e' is lexicalized as *way*, expresses a locative relation between the Theme *the bridge* and *the ship*, the latter in possessive guise (thus the genitive mark in *the ship*). In turn the verb coding event e, *float*, somehow incorporates to a higher element: either directly, to a light v (yielding the 'x way' construction in (30)), or indirectly, via the event lexicalization *way* associated to *under* (yielding the dynamic 'underfloat' reading in (31)). We return to a more detailed presentation of this sort of incorporation, and why it is not systematic even in a language where it's possible.[23] What matters now is that syntactic incorporation of an element carrying e into an element carrying e' (directly (31) or indirectly (30)) *results in identification* of these two sub-events. This – chapter 2 admits – poses the XTRA issue: things only work with user-friendly phrasal axioms.[24] So what can be done about that?

---

23 Thus observe: *Jack elbowed *(his way) out of the party.*
24 Note that *the ship*, which starts the derivation inside the VP complement, is taken to somehow associate to *under*, to undergo 'possessor raising', thus being promoted to subject position. This in turn must again result in identifying the variable y associated as a Theme to *float*, in

3.5   A syntax/semantics for identification

Let's first generalize 'semantic identification', and next consider a syntax for it. It is only after this is achieved that we can return to the quantificational problem posed in section 3.4 for complex relational nominals (why we need to resort to an identification process within them).

3.5.1   *Generalizing semantic identification*

Semantic identification is very general. Consider:

(32)   I (won't) declare [Dr. Jekyll Mr. Hyde]

Dr. Jekyll and *Mr. Hyde* are referring expressions, yet in situations of iden-tificational predication we combine them, to yield an expression whereby the reference of one is identified with that of the other. Moreover, Higgins observed in (1979) how 'reversibility' is possible just then:

(33)   I (won't) declare [Mr. Hyde Dr. Jekyll]

(34)   a.   I consider [Dr. Jekyll a troubled man]
        b.   *I consider [a troubled man Dr. Jekyll]

Another well-known instance involving identification involves individual adjectives of the sort in *a dead man* (denoting an individual who is both a man and dead). Higginbotham (1985) proposes his thematic-discharging mode of theta identification for precisely this purpose. Logically, one can imagine entities, for instance Siamese siblings, one of whom is dead while the other is a man; but obviously such an entity cannot be denoted by *a dead man*. We can surely make our phrasal axioms work in such a way that they prevent non-identificational modification by way of discharging reference to two separate individuals. Consider, for instance, the expression *the two dead siblings*, side by side with the expressions *two siblings* and *the dead*. Why can't the former be used to denote two individuals each of which satisfies the description encoded by the other two expressions? It may seem as if strict compositionality does the job, but this is unclear if the input syntactic structure involves displacement as in (35).

---

the incorporated *float+V*, with the variable x initially associated to *under*. This result must be true also in the static reading of *the ship floated under the bridge*. In other words, the floating ship in this reading must be the same as the ship under the bridge. Let's set aside this aspect of both readings, concentrating on the one yielding the dynamic one – the event identification via incorporation.

(35)   ∧
        the ∧
        dead$_i$ ∧
         two ∧
          t$_i$ siblings

Granted, for the reading we are asking about to arise, *dead siblings* in (35) cannot be taken as an argument of *two*. But why should it be? Suppose we respond: 'because they form a constituent'. However, unless we say this explicitly, that should not be decisive, especially in the neo-Davidsonian system. Thus consider (36a), with the semantics in (36b).

(36)   a. God appeared Monday.
          b. ∃e appear(e) [Theme (God, e) & Monday (e)]

Monday arguably forms a constituent with VP, but that doesn't mean it has to be its argument; a neo-Davidsonian argues that it's not. We can then complain that *dead siblings* in (35) is not just a constituent of the immediate projection of *two*, but it is its *complement*. Still, why should complements *necessarily* map to an argument? We can make that happen if our phrasal axioms say so; the issue is why they should. Suppose they did not. We could then treat the relation between *dead* and *two* conjunctively, as we do with the adjunct in (36). That would allow for a paratactic combination of the sort in *the dead (, and) two siblings appeared in my dream*. All that strict compositionality demands is that rules of semantic composition be *interpretive* (ours above are) and *local* (ours in (35) are that too – at no point have we contemplated a relation between, say, a quantifier and a *distant* dependent). What has been allowed for is the possibility of ignoring constituency links, thus permitting, in principle, the possibility of conjunctive readings of 'visually' hypotactic dependents (a head/complement relation) which are nonetheless interpreted 'paratactically'. If the grammar is to disallow that, it ought to be made explicit and follow from something natural. Logic alone doesn't do the job.

The other constraint on the syntax/semantic mapping that we have considered is what was called in chapter 2 the P/W^2 thesis. But that won't be of any use now, as the issue is not mapping a P/W relation to anything, but rather a head/complement pair, neither one of whose terms is part of the other. What we need is another kind of syntax/semantic constraint that explicitly and naturally *disallows mapping merged structures to anything with parallel or independently referring semantics*. This is not to imply that axioms in the market lack this consequence; Higginbotham's theta identification in (1985), for instance, requires that each of the predicates in (35) be bound by the same quantifier, which forces a modificational interpretation of *two*, short of violating the Principle of Full Interpretation. But what is it about axioms like these that conditions the desired result? That is the question.

In that respect, it seems curious that theta identification shares with predicative identification what looks like an adjunctal syntax: adjunction to a head N in the adjectival instance, adjunction to the predication subject in the small clause instance. Moreover, in the analysis of identification in the 'x way' construction, as in (31) above, we also presuppose adjunction via the process of incorporation (in Baker's [1988] sense) for the purposes of event identification. The obvious concern then is whether there is a way to require that *syntactic adjunction at large* bijectively correspond to semantic identification; if so, we will not be able to separate the predicate *dead* from the predicate *siblings* in the manner being sketched, and the rest of the discussion becomes moot. In effect, what does *not* involve the syntax of adjunction, from this viewpoint, will have to involve something *more* elaborate than semantic identification.

3.5.2   The Trivial Structure hypothesis

A postulate like (37) below can have a defence along the lines discussed in section 2.4.1 for the other syntax/semantic mappings: assuming that it results in a narrower mapping between syntax and semantics, it is a more elegant way for learners to acquire the lexicon.[25]

(37)   The Trivial Structure (TS) Hypothesis
        If X and Y are trivially related in syntactic terms, the denotation [|X|] of X must be trivially related to the denotation [|Y|] of Y assigned by interpretive axioms.

Precisely one form of trivial syntax is assumed here, which doesn't involve any recursive procedure of the sort involved in Merge or similar context-free operations: adjunction (more on this in chapter 6). In turn, let's take semantic identity to be the most trivial form of semantics.[26]

The TS hypothesis entails that the trivial syntax connecting two referring expressions corresponds to a trivial identificational relation among them – which describes the situation in identificational small clauses. Predicational

---

25 We return to a minimalist argument for theses of this sort in section 8.2.
26 Assume the other form of trivial semantics is listing. As will become apparent in chapter 6, when talking about finite-state systems, both identification and listing are exploited by grammars in 'label-less' finite-state conditions.

small clauses generalize this result, combining an expression referring to an individual with one that does not. Here identification proper between the expressions is impossible; nonetheless, nothing fancy can happen in the semantics if (37) is correct. Predication, however it ultimately works, appears to be all that the semantics has in stock. What is important for us now is that predication has an identificational part to it: the newly combined predicate holds as a new predicate *of the referent of the initial one.* Given the TS hypothesis no other possibility arises, as the opportunistic semantics makes do with whatever meager structure the syntax provides. Similarly, this hypothesis prevents crazy readings of modification-turned-into-referring-predicate in circumstances of theta identification: if we take 'adjunction' to be too weak a relation to have any complex semantic function associated to it, then *n* particular expressions that stand adjoined to some given element K (and adjunction has no principled upper boundary) can simply be said to 'hold', in the weakest predicational sense, of whatever we take the denotation of K to be. Finally the TS hypothesis predicts that, given an incorporation syntax, Higginbotham's semantics for 'x way' constructions follows.

To repeat, we have one identification process there, whereby events *e* and *e′* become one. If (37) holds, this could simply be because the expression syntactically representing *e* and the one syntactically representing *e′* end up with the same trivial syntax, adjoined to the same V. These are all instances of 'naturalizing meaning'.

3.6   A syntactic solution to an apparently semantic problem

Let's return now to (28a) and (28b), and why they can't be used to invoke logically possible P/W relations involving separate quantifications for the whole, the part, and their combination.

3.6.1   *Grammatically impossible integral expressions*
The relevant examples are repeated now as (38a) and (38b).

(38)   a. $(Qx: city(x))$ $\{(Q'y: city(y))$ $[(Q''z: neighborhoods(z))$ $<$WHOLE(x, y) & PART$(x, z)>]\}$

b. $(Qx: neighborhoods(x))$ $\{(Q'y: city(y))$ $[(Q''z: neighborhoods(z))$ $<$WHOLE(x, y) & PART$(x, z)>]\}$

Suppose that either the expression representing the whole in the examples in (38) – which will be called the *space* – or the one representing the part – the *presentation* – must for some reason incorporate to the expression representing the *relation* between those two. Then it will follow from the TS hypothesis that the two incorporated elements must bear identificational semantics.

Needless to say, we must evaluate the reason behind the necessary incorporation in relevant examples. Consider again the syntax assumed for these integral expressions, (17a) and (17b), repeated now as (39a) and (39b), corresponding to the semantics in (38a) and (38b).

(39)   a.

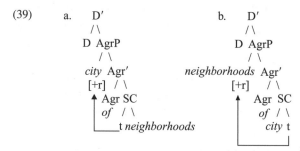

In structures of this sort the expression bearing the [+r] feature relates to the Agr head in each instance; in (39), for concreteness, the relation is expressed as one of *specification*, involving the AgrP specifier; the other possibility is that the relation in question should be *incorporation*.[27]

Now suppose that the Agr head projects a structure which the D introducing the entire expression must *theta-bind*, in Higginbotham's (1985) sense; this is to say that the Agr head represents the variable that D binds. Then for the incorporation scenario just raised, the TS hypothesis predicts that *neighborhoods*, having adjoined to Agr, results in its variable being identified to the one gluing together the entire quantificational expressions in (39), as desired (i.e. we cannot have two different variables for the theta-binder and whatever incorporates to Agr). That useful reasoning also extends to the instance involving displacement of *city* to the Agr specifier if, as per the proposal in Chomsky (1995, chapter 4), this type of displacement too involves featural operations in the Agr head. In fact, an operation targeting the XP specifier of YP is the mere *ancillary reflex* of a more basic operation involving the corresponding heads X and Y. If such head-to-head matchings are intended as involving trivial adjunction also (of relevant and crucial features),[28] then the main conclusion of identifying the heads involved in the

---

27 When the matter is studied in section 3.6.2, we will conclude that (39a) does indeed involve specificational syntax, whereas (39b) should instead make use of incorporation.
28 Or some variant syntactic process (of the valuation-via-agreement sort) also subject to the TS hypothesis.

dependency will still hold, and consequently it will still be true that theta-binding of the (in the extended sense) identified Agr head and the corresponding lexical element will be theta-bound by the D element. Then no complex quantification can ensue, again as desired.[29] However, we must immediately raise two questions: whether this state of affairs is necessary in syntactic objects of the form above; and why it doesn't extend to standard quantification over events in sentential instances. These questions are arguably related.

3.6.2   *Not enough cases?*

Chapter 5 will be arguing for a Case hierarchy whose main consequence is easy enough to observe, regardless of what explains it. Whereas verbal domains present three sorts of structural Cases ('object', dative,[30] and 'subject' Case), nominal domains present at most one structural Case (genitive); in addition there can be one extra systematic source of inherent Case in each domain. This is central in understanding why (38), (39) and the like require, in effect, some sort of 'valence reduction'. Although it would have been semantically possible to assemble the sort of complex structure assumed in nominal instances stemming from relational notions, it is syntactically impossible for the structures in point to surface as multi-valence dependents; arguments require Case valuation, and there aren't enough Case values in nominal domains to do the job. Or to be more precise, the Case situation in these nominals is very delicate, since they depend on a conspiracy of factors to have all imaginable dependents Case licensed (a high source of genitive, a low source of prepositional/inherent Case via *of*, and a configuration such that the entire DP has an external source of Case somewhere even higher within the clause taking this whole DP as a dependent). As it turns out, it is impossible to get such a conspiracy to work beyond two Case sources, for reasons to be discussed in chapter 5. This idea works nicely, but there is one problematic instance to worry about – which forces us to spell out important details.

Let's observe (39) in the light of the Case issue just raised. We cannot have a structure along the lines of (40), *base-generating an otherwise coherent extra lexical head* associated to the Agr projection, without originating inside

---

29 We return in section 8.4.6 to comparable displacement instances where we do not obtain the ensuing identification – in fact quite the opposite. A major structural 'reprojection' can be shown to obtain in those instances.

30 On the nuances of dative Case, and how it sometimes cannot be merely 'inherent', see section 5.3.1.

the small clause SC (see 3.4.2 above). Bear in mind that, to cover all grammatical possibilities, we are using derivations involving either the specifier *or the head* of the Agr projection, both of which are in principle possible.

(40)

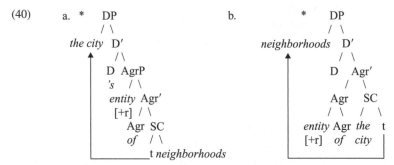

The signaled movement in (40a) violates the MLC (displacement of *the city* over the AgrP specifier). (40b) is more problematic: the additional referential element *entity* now *heads* the Agr projection, which eliminates (at least any simple-minded) violation of the MLC. Why can't this expression be grammatical with: (i) *entity* getting its Case demands met in terms of whatever Case the DP is checking as an argument, (ii) *the city* satisfying (inherent) Case via the pleonastic *of* preposition – which for Kayne (1994) was a possible realization of the Agr head, although more on this below, and (iii) *neighborhoods* getting genitive Case in the D specifier?[31]

As it turns out, for the displacement of the small clause predicate – which is being called a *presentation* – movement as in (40b) is not definable. This is because, if small clauses are as standardly conceived since Stowell (1983),[32] then SC is some *projection of the presentation* (more generally the predicate) not the space (more generally the subject), and thus this space must be a *maximal projection*. In contrast, the presentation itself may be either a mere head or an intermediate projection (depending on whether it has dependents). This projection status affects how each, the space and the presentation, displaces to the Agr projection (or beyond). In its strict head guise, a presentation should move to the next head up, adjoining to it – which is violated in

---

31 The same could be asked of a version of (40a) with the extra element adjoined to the Agr head.

32 Prima facie this is incompatible with the view of perfectly symmetrical small clauses presented in Moro (2000). We see in section 6.4.2 (when discussing how to make sense of the head/non-head relation even in simple finite-state terms) that the incompatibility is only apparent.

(40b);[33] in contrast when the *space* displaces it should not involve head adjunction to Agr, but instead displacement to the Agr specifier. Although displacement to a specifier does happen in (40a), the relevant movement skips the Agr specifier, as we saw – violating locality conditions.

That conclusion actually affects the analysis suggested above for (18), about which we can now be more accurate. The issue in that instance was the putative displacement of a presentation over a space which has itself associated to the Agr projection (yielding the impossible **neighborhoods' city*). Now we can see that such a displacement would have to be head-to-head, thus involving the Agr head in its way up to the D head. Under one possible derivation, where the presentation has a [+r] feature to allow for such a displacement, the move to the Agr checking domain would conflict with the displacement of the space to such a domain. Either that extra movement would not be motivated or else the checking features of Agr would have to be involved twice. If, on the other hand, the presentation does not have the [+r] feature, it would not be legitimate for it to move to Agr to start with in satisfaction of the LRC, and its movement higher up in the tree would violate head-to-head conditions (another MLC effect). Either way we still have a syntactic analysis of the paradigm gap.[34]

A more challenging, and still ungrammatical, derivation combines the basic tenets of both (40a) and (40b), as in (41).

(41)　　*　DP

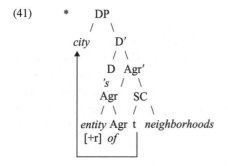

Why can't this time the space *city* move *as a maximal projection* (which it is, as well as a head) over a head Agr *already associated* to the referring *entity*

---

33 The item *neighborhoods* as such could move as a head, but not skipping the next head up, namely Agr (short of violating the MLC); in the present instance this Agr head is associated to a lexical entry, *entity*, and thus the sort of incorporation that would have been viable to Agr has now been barred.

34 The argument in section 3.3 was that no such explanation is obvious if the relevant relations are merely lexical; this continues to be the case in the present analysis.

(supposing an appropriate [+c] feature carries the item to the DP specifier)? This is puzzling, since (41) looks similar to the viable (42).

(42)

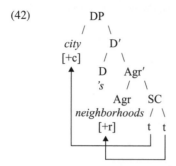

There are two difference between (41) and (42): first, in the former instance there is an *of* before the trace in the SC subject position, which is arguably important to Case-license *neighborhoods*; in the latter instance there isn't one, which entails that *neighborhoods* in this instance will be Case-licensed in terms of whatever source of Case takes care of the entire DP within the clause. Second, in (42) the head associated to the Agr projection has been *displaced* to that position, whereas in (41) we have base-generated the relevant element in such a disposition. Either one of these differences may be relevant, so we should study them in turn.

3.6.3   Chain uniformity and its consequences

Descriptively, the Agr head does *not* surface as *of* and similar elements when not followed by any lexical material (see Castillo 2001). That is, together with, say, *neighborhood of the city* or *city of neighborhoods* we have *city's neighborhood*, but obviously not **city's neighborhood of*. One possibility to consider is that whatever explains this ungrammaticality should also extend to explaining the impossibility of (41). Observe the relevant structures.

(43)   a.   [*city*$_i$'s [*neighborhood*$_j$ [t$_i$ [t$_j$]]]]
        b.   *[*city*$_i$'s [*neighborhood*$_j$-*of* [t$_i$ [t$_j$]]]]

Given what was said above, the presentation *neighborhood* must be moving head-to-head in this instance, adjoining to *of* in (43b).[35] In itself this cannot

---

35 There is no other way of moving head-to-head in 'last-resort' terms. Early minimalist works also contemplated the possibility of head-to-head movement by 'substitution'; however, as a Bare Phrase Structure is assumed, no such substitution target can be postulated. Thus incorporation is the only relevant option here.

be a problem, or we would never generate *neighborhood of the city*, which also implies incorporation of *neighborhood* to the Agr head and a trace after *city*. But it could be that the presence of *of* in (43b) affects *the other* trace, the subject one left by *city* on its way out. This recalls the complementizer-*t* effect.

(44)   a. Who do you think [(*that) [t left]]?
         b. Who do you want [(*for) [t to leave]]?

Lasnik *et al.* (2005: chapter 7) interpret that effect in terms that have an interesting independent consequence for the present analysis. Consider their approach.

Argument chains are curiously non-uniform (they start in an A-position and displace through A′-positions). Following Browning (1987), Chomsky and Lasnik (1993) argue for (45).

(45)   Condition on Chain Uniformity (CCU)
         A chain must be uniform, where a given chain C= $(a_i^i \ldots, a_i^j)$ is *uniform with respect to P* if each ai has property P.

Chomsky and Lasnik also assume that lack of chain uniformity (e.g. in A/A′ status) can be remedied by deleting offending traces. The version of this proposal in Lasnik *et al.* assumes that by erasing an intermediate trace – in conditions where such an information-losing operation is even possible – the entire offensive chain will cease to be. The point is, then, which intermediate trace to delete, and when, especially in a cyclic derivational system that works bottom-up. Intuitively, the sooner an offensive trace is deleted, the better off the system will be, since a grammar that transfers derivational material to the interpretive components in phase fashion is in the position of having to deal with an ill-formed chain (according to the CCU in (45)) already in an early cycle. Lasnik *et al.* also assume, in the spirit of Cinque (1990), that destroying a chain relation via an intermediate, uninterpretable, trace that can be erased forces the system into a pronominal-antecedent (binding) dependency, between the original gap in an A-position and the head of the chain in the A′-position.[36] Two asymmetries then arise between object and subject chains: the former have their first link within a *v*P phase (from V complement to *v*P specifier), whereas the first link of the latter must be established *across* phases (from the *v*P specifier to the TP specifier,

---

36 In other words, we must allow (to some extent) a functional determination of some gaps, thus reinterpreting a trace as a pronominal element.

the latter in the CP phase). In addition, whereas the specifier of a *v*P is arguably an erasable site, the specifier of TP is not if the extended projection principle (EPP), demanding surface subjects, is operative. As a consequence of these asymmetries, when evaluating chain uniformity the system can take care of the lack thereof in the complement instance already at the point that the *v*P phase is transferred to interpretation. At such a point there isn't, still, a subject chain (the subject hasn't displaced yet); the relevant displacement takes place in the CP phase, when both the creation of the link spanning to the TP specifier happens, as well as the subsequent link spanning to the CP specifier. Crucially the trace in the TP specifier cannot be eliminated – in languages obeying the EPP – and thus the phase is stuck with a non-uniform chain. Why does a null complementizer help? Because it signals, Lasnik *et al.* argue, the system to *halt* a phase-transfer at the CP level. If the transfer can be delayed until the next *v*P phase up, the system can invoke that *v*P specifier instead, thereby being able to erase the intermediate trace *at the CP level* (where it is not demanded by the EPP). This results in a dependency of the antecedence sort.

For that reasoning to be relevant now we must suppose that those mechanics are operative, also, within the small clause associated to the Agr heads we are studying. The hope is that – unless something interesting happens – the computational system is facing a non-uniform chain, in violation of the CCU. This presupposes a prior question: are relevant chains indeed non-uniform? The issue does arise for at least the small clause subject, customarily assumed to be adjunct on its predicate (we return shortly to the small clause predicate). If such a subject/adjunct remains in situ, satisfying its derivational demands in place, nothing else needs to be done. However, if this element displaces to either the Agr or D specifiers, assuming these are A-positions, a non-uniform chain will emerge (foot in an adjunct position and head in an A-position). Two questions arise, then: (a) how to prevent such a chain (which chain link can be eliminated to turn the chain into an antecedent/gap relation for which uniformity conditions are irrelevant) and (b) why presence of an element like *of* should make a difference in that respect. As for (a), the Lasnik *et al.* logic forces us to have an erasable intermediate trace. If things are as presented so far, such a trace actually doesn't exist: we just have the initial trace associated to the small clause. However, things can proceed in the appropriate direction – a matter that will be justified further in section 5.5.2 – by treating the *of* head not so much as *realization* of Agr, but rather as its own *separate* projection. A relevant derivation would be as in (46).

(46)

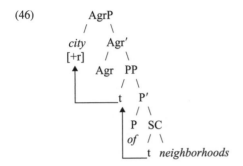

The *city* chain now has an intermediate trace, and is non-uniform as desired (assuming the *of* specifier constitutes an A-position). Thus the possibility of erasing the key intermediate trace emerges, that making the non-uniform chain collapse into an antecedent/gap binding relation.

(47)
```
          AgrP
         /    \
     cityᵢ    Agr'
             /   \
          Agr    P'
                / \
               P   SC
              of  / \
                Øᵢ  neighborhoods
```

Having addressed question (a) – how to prevent the non-uniform chain by deleting an intermediate link – we must now concern ourselves with (b) – when presence of *of* has an effect on the derivation. In (46) it makes no difference. However, it does in (48) below. One clear difference between these examples is in terms of the *of* head being de-activated in (46), after it is involved in Case determination for *neighborhoods*, a task that never takes place in (48): where *neighborhoods* will check its Case in terms of some category higher up in the derivation. Evidently *city* is irrelevant to the present point, in both instances. (If we don't introduce the *of* in (48) – assuming that possibility even exists, a matter we come back to in section 5.5.2 – then we won't take the intermediate step that we motivated for (46) to start with, and the relevant chain will directly violate the CCU; so that particular derivation cannot be the source for the grammatical (43a), to which we return shortly.)

(48)

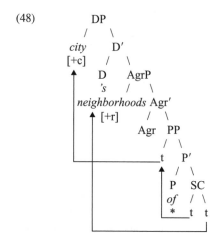

Plausibly Case deactivation makes a difference in the possibility of trace erasure, in terms of an erasure convention that we can express as in (49).

(49)   *Erasure Convention* (EC)
        Only uninterpretable items in inactive sites are erasable.

The intuition behind the EC is simple, and it reduces to a sub-case of what Lasnik *et al.* (2005, chapter 1) call the First Conservation Law of derivations.[37]

(50)   First Conservation Law: Conservation of Lexical Information
        All information in a syntactic derivation comes from the lexicon and
        interpretable lexical information cannot be destroyed.

The EC in (49) simply prevents wild erasures, in particular because, in a bare phrase structure system,[38] erasing a term in a relation of Merge (in the instances in point, a specifier) entails erasing the projection that results from that merge. Given the EC, such a drastic mechanism is possible *only if the two terms in the merge are uninterpretable*. The cases Lasnik *et al.* study within the *that*-t paradigm conform to that pattern: they involve the *v*P specifier when theta roles associated to the *v* head have already been established and the Case this head activates has already been checked.

---

37 In effect this combines the traditional recoverability condition with Chomsky's (1995) inclusiveness condition.

38 The present system, though different in details from standard ones, is still a bare phrase structure system in all relevant respects. In particular no superfluous operations or symbols are allowed, and all phrasal (or even simpler or, of course, more complex constructs) are obtained through standard syntactic processes.

An analogous situation takes place in (46), where *of* has already introduced the small clause and determined inherent Case to *neighborhoods* within it. However, the same is not the case for (48), as in this instance *of* hasn't been deactivated by Case assignment. Note that, from this perspective, (43a) must be analysed as in (51) below. In this instance the abstract P in (51) must displace with the predicate head that moves in head-to-head fashion, to the Agr projection. Thus, although the P doesn't involve in any Case assignment here (so any 'deactivation' either), the erasure of an uninterpretable trace, in *whatever remains of P's projection* (also a trace) after P incorporates, arguably doesn't violate the EC.

(51)

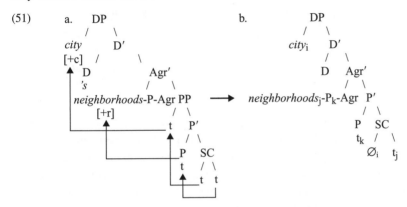

So to sum up, let's look at all the relevant structures side by side:

(52)   a.   [*neighborhoods*$_j$-*of*$_k$ [$_{P'}$ t$_k$ [*city* [t$_j$]]]]
         b.   [*city*$_i$ [$_{PP}$ t$_i$ [*of* [**t$_i$** *neighborhoods*]]]]]
         c.   [*city*$_i$'s [*neighborhoods*$_j$-P$_k$ [$_{PP}$ t$_i$ [t$_k$ [**t$_i$** [t$_j$]]]]]]
         d.   *[*city*$_i$'s [*neighborhoods*$_j$ [$_{PP}$ t$_i$ [*of* [**t$_i$** [t$_j$]]]]]]

In all these representations, except (52a), an issue arises with the highlighted trace of the underlined-small-clause subject *city*, namely t$_i$ – whether we can succeed in reinterpreting it as a gap bound by an antecedent to which it doesn't relate as a chain, after destroying some offending intermediate link, as the relevant chain otherwise violates the CCU. The trace erasure has to proceed in satisfaction of an EC. The trace of a preposition like P in (52c) constitutes a valid target of erasure when associated to an also uninterpretable trace. Overt *of* can have a similar effect *if* it has been deactivated after inherent Case assignment, as in (52b). Finally, the overt *of* in (52d), which has not determined any Case within the small clause and is thus accessible to the computational system, does not constitute a valid point of erasure in satisfaction of the EC, with the consequence ensuing that the chain it constitutes a link of never ceases to be non-uniform and is thus illegitimate (alternatively, movement of the head *neighborhoods* over *of* in this instance violates the MLC, also predicting the ungrammaticality).

Finally re-consider (41), with the extra prepositional projection just discussed.

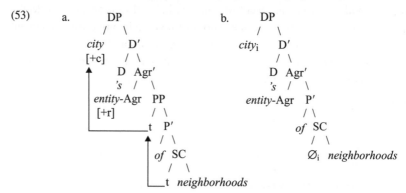

In this instance, given everything said so far, we should be able to delete the intermediate trace in the PP specifier, yielding (53b) as grammatical, contrary to fact. Note in particular that *of* is deactivated here after determining inherent Case in *neighborhood* (53a), so erasure of a trace in its specifier as in (53b) should be sanctioned by the EC as much as it is in (47) above. This suggests that, although a *that*-t-style approach is necessary and straightforward in accounting for the sort of grammaticality in (43b), the explanation actually does not extend to the problematic (41). This is, however, not all bad news. First, we have explored a mechanism, involving the reasonable property of chain uniformity, which will be of central use in various other places in this book (see sections 6.4.3 and 8.5). Second, there is another difference we observed in section 3.6.2 between (41) and (42): the referential head in the first instance has reached the Agr projection by movement, whereas in (42) the referential head is base-generated associated to the Agr head instead. Could that, then, be the culprit for the ungrammaticality of (41)?

3.6.4   *Lexical and functional projections*

Since Chomsky (1957) we separate such elements as head verbs from corresponding agreement projections (either of the *v* or the T sort), and similarly for other substantive (N, A, P) items and corresponding formal projections that, in many languages at least, are overtly associated to the latter. This can be made explicit as the thesis in (54), often tacitly assumed for verbal elements.

(54)   Lexical Projection Thesis (LPT)
         (a) Formal items involve transformationally driven event-quantification
             semantics.
         (b) Substantive items involve configurationally expressed predicative
             semantics.

The problem with (53), then, must be that the predicate *entity* goes against
(54b): it is not in a *configurationally* expressed predicative relation, as it is
adjoined to the Agr head. We return to adjunction as a process in chapter 6, but
it clearly is never a standard (e.g. 'head/complement') configuration. Moreover, unlike other substantive elements of the sort we have discussed at length
throughout this chapter (*city, neighborhood* and the like) *entity* in (53) is never,
at any given point in the derivation, in one such configurational relation.

    Given the character of a law, the LPT rules out any substantive item that is
not configurationally introduced into the derivation. As stated, the thesis
predicts that the lexical dependencies in a small clause (which by hypothesis
involve adjunction) are actually neither substantive nor formal. This matter
will be clarified further in section 6.4, when we discuss a variety of finite-
state processes involving elements that could in fact be categorized as neither
substantive nor formal, but as something more elementary. At any rate, what
was referred to as 'identification' in section 3.4 and 3.5 above puts the item X
that identifies (after head/adjunction) with a different item Y in the position
of *inheriting the LPT status* that Y may have on its own. So if Y is a head of a
formal sort (e.g. one expressing a referential variable), the identified X will
assume a formal status too (in particular one identifying its predicate
denotation with the denotation of the variable that we are taking X to
express). This is possible only if we take the phenomenon of referentiality to
be of the formal, not the substantive sort, as a category cannot be in a position
to inherit an identificational status other than through base-generated
adjunctions or those obtained via movement, neither of which counts as
configurational. In the most minimalist scenario, this entails that even simple
expressions like *the man* or *water*, which obviously can be used to refer,
ought to achieve their referentiality by way of complex relational procedures
of the sort discussed in this chapter. Although we will not go into this matter
here, Muromatsu's (1998) exploration of the syntax of classifiers makes
precisely that point.[39]

---

39 Essentially Muromatsu treats the classifier as what is being called a presentation on the
   nominal space, and then shows some consequences of this move for various syntactic
   properties of these elements in several languages.

We started this analysis by asking, at the end of section 3.5.1, whether having to identify two predicates is necessary in the cumbersome quantifications that the relational system we are studying allows (in effect reducing the complexity from three imaginable lexical predicates to only two usable ones). We have now seen that, given the Case properties of relevant nominal expressions manifesting the syntax under scrutiny, coupled with standard syntactic conditions, the answer is 'Yes'. Whether it is necessary for UG or just for the languages we have looked at depends on whether the impoverished Case system within nominals is universal; chapter 5 will suggest it is. Note also that the analysis of the impossible (53) in terms of the LPT in (54) has nothing to say about a structure where, for some reason, a head analogous to *entity* manages to reach a functional projection in the course of the derivation. This is actually good, because after all we have plenty of structures with the format of *Picasso's portrait of Gertrude Stein*, which seem tantalizingly similar to the impossible **city's entity of neighborhoods*. But to examine this matter seriously, we must concern ourselves with why the considerations above do not directly extend to standard quantification over events in sentential instances, where it is obvious that relevant quantifications can be extremely rich.

3.7   Consequences for thematic relations within VP

The main reason to worry about the relational matters just examined is how they may affect thematic relations at large. The appropriate extension is mentioned in Castillo (2001), who suggests a simple parallelism ought to obtain between *a portrait of Gertrude* (or similar examples) and *a neighborhood of the city*. More centrally to our purposes here, there ought to also be a parallelism between *a portrait of Gertrude* and the verbal expression *to portray Gertrude*, which in present terms gains an intriguing significance that we return to in section 5.4.3. Thus, we should obtain (55) for the nominal instance and (56) for the verbal counterpart:

(55)

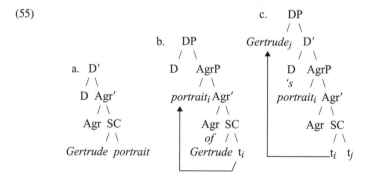

(56)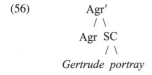

(56) is less radical than it may seem. In chapter 5 the 'clausal' structure in (56) is reduced to something more familiar (by way of what will be referred to as 'complement assumption'), albeit without losing the complexity implied in the clausal extension, which we want for implicational reasons of the sort raised in chapter 2. Moreover, a proposal along the lines in (56) has been around since Kayne (1984) invoked a small clause analysis for double object constructions.[40] That intuition goes back to relational grammar studies relating 'clausal reduction' to argument taking.[41] Basically, *every verbal argument is a subject of sorts*, even when it gets assumed into the complement skeleton of the verbal projection. That is, to *portray Gertrude* involves Gertrude as participant in some portrayal situation. Moreover, n-adic predicates essentially involve n such situations, and thus *for Jack to boil the soup* involves not just the soup as articulating a boiling situation, but also Jack as participant in a causing of that boiling of the soup, and so on (see Pietroski [forthcoming], Mori [2005] on these matters).[42] Finally, even standard syntactic proposals indirectly make the same point; take Lasnik (2003), building on Koizumi's (1995) idea involving overt object shift to some functional category. Lasnik argues that each relevant argument (direct object, indirect object, subject) starts its derivational life *above* the functional projection whereby the previous, thematically lower argument does. The intuition behind that approach is clear: Case checking or similar 'grammatical' dependencies are, in this view, interspersed with thematic relations. That comes close to asserting that each 'grammatical' dependency is 'subject-like', even if other factors intervene to determine 'objecthood'.

Without attempting to be explicit yet about the mechanism of 'complement assumption', but just to give a picture of how n-adic dependencies work, the schematic representation in (57) can be offered, where SC_1 in (57a)

---

40 A more modern version of this approach is Déchaine *et al.* (1994).
41 For references and a discussion of clause union and similar processes, see Perlmutter (1983).
42 The notions 'articulating' and 'participating' role were introduced in section 2.4.2. From the present perspective, the lowest small clause articulating an event matrix will establish the first articulating role: the Theme. Other small clauses built on that first space will generally add mere participating roles.

introduces the direct object (a DP signaled as direct object (DO) after incorporation) and SC$_2$ introduces, after the complement assumption in (57b), the next dependent (either a subject or an indirect object – this being orthogonal to our concerns right now – simply signaled here as ' ... '). This view of the VP is to be contrasted with more traditional ones, for instance Hale and Keyser's in (2002) and elsewhere. At some point (after 'complement assumption') all proposals are intended to be roughly identical; however, initial phrase-markers here have a clausal structure to them, with relevant predications playing a crucial role at a lexico-conceptual level that articulates the implicational structure of the VP – its Aktionsart:[43]

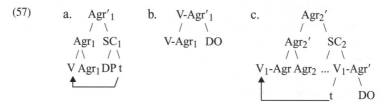

This suffices as a sketch, although we will later be making much of the syntactic consequences of 'complement assumption' (see chapters 5 and 7). Within the narrower concerns of this chapter, concretely the LPT introduced above, complement assumption is taken to generate a configuration, one in particular of theta-dependency, which is assumed to be substantive in the intended sense.

As to why syntactic limitations in relational expressions within the DP – preventing otherwise sensible expressions like *my wife of yours* – do not extend to standard quantification over events in sentential instances, observe that, aside from the (main) predicate introduced by the event quantifier, we have as many *further* predicates as lexical nuances that the relevant verb allows – from no further argument in presentational or weather predicates to up to three in ditransitive verbs, or more if we start involving oblique dependents (Mori 2005 counts up to five). Such riches are a mere consequence of the corresponding richness in the Case system for verbal instances, which will be examined further in chapter 5.

---

43 This is proposed as an *alternative* to generative semantics. The predicational (multi-clausal) layers presented so far are meant to be extremely restricted: to start with, not all 'clausal' relations count for the purposes of the articulation of a VP – not even all 'syntactically viable' clausal relations do. Moreover, the generative power of this machinery is reduced once 'complement assumption' is discussed in chapter 5. These points are discussed more fully in chapter 7.

But not all imaginable combinations that emerge in relational expressions within DP are immediately expressible at the VP level. Recall that the procedure we discussed in section 3.6.3 to get a successful referential object when the subject of the small-clause displaces is fairly cumbersome, entailing a trace-erasure that all but breaks the direct syntactic connection between a lexical item displaced to a referential site and the lexico-conceptual 'inner variable' that it starts from. The relation between the theta-identification site with referential import and the integral site with conceptual import is eventually one of mere binding, even if it originates through movement. Such a drastic chasm should not be operative for the corresponding predicate, simply because *it can move as a head* and therefore enter into a head/head relation, whereby as Chomsky (1995, chapter 4) argues, uniformity considerations become immaterial upon entering the Word Interpretation realm of heads. We see in chapter 5 that this is consistent with the shape of most productive referential dependencies formed from the elements of an integral small clause, especially verbal ones, which normally are predicate-driven (e.g. *city neighborhoods*) instead of subject driven (e.g. *city of neighborhoods*). In other words, we find plenty of verbal expression of the sort of *skin the beast* – where the part, or in present terms presentation, heads the verbal projection – but not **beast the skin* – where the whole, thought of here as a mental space, is what is responsible for the verbal denotation.

Nonetheless, in this sort of mechanism for the successful completion of referential derivational dependencies a chasm is created, as the interpretive nuances of a head chain are resolved *within a Word Interpretation component*. This entails that we don't expect the resulting representation to present an active syntax, whereby for example reconstruction (in the sense of section 1.5.1) or similar effects could be displayed, since in both instances the derivation destroys the representational history that could have allowed the system to reconstruct the appropriate derivational origin. This is quite important in understanding why these otherwise syntactic processes do not leave syntactic vestiges that can testify to their active presence beyond lexical entailment, the central point of contention in the Linguistic Wars (see chapter 2). We return to these matters in section 8.5.

Note to conclude that, in situations like *Picasso's gift of flowers to Gertrude (moved her)*, each nominal manages to find a way to survive the derivation, relevant Cases to be studied in Chapter 5 appropriately emerging in their final destinations. This includes a Case for the entire expression associated to *gift*, assuming an external source.[44] The idea is thus confirmed that the specific problem with expressions like **NYC's entity of neighborhoods (shines)* is not so much with how the various nominals get Case. Rather, it is the fact that there is no lexico-conceptual source for *entity*. The difficulty is derivationally taken care of in the much more complex DP at the beginning of this paragraph, a nominalization from the, in itself complex, verb *give*, an achievement with various internal layers of small clauses (at least one per obvious argument). As the derivation unfolds, no substantive item is ever introduced in the derivation other than through the lexico-conceptual (space, presentation) relation discussed here. If that is taken care of, however, and in addition all appropriate nominals find themselves in a valid Case context, then the result will be grammatical. In general verbal domains will be more flexible, as they don't depend on external sources of Case to meet their Case demands; but relevant Case conspiracies can also result in pretty generous dependencies at the nominal level, as desired.

3.8   Conclusions

Relational nouns, it would seem, abound – it is easier to find them than not. Coding their properties as lexical idiosyncrasies is not illuminating, and invoking syntax for their subtle distributions is much more promising. In turn the syntax that we need for them is quite relevant for argument structure more generally, which is where the dimensional syntax we will be examining in this book ought to be grounded. Addressing the puzzles that this sort of syntax poses for the appropriate interpretation of corresponding semantic expressions moves us in the direction of a relativistic notion of intentionality, whereby elements don't come from the lexicon equipped as 'referential' or otherwise. Rather, they *become* referential, or in fact contextually confined if quantificational, if in the appropriate (transformationally determined) syntactic structure. This view of things places referentiality in the hand of users, for it is they, ultimately, who decide whether or not to place relevant [+r] (for reference) or [+c] (presumably for context confinement)[45] features in

---

44 Similar considerations obtain for a version of this expression with noun incorporation:

(i)   Picasso's flower gift to Gertrude (moved her).

45 We return to contextual specifications in section 4.3, and again in section 8.4.7 more broadly. Displacements for contextual purposes are related to those studied in Jeong (2006), based on an important literature on 'applicatives'. The main difference with that work is that the

relevant numerations, to drive the transformational machinery under 'last resort' conditions.[46]

In addition, this approach raises interesting puzzles, the deepest one of which is that it allows, semantically at least, the possibility of as many 'nominal-internal' quantifications as one sees in a clause (where a priori there could be as many as arguments plus one, for the event quantification that glues argument structures together). The solution to this puzzle explored here is syntactic. By way of a detailed analysis of apparent incorporations internal to nominals, the Case system is shown to be centrally involved in these matters: essentially 'not enough cases' is what rules out something like *my wife of yours*, adding a new twist of irony to familiar 'three-body problems'. Given these ideas, we must commit to a specific syntax/semantics for incorporation and other instances of what was called 'trivial syntax' (basically involving adjunction), aside from independently established derivational conditions like the LRC, MLC, or CCU. In chapter 7 we discuss how the assumption that trivial syntax should correspond to trivial semantics is yet another instance of the general Transparency Thesis. For the specifics of the proposal here to work inside nominals, it must be true that Case dependencies in these contexts are reduced vis-à-vis those in clauses; factually this is obviously true, but we also discuss in chapter 5 why it should be true in a minimalist system. In any event, these all constitute instances whereby semantics is forced into the tight conditions left open by syntax, illustrating a brand of 'naturalizing meaning'.

present approach does not force us to postulate movement into theta positions, even if the movements examined here have interpretive consequences that can be construed as 'thematic'.

46 Ultimately, these features may themselves reduce to formal ones, as implied in section 8.4.7.

4 *Online conditions and parametric variation*

4.1   Introduction

In this chapter two analyses will be presented of rather puzzling phenomena, which can be naturally stated as conditions on narrow and broad *online* derivational stages, respectively. Importantly, these are not obviously reducible to 'virtual conceptual necessity', as relevant conditions within them exploit a substantive connection with semantic interfaces. Yet in these two cases systemic interactions are not *output* ones for the derivation (i.e. LF conditions), but are rather stated in terms of domains of lexico-conceptual dependency and so-called *surface syntax*. This, if correct, reinforces the distributed interpretation thesis. The arguments will each occupy a long section of this chapter, and can be examined in more detail in their published versions (Uriagereka 2003, 2006). Things get wrapped up, both technically and conceptually, in a unifying fourth section, which leads to a concluding discussion.

4.2   The null Case issue

Null Case was proposed by Chomsky and Lasnik (1993) in order to resolve some interesting empirical problems associated with the distribution of PRO.[1] But as Hornstein (1999) points out, it is *ad hoc* to have a Case whose sole purpose is to be used this way. Uriagereka (2006) agrees that, therefore, either null Case should not exist, or else it must also be assigned to elements other than PRO.[2] The part of this discussion that interests us now concerns the rationalization of null Case *application*, and whether that can help us address two interesting issues: (i) how the presence of 'referentially low key' elements like PRO, clauses, and perhaps some indefinite

---

1 See Martin (1996) for a detailed presentation.
2 A different possibility explored by San Martin (2004) is that PRO receives *regular* Case.

expressions, interacts with conditions on Case valuation and their relation to the person system;[3] and (ii) how we can account for the serious variation apparent in successive cyclic A-movement. Uriagereka (2006) suggests that having null Case in the system allows us to address these apparently unrelated puzzles, if this sort of Case is peculiar in needing to be established *in context-free terms* – instead of the Agree conditions that Chomsky has been recently exploring for regular Case valuation. In what follows, each of these problems is presented in turn, first, and the solution just alluded to is then sketched.

4.2.1 Case puzzles related to complement clauses

Within the P&P system it was assumed (a) that arguments require Case (Aoun's [1979] Visibility hypothesis) and (b) that an element like *him* in (1) involves the accusative Case associated to the *v-believe* complex (exceptional case marking, or ECM).

(1)   I believe [him to be smart]

Since [him to be smart] is the direct argument of *believe*, this creates a contradiction.

This is not the only problem that complement clauses raise for the Case system. Consider the facts discussed in San Martin and Uriagereka (2003), where it is shown that contexts of obligatorily controlled PRO in Basque effectively render a transitive verb selecting the controlled clause into an unaccusative.

(2)   a. Ni   [PRO pisua   galtzen]   saiatu naiz.
           I.ABS   weight-ABS lose-nominalizer-LOC try-part I.be
           'I have tried to lose weight.'
        b. Nik   hori   saiatu   dut
           I.ERG that-ABS try-part I.have.III
           'I have tried that.'

The situation in (2b) is normal: the transitive *saiatu* 'try' goes with transitive auxiliary *dut*, coding agreement with the ergative subject *nik* 'I' and the absolutive object *hori* 'that'. But this Case/agreement array is altered when the direct object is the clause: this time around, the auxiliary accompanying *saiatu* 'try' is the unaccusative *naiz*, signaling agreement with the now absolutive subject *ni* 'I'. In other words, the clause is taken as invisible for the

---

3 See Ormazabal (2000) for discussion in this general direction.

regular Case/agreement system when it involves an obligatorily controlled PRO subject. One might think, then, that there is *no v* element here. That, however, is unlikely if *v* is responsible, à la Hale and Keyser (1993, 2002), for the agent theta role associated to *saiatu* 'try'. Assuming theta roles haven't changed from (2a) to (2b) (involving the same verb), *v* in (2b) must be somehow activating the regular Case system ('object Case' to the object, 'subject Case' to the subject); but then it is unavoidable to conclude that in (2a) *v* (or whatever is involved in the process) does not behave in the same way, and the regular Case system now acts 'intransitively'.

Uriagereka (2006) shows that the paradigm is not circumscribed to instances where PRO is involved, and it extends to Basque subjunctive complement clauses as in (3a). This example presents no PRO in the embedded clause, just plain hypotaxis. Here too, as in (2a), the matrix verb acts in a surprisingly unaccusative fashion, again indicating that its *v* does not activate the regular Case system, for reasons we would expect to be related to those in (2a):

(3)   a. Jon   [Mirenek   pisua   gal   zezan]   saiatu   zen
          Jon-ABS Miren-ERG weight-ABS lose have-subj-LOC try-part III.be
          'Jon tried that Mary lose weight.'
       b. Jonek   [Miren   polita dela]   pentsatzen du
          Jon-ERG Miren-ABS pretty is-Comp think-part III.have. III
          'Jon thinks that Mary is pretty.'

The example in (3a) contrasts with domains involving indicative embedded clauses, as in (3b); here the regular Case system is again deployed, with the embedded clause triggering accusative auxiliary selection and preventing the subject from taking absolutive case.

The interaction, or lack thereof, between clauses and Case systems goes back within the P&P system to Stowell's (1981) Case Resistance condition, which actually *prevents* clauses from receiving Case altogether. If such a measure is taken, the two clauses in (3) have to be analysed differently. This has been suggested, for instance, by Torrego and Uriagereka (2002): hypotactic dependents are true CP complements of the verb, while paratactic dependents are more complex cataphoric associates of null (or occasionally overt) default referential pronouns, of the sort in *I take **it** (for granted) that this is an issue*. If *it* (or some null variant) is what engages the Case system in instances of embedded parataxis, perhaps what we see in the Basque cases of true hypotaxis (embedding with subjunctive or infinitive moods) is *no activation* of the Case system other than by the subject of the expression, which (thus being the only element in need of Case) comes out unaccusative. That said, however, there is reason to doubt that clauses simply resist Case marking. To start with, it is an observable fact that in the Basque hypotactic instances the clauses are actually overtly marked with a curious *locative* Case.

Moreover, as Plann (1986) argues, the Case Resistance hypothesis is questioned by the fact that clausal dependents of nominals systematically get marked with case-marking prepositions in a language like Spanish, yielding instances as in (4).

(4)   a. La idea **de** [que la tierra es plana] es muy sensata.
            the idea of that the earth is flat   is very sound.
            'The idea that the earth is flat is very sound.'
        b. Mi intento **de** [que nos   llevemos bien] ha fracasado.
            my attempt of that ourselves get.SUBJ well   has failed
            'My attempt for us to get along has failed.'

Stowell claimed that nominal dependents are not complements; they are instead predicates, as suggested by the fact that the nominal in (4a) can be paraphrased as in the identificational (5a).

(5)   a. La idea es que la   tierra es plana.
            the idea is that the earth is flat
            'The idea is that the earth is flat.'
        b. ?* Mi intento es que nos   llevemos bien
               my attempt of that ourselves get.SUB well
            ('My attempt is for us to get along.')

It is not altogether clear how that should make the clausal dependents less case-marked (presence of preposition *de* 'of' is just a fact, regardless of the inter-pretation the clause gets); but moreover that situation seems to be restricted to epistemic/declarative nominal dependents.[4] It is impossible to have, as in (5b), an identificational paraphrase of (4b) (which involves hypotaxis when the nominal head is of the volitional/desiderative sort). So even though we plausibly have, in this instance, a form of argumental dependency between the nominal head and the clause, it nonetheless is signaled by the case-marker *de*.

We are, then, led to reject the idea that clauses simply resist Case, which is consistent with the Visibility hypothesis: clause or not an *argument* needs Case. At the same time, if we go in this direction we must have a different source of abstract Case for clauses. We may then suppose the following, for now without worrying about justifying it within a larger system:

(6)   a. Clauses receive abstract null Case.
        b. V assigns abstract null Case.

4 Stowell argued that only non-finite control clauses are true complements within nominals. Safir (1985) showed that the generalization extends to some nominal finite complements as well.

Then the peculiar Basque examples above could receive an analysis as in (7).[5]

(7)   ... v [V [EMBEDDED CLAUSE ...]-*loc.*] ...

         null Case

In addition – and so that the regular Case system is not automatically 'activated' in a transitive guise in these instances – we have to assume a condition along the lines of (8).

(8)   The Minimal Array Condition (MAC)
        Given a collection of substantive items, select into the array only those Case/
        person specifications that are necessary for convergence.

Lexical arrays are thus built economically, so that unspecified Case features are added *only if necessary* for convergence. For some reason that we return to, full (as opposed to null) Case features are required only on personal nominal expressions, not on clauses. In (7) the MAC does not associate more than one full Case feature to the matrix verbal system because there the lower argument is saturated by an element that doesn't require that sort of marking, as it can (perhaps must) be signaled by the arguably default – at any rate, more basic – null Case system. This is an economy argument that takes the lexical array seriously, as indicated in chapter 1.

The phenomenon just studied is not easy to detect in a 'nominaccusative' language, where subjects get subject Case, period. However, Basque being an 'ergabsolutive' language, an absolutive Case 'unused' for a complement is free to go to the first element that needs it, the subject in (2a).[6] In (2b), in contrast, the direct object is *hori* 'that', which takes the absolutive Case for itself; then ergative Case is the one left for the subject in (2b). But even in English we can detect similar effects in ECM sites, where we want to deal with the problem associated to, for instance, (1) above. (9) repeats this example with a representation highlighting the point.

(9)   *accusative*

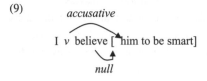

I v believe [him to be smart]

         null

---

5 We could take the curious locative as a manifestation of null Case.
6 The implied Case hierarchy will be deduced from derivational dynamics in chapter 5.

Here the *v* element associated to the main verb assigns accusative Case to the subject of the embedded clause, via Agree in the sense of Chomsky (2000), whereas the verb itself *locally* assigns null Case to the complement clause. The paradox for the Visibility thesis thus disappears.

Given that analysis we must then worry about what happens in a finite version of (9). Are there *two* Case assignments in such an instance as well? If so, involving what elements? Or is it rather that in this instance the embedded clause is receiving *only null Case*? As it turns out, each of these options arguably correspond to parataxis (involving indicative dependence) and hypotaxis (involving subjunctive dependence). The latter possibility is illustrated by a subjunctive-embedding version of (7) above (the other possibility being an infinitive-embedding one), and it is straightforward. For parataxis, we can assume the analysis in (10b), based on the paratactic dependency in (10c) that was alluded to above.

(10)   a. I believe [that the earth is flat]

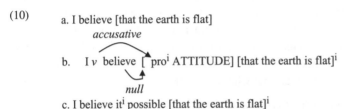

b.   I *v* believe [pro^i ATTITUDE] [that the earth is flat]^i

c. I believe it^i possible [that the earth is flat]^i

Hinzen (2003) argues that embedded propositions, whose veridicality the subject of the main clause has an attitude towards, involve a small clausal structure that is overt in instances like (10c). If so, the small-clause generated as a complement of the epistemic/declarative verb (and thus the attitudinal predicate) can receive null Case – very much as the infinitival complement in (9) does; in contrast, the dependent clause itself is cataphorically associated to a (null) pronominal that receives accusative Case – also in line with the situation in (9). In other words, parataxis reduces to nominal elements receiving Case in ECM conditions.

If a verb can assign null Case to a complement clause, an interesting question is what happens when it has *merely a direct object nominal*, checking its accusative Case via *v*. The most straightforward approach is that in those circumstances, too, verbs can directly assign null Case. We return to this situation in section 4.2.4.

4.2.2   The puzzling cross-linguistic distribution of A-movement
After introducing (6b) to have V determine null Case, and given Chomsky and Lasnik's assumption that defective T checks null Case as well, we must

worry about what specific elements involve this sort of Case. Uriagereka (2006) proposes the following hypothesis, as an attempt to rationalize these matters:

(11)   Null Case Visibility (NCV)
        Null Case is determined by a context-free dependence between an element X and an overt head Y; it has a freezing effect on X if X's features overtly mark Y.

We will return to justifying this proposal; for now let's just clarify what it says. First, null Case is associated to any overt head Y.[7] This is to say that, given the NCV thesis, not just defective T in control structures, but even the sort of T that Martin (1996) shows inducing raising structures, or complete T in regular clauses, *can* assign null Case. As a consequence, null Case affects the workings of the extended projection principle (EPP) in embedded contexts:[8] This could arise via null Case-checking requirements or licensing effects. Granted, if this particular mechanism is to be pursued, the issue arises as to whether *successive-cyclic* displacement across tenseless domains should be even possible, assuming that null Case checking, as does Case checking more broadly, renders the DP where it occurs *inactive* for computation (Lasnik 2001, Parts iv and vi; Chomsky 2000):

(12)   Case Freezing Condition (CFC)
        All other things being equal, Case checking effected on X stops further computational access to X.

The hedge in (12) is central to continuing with the reasoning, as we see next.

Consider the following contrasts, from a variety of languages, starting with English.

(13)   a. Jack is likely [t to seem [t to be the leader of this group]].
        b. Jack was [t seen [t to be the leader of this group]].
        c. *Jack is likely [t is the leader of this group].

This contrast is usually taken as the baseline: successive cyclic A-movement is possible across tenseless domains, as in (13a) or (13b),[9] not across tensed ones ((13b), an instance of so-called hyper-raising). The CFC in (12) predicts these contrasts if only in the latter instance is the lowest trace in a (here nominative) Case position, which freezes the Case-checked nominal in place.

---

7 So long as it is *of the Case-assigning sort*, e.g. V, T, etc., a matter analysed in chapter 5.
8 Where Lasnik (2001) has argued it holds, problematically as it doesn't involve any feature checking.
9 Whether it involves pure raising verbs like *seem* or rather passivized expressions like *seen*.

But, of course, ever since Xu (1993) and Ura (1994), there is reason to believe that some languages do exhibit hyper-raising, a phenomenon observed already in George (1980) for Greek. We can illustrate it with Rumanian data from Rivero and Geber (2003):

(14)   Noi părem   [să   [t incepem [să   [t lucrăm bine]]
        we seem-agr Comp   begin-agr comp   work-agr well
        'We seem to begin to work well.' (Lit.: 'We seem that begin that work
        well.')

Uriagereka (2006) shows that A-movement needs to be parameterized also within tenseless domains, as is shown by the Galician/Portuguese data in (15):[10]

(15)   a. ?*Ti fuches [t feito [t   ser capitán do   equipo]]
            you were   made-agr be captain of-the   team
            'You were made to be the captain of the team.'
        b. Ti podes [t parecer [t ser capitán do equipo]]
            you can   seem   be captain of-the team
            'You are likely to seem to be the captain of the team.'
        c. *Ti pareces [t es capitán do equipo]
            you seem   are captain of-the team
            ('You seem are the captain of the team.')
        d. Ti fuches [t feito [t   capitán do equipo]]
            you were   made-agr captain of-the team
            'You were made captain of the team.'

In all these instances we are attempting to displace a nominal in reasonable circumstances, via successive-cyclic A-movement. In languages like Galician or Portuguese, as in the English examples above, displacement is possible across tenseless domains (15b), though not across tensed ones (15c). However, when displacement is across tenseless domains involving *passivized verbs* (15a), the result is unacceptable (and cf. (13b)). (15d) is added to the paradigm to show that the problem is not merely in the A-movement, or when it takes place over an overt agreement category *per se*, possible here; the issue arises only when the displacement is *long distance*, of the successive-cyclic sort. Let's call *radical* hyper-raising what we witness in Rumanian (14) – movement across a tensed domain – and *moderate* hyper-raising what we witness in English (13a) – raising across a tenseless domain.

---

10 The situation is different from that shown in Kayne (1987) for French, where apparently movement through a past participle domain actually *forces* agreement. So, internal to Romance languages, we find conditions where agreeing participles either correlate with or freeze movement.

In Galician we see no radical hyper-raising (15c), while we do see moderate hyper-raising (15b); but we can also build a *hybrid* hyper-raising case, with movement taking place across a domain that is tenseless, as in moderate hyper-raising, but exhibiting overt agreement (triggered by the matrix passive) as in radical hyper-raising and the result is then ungrammatical.

That doesn't exhaust the array of variation. Consider also the Russian data in (16).

(16)   a. ? [Ivan byl uviden   t]
           Ivan was seen.agr
           'Ivan was seen.'
        b. Ivan kažetsja [t glupym]
           Ivan seems   silly.agr
           'Ivan seems silly.'
        c. *Ivan byl [t uviden [t uxodit']]
           Ivan was   seen.agr leave
           ('Ivan was seen to leave.')
        d. *Ljudi kažutsja [t priezžat' po-odnomu]
            people seem   arrive   one-by-one
            ('People seem to arrive one by one.')

Although (16a) and (16b) show that A-movement is possible in Russian, the other examples in (16) show it to be unacceptable across TP domains, regardless of whether they are of the (hybrid) hyper-raising sort (16c) or even *simple* raising.[11] This pattern is common in Slavic.

Finally, observe the German examples in (17).

(17)   a. Hans schien [t der Führer dieser   Gruppe zu sein]
           Hans seems   the leader this-gen   Group to be
           'Hans seems to be the leader of this group.'
        b. ?*[Hans kann wohl [t [t der Führer dieser   Gruppe zu
           werden] zu scheinen]]
           Hans can   certainly the leader this-GEN group to be
           (come) to seem
           ('Hans is likely to seem to be leader of this group.')
        c. ?*[Hans wurde [t dazu gebracht [t [t der Führer dieser
           Gruppe zu werden] zu scheinen]]
           Hans was   PART brought   the leader this-GEN
           group to be(come) to seem
           ('Hans was made to seem to be leader of this group.')

---

11 Radical hyper-raising is not an option in Russian either.

Table 4.1. *Cross-linguistic variation in A-movement*

Languages	Radical H-R	Hybrid H-R	Moderate H-R	H-R (across TP)	Passive
Rumanian	Yes	Yes	(Yes)	(Yes)	Yes
English	No	Yes	Yes	Yes	Yes
Portuguese	No	No	Yes	Yes	Yes
German	No	No	No	Yes	Yes
Russian	No	No	No	No	Yes

H-R: Hyper-raising

The contrast here is between simple raising as in (17a), which is possible in the language, and moderate hyper-raising (17b), which is not.[12] This signals a dividing line in German: movements shorter than (17a), as in passive, are possible; movements involving more steps than (17b) are not, including the hybrid hyper-raising instance in (17c).

Table 4.1 summarizes these possibilities.[13]

How can we predict the variety of raising options we witness in Table 4.1? Following Alexiadou and Anagnostopoulou (1998), suppose we assume that not all languages satisfy the EPP. But that ought to give us languages with and without movement to *any* subject, and, although such languages arguably exist, this is not the issue here. All the languages we are discussing *have A-movement*, for instance in passive constructions. One could, however, couple EPP parameterization with an associated parameterization of the CFC in (12). To be specific, suppose that languages with 'funny' EPP properties (call them F-EPP, characterized as in (18)), for some reason do not invoke the CFC in (12), thus allowing radical hyper-raising.

(18)   *F-EPP language*
        A language that may have no categorial representation *in an EPP site.*

---

12 Some traces 'pile up' because German is a head-last language, which appears orthogonal to our discussion.

13 The caveat associated to Rumanian (the reason the possible raising across one TP, and possible moderate hyper-raising across more than one TP, are parenthesized) is because whether this language has bona fide tenseless clauses is debatable. This is a factor that is now being set aside, as other languages involving possible hyper-raising (e.g. Bantu variants studied by Carstens [2005]) do not present a similar profile.

Unfortunately, this array of conditions overgenerates, allowing for hyper-raising in *any* F-EPP language; while it is true that many languages for which hyper-raising has been observed (paradigmatically, East Asian variants) are arguably F-EPP languages, many that would fall under the F-EPP rubric only exhibit hyper-raising in some variants (e.g. Portuguese, rather than Rumanian). So we need another variable, one implementing the intuition that an *embedded* subject, indeed of the tenseless sort, is what suspends the CFC. Let's call that the 'funny' F-EPP.

(19)   *F-F-EPP language*
        A language that may have no categorial representation in a *tenseless* EPP site.

Things starts looking strange, since we are now gearing CFC application to a bizarre sub-case (subjects of tenseless clauses). It is not obvious that the F-F-EPP option in (19) plays any role *in itself*, other than as the condition to suspend CFC application in relevant languages. An example of a language that would fall under the F-F-EPP type, other than in the terms being discussed now, should involve obligatory subjects in tensed clauses but optional subjects in tenseless ones.[14] Moreover, it is not obvious that the CFC plays any systematic role. Although some of the subjects falling under the description in (19) have been argued to involve some form of Case (exceptional accusative, null), the subjects that are relevant to our paradigm (embedded EPP subjects where mere traces end up surviving, if anything) are not traditionally considered worthy of any form of Case (even abstract or null ones). So at this point we couldn't be parameterizing Case-*freezing* conditions, since by hypothesis not even Case obtains here.

To go on with some analysis of the form just begun, suppose there were some freezing condition analogous to the CFC that would obtain in these domains, the 'funny' CFC.[15]

(20)   *F-CFC*
        All other things being equal, 'funny'-checking effected on X stops further computational access to X.

This approach would distinguish languages for which radical hyper-raising is possible from those in which only moderate versions of the process (including

---

14 It would be like English, except that the embedded subject in *I believe this to be crazy* would be optional.
15 'Funny'-checking in (20) can be thought of as 'embedded EPP'-checking. The F-CFC is, thus, a freezing condition demanding that when the '*embedded* EPP feature' is checked, no further availability exists for checking said feature.

hybrid ones) are. Since we have seen in Table 4.1 that among the latter we must distinguish those languages (e.g. Portuguese) in which the hybrid version of hyper-raising is disallowed, while the moderate version of the process is still available (vis-à-vis languages like English where both options exist), then we need yet another variable, one implementing the intuition that an embedded subject, crucially *not* involved in overt agreement-checking, is what suspends the F-CFC. Let's call that the 'funny' F-F-EPP:

(21)   *F-F-F-EPP language*
        A language that may have no categorial representation in a tenseless, *non-agreeing* EPP site.

The conceptual caveats raised for (19) only compound now. Languages that independently present variation specifically in terms of (21) should involve obligatory subjects in tensed clauses and tenseless clauses whose subject position is of the non-agreeing sort, but optional subjects otherwise. The situation would distinguish languages for which radical, hybrid, and moderate hyper-raising is possible from those in which it isn't. But again, we have seen in Table 4.1 that among the latter we must distinguish those (e.g. Russian) in which even simple raising across TP is barred from those (e.g. German) where it's possible. So we need one more variable, and of course following the analytical procedure we could implement the intuition that an embedded subject not involved in overt agreement checking is what suspends the F-CFC in relevant languages, but only *once* (thus allowing only simple raising).

(22)   *F-F-F-F-EPP language*
        A language that may have no categorial representation in a tenseless, non-agreeing EPP site *once*.

What's going on seems simple enough. To separate German from Russian, we want to parameterize the situation for which the freezing effect implemented by the F-CFC doesn't obtain in a tenseless, non-agreeing EPP site, precisely once (German), from one in which the CFC does obtain even there (Russian). Unfortunately, expressing this as in (22) is just coding it.

We can implement the idea above in terms of a markedness hierarchy, to describe the space of possibilities we have encountered; if we find counter-examples to that hierarchically organized chart, or different arrangements of the observed facts, we re-rank the relevant constraints. But of course the issue is the nature of our conditions and definitions, specifically the ones we have prefixed an F to. Do we want our parameters to have this expressive power? One could also attempt to account for the paradigm in Table 4.1 in a non-unified way. For instance, it is customary to say that Slavic languages exhibit no IP/TP selection for raising verbs and one could raise equally stipulative conditions for the other languages.[16] In what follows let's attempt a different, albeit still unified, approach to the causes behind the observed variation.

4.2.3   Null Case realization in inflectional specifiers

Genuine variation in a P&P-style system implies having a principle P (or some relevant such set) to yield a structure S in a given context C in language L, and then via some parameter having P somehow yield an *alternative* structure S' within C in some language L'. That whole reasoning is vacuous if there is no P to start with. In the cases that occupy us now, we have attempted to invoke the EPP and the CFC as our P set, to then have the EPP and CFC parameterized, such that freezing doesn't obtain in some relevant EPP contexts. That's where we encountered problems, for the more we parameterized relevant sub-cases, the more we distanced ourselves from any plausible version of a mere subject condition (the EPP) and a mere Case condition (the CFC).

Uriagereka (2006) suggests that a line of reasoning in terms of null Case in these contexts involving functional structure (T, and *v* in particular) is more promising. This is, if nothing else, because a priori this sort of formal Case requirement may or may not entail freezing in the relevant domains, in terms of the mere CFC;[17] this would be *instead of* the stipulative F-CFC discussed in the previous section. But there's more. By its very nature, if null Case does exit as argued for in section 4.2.1, it *ought to be a local phenomenon*. That is to say, it shouldn't be satisfiable in context-sensitive terms. The reason is simple. Transformations involve context-sensitivity, thus a characteristic discontinuity posing grammatical and processing complexity. In standard instances this is addressed via the grammar signalling the process dually: by uninterpretable (triggering) morphological markings at the Probe and corresponding interpretable matches at the Goal. There are much debated exceptions when characteristic interpretive consequences ensue, for instance in Quantifier Raising of the sort discussed in Fox (2000). But null Case doesn't show either morphological marking or specific interpretive consequences, so it ought to be resolved in less cumbersome, context-free, terms.

---

16 Even that is unclear, since in many instances the issue is not selecting some XP, but allowing movement *past* XP in certain conditions – e.g. in German, where movement across one TP is possible, but not across two.

17 Null Case may or may not enter standard conditions on freezing, an option that even radical hyper-raising attests to.

That being the case, we can ask what kinds of narrow manifestations the grammar allows for this process, leading to the observed variations.

First, locality in checking limits relevant instances to those involving displacement to a specifier or association to a complement, in particular preventing long-distance Agree manifestations, contrary to what obtains for regular Case checking (see chapter 5). Second, the appropriate narrow checking may be affected in two circumstances: (a) there could be something special in the checking head or (b) the checked element could be peculiar. This isn't as trivial as it may seem: we're dealing with something very abstract, *null* in the receiving end and without semantic consequence. Overt syntax is readily parseable or acquirable. But tacit processes depend on underlying grammatical conditions and how they interact with independent elements, so there could be several curious interactions in this domain – which, given what we observe, is precisely what we need. Although this won't be presented in any detail now, we can give a flavor of the analysis proposed in Uriagereka (2006) in this respect.

Thesis (23) below ((11) repeated) pursues, first, the intuition that morphologically manifested Cases (in terms of Case morphology on pronounced nominals) are easy for a learner to detect, so they can relate to null inflectional elements like v and the like. Null Case is in contrast undetectable unless signaled by the element that determines it, since it lacks morphology and may appear on silent elements like PRO – so its range should be narrower:

(23)   Null Case Visibility (NCV)
        Null Case is determined by a context-free dependence between an element
        X and an overt head Y; it has a freezing effect on X if X's features overtly
        mark Y.

Given this NCV thesis, we expect elements like the inflectional *to* or lexical heads to, in principle, be able to determine null Case. Infinitival heads involve their specifier (e.g. PRO), whereas lexical heads like verbs involve their complement (for instance complement clauses in need of null Case), thus rationalizing (6b) in section 4.2.1 above. Given NCV, we expect the checking that is relevant for null Case – which we may assume is simple *Concord* – to be absolutely local, unlike similar, though context-sensitive, Agree dependencies. In addition, (23) specifies the particular freezing effect ensuing in these Concord instances: under normal circumstances, only *overt* Concord entails the immediate freezing of the agreeing nominal. This is reasonable. The freezing effect captured via the CFC is a consequence of feature valuation on the nominal, after being Probed in Agree instances or, more generally, engaging in a checking process of the Concord sort. The unvalued Case feature in the nominal makes it accessible to further computation (e.g. movement); as the Case feature is valued, computational inaccessibility ensues.

However, one may also consider a special situation where feature valuation does not entail value *fixation*, especially for the purely formal null Case that, unless signaled overtly on the determining head, has no effect on the receiving nominal. NCV captures a related property of null Case when demanding that heads determining null Case be overt; the requirement presently being considered is a counterpart of this idea on the receiving nominal, which predicts viable moderate hyper-raisings vs. unviable hybrid ones, in languages like Portuguese where the relevant Concord is manifest. In Portuguese the overtly agreeing participle involves Concord and, furthermore, a freezing instance of this operation given its overt morphological involvement; in English, although Concord drives the relevant hybrid and moderate hyper-raisings as well, since it involves no overt feature marking on the heads determining null Case, no freezing ensues. The same is true of Portuguese instances involving moderate hyper-raising across no overt Concord.

Uriagereka (2006) then goes on to show how this approach to the descriptive problem in the previous section dispenses with the need of a *separate*, now arguably unjustified, EPP requirement: displacement to embedded EPP-sites is in terms of null Case checking via Concord. The paper also discusses the difference between languages in the middle of the chart in Table 4.1 and, on the one hand, languages of the Rumanian type – with radical hyper-raising – and, on the other, languages of the German and Russian type – with no hyper-raising. For the former, the following 'slipping' condition is postulated:

(24)   Slipping Condition
        A weak D element does not result in inaccessibility upon Case checking.

In effect, the D system has to be robust for Case valuation (of either the full or the null sort) to affect it representationally, even when the appropriate checking conditions are otherwise derivationally met; when D is not pronounced or is merely a morpheme/clitic on nominal associates (the situation in languages of the radical hyper-raising type), Case valuation 'slips' through its target, and so it does not have a deactivating effect on the relevant phrase associated to D. Being representationally visible, this phrase continues to be accessible in the derivation. To deal with languages that present an absolute ban against any form of hyper raising, (24) is proposed, as a condition on all sorts of Case checking (full or null).

(25)   Bracing Condition
         A domain undergoing morphological dependency results in inaccessibility
         upon Case checking.

This condition concentrates on the presence, within the domain where Case checking will be relevant, of other morphological processes that may make Case valuation avoid 'slipping' in the sense of (24). Both German and Russian present systematic case Concord internal to the D/N domains under consideration. This process has its own representational effect. Even if D, in itself, is in some sense weak (the situation in Russian), its presence is representationally signaled via internal Concord, enough for the ensuing visibility to constitute a necessary condition for 'bracing' the Case valuation process. Morphological conditions internal to the D/N distinction also make a difference. For instance, having a weak D, Russian exhibits case morphology on the N-related elements (N itself and the adjectives), whereas German also exhibits case morphology in its overtly pronounced D's. Uriagereka (2006) argues that this dual manifestation of case morphology in German allows for one further degree of freedom in this language with respect to A-movement. Although in both Russian and German case Concord internal to the D/N domain triggers the Bracing Condition – which entails immediate action of the CFC – there are in principle *two* triggers for A-movement: full and null Case. This won't make a difference in Russian, as only the N system can be morphologically active in this language; thus, whether the displacement is driven by full or null Case considerations, the moment these are met access to the element that has undergone Case-checking-plus-movement terminates. This predicts precisely one A-movement in this language, for instance of the sort we see in passives. German is more permissive, although relevant structural conditions are identical to those in Russian; the difference is that whereas the N system in German can gear one possible A-movement, it still has the D system to gear a second A-movement. This is enough to allow for both passive and raising, though not hyper-raising.

The Table 4.1 paradigm is thus modeled, through the CFC and associated morphological conditions ((24) and (25)) which make explicit the 'visibility' part of the Visibility hypothesis on Case. Case valuation is a delicate process requiring a fine balance: the element(s) that undergo the process cannot be too weak (short of having the Case value 'slip' through) or too engaged in other morphological processes (or they will result in Case freezing, even in situations that could otherwise be grammatically prone to permissiveness with regards to such a putative freezing). This morphological subtlety is even more apparent in instances of null Case valuation, subject to NCV conditions geared towards both context sensitivity of the relevant process and its overt manifestation, which used to go by the name of Concord in traditional accounts. Arguably these NCV conditions are independently needed, as discussed in section 4.2.1, and they have the effect of allowing us to dispense with residual EPP instances (see Martin [1999]).

4.2.4   More instances of null Case visibility and the person generalization

When studying Basque hypotactic clauses, we saw that the flexibility of the MAC allows v not to assign a full Case. As the true complement clause did not need accusative Case in relevant instances, the 'next argument up' was treated as the argument of an unaccusative verb. Uriagereka (2006) shows that a situation along these lines surfaces also with regular transitive constructions that need not assign accusative Case to their nominal direct object.

(26)   a. Nik   hori   saiatu   dut
         I.ERG that-ABS try-part III.have.I
         'I have tried that.'
        b. Ni   horretan saiatu   naiz
         I.ABS that-LOC try-part I.be
         'I have applied myself to that.'

(26a) is (2b) repeated. A pattern along the lines discussed in (2a), but involving what looks like a regular direct object (not a clause, though see fn. 19), is shown in (26b).[18] With two conditions: (i) the ensuing predication should be atelic, and (ii) the direct object should be interpreted as a mere theme that measures out the corresponding eventuality, not a personal event participant.[19]

The situation just discussed recalls conditions on so-called Split Ergativity, which for instance Laka (2006) argues are exhibited in Basque progressive sentences. Consider:

(27)   a. Emakumeak   ogia   jaten du.
         woman-det-ERG bread-det-ABS eating III-have-III
         'The woman eats the bread.'
        b. Emakume-a   ogi-a jaten   ari da.
         woman-det-ABS bread-det eat-nominalizer-LOC prog III-be
         'The woman is eating the bread.'

---

18 Again the locative that was associated to null Case in section 4.2.1 is seen in this instance.
19 It must be noted that *saiatu* 'to try' seems exceptional in allowing the expressions under discussion. So this doesn't appear to be a regular paradigm, except for the 'split ergativity' conditions discussed immediately below.

c. Emakume-a   ogi-a-ren   jaten   ari da.
woman-det-ABS bread-det-GEN eat-nominalizer-LOC prog
III-be
'The woman is eating of the bread.'

These examples track all the features of (26) that matter. Note, by comparing first (27b) with (27a), how the subject demotes its Case realization from ergative to absolutive (with an associated change in the auxiliary from transitive to unaccusative), and a locative appears in the structure – in this instance associated, Laka argues, to the entire nominalization of the verbal expression, to express progressiveness. The main difference between the split in (27) and that in (26) is that in the former instance the locative goes directly on the direct object. Based on previous insights by Ortiz de Urbina and Hualde (1987), Laka makes much of this locative in her examples, arguing for a bi-clausal analysis of progressive constructions in Basque – cf. the one proposed in section 4.2.1 for hypotactic dependence more generally. From that perspective, the absolutive showing up within the nominalized verb is not surprising. This is the Case that should appear in the lower clause (part of a separate derivational phase), without affecting the interesting Case conditions that we are now exploring for the subject, in a separate cycle. What's curious about the 'split' in (26) is that, this time, a true bi-clausal analysis seems less plausible.

An interesting issue to pursue is whether (26) is just a fluke, and whenever systematic splits obtain, there is always clausal embedding involved,[20] or rather nothing requires that what causes these 'splits' should be *a second clause per se*, given how the MAC operates. Perhaps the MAC can choose not to activate the full Case system in *v* under other conditions. Maia Duguine observes in this regard that in the Navarro-Labourdin dialect (27c) is the surface form, where the direct object associated to *jaten* 'eat' shows up as genitive, not absolutive. This suggests that in these circumstances biclausality is not at issue, or the argument of the extra embedded clause would show up with a verbal Case (ergative/absolutive, instead of genitive). From the alternative perspective, the MAC simply doesn't activate the Case system in the standard way, and instead an inherent genitive is deployed, still thereby freeing up the absolutive Case for what ends up being the single subject of a single clause. It is not crucial to choose between these analyses here.

---

20 In other words, it is always a lower *clause*, whether hidden or patent, that receives the null Case that 'frees up' the regular Case system, so that the first DP in need of full Case gets absolutive, not ergative.

Uriagereka (2006) also observes that something much along these lines should be operative for *John drinks (heavily)*, which is grammatical together with *John drinks brandy*. In the second example accusative Case is apparently involved; however, in the first it can't be, or it won't be checked under standard conditions. That said, a 'canonically indefinite' object meaning is clearly involved in these instances.[21] If that extra object is not an argument, it is unclear how we obtain the compositional meaning of the expression in its transitive guise (with the tinge alluded to in fn. 21) or how we satisfy the lexico-conceptual requirements of an obviously transitive verb. If the complement is an argument, what Case does it check in accordance to the Visibility hypothesis? Given the present analysis, we can have the implicit object check null Case via V. In turn the accusative Case is not involved because MAC doesn't force us to engage it. Note, incidentally, that a nominal for which both null Case through V and accusative Case through *v* are available can have its null Case slip in most circumstances, resulting in no freezing effect.

What Belletti (1988) calls 'partitive' Case looks suspiciously like null Case as is being explored here, both in that it is assigned locally and in that it corresponds to vaguely indefinite (i.e. impersonal) nominals, which affects aspectual and related matters at the VP level. Moreover, 'personal markers' in direct objects in Spanish or Turkish (see Torrego [1998]), as opposed to instances without such markers, may arguably be treated in terms of the accusative vs. null Case divide. In particular, we could, in the spirit of de Hoop (1992), take *v* to assign 'personal' accusative Case (with ensuing animacy effects, see fn. 22), while letting V assign 'impersonal' null Case to indefinite arguments. This would mean that null Case is assigned by V to XPs (clausal or nominal) receiving what were called 'articulating' roles in section 2.4.2, whereas regular Case associates, via *v*, to DPs determining 'participating' roles, in the sense also given in that section. Some DPs could receive both forms of Case without contradiction.[22]

---

21 *John drinks heavily* cannot be used to mean that every day he drinks two gallons of milk, and nothing else.

22 Such DPs would also determine articulating and participating roles discussed in section 2.4.2. This duality may relate to whether theta roles are features or configurations (Hornstein *et al.* 2005). Perhaps only articulating roles are truly configurational, while participating ones are a combination of a configuration determining compositional meaning, plus elaborate Probe/ Goal dependencies establishing intentional nuances involving context-confinement conditions. It remains to be seen how this relates to 'surface semantics' notions to be discussed below, and how that affects 'discourse configurationality'.

Given the logic of the proposal, it's not just the v/V system that could engage in full vs. null Case determination. The same is true for T. We have already argued that, in many instances, defective T is involved in null Case determination. How about complete T, the one that we normally associate to nominative Case checking? The very fact that we don't have two categories at stake in this instance (e.g. V vs. v) simplifies matters, if we assume the familiar (28).

(28)   Case Uniqueness Condition (CUC)
        Any given category X can only determine one structural Case Y.

The CUC, in conjunction with the MAC, forces T to assign null Case by default (within NCV conditions). However, if the MAC identifies a grammatical need, it will 'turn on' nominative valuation. Conditions on what is promoted to a categorical judgement by visiting the T projection in terms of full Case visibility, as discussed in Raposo and Uriagereka (2002), should arguably be explicated in the present terms as well. Observe:

(29)   a. Un lobo es una bestia.
           a wolf is a   beast
           'A wolf is a beast.'
        b. Un lobo está acorralado.
           a wolf is   cornered
           'A wolf is cornered.'

In (29a) we have a so-called individual-level predication, while in (29b) we have, instead, a stage-level one. Raposo and Uriagereka argue that those are the wrong categories, the phenomenon in question being not lexico-conceptual but rather more along the lines of the thetic vs. categorical distinction that Kuroda (1972) rescued from the philosophical tradition. In the categorical (29a) a generic interpretation is required of the indefinite subject, unlike what is obtained for (29b), where such an interpretation is barred if no further qualifying expressions are added to the example. Raposo and Uriagereka signal these distinctions in terms of the Case/agreement system, which could be now extended along the lines explored in this chapter: arguably the categorical subject in (29a) is receiving nominative Case, while the subject in the thetic judgement, instead, receives null Case.[23]

---

23 This may relate also to the traditional phenomenon of *nominativus pendens*, an overtly nominative Case classically associated to topics in many languages; topics, too, typically involve categorical judgements that hold for their referent.

Implicit in all of the discussions above has been the following general-ization:[24]

(30)   The Person Generalization
        Full (vs. weak) generalized Infl ⟷ Person (vs. only number) features in
        inflections.

For some reason, morphological fullness in inflections correlates both with their ability to determine full, as opposed to null, Case and also their mani-festing person, as opposed to only number distinctions. As a consequence PRO, indefinites, implicit arguments or CP go with null Case, as opposed to personal elements. Of course, the question is why (30) should hold. We briefly return to this after introducing a very different set of facts.

4.3   Towards a syntax of evidentiality and related phenomena

Next let's summarize the central ideas in Uriagereka (2003), where a connection is explored between syntax and pragmatics, by way of 'surface syntax'. It is illuminating to consider how to resolve the issues posed by such a syntax, if it affects interpretation. These ideas go back to Uriagereka (1988), where various syntactic phenomena led to the postulation in the periphery of the clause of a surprisingly evidential site, which was then dubbed F (for 'further' position). The relevant argument was comparative, concerning Romance clitics and their familiar, and very different, placements (see Raposo and Uriagereka [2005]):

(31)   'I have tried to do it.'
        '... that I have tried to do it.'

        Spanish
        a.   **Lo** he intentado hacer
        a'. ... que **lo** he intentado hacer

        Portuguese
        b.   Tenho-**o**   tentado fazer
        b'. ... que **o** tenho tentado fazer

        French
        c.   J'ai essayé de **le** faire
        c'. ... que j'ai essayé de **le** faire

---

24 This generalization bears on the surprising fact that PRO is not pronounced, which hasn't been accounted for – short of directly assimilating it to a trace as in Hornstein (1999) – in Chomsky (1981), in terms now given up (see Lasnik and Uriagereka [2005: chapter 7]). See San Martin (2004) for extensive discussion of this and related points.

Taking inspiration from Kayne (1991) – though departing from some of its essentials – some functional F had to be assumed, as in (32), that is either morphologically there (as in the (31b) examples from Portuguese) or not (as in the (31a) examples from Spanish). This element is supposed to trigger verb movement past the clitics in root clauses, but not in embedded ones, where it can be hosted by 'governing' elements. For French, where the clitic facts are significantly different ((31c) merely scratches the surface), it was postulated that F is not present in overt syntax, which was taken to have a variety of consequences for the clitic system.

(32)   a.   [F-lo [he intentado [[hacer]]]]
          a′. [que [F-lo [he intentado [[hacer]]]]]
        b.   [Tenho-*F*-o [t tentado   [[fazer]]]]
          b′. [que- *F-o* [t [tenho tentado [[fazer]]]]]
        c.   [J'ai essayé [de [**le** faire]]]
          c′. [que   [j'ai essayé [de [le faire]]]]

(**F** is a syntactic formative and the italized *F* is a morphologically heavy version of **F**.)

Uriagereka (1992, 1995) argues that F plays a role independently of the facts just alluded to, a matter systematically witnessed in languages like Portuguese (called *archaic* because many medieval Romance variants appeared to act like this), much less systematically in languages of the Spanish sort (referred to as *standard*), and not at all in a language like French (described as *radical*, likening some of its properties to those observed in Brazilian Portuguese). The idea was that F may be a trigger of the 'hot' behavior of languages, in the sense of Huang (1984), for topics, foci and the like, as in the Spanish instances in (33):

(33)   a. Juan dice que [**ese hombre** [María piensa que es un burro]].
          Juan says that that man   María thinks that is an ass
          'Juan says that this man María thinks is an ass.'
    b. Juan dice que [**muchas cosas** [ha tenido que soportar en esta vida]].
          Juan says that many   things has had   that endure in this life
          'Juan says that he had to endure MANY THINGS in his life.'

Of course, inasmuch as a focus (expressing non-presuppositional material) and a topic (expressing narrowly presuppositional material) are in this approach *both* associated to F, the association cannot be classically semantic, in any trivial sense. What was taken to be common to both sorts of elements in the examples in point was the expression of an attitude. This is significantly different from proposals in the Cartographic program (Cinque 1999;

Rizzi 2004), where each lexico-semantic property is associated to a separate category.[25]

4.3.1   *Some place(s) for pragmatic interfacing*

Since the earliest studies of these pragmatically-related notions by Jackendoff (1972), it has been clear that they have a peculiarly overt manifestation: direct displacement in the case of topics, and that or phonological prominence in the case of foci. Such overt properties were central in arguing for the existence of S-structure as a level of representation, different from the thematically oriented D-structure, and also the scopally-driven LF. In current terms, this entails that discourse dependency must be coded prior to the PF/LF split, which creates a puzzle for minimalism as is often presented. Indeed, it may create a puzzle even for the sort of system sketched here, since after all any standard syntactic 'flow' goes from lexico-conceptual information to transformationally derived intentional information of the LF sort. Any simple version of that allows for a maximum of *two* interface levels: one at the input and one at the output. But we appear to need more.

We should clarify what a 'pragmatic phenomenon' is. Some are clearly not constrainable to contexts of the F sort (much less to root ones). Consider for instance nominal displacements of the sort independent of Case/agreement reasons. Shifts within the VP have been observed in the *various* layers that correspond to small *v*'s, involving what has come to be known as *inner topics*. Even worse, observe these contrasts.

(34)   a. The CIA is following [every step of his/Osama's], although he hasn't
             taken any.
         b. The CIA is following [his/Osama's every step], #although he hasn't
             taken any.

The locution *his every step* invokes a presupposition in this environment that, in the same domain, *every step of his* doesn't. The only obvious difference between the expressions is that in the latter *his* has been displaced to the nominal periphery. But this is enough to alter this nominal's intentional specifications, so that *every step* becomes contextually confined to *his*, in such a way that this contextual specification affects verifiability conditions: the expression cannot denote vacuously in these sorts of domains, unlike

---

25 Separate focus and topic positions, among many other categories, are assumed in this alternative. In the proposal under discussion, instead, there was a single evidentiality site. In what follows we explore a way to dispense even with that, as a category at least, although that will require a different treatment of the phenomena just alluded to.

every step of his, as the infelicitous continuation in (34b) shows.[26] *His every step* is thematically and scopally indistinguishable from *every step of his*, which means that, in D-structure and LF properties, the expressions are alike. Yet they exhibit an interpretive difference, which involves a kind of DP-internal topicalization. Uriagereka (2003) mentions other phenomena along these lines, which forces the discussion in one of two mutually exclusive directions.

The first option is to posit elements like F every time there is a pragmatic effect, pursuing an intuition that goes back to Banfield (1973) and which capitalizes on root nodes being special, for some reason anchored to speakers (see Etxepare [1997] for much useful discussion in this regard). This view must postulate essentially root nodes internal to nominals, to account for facts along the lines of (34) – and more.[27] The alternative is to forget about F being involved in these pragmatic instances. But then we still have to say something about how we obtain a surface syntax that interpretation manages to be sensitive to. Chomsky (2001) sketches an interesting idea in this regard, suggesting that this kind of interpretation arises *at phase borders*.

Chomsky is concerned with languages that involve object shift, an option he takes to be universal. What results in its being *obligatory* in some languages, though, derives from independent 'surface' semantics requirements, a kind of interpretation that is assigned to the head of a chain (35a). At times the head and the foot are the same (35b), a circumstance for which Chomsky allows either 'deep' or 'surface' interpretation to the head of the chain. But when displacement to an 'EPP' (in section 4.2, null Case) position occurs as in (35c) – thereby creating a non-trivial chain – then only the head of the chain can receive 'surface' interpretation, assigned to EPP sites.

(35) a. Normal interpretation for Ch = (a_i, t_i): $[a_i \ldots \quad [\ldots t_i \ldots] \ldots]$
      SURFACE   DEEP

  b. Interpretation for trivial chains Ch = a_i: $[\ldots a_i \ldots]$
      DEEP
      SURFACE

  c. Obligatory interpretation for chains involving P(eripheral) (EPP) features Ch = (a_i, t_i): $[[a_i]-P \ldots [\ldots t_i \ldots] \ldots]$
      SURFACE   DEEP

---

26 Phenomena along these lines have been already discussed in section 3.6, as involving the contextual feature [+c].

27 Obviously this view of things shares much in common with generative semantics as discussed in chapter 2.

A parameter is also needed to make the system work, Chomsky proposes (36a).

(36)   a. PARAMETER: In L we interpret the *phonological border* of *v*P as 'surface': Yes/No
         b. IMPLICIT UNIVERSAL REQUIREMENT IN (35c).

The idea is to code the fact that some languages require the assignment of 'surface' interpretation to elements at the phonological border of *v*P, defined as follows:

(37)   Phonological Border
         The phonological border of a phase P is its leftmost element with PF support.

For Chomsky's point to go through, it's not crucial to know precisely what a phase is, so long as in particular *v*P counts as one such cycle.[28] The key to the parameter in (36a) is whether a given language L forces speakers to interpret the phonological border of the *v*P phase as a 'surface' position, irrespective of considerations pertaining to the universal EPP requirement in (35c). Languages with obligatory object shift involve a 'surface' interpretation in the phonological border of *v*P. If a given object, whose internal properties force it to be 'specific', happens to fall on the phonological border of *v*P because everything else c-commanding it has conspired to move out of that *v*P cycle, the object will then be forced to undergo object shift to a 'surface' site where it can be legitimately interpreted as 'specific'. In contrast, in a language where no such surface requirement is active (where parameter (36a) is set to 'No'), the phonological border of *v*P need not be interpreted as 'surface', thus an element in the circumstances just described can remain part of a trivial chain, where 'deep' and 'surface' interpretation co-exist (as in (35b)).

The key then is that the phonological borders of phases highlight concrete material, in relevant languages, as destined for 'surface' interpretation, which eliminates the possibility of interpreting a chain trivially in those languages, as an object with both 'deep' and 'surface' properties. Uriagereka (2003) develops this idea in a less stipulative fashion. In so doing, some light is shed on how the syntax may interface with the pragmatic components.

4.3.2   *Syntactic involvement in context confinement*

Pragmatic considerations must involve specification of contextual cues. Uriagereka (2003) explores the possibility that this is all there is to the

---

28 Recall the discussion in section 1.4.2. We return to these matters in section 6.4.2.

syntactic manifestation of pragmatics: *it expresses context*. As is well-known, human quantification is contextually restricted. The idea is to take this semantic need and turn it into an interface demand. The syntax links to the pragmatics by coding contextual specifications in designated areas, which may entail syntactic displacement. Movement of the sort analysed in chapter 3 as involving [+c] features is of this sort, with an interpretation related to the intentional matters raised in Higginbotham (1988) when it comes to context confinement. For example, for the central DP in (34b):

(38)   a. Syntax: DP   b. Interpretation: the speaker confines the range of

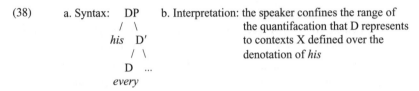

the quantifacation that D represents
to contexts X defined over the
denotation of *his*

As was implicit in chapter 3, the genitive occupying the DP specifier forces speakers to confine the range of the relevant quantification over its denotation (here, *his*) in characteristic fashion leading to a presuppositional reading (in (34a), of steps already taken by Osama).[29]

Implicitly, we saw already in chapter 3 that DPs specified as just indicated have interpretive differences vis-à-vis unspecified versions of the same phrases. We need not be overly technical about this, but recall the discussion of examples of the sort in (39) below, involving several sub-events of the main event, represented in various *v*s. If these *v*s are visited by moved nominals (in terms of a [+c] feature), as in the process of 'possessor raising', then corresponding sub-events are interpreted as forcing the confinement of their range to situations relevant to the moved possessor.

(39)   a. Le   vi   el cordón umbilical a mi   hija. [POSSESSOR RAISING OF *le*]
            dat saw. I the cord   umbilical to my daughter
            'I saw the umbilical cord on my daughter.'
        b. Vi   el cordón umbilical de mi hija.   [NO POSSESSOR RAISING]
            saw. I the cord   umbilical of my daughter
            'I saw my daughter's umbilical cord.'

As we discussed in section 3.2.2, for the example with 'possessor raising' to be felicitous, the chord must be attached to the baby, in a way that it need not be for (39b) to work. The analysis given for these facts was in terms

---

29 This must be spelled-out: how the relevant second-order predication results in the added
  presuppositionality.

of the raised possessor moving through the inner topic position at the *v*P phase (the *v* spec), with the associated contextual confinement (to my daughter) of the sub-event of the cord being seen. This is what ensures the 'attachment'.

Uriagereka (2003) simply makes this point: if we need context confinement for the precise semantics of quantification, and we have reason to believe this process involves a Q specifier, let us assume that this *is* how the syntactic derivation interfaces with pragmatics.

(40)   The Pragmatic Assumption
        Context effects arise wherever there is a quantification Q that needs context confinement, which is syntactically coded in Q's specifier.

Nothing forces the system to be narrowed down specifically to the IP/TP periphery; we can get context effects *wherever there are quantifications* that need context confinement. This is central to the reasoning, as instances were shown in the previous section of pragmatic effects that, although 'peripheral' to *v*P or comparable nominal cycles, are not peripheral to IP/TP, as the original F was. This leaves two questions open. One is why the syntax has chosen the mode of representation implicit in the Pragmatic Assumption for context confinement, as opposed to other a priori imaginable restrictions. The second is why this sort of process is more obvious in 'hot' languages, and also why it takes place *at phase borders*. These matters are addressed in the next section, where we also return to the questions left looming with regards to the Person Generalization, which relates full morphology in the clausal inflectional system to person features – a pragmatic notion.

4.4   'Surface' semantics matters

Let's now tie up the two sets of facts discussed above: null Case distribution in context-free terms with its associated non-personal semantics, and all the matters just seen pertaining to the conditions where 'surface' semantics – of the personal sort – manifest themselves.

4.4.1   Specificity, the Elsewhere Condition, and multiple spell-out
Uriagereka (2003) suggests that 'surface' interpretation is a consequence of the Elsewhere Condition. Learners are conservative, so in situations of interpretive conflict they must assume the 'most specific' option. The following seems reasonable, even uncontroversial:

(41)   (i) The subtle difference between a contextualized quantification and a decontextualized one counts as a possible source of *interpretive conflict* in learning.[30]

(ii) A contextualized reading is *more specific* than a decontextualized one.

(iii) A structure involving extra PF assumptions, either in terms of overt movement, a phonological border, or some form of prominence, is *more specific* than a corresponding structure without any of the above.

There are two notions of specificity being used here, related on purpose. On one hand, in (41iii) we are dealing with *information* specificity, which correlates with information *amount*. To illustrate, *the man who wrote this* is more informative than *the man*: it involves more information (just as 3.141592 is a more specific approximation to *Pi* than 3.1416). In this sense, comparative specificity just means accuracy in terms of representation, which is directly proportional to *extra* symbolic specifications, given some shared symbols. As for specificity in the sense of (41ii), books have been written on the topic. But we can cut to the chase: interpretational specificity in the linguistic sense can be seen in terms, again, of extra symbolic baggage. *One idea* is less specific than *the one idea I'm trying to push*. The former is a proper sub-case of the latter in terms of symbolic representation, and thus the latter is saying, thus specifying, *more accurately* (and see fn. 30). In addition, Uriagereka (2003) assumes a third sense of 'specificity', and taking the idea from work on this topic stemming from phonology and morphology (following Lasnik [1981]), explicates it in essentially the same information-theoretic sense, albeit cued to learnability considerations. This is achieved

---

30 A learner must decide, when facing an expression like 'cat', whether what is being acquired denotes a kind or, instead, describes an exemplar of that kind. Exemplary readings are more specific than kind ones, across languages, and moreover the latter are typically used in vaguer or even decontextualized situations. For example, compare:

(i)   a. The/a portrait of Mary Magdalene.
           b. Mary Magdalene's portrait.

It is much easier to use the decontextualized (ia) with a prototypical or generic use than it is with (ib), where *Mary Magdalene* is promoted to a context-specifying site.

(ii)   a. The portrait of Mary Magdalene wasn't developed as a genre until the Italian Renaissance.
           b. # Mary Magdalene's portrait wasn't developed as a genre until the Italian Renaissance.

through the one principle of learning that studies on learnability converge on:

(42)   Sub-case Principle
        Conservative learners choose the more specific option, within sub-case
        conditions.

What's at stake is fixing learning options in conflicting (sub-case) instances (e.g. the one alluded to in (41i)), whereby for the learner to bet on the *less* specific option would be risky, assuming human learners do not employ negative generalizations over data. The learning, semantic, and syntactic facts in (41) that touch on specificity can be coupled together in terms of the over-arching co-linearity thesis (CLT) in the present book, concretely a version tailored to those facts in terms of a *learnability wager*, to be coupled with the sub-case principle in (42), which demands that learners assume the results in (41) *as their first guess*:[31]

(43)   Learnability Wager
        In situations of learning conflict, let whatever involves a more specific
        form correlate with whatever involves a more specific interpretation.

Descriptively, the issue arises in 'EPP environments', where a given element is detected as displaced. Thus, by the co-linearity assumption in the Learnability Wager, the element is signaled as involving a 'surface' interpretation correlating with salient syntax.

But why are *phase borders* significant? Uriagereka (2003) suggests that this is because they are one of only two phonological cues left in a domain after its 'radical' spell-out, its phrasal-structure being destroyed at this point;[32] the only other cue left after spell-out of this kind is provided by the top category itself. Uriagereka (1999) contemplated both *radical* and *conservative* versions of multiple spell-out. (44) compares each possibility. In the radical version in (44a) each spelled-out chunk leaves the phrase-marker; in the conservative version in (44b), instead, the material remains in the phrase-marker, albeit flattened. It was also suggested that the radical version of online spell-out may give us a rationale for morphological Concord of the Case/agreement-marking sort showing up with regards to specifiers only (no such phenomenon is

---

31 In the spirit of Manzini and Wexler (1987), matters are expressed here in terms of 'sub-*case*', instead of 'sub-*set*' situations. Still, an interesting issue is how this 'wager' is instantiated in the learner's mind.

32 All forms of spell-out entail destroying phrasal information upon mapping it into a speech signal; however, in radical systems this is done more dramatically, as spelled-out material is not just devoid of phrasal boundaries but furthermore entirely sent to performance without residues in the derivation.

witnessed for pure complements): structural chunks that abandon the derivation have to be relocated in performance for the purposes of interpretation; overt Case/agreement counts as an *address* system or pointer.

(44) a. Radical spell-out of specifiers: b. Conservative spell-out of
                                                       specifiers:

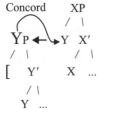

                                                            XP
                                                           / \
                                                        YP   X′
                                                     [...-Y-...] / \
                                                              X ...

                                                       Interpretation of flattened
                                                       YP in place

Construal of YP in Y in performance
through Concord addressing
(system only sees label Y and border [ )

The radical version in terms of Concord makes little sense in languages with poor Case/agreement markings. Therefore Uriagereka (2003) proposed that the two theoretical *versions* of spell-out contemplated in the past are two parametric *options* that correlate with morphological specifications. In languages with robust morphology spell-out is radical, while elsewhere spell-out must be conservative, dependent on configurational attachment. The parametric differences that then surface are summarized in Table 4.2.

In languages of the conservative spell-out sort, where configurational attachment of flattened spelled-out chunks is the mechanism employed, the phrase marker is not radically split on its way to the interpretive components (44b). In a language of this kind it is thus possible, in principle, to have trivial chains with 'deep' and 'surface' interpretation associated to them, as we can reconstruct 'deep' characteristics of the configurational sort (context-free) and also directly read 'surface' properties of the chain sort (context-sensitive) from the phrase marker itself. It may be flattened by the spell-out procedure, but it hasn't lost all its derivational information. But such a conservative procedure is impossible in languages that deploy the radical spell-out mechanism, where each spelled-out chunk follows its path to performance and unification takes place only in the interpretive components, and due to a dynamic concord system (45a). In those conditions, phase borders (for phonological purposes) and top-labeled categories (the basis of the Concord unification) are the only grammatical notions visible to the system, and the grammar anchors the labeled top to the 'deep' interpretation and the border to

Table 4.2. *Multiple spell-out possibilities and their effect*

Language type	Radical spell-out	Conservative spell-out
Syntax Interface	Trivial chains impossible Labeled top **Y** assigned to 'deep' interpretation Border **I** assigned to 'surface interpretation'	Trivial chains possible 'Deep' characteristics reconstructed from configuration 'Surface' characteristics read off a phrase marker
Observations	Syntactic object can be directly reconstructed in split phrase-marker	Reconstruction possible

a 'surface' interpretation. This makes sense: the label designates a configuration type, and configurations are the subject of 'deep' semantics or lexico-conceptual dependencies. The phonological border is simply the 'elsewhere' scenario: the grammar needs to involve an extra interpretation of a different sort, and it goes with the other available cue to anchor it. It would make no sense, design-wise, to conflate 'deep' and 'surface' interpretations in a given object in this sort of language, as it involves no reconstruction source to disentangle such conflations.

Uriagereka (2004) also adds the condition in (45).

(45)   Spell-out Economy Metric
        The radical spell-out system is more economical than the conservative one.

Radical spell-out allows phrase markers which are representationally simpler, and in that sense is less taxing in terms of online memory for the system. But some grammars cannot go with the simplest option because they lack the appropriate Concord systems to serve as overt addresses, thus they stick to the more complex configurational flattening, the one converging.

The idea that languages with robust morphological dependency should allow arguments to be more 'separated' from the phrase marker than languages without morphological cues of this sort, which rely instead on configurational ordering, is actually traditional. The new twist given to this intuition is that in 'partially configurational' languages spell-out is of the radical sort, and thus phase borders and top-labeled constituents matter to an extent that they do not in fully configurational languages where the phrase marker is never dismembered.

This seems to accord with the facts. Languages without peripheral F effects, in the sense discussed in the previous section – for instance French and English – happen to present impoverished Case/agreement systems, vis-à-vis languages where these sorts of effects are present, like Portuguese or many Slavic and Germanic languages, which rather clearly tend to show robust agreement, Case, or both. In the original work on these matters that was correlated, without an explanation, to the morphological properties of F. From the present perspective the correlation is a consequence of whether the languages undergo radical or conservative spell-out. If spell-out is morphologically sanctioned as radical, border effects in phases will be significant, and consequently we expect Chomsky's phenomenology with regards to 'surface' syntax in these instances. If spell-out must be of the conservative sort that results in a unified phrase marker, because of morphological impoverishment, then relevant languages will tolerate ambiguous 'deep'/'surface' interpretations on trivial chains.

Recall also from (31) and (32) that three settings for F-related variation were being assumed, exemplified in the French vs. Portuguese extremes already discussed in the new light, vis-à-vis the intermediate case of Spanish, which presents peripheral phenomena as in (33) but no verbal displacement to result in enclisis, as in (32b). This third setting ought to result from a *mixed* pattern of spell-out, a straightforward possibility: those parts of the derivation that obey robust morphology (for whatever reason) go with the more economical radical spell-out, and those parts where morphology is absent (again for reasons that do not affect the logic of the proposal) go with the more costly conservative spell-out.[33] This is quite plausible for a language, like Spanish, that exhibits robust Concord at some level (typically a structurally higher chunk) but not lower in the inflectional skeleton. In such a language, radical spell-out would be possible with TP specifiers, in particular, but not *v*P specifiers. Consequently, border effects should arise in higher, but not lower phases, internal to a clause.

That is what one finds: border effects high up in the Spanish clausal periphery, such as fronting for emphasis purposes, but no systematic scrambling effects at the *v*P phase. It then should be the case that scrambling should be more of an option in archaic languages of the Galician/Portuguese sort, although its effects may be masked by the fact that the verb itself, in this sort of language, will normally raise even higher. We could however witness scrambling in situations where the verb manages to stay low, a possibility explicitly

33 See Gallego (2007) for much related discussion.

discussed – as an explanation for why infinitival proclisis is the norm in Portuguese, though not in Spanish – in Raposo and Uriagereka (2005).[34] It may be added, also, that the verbal displacement observed in some Romance variants ought to correlate with 'surface' semantic effects, for the reasons discussed which it does. A displaced verb expresses a thetic judgement, whereas a non-displaced verb allows for a categorical judgement instead, a distinction analysed by Raposo and Uriagereka (2002) in context-confinement terms.

4.4.2   Local transformations

Implicit in Chomsky's approach, clarified and extended here, is the fact that not all syntactic displacement can be confined to standard formal triggers. Once we have explored matters along the lines suggested, it may not be necessary to postulate formal features of the [+c] or [+r] sort, which geared movement in terms of the LRC in chapter 3. The LRC seems to be beside the point in scrambling and related surface–driven phenomena. In effect, Chomsky's proposal can be seen as a rationalization of Emonds original (1976) local transformations, which differed from his structure preserving ones in terms that are relevant to us.

(46)   Classical formulation:

  (a) Core transformations:
     i.   are triggered.
     ii. can be unbounded.
     iii. are structure preserving.
     iv. may have scopal effects.
  (b) Stylistic transformations:
     i.   are not triggered.
     ii. are extremely local.
     iii. are sensitive to phonological demands.
     iv. typically have surface effects.

---

34 Compare the Portuguese (i) with the Spanish (ii)((iia) was correct in Spanish up to the sixteenth century):

  (i)   Não **te** convidar para a   festa...
          not you invite for   the party
          'Not to invite you to the party...'
  (ii)   a.   No **te**   invitar a la fiesta...
                not you invite to the party
          b.   No invitar**te** a   la fiesta...
                not invite.you to the party
                'Not to invite you to the party...'

(47)   Minimalist formulation
  (a) Transformations associated to Agree:
    i.   obey the LRC.
    ii. obey the MLC.
    iii. obey the CCU.
    iv. may have scopal effects.
  (b) Operations without Agree:
    i.   are not subject to the LRC.
    ii. must take place within phases.
    iii. are sensitive to borders.
    iv. typically have 'surface' effects.

Minimalism has substituted the chain conditions introduced in chapter 3 (LRC, MLC, and CCU) for what used to be thought of as 'triggers', 'locality', and 'structure preservation', but the spirit remains: core transformations, of the sort that affect scopal relations, are different from the 'untriggered', more 'local' and less 'sensitive to syntax', *adjustment* processes of the scrambling type, which do not affect either lexico-conceptual relations or scopal specifications. For the minimalist treatment of the operations where Agree is not relevant, the system must have concrete specifications about cyclicity: a definition of *phase* plus syntactic inaccessibility and interpretive transfer conditions. Chomsky (2000) assumes the following:

(48)   Phase Impenetrability Condition (PIC)
         Where ZP is the least phase dominating a phase H, the domain of H is not accessible to operations at ZP; only H and H's edge are thus accessible.

(49)   Where a is a derivational phase, the effects of related syntactic processes spanning over a are evaluated at the point of a's TRANSFER (to PF and LF).

This defines characteristic cycles,[35] within which the syntax can act disregarding LRC conditions (possibly also MLC and CCU, concentrating on phonological clues and predicates, such as *adjacency*). Stylistic processes are trapped within these confines.

The real issue is why things turn out to be as in (47). The gist of the proposal has been that *derivational dynamics* determine these 'local adjustments' of the stylistic sort. Since we return to core transformations and their interpretive correlates in chapter 8, we can set them aside now. As for the other phenomena, the matter of their triggering is contentious – boiling down

---

35 These phases are compatible with although different from, multiple spell-out cycles, which we return to in chapters 5 and 6.

to what we make of the EPP. In the first half of this chapter it was suggested that a residual form of Case may be at stake. But this need not be, in any case, a normal 'trigger' in satisfaction of the insight behind the LRC; things work in 'last resort' terms for null Case, but that doesn't seem to be central to the process, suggesting it reflects something deeper. Understanding why the grammar may have null Case presupposes understanding, also, why full Case exists. The view on this in Uriagereka (1997), which we return to in section 8.4.5, is that Case distinctions serve the purpose of tokenizing DPs, in the sense already alluded to in sections 1.4.2 and 1.6. The logic of that idea is that *specific* Case valuations relate to *specific* configurations (e.g. nominative to TP, accusative to v, etc.).

To put it simply, if our system has difficulties distinguishing a token D_i from another token D_j,[36] their configurational *context* will do it. Having a D sister to the v projection is not the same as having a sister to the T projection – even the dullest syntax can express that, so long as it has the appropriate online memory.[37] If this is the rationale behind full Case, null Case, as understood in this chapter, has nothing to do with (successful) tokenization. We have seen V, v and T all assign null Case; in fact this was central in addressing Hornstein's worry that null Case as in Chomsky and Lasnik's proposal (where it is restricted to defective T of the raising sort) is *ad hoc*. Null Case thus appears everywhere (modulo NCV conditions), but precisely for that reason it has to be orthogonal to any form of contextualization. Indeed, for all practical purposes null Case is used to signal non-personal arguments and movement targets. But the system shouldn't then have this form of Case *because* of those consequences.

Suppose grammar has Case for tokenization purposes; this implies the system can identify a configurational context X, and associate it (arbitrarily far, via valuation, within a derivational cycle) to a given D; this then becomes *token* D_x. Once this process is assumed, the grammar can't help but have null Case as well, as a trivial instance of full Case *where configurational context X is devoid of any substantive content*, and thus has to be matched locally (in context-free terms, as was argued). In other words, null Case is what the MAC activates without worrying about whether X is T, v, or anything else; it's simply a category, and as such a configuration at the point of context-free Merger – *any* configuration. Full Case is much more costly for the MAC, as it

36 In particular, without trivial annotations or allowing the syntax access to interpretive information.

37 See Drury (2005) for further discussion of these and related ideas.

involves 'knowing' T from v and so on, hence its tokenization consequence. That said, null Case satisfies the LRC, but LRC conditions don't seem central to its mechanics, as they are for full Case. Identity elements in arithmetic behave similarly:[38] they do not participate in the effects of relevant operations, although they are key to the architectural properties of the system. Null Case, too, is trivial in one sense but central in other: it provides (embedded) EPP effects that gear the surface semantics system we have discussed in the second half of this chapter.

As for surface semantics, it may ultimately not be very sound to propose (as I did in the past) a category or even a category zone to code pragmatic effects. This is, first, because pragmatic effects, even if prominent at the clausal periphery and highly visible at the root, are present elsewhere in a complex structure. One can hardly pin them down to a category (zone) without going back to generative semantics. Second, even if we do detect *the* place(s) where pragmatic effects arise, we must still determine what it is that they *are*, and how they affect interpretation. Surely one can also code a phenomenon with interpretive consequences into a category. But if syntactic categories have deep properties of the lexico-conceptual sort, it seems questionable to start also categorizing notions that pertain instead to the way in which speakers intentionally anchor their concepts to the world around. That is, a nominal space with all its nuances (of the sort studied by Muromatsu [1998] or Castillo [2001]), or a verbal space with *its* nuances (which Mori [2005] explores, among many others looking at vastly rich intricacies of entailment), are not at the same level as the context specifications that determine the important, though non-conceptual, workings of surface syntax. When saying that I boiled the soup it is entailed that, then, the soup boiled. But when saying that they are following Osama's every step, an entailment cannot be ascertained to the effect that, then, they are following every step of Osama. The latter assertion is, as was shown, compatible with Osama not taking any step. In other words, lexico-conceptual entailment is beside the point in instances involving context confinement, and *categorizing* both sorts of phenomena by way of functional structure clouds this distinction.[39]

---

38 For instance *0* for addition, *1* for multiplication, and so on. Such elements are entirely central in numerical analysis, as the basis of inductive procedures that support numerical architecture.

39 This criticism extends to aspects of the Cartographic project (Cinque 2002; Belletti 2004; Rizzi 2004), which only compounds the matter by introducing not one, but in fact as many categories (of the relevant sort) as detectable, thinly cut, interpretation effects (see Lambova [2003] for much relevant discussion).

It was suggested above, instead, that pragmatic effects with a syntactic correlate involve *context confinement* of relevant quantificational elements, which can thus be anywhere in the structure where a quantifier is allowed. Syntactically, it was indicated that this involves the specifier of whatever category supports the quantificational element, which is in line with what was said about referentiality in chapter 3.[40] This, *per se*, doesn't say anything about whether the phenomenon ought to involve deep, surface or covert syntax. It was argued that this is a more subtle matter relating, in terms of the Learnability Wager instantiation of the CLT, to learnability considerations and how a surface, specific semantics is read off a prominent syntax, for instance of the EPP sort. Languages were in turn separated in terms of whether they exhibit robust Case/agreement systems, if not allowing a radical, and simpler, form of spell-out recovered in performance through a morphological address system. In these languages phase borders are significant domains that the system must align with surface interpretation.

Concord processes, in the specific sense of null Case determination, and arguably associated stylistic phenomena with surface effects, plainly exist. It makes sense to treat this as a context-free phenomenon, thus forcing extreme locality (extended forms of sisterhood),[41] leaving context-sensitive dependencies for probing relations that demand a search space. In addition, possible associated displacements affect surface semantics, but only within the confines of phases, arguably because there is no way of pushing forward, in the derivational flow, this context-free information. Since languages differ in how they treat cyclic matters – how their specifier cycles are cashed out – in addition this also entails interesting linguistic variation. The parametric cues for it are just rich morphology; however, the observable consequences are drastic – a 'hot' vs. a 'cold' behavior in surface semantics.

To rationalize the system, the Person Generalization in (30) was assumed: morphological fullness in inflections correlates both with their ability to determine full, as opposed to null, Case and also their manifesting person, as opposed to only number distinctions. What would go wrong in a syntax that

---

40 This time the intentional issue being the support of the variable that a given quantifier theta binds.

41 Chomsky (1986) treated the complement and specifier of the T (I) projection as 'extended' sisters. In Chomsky (1995) intermediate categories are inaccessible to the computational system. So in effect the head/spec relation is as context-free as the head-complement relation. This is obviously true for the (X′, spec) relation, and if in a bare phrase structure system X^0 is feature-wise indistinguishable from X′, then context-freeness holds for the entire X projection.

mapped null Case to personal pronouns and full Case to PRO? In terms of the CLT, the Agree relation – which involves a context-sensitive Probe/Goal dependency – should have an interpretive consequence that is rather different from that of a related, albeit context-free, syntactic process also involving feature-match: Concord between a head and its specifier. Observably, Agree exhibits personal semantics, while Concord does not. This follows from the architectural concerns we're entertaining, if personal semantics involve a system of *paradigmatic dependencies* of the pragmatic sort, inexpressible via binary oppositions like [+/− plural] (number) or [+/− masculine] (gender). Personal relations are the systematization of context-sensitive dependencies, now using the word 'context' in the pragmatic sense. First person is an anchoring of the propositional content in a sentence to the speaker (responsible for context confinement), second person is a similar anchoring to the addressee (responsible for decoding the speaker's contextual confinements, over imaginable alternatives), and third person is left unanchored. Thus is the referential repository that intentionality can systematically use. How does interpretive context relate to syntactic context?[42] The implicit co-linearity of the CLT invites this inference: *because* the relation between X and Y is syntactically context-sensitive, semantic context-sensitivity (i.e. 'pragmatic dependency') will be its natural interpretation.[43] This justifies the Person Generalization. It could not have been that the context-free Concord involved in null Case is responsible for context-sensitive pragmatic relations; these also demand context-sensitive syntactic dependency.

4.5   Conclusions

In this chapter we have taken a look at syntactic processes that are not well understood in terms of mere output conditions in the derivation, instead implicating online derivational dynamics. Moreover, although there are aspects of the mechanisms involved in such a syntax that arguably respond to

---

42 Another way of asking this is how a second-order context variable, holding as a predicate of intentional variables in a quantified semantic representation, relates to the history of a syntactic derivation.

43 In the more radical interpretation of this project, semantic context-sensitivity ought to follow from syntactic context-sensitivity, not just be co-linear with it. It is unclear, with present understanding of these matters, how such a deduction would work, as the syntactic notion is much better understood than the semantic correlate. This is one of the reasons I have not committed to the interesting implementation of these ideas that Wolfram Hinzen (2006, 2007) has attempted in his work.

design and operational economy considerations, not all of their facets allow for such a reduction, and instead several seem to depend on interface demands. But these crucially happen *prior* to the derivational output at LF, and they appear to revolve around matters of information and context – in a word, pragmatics. That such pragmatic cues affect syntactic derivations in some languages is undeniable, as is the fact that these are neither specifications of lexico-conceptual matters pertaining to the shape that predicates or arguments take, nor of the logico-intentional sort, involving scopal interactions. Instead, what seems relevant with regard to the phenomena in this chapter is how grammatical features correlate with the personal axis in discourse, linking speakers to addressees, or how informational specificity is affected by the relative position of expressions. In the process, massive linguistic variation can be observed, which ought to be explainable also in terms of a sound parameterization, hopefully geared by the mechanisms under study. The co-linearity in the CLT allows us to connect the syntactic and interpretive aspects of the phenomena, within a cyclic derivation obeying the distributed interfaces thesis. From this perspective it is natural to make syntactic specificitiy (*complexity* of the sort resulting from the transformational component) correspond to information specificity (a contextually rich presentational array of a referring expression), especially so when learnability (the need to fixate on specific options) is at stake. This is a model story for the present framework.

5 *Prepositional case throughout*

5.1 Introduction

In previous chapters a core syntax was introduced, and a basic sort of mapping outlined between that syntax and a corresponding interpretation. In the process, various paradigms and related puzzles were studied that emerge around the notion 'argument', especially when considered vis-à-vis conditions on Case assignment. In this chapter, a more detailed analysis is given of the Case mechanisms themselves.

Most significant progress within Case Theory has been made in clarifying the conditions under which Case is determined, traditionally via *government*. Classical minimalism rethought this in terms of head/specifier relations achieved by way of displacement of a Case assignee into a *checking* (as opposed to assigning) position. However, as the primitive nature of this dependency came to be questioned, it became reasonable to treat Case valuation as a process of long-distance Agree. In what follows Case conditions are reexamined from this perspective, in an attempt to unify various instances of Case determination as involving a preposition. In the second section various puzzles are sketched that relate to Case. A way is suggested to unify the bizarre results of having only prepositions assign Case, which forces intriguing readjustments in the system. In the third section Case conditions are studied that go beyond that core situation, arguing that cyclic derivational dynamics play a central role in the nature of the valuation they imply. An account of the Case hierarchy is given in section 4, which presupposes distinguishing context-free from context-sensitive conditions. Section 5 analyses some consequences and presuppositions of the proposed system – especially in terms of the complexity it implies for the syntax deployed – and some conclusions are drawn in the sixth section. The analysis in this chapter, although original, owes much to several works on Case theory.[1]

---

1 My interest in Case stems from an early reading of Hjelmslev (1935, 1937) and Fillmore (1968), and became focused after working through Chomsky (1981) and related pieces: Lasnik

5.2   Case conditions, Case puzzles, and steps towards a unification

Even if conditions on Case determination received a proper structural characterization, we'd still need to address seven additional Case puzzles.

(1) i.   What constitute the valid Case 'assigners'?
     ii. What does it mean to have both 'structural' and 'inherent' Case specifications?
     iii. Why does Case have a possible 'freezing' effect on displacing items?
     iv. Why does language have more than one Case value?
     v.   Why doesn't language have indefinitely many Case values?
     vi. Why are there Case hierarchies in grammar?
     vii. Why does language have Case at all?

Puzzle (1i) is easily answered. Prepositions systematically determine Case but everything else is more complicated. Most verbs do, nouns don't, although they directly associate to D categories that do determine Case. Adjectives don't determine Case and they don't directly associate, either, to those D categories that invoke genitive Case for nouns. Functional categories are a mess: some determine Case ((obligatorily) tensed T, (optionally) D), while most others (untensed T, C ...) either do not determine Case or determine some residual (null) Case in the sense of section 4.2. About the 'structural' vs. 'inherent' Case distinction (1ii) we only know that it relates to lexical dependencies of the thematic sort for inherent Case, which force this type of relation in 'base' configurations; we have no idea why the distinction exists. We are similarly in the dark regarding the freezing effect of Case valuation (1iii): we simply know that for some reason it prevents further A-movement after Case valuation has taken place (the Case freezing condition in (12), chapter 4) – although recall the variation we saw in this respect. Regarding the issue of different Case values (1iv), we typically encounter value systems that involve accusative, nominative, dative, genitive ... , but the list does not go on forever. One could imagine a system (like that associated to Tense) whereby only one or

and Freidin (1981), Hornstein and Weinberg (1981), Raposo (1987), Baker (1988), and Larson (1988), at least. Large chunks of my (1988) dissertation were devoted to my takes on these topics. Raposo and Uriagereka (1990) anticipated my current view on Case, which other than obvious conceptual debts to Halle and Marantz (1993), owes much to the comprehensive Bittner and Hale (1996), as well as to a mechanism in Watanabe (1993). A recent piece that has been useful in clarifying the morass of questions involved is Legate (2006). In addition, some of the proposals to be explored below emerged through collaborative work with Roger Martin during the writing of his thesis (Martin 1996).

perhaps two, marked and unmarked, values are involved;[2] or, rather, a system where innumerable values could be invoked, depending on argument complexity (1v) – yet neither of those limiting conditions are apparent for Case systems, nor do we have situations whereby case features combine (in the manner of Tense and Aspect specifications) to compose new Case conditions. The puzzle compounds when we observe that Case values obey some sort of hierarchy (1vi), so that (for instance) accusative values are fixed before dative ones. Some of these puzzles may reduce to one another, but prima facie, they have no obvious solution, especially, of course, with the puzzle of why Case exists (1vii). We aim to have as many of these puzzles deduced from as few assumptions as possible, inevitably forcing certain abstractions. Perhaps the most extreme of these relates to the conditions on Case determination itself, as it will be suggested (arguably in the spirit of Bittner and Hale [1996]) that Case is *systematically* a prepositional phenomenon, even in instances where this isn't obvious.

5.2.1   The Case of prepositions and beyond

Prepositions are relatively well-behaved elements with regards to the Case system: they all determine Case, and they all can do so locally. Suppose, then, that thesis (2) obtains:

(2)   Case is determined by P.

Structurally, this could associate to two different configurations, exemplified as in (3):

(3)   a.   P′   b.   C′
              / \   / \
             P   DP   C   IP
            for   *for*$_i$ / \
                                         DP$_i$ ...

It will be assumed that (3a) corresponds to *inherent* Case 'assignment', thus is associated to 'base' positions. In contrast, we may take (3b) to correspond to a form of *structural* Case 'assignment' (to *all* relevant forms, via a checking process that we return to). Whereas the former instance involves (external) Merge between the preposition and the Case checker, the second instance

---

2 Tense is mentioned for concreteness; the point is about any system where only one value is relevant.

involves Agree (presupposed for internal Merge) between the preposition and the Case checker, and this may result in additional pied-piping of material containing the latter. If this is the correct implementation of Case specification, it directly involves the logical possibilities that Chomsky (2004 and elsewhere) has examined for Merge conditions.

(2) holds uncontroversially as a simple material implication, which we want to turn into a stronger, natural implication, so that not just *if* a preposition exists in a structure can Case be released, but that indeed *only if* this is true can Case valuation obtain as a direct consequence. The problem is what to do then with verbs, T, D and so on. But suppose (2) is refined to (4).

(4)   Case is determined by $[-N, -V]$ elements.

This is extensionally equivalent to (2), but the formulation in (4) addresses the *component parts* of P. That gives us some hope in the verbal instance, if we manage to devise a system whereby in effect the relevant features in (4) are also somehow involved. Suppose, in the spirit of an operation in Watanabe (1993), that specific combinations of verbs and something 'anti-nominal' result in the missing property for verbs that somehow produces a Case context in terms of (4) – perhaps not unlike certain sub-atomic particle interactions resulting in new particles.

This analogy will be pursued in what follows, arguing for two related ideas. One is borrowed from the Distributed Morphology model (Halle and Marantz [1993] and elsewhere) and is that categoricity (of the V or N type) is encoded by way of a separate formative of grammar associating to a lexical root, the latter being added late in the derivation. The second idea, original to this work if inspired by Watanabe's 'passing' features,[3] is that such categorial markers can be 'liberated' from syntactic interactions. It will be suggested that the phenomenon of Case determination is closely related to the particular sort of categorization that emerges in this sort of derivational process.

5.2.2   *Substantive and formal categories*
To make sense of that suggestion, let's start by supposing the following specification of the lexical projection thesis in section 3.6.4, as a way of

---

3 The idea of passing features is not unique to minimalism: although for different conditions, it features prominently in the 'slash' notation of GPSG (Gazdar *et al.* 1985) and other models (e.g. Bresnan and Kaplan [1982, p. 234]).

relating substantive and formal categories in terms of features from an abstractly common conceptual vocabulary.[4]

(5)   a. Substantive (predicational) categories are +N.
        b. Formal (grammatical) categories are +V.

If (5) obtains, major categories actually translate as in (6):[5]

(6)   a. [−N, −V] elements (P) are neither substantive nor formal.
        b. [+N, +V] elements (A) are both substantive and formal.
        c. [−N, +V] elements (V) are not substantive but formal.
        d. [+N, −V] elements (N) are substantive but not formal.

Intuitively, (6a) is true: prepositions are *merely relational* items from a closed and frozen class, and not predicational in any obvious sense, yet they do not normally behave like formal items. For instance, Ps don't systematically compose to further formal items in the manner *v* does to T or T to C, nor do they allow adverbial modification even when it would be reasonable (**in now/usually/perhaps the park*). (6b) seems also true: adjectives are predicational and items from an open class, but they also behave like formal items, for instance in combining with Degree elements (*the very tall man, a man taller than a giant*) or allowing adverbial modification (*the now/usually/ perhaps irresistible Mary*). However, whereas verbs seem more formal than nouns (e.g. verbs combine with all sorts of formal categories and they take adverbs, unlike nouns), and nouns seem more substantive than verbs (we use nouns to *designate* substantive classes, unlike verbs), it is no less true that nouns are somewhat formal in that most of them combine with some formal categories, and verbs are somewhat substantive in that the events they introduce are described in terms of some predicate. Note finally that, from the perspective in (6), there is a sense in which prepositions are featureless categories, involving the fewest assumptions within this category system. The opposite is true for adjectives, which have the most properties.

Suppose next that *all* substantive categories live in the lexicon, as lexical roots, *in their most marked/specific guise*, or with the most properties, thus as

---

4 As Baker (2003) observes, no one has seriously studied the [N]/[V] distinctions. The present system will diverge from the one explored by Baker, for whom [+V, +N] elements do not exist. These will be crucial to the present approach (their existence constituting the null hypothesis, as they follow from logical combination without added stipulations).

5 What follows is an attempt to ground familiar distinctions among the 'parts of speech' on more than the usual feature combinations introduced in Chomsky (1970) and Jackendoff (1972, 1977). Baker (2003) and Borer (2004, 2005), are the only recent works that even discuss these matters; the present take is sympathetic to these sources, although quite distinct.

$[+N, +V]$.[6] Such a state of affairs is natural on mere learnability grounds already reviewed in section 4.4.1 – sub-case conditions force learners to posit the most marked forms as their first hypothesis. The logic, in relevant circumstances, is simple. Hypothesizing sub-case (marked) forms is the most conservative route to take: either learners happen to be right on their first pass at a word, or else positive data will take care of the 'unlearning' by exhibiting a falsifying context for the wrong guess. This issue is quite real for substantive items, such as the word *cut*, which can appear nominally (*a cut of beef, missing the cut*), verbally (*cut the grass, cut across a field*), or in adjectival guise (*cut stones, a cut man*),[7] a matter that only compounds in other languages (see Baker [in press]). So we can take *cut* to be listed as $[+N, +V]$ in the lexicon; with something contextual happening in instances where the relevant interpretation is not adjectival. The original $[+N, +V]$ *cut* must *become* $-V$ if used as a noun, or $-N$ if used as a verb. The issue, then – as broadly posed within the Distributed Morphology framework – is what 'verbalizes' or 'nominalizes' given predicate roots.

Let us now assume opposing conditions as in (7).

(7)   a. An 'anti-noun' *v* verbalizes a predicate (providing a $-N$ feature to the complex).

       b. An 'anti-verb' *n* nominalizes a predicate (providing a $-V$ feature to the complex).

We may take 'anti-categories' to be categorial shells, in the general sense of Larson (1988). Intuitively, we can think of *v* as a content-less or light verb, a $[-N]$ 'auxiliary'. In turn *n* is perhaps a $[-V]$ classifier, which somehow eliminates combinatorial possibilities (in a manner we return to). What remains to be seen is what role, if any, these sorts of bare elements have in Case release, as suggested in the previous section. And incidentally, if (7) is a general mechanism, it shouldn't be only active in those ambiguous instances, like *cut*, that create a learning issue; presumably this *is* the way UG codes 'nominality' or 'verbality'.

5.2.3   Category collision and feature release

We can now provide 'anti-categories' with a dual role. On one hand, in context-free terms and via (external) Merge, they act as, in effect, categorizers, somehow turning roots that are $[+N, +V]$ into $[-N, +V]$ or $[+N, -V]$

---

6 This is different from what is normally assumed within standard Distributed Morphology, where roots are taken to be featureless elements.

7 Although most lexical items can have nominal and verbal manifestations in English, it is for some reason less common to find all three situations just described.

elements. This is, in effect, the idea of Distributed Morphology. The question is precisely how the categorization takes place, if categories are mere sets of privative features, and thus they can't be both $+F$ and $-F$.[8] Assuming all predicates are 'adjectival' [$+N$, $+V$], the only possibility is that upon being 'infected' with an 'anti-category' of a given sort, the original matching feature gets literally *expelled* from its host. To be precise:

(8)   When category X with features [aF_i, $+/-F'$, ...] combines with anti-category Y with feature [$-aF_j$], then category X becomes [$-aF_j$, $+/-F'$, ...] and feature aF_i gets released.

The subscripts in (8) are merely expository, to keep track of token features of the same categorial type (which may differ in polar value). The variable a ranges over ' $+$ ' or ' $-$ ' values, so that their polarity can be reversed when (8) takes place. The mechanics will become clearer shortly.

The next question is what happens with the feature released in a 'category collision'. Let's take it as a (non-trivial, indeed foundational) axiom, adopted from Chomsky (1995, chapter 4), that features cannot 'freely float' in derivational space, they must integrate into categories.[9]

(9)   Grammatical formatives are *sets* of privative features, not mere features.

Then, when expelled from a category upon a 'category collision', a feature must either be successfully absorbed into a new category or somehow turned into something categorial, by itself. Let's assume that, otherwise, the derivation cancels, as a consequence of the 'unintegrated' feature. We can put aside, for now, the possibility of a released feature being absorbed into another category. Unfortunately for the released feature, it does not have a categorial status, and if it is to 'turn into' a category in order to survive the derivation, the only thing it can exist as is a *featureless* category.[10] In instances where a mere

---

8 This is a substantive claim about categorization, going back to Trubetzkoy (1969) and Jakobson (1941).

9 The oblique reference to the Foundation Axiom in Set Theory is intended. This Axiom prevents an individual from being identical to the set containing it. Without it, Russell's paradox emerges (more simply, the empty set would be identifiable with the set containing the empty set, that is number one, and so on, with the number system collapsing). By this very axiom, at least it is true that a category (set of features) cannot be identified with a mere feature, even if we are speaking of a category set containing precisely that very feature and nothing else. A different question is why Merge operations must be on (category) sets, while valuation processes are, instead, directly on features, a matter to come back to in sections 8.4.3 and 8.4.4.

10 It is being assumed that because the feature has no categorial status, it does not relevantly retain its informational content if it succeeds in becoming categorial (with a caveat discussed further in the following footnote). An analogy might help. A person is not a legal organization, for instance a not-for-profit association; a person can *become* one such

feature gets released after relevant categories collide, the resulting element will have to be of the $[-N, -V]$ type – a preposition – which in turn means *a Case determiner* as per hypothesis (4). That is, then, the second role of an anti-category, specifically of the sort whose released feature *cannot absorb into a further category*: it in effect creates a P element that has no place in the system once the interface is reached. It must thus be eliminated. This can be achieved in context-sensitive terms via Agree.

Consider the collision of an anti-noun v shell and a predicate root. Graphically:

(10)   Case′
            / \
    +N = P$_N$ v′
          ↖   / \
            v ↘ ← [+N, +V]
          [–N]

In (10) the light v with $[-N]$ features collides with the predicate $[+N, +V]$, as a result of which a single $+N$ feature is released. This feature cannot exist as such, and the system interprets it as a featureless, default, $[-N, -V]$ P. As per assumption (4), this sort of element determines Case properties. Upon checking Case by way of Agree with some relevant category, in a manner that we return to, the Case projection is eliminated from the system. Actually, we know that relevant 'Case receivers' have to be *nominal* in character, for unclear reasons.[11] That goes well with the fact that the way we obtained the Case P element in (10) is through the system interpreting a mere feature $+N$ as a category; we may suppose the computation is sensitive to this information (coded as a subscript N attached to P), indicating that the featureless $[-N, -V]$ element originates from a $+N$ feature expelled from a predicate, and is thus in effect a 'nominal' preposition.[12]

That last comment raises the question of what happens when the released feature is not $+N$, but $+V$, as would presumably be the case when, *mutatis*

---

organization if meeting certain legal standards and upon notarizing several documents; in so doing the attributes *of the person* normally do not matter, so long as they are not contradictory to the legal requirements for the organization.

11 Case phenomenology manifests itself in nouns, determiners, and adjectives, but not in prepositions or verbs, which are both $-N$ elements.

12 To continue with the analogy in fn. 10, retaining a residue of the origin of the preposition would be similar to a pre-condition on the *type* of organization that becomes possible given the attributes of their members. For instance, a person who is not a musician is prevented from joining a musicians' guild.

mutandis, a [+N, +V] predicate root combines with an anti-verb [−V] shell to result in a [+N, −V] nominal. Graphically:

(11)

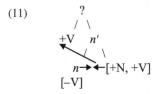

What sort of object is this V feature associated to a noun? Again, let's assume that Case valuation is, for reasons that do not affect the reasoning, undertaken by [+N] elements. We may thus suppose that the emergent category in (11) will not resolve its problematic existence in terms of Case checking, as there won't be a Case-checking target to take care of it. But then we need to resort to something else to deal with the category. The possibilities are two: a grammatical formative is either interpretable, thus making it into the interpretive interfaces where it is appropriately read, or uninterpretable, and thus it gets eliminated from computation prior to the interfaces. The latter, however, is not a haphazard process: there are well-behaved elimination mechanisms – e.g. Case checking – to take care of problematic instances. Unhappily for the verbal feature in (10), the mechanism the grammar provides for featural elimination is of no use.[13] Then the released feature must make it to the interfaces.

5.2.4   *Interpretable Concord*
The situation just outlined correlates with another curious property holding inside nominals, already alluded to in section 4.2. The nominal projection – including the noun, the determiner that binds it, and all adjectives theta identified by the head noun – may exhibit Concord throughout. This is entirely unlike the verbal projection: verbs don't obviously agree (internal to themselves, not via extra dependents)[14] with auxiliaries or even adjuncts. In addition, it is almost a necessity that Concord involves interpretable features. This

---

13 Raising the question of why the Case system falls in the 'nominal side of things', instead of the verbal one. For now this is being assumed as a matter of fact, although see section 8.4.

14 Often (e.g. in the Bantu languages (see Carstens [2005]) or Arabic (see Soltan [2007])) one does see agreement on a sequence of verb/auxiliaries. That, however, is agreement *with some argument*, an irrelevant matter now. What doesn't appear to exist is the verbal equivalent of the Concord between a head noun and its adjectives, an agreement holding internal to the projection, in terms of the referent of this expression. If such a situation existed for verb/auxiliaries, the elements (perhaps also corresponding adjuncts) would all agree in tense, mood, aspect or similar features – but these are each represented on a separate head. There are, to be sure, tense and even mood/aspect, or for that matter negative, Concords in various

is because, unlike agreement of the sort associated to verbal arguments and checked in terms of Case valuation, Concord spreads (for instance in languages where nominal heads match indefinitely many adjectives in their features). There is no trivial mechanism that would eliminate *all* these iterated features, and we must thus assume that they carry some sort of interpretation.[15]

Language seems to have resolved the matter of the released P_V feature in (10) in the other way – by interpreting it. Factually, the system involving that interpretation is given a useful classifier interpretation, e.g. coding gender and number.[16] The classifier feature manages to signal both theta-binding (from whatever quantifier selects the nominal predicate that resulted in the released verbal feature) and any further predication associated to that binding relation (e.g. relative-clause expressions). That is not a necessary mechanism – after all, the binding of verbal events or further predications associated to adverbial modification doesn't exhibit Concord of the sort now being explored[17] – but at the same time, nothing goes wrong with the grammar explicitly coding these interpretable relations, which in addition allows for a classificatory system. That is, an abstract binding won't allow the system to sortalize the process; however, once we are in the business of coding features, we can invoke *sorts* of them, and then separate binding into inanimate vs. animate entities, and among the latter male-like vs. female-like, and so on. What we have to understand is how this is done.

In fact, once they enter a given projection, Concord features *replicate* with any new lexical dependency that relates to that projection. This obtains if the $+V$ element we are dealing with manages to create a *further* $+V$ release upon its Concord projection colliding with an adjectival position, as many times as adjectives are invoked. In order for that to take place, the mediating Concord itself has to be a real category, a clitic-like element that has a nominal character. Suppose that Concord is *inherently* non-verbal, a possibility that arises if this sort

---

    constructions in grammar, but those involve separate derivational cycles, and seem to invoke issues that go beyond the narrow system being explored.

15 One can modify the Agree operation so that it becomes multiple (Richards 2004; Henderson 2006; Hiraiwa 2005). Note however that a phi feature on a verb plays no role in terms of its denotation, and thus it is natural to attempt to expunge it prior to LF. In contrast, a phi feature on a noun is in synch with the referential specifications of this expression, and thus plays an obvious role in the semantics: it instantiates a variable. If relevant phi features on nouns/ adjectives were not interpretable, we'd have to explain how variables 'pop up' in the semantics, without a grammatical reflex to carry them. (A different issue is to claim that it is *because* of the need to interpret these elements that the system has them.)

16 Or more subtle distinctions in relevant languages, a matter that doesn't affect the reasoning.

17 Though see below for a suggestion that this sort of binding also involves a grammatical marking.

of element doesn't carry any lexical content, and given that it doesn't show up in verbal contexts.[18] As per assumption (8), a [+N, −V] element cliticizing onto a +V element, if this process too involves category collision, will release a −V feature, which in turn – when combined with a [+N, +V] adjective – forces the release of a new +V feature, sending us back to the situation in (11).The grammar is then able to invoke yet another Concord element, which repeats the process when colliding with a further adjective, and so on, potentially *ad infinitum.*

Eventually that system has to be capped off, which is done in practice in terms of introducing a quantifier that, unlike the adjective, is not specified for V features. Quantifiers are peculiarly dual elements. We know they have nominal properties, so it is natural to think of them as [+N]. At the same time we want them to somehow *become* verbal-like in the course of the derivation, so that they can eventually act as predicates with regards to their scope. In this respect, it is handy to have a quantifier associate with a +V feature that emerges in the Concord dynamics, via standard Merge (here denoted by X← →Y), and not category collision in this particular instance (denoted by X→←Y); cliticization – another form of category collision, albeit internal to words – is denoted by '>' in (12) and throughout.

(12)

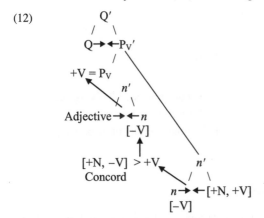

Note, first, that the adjectival projection is in a 'separate dimension' (created upon treating the released +V feature as its own source of projection, via Concord).[19] The role of Concord is to change the polarity of the released +V feature into a −V element, which upon collision with an adjectival element

18 This relates to the matter raised in fn. 11, in equally puzzling ways.
19 Such parallel mergers were explored in Uriagereka (1998, p. 279ff.), for adjuncts. We return to 'separate dimensions', precisely for adjuncts, in section 6.4.

will produce a further +V element; that new release can further enter the Concord process. Second, this adjectival projection is unnecessary for the quantifier to assume a +V feature: it could have used the very first +V feature released upon the collision of *n* with the nominal predicate. In other words, from the perspective of its lexico-semantic consequence, though possible given this syntax, theta identification by adjectives is orthogonal to theta binding of nominal predicates by quantificational elements.[20]

To round up the analysis, we must assume that morphological fusion in the PF component, to the closest lexical item as in (13), takes care of the Concord features showing up where they do.

(13)

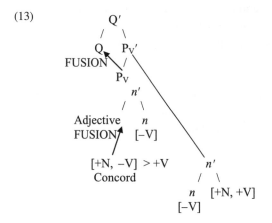

This sort of fusion is an essentially finite-state process, involving basic adjacency (see Raimy and Idsardi 1997).[21] We return to further such Markovian processes in chapter 6, and in chapter 7 to the architectural presuppositions and consequences of such a move.

5.3   Case beyond the Core Case

In the present approach, lexical predicate roots are [+N, +V], and they *become* verbs or nouns by colliding with anti-categories, shells with negative N or V features. Category collision is just an instance of external Merge, albeit one whereby a feature is released by way of another, with the opposite polarity,

---

20 We return to the verbal feature that, associated to the quantifier, must be seen as syntactically *prepositional*.
21 If so, perhaps the element notated as *n'* in (12), which dominates the pair (Adjective, *n*) does not exist as a phrase, and it instead constitutes a mere Markovian chain.

entering the feature set. This released feature is seen in one of two ways, depending on whether the system attempts to integrate it: as a Concord complex, originating from a V release coupled with a nominal morpheme; or as a Case marker (featureless preposition), if its origin is an N release. The Concord complex is interpreted as a classifier, which iterates until a quantificational element in demand of its $+V$ feature is found. The Case marker must be eliminated, which results in a unique agreement relation with a nominal. From this perspective, the Case system associated to a verb is identical to the one in (3) and (4), in structural terms. We haven't yet specified the Agree details of the emergent P as in (10), but they won't differ from whatever the details are for the more familiar situation in (3b), involving 'long-distance' Case. Our next main concern should be whether this specific Core Case generalizes to other instances where Case is at issue (it will be argued that it does not), and whether prepositional Case determination is the manner in which Case relations get established elsewhere (it will be argued that it is).

5.3.1   *Dative Case*

The key in the line of reasoning for the Core Case above is the released P_N element. It is not clear how we could obtain the release of a $+N$ feature in contexts that emerge beyond the first combination of V with an anti-nominal, which as we saw produces a P_N element. Once the $+N$ feature is released from the verbal projection, only a stipulation would put it back, just so that the system again expels it. Then again, to fit into the 'prepositional frame' we are exploring, one doesn't need an *emergent* preposition like P_N. A real one would do. Interestingly in this sense, higher VP cases are prepositional: dative and oblique (locative, instrumental, etc.). Oblique instances reduce to the (3)/(4) situation, in particular (3a), as these are taken as instances of lexical case. Dative is more interesting, especially where it cannot reduce to an oblique Case.

Consider, for instance, the Basque examples in (14).

(14)   a. Jonek   Peruk   Miren   jo zezan   egin zuen
          Jon-Scase Peter-Scase Miren-Ocase hit has-agrO-AgrS-Comp make
          had-AgrO-AgrS
          'Jon caused that Peru hit Miren.'
       b. Jonek   Peruri   Miren   joerzsi zion
          Jon-Scase Peter-IOcase Miren-Ocase hit-cause had- AgrO-AgrIO-AgrS
          'Jon cause-hit Miren to Peru.' (Jon made Peru hit Miren.)

Thematically, (14b) is akin to (14a): they are both causative expressions involving identical events. This is important only because the theta role that *Peru* bears in (14b) is the same as in (14a), that of agent. But dative subject of causative expressions can be formed with all sorts of thematic imports, simply depending on whether the subject of an embedded clause of the sort in (14a) happens to be an experiencer, a goal, a source, an instrumental or whatever. There is no correspondence between thematic structure and dative Case in a causative construction, much as there is no correspondence between thematic structure and exceptional accusative in any exceptional case marking (ECM) environment. Differently put, it may be that some instances of dative Case are inherent (when they typically associate to source/goal arguments), but not all dative Case can be explained away in that fashion, which is what matters for present purposes. How does a Case like the, as it were *exceptional*, dative in (14b) get determined?

If the structure in (3a) doesn't work in generalizing prepositional Case, in the absence of relevant thematic relations, we must attempt (3b) next – in effect an extension of (3a).[22] Note that, for an example like (14b), that would force us to treat dative-determining prepositions as Comp heads, as in Kayne (1999), an idea that goes back to (Emonds 1985):

(15)
$$
\begin{array}{c}
\text{C}' \\
/\ \backslash \\
\text{C}\quad \text{IP} \\
DAT_i\ /\ \backslash \\
\text{Peru}_i\ \dots
\end{array}
$$

This reduces to a familiar context, pending the Agreement details, in this instance between the dative element in C and the subject of its complement clause. This is discussed more thoroughly below. If we want to use (15) also internally to apparently simplex VPs (as instances of the causative sort where two clauses surface in PF), we will have to consider some form of bi-clausal analysis for the relevant VPs, in the spirit of the proposal in Kayne (1984).

Constructions of the sort in (15) do not emerge for nominals. Observe:

(16)   a. [John's gift of goods *to the Red Cross*] was generous.
        b. [John's causing [Peter to punch Mary]] was unfortunate.
        c. [John's cause [(* to) Peter to punch Mary)]] was unfortunate.
        d. [John's punch (* to) Peter Mary)] was unfortunate.

---

22 At first this would seem to presuppose a certain representational economy, of the sort argued for in Cardinaletti and Starke (1999), Brody (1995), Rizzi (1997), or Boskovic (1997). As we construct our own deduction of the Case hierarchies, it will turn out that a derivational approach is preferable.

We have instances where dative is possible inside a nominal expression (16a), but whenever that happens, dative is lexical; we do not have, in contrast, nominalizations of causative constructions equivalent to (14b) – thus do not accept (16c) with the intended meaning in (16b). In fact versions of (16c) or (16d) are impossible regardless of whether the Case we determine on the subject of the embedded clause is exceptional accusative (as it normally is in English), exceptional dative (as is normal in Spanish), or either one depending on the transitivity of the embedded clause (the situation obtaining in many languages). This is striking because the differences between especially (16c) and (16b) are minimal. In gerundial guise the appropriate expression obtains, so the only difference between the examples – the nominal character of the latter as opposed to the verbal character of the former – must be the deciding factor in allowing the extra source of Case. As we saw, nouns do not involve the Core instance of Case determination because they never release the P_N element that is central in this basic instance; instead they release the P_V element that enters into Concord complexes. If access to the sort of structure in (15) is possible *only in local domains where the Core Case has been determined*, it follows that (15) is not an option for nouns. This constitutes the first instance where Case Hierarchies are central.

5.3.2   *Nominative and genitive Case*
Once we have seen 'higher' verbal Cases reducing to our instances in (3) and (4), could something along these lines extend to the sort of Case that associates to T (nominative) or D (genitive)? The factors that enter the problem of nominative/genitive determination in prepositional conditions seem clear: (i) the relevant configuration ought to be of the form in (3b) or (15); (ii) since in this instance we don't normally see overt prepositions take on a Case determination, a 'preposition' somehow ought to emerge in the derivational dynamics; and (iii) it probably should be relevant that nominative and genitive Cases are determined *under personal agreement* with an inflectional projection. The latter point is interesting, since personal agreement is of the sort that must be eliminated by the system before reaching LF, as it has no interpretive consequence.

Assuming personal agreement is pronominal,[23] this feature may be there to provide a 'nominal' character to the relevant configurations. But why should this be necessary? We saw above that the +N character of certain emergent

---

23 This is an insight that Rizzi (1982) borrows from traditional grammar (agreement markers emerging from the 'grammaticalization' of pronominal elements, see Barlow and Fergusson [1988]).

prepositions (created upon a verb colliding with an anti-nominal) is central in determining Case conditions. Perhaps the uninterpretable nominal agreement exhibited wherever nominative and genitive is determined is a clue to the sort of Case involved here: *it requires nominal features to be added.* Supposing these features can be made to combine with P, the resulting conglomerate could well be the sort of thing that does determine Case. And given what we have said so far about how truly featureless Ps ultimately are, perhaps all we need for the system to functionally determine a category as prepositional is mere *absence of intrinsic N and V characteristics.* That is certainly consistent with the fact that complementizers can be headed by prepositional elements, and even with the fact that the infinitival version of the inflection in English is *to,* which is either homophonous with or an actual preposition. (Examine in that regard the discussion in Pesetsky and Torrego [2004], and see below for an alternative.)

The present suggestion is reminiscent of the analysis proposed by Raposo (1987) for inflected infinitivals licensing nominative Case in Portuguese.

(17)   a. Para eles falarem, ...
           for   they talk-agrS
           'For them to talk, ...'

    b.   C′
             / \
            C   IP
         *para*ᵢ / \
            *eles*ᵢ I′
                  / \
                 I ...
              falarem

(17b) is not unlike *for them to talk ...* , although in Portuguese the case showing up in the pronoun is not accusative, as in English, but nominative. This proves that nominative can have a preposition as its source, for as Raposo showed inflected infinitives require both agreement *and a source of Case.* That poses an interesting follow-up question: why does the construction – licensing nominative – itself require Case? A natural answer is that *the nominal* requires the Case the preposition provides, in effect treating the relation between that preposition and that nominal as another instance of ECM. Granted, in standard ECM, accusative shows up in the nominal, but we already saw in (15) above that at least the dative Case too could be determined 'exceptionally'.[24]

---

24 It is suggested below that, in effect, all structural Case is determined 'exceptionally', in the ECM sense.

Then we may generalize Raposo's situation to nominative determination in all cases, supposing that they all involve a preposition associated to Comp (a consequence of Comp being interpreted as a preposition by default, or perhaps a separate preposition, as suggested below). Similar conclusions could obtain for D and genitive Case, especially if we follow Szabolcsi (1983) in her analysis of the Hungarian DP, given data as in (18).

(18)   a. (a) Peter kalap-ja
            def Peter-nom hat-3sg
            'Peter's hat'
        b. Peternek a kalap-ja
            Peter-dat def hat-3sg
            'Peter's hat'

The situation in (18b) exhibits dative Case in the possessor, and it resembles processes of 'possessor raising' in other languages, whereby a possessor ends up as a grammatical dependent of higher components in the clause. The interesting example is (18a), where the nominal-internal possessor exhibits *nominative* Case, which makes Szabolcsi postulate an Infl head internal to DP. In turn, since the possessor appears to the right of a crucially definite article, she argues that the latter element is akin to a Comp site. The parallel between (18a) and (17b) is then quite obvious.

(19)   C′
           / \
          C   IP
          a_i / \
        $Peter_i$ I′
                  / \
                 I ...

Two further facts, one formal and one empirical, support that overall conclusion. First recall from (12) above that, given the dynamics of the system, in nominal projections a verbal feature is released which combines with the quantifier in prepositional guise. That preposition comes in handy at this point as a vehicle for genitive Case, when enriched with nominal characteristics provided by Concord.[25] Second, when Kayne (1994) adopts Szabolcsi's analysis, he is forced to conclude that in some instances her D element shows up *as a preposition*. This curious line of reasoning has consequences well worth investigating.

---

25 To make that suggestion cohere with the sort of structure in (19), extended by Szabolcsi to nominals, we may have to enrich nominal projections, in a manner we return to shortly.

The idea is pursued by Hornstein *et al.* (1996) when analysing the integral (20a) as analogous to (20b), in both instances the car being whole to its engine.

(20)   a. There is a Ford T engine in my Saab 900.
        b. My Saab 900 has a Ford T engine.

The assumed *source* structure for either example is as in (21).

(21)
```
          D'
         / \
        D  Agr'
           / \
         Agr  SC
              / \
      my Saab  a Ford T engine
```

The idea, taken from Kayne (1994), who in turn follows Freeze (1992) in essential respects, is that in (20b) *my Saab* raises out of the DP; if this was a Hungarian structure, it could then surface with the format in (18b). But English doesn't have dative at its disposal to determine on the raised element, so the raised possessor has to go all the way up to subject position, where it becomes nominative. In contrast, in (20a) it is the possessed *a Ford T engine* that raises to the DP specifier. Then, in order to get the surface order, Hornstein *et al.* must assume that D surfaces as preposition *in* (and see fn. 13 in chapter 3), for which they provide constituency tests showing that the preposition is not a sister to the nominal.

(22)
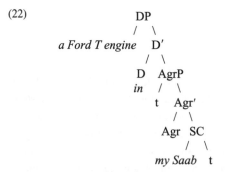
```
                    DP
                   / \
    a Ford T engine   D'
                     / \
                    D  AgrP
                    in / \
                      t  Agr'
                         / \
                       Agr  SC
                            / \
                     my Saab   t
```

If this analysis is generally correct, we have prima facie evidence that just as Comp can surface as a preposition as in (17b), so too can D surface as a preposition as in (22). In both instances we can take this preposition to be the source of Case that we need for the inflectional specifiers in each example, in accordance with the general idea explored throughout this chapter that Case determination is a prepositional phenomenon.

Alternatively, to unify the present analysis with the sort of structure we saw in (12) (and also with conclusions independently reached in section 3.6.3), perhaps it is not so much that D or C are *interpreted* as prepositions, but rather that they are somehow *associated to* abstract prepositions. As for the C projection, in recent versions of his analysis (e.g. 2000), Raposo assumes the presence of a crucial functional category F (alluded to in section 4.3) between the CP and TP projections, the actual source of infinitival Case. It is natural to reinterpret such an element in prepositional terms,[26] which makes the DP and CP projections entirely analogous.[27]

Two more comments are in order to conclude this section. First, it does not seem crucial for specifiers in DP to be specifically genitive: as we saw in (18), in Hungarian they are nominative, suggesting they are indeed very similar to whatever takes place in TP specifiers. We will return to matters of specific Case valuation. Second, contrary to what happens with dative Case valuation inside nominals, whatever structural Case is involved in the DP specifier cannot be subservient to the Core Case. Plainly, the Core Case doesn't exist in nominals, and yet structural genitive (nominative in Hungarian) does. We know the Case is structural because, quite obviously, it presents no thematic restrictions, including the marking of elements displaced internally to a nominal projection (23b) – and indeed even *adjuncts* (23c).

(23)   a. [Bush's destruction of Baghdad] was horrendous.
        b. [Baghdad's destruction t] was horrendous.
        c. [Yesterday's destruction] was horrendous.

5.4   Towards an account of the Case hierarchy

We have examined the Core Case involving prepositions and anti-nominal *vs*, and one instance that seems subservient to that Core Case (structural dative Case determination) and one that doesn't (structural nominative/genitive Case determination). What does 'subservience' mean?

5.4.1   *Where do Case hierarchies reside?*

The existence of hierarchies poses an issue for any system – like the one implicit under most versions of minimalism – which both attempts to

---

26 This is especially so if, as argued in section 4.3, F is a purely emergent phenomenon, given derivational dynamics of the radical spell-out sort.

27 This element could also mediate binding between the event operator, perhaps associated to the CP projection, and its event variable in the TP projection.

eliminate any representation of context-free characterizations of structures (possibly amenable to hierarchical analysis, as seen in section 2.4) and insists on syntactic representation being context-sensitive (which produces a characteristic transformational structure that is not obviously hierarchical in any direct sense, see section 8.2). In addition, a putative Case hierarchy raises a logical puzzle of its own: even if one wants to admit the possibility of context-free conditions in syntax, inasmuch as at least structural Case conditions are context-sensitive, it is perplexing that they should track hierarchical restrictions that are not. We will consider next whether we can deduce the hierarchical properties of Case systems from conditions that do not compromise their context-sensitivity.

Two broad proposals exist in the recent literature regarding the multiple spell-out of structural chunks on their way to the interpretive components. Chomsky's proposal (2000 and elsewhere) is based on the notion of a *phase*, while my own proposal (1999) is based on the notion of a *command unit*. Each of those domains can be characterized as follows:

(24)   a. A *command-unit* is the maximal amount of structure that can be assembled through Merge without abandoning a derivational work-space.

   b. A *phase* is the minimal amount of structure where a set of grammatical dependencies can be exhaustively satisfied.

A phase turns out to be the head-complement space of a *v*P, a CP, or possibly DP, domain where a set of theta relations find corresponding Case/agreement relations; phase-specifiers (the phase *edge*) are, as matters are defined, not a cyclically transferred part of the phase, thus are accessible to further computation in subsequent phases in the derivation. Given Chomsky's phase impenetrability condition (PIC) ((48) in chapter 4), a characteristic derivational cycle is specified around phases, from one probing element determining a given phase in its complement domain all the way down to the edge of the next phase in the derivational history, as in (25). (Accessible structure for context-sensitive dependency, of the Agree sort, is enclosed.)

(25)

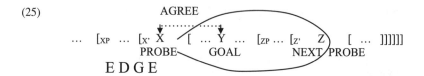

In contrast, command units (CU) are at right angles to the grammatical relations they sanction; for a command unit to be identified we need not consider whether some features are still active within it, but merely whether we are forced to leave a given derivational space to satisfy Merge.[28] This situation emerges if Kayne's (1994) linear correspondence axiom (LCA) is reduced to a natural minimalist theorem, as in (26), in which case it is not a complete procedure.

(26)   If A asymmetrically c-commands B then A precedes B.

Of course there are situations in which we encounter A preceding B where A doesn't c-command B: for example, if A is dominated by C which c-commands B, the case of specifiers. In those instances, Uriagereka (1999) has relevant linear relations follow from the application of spell-out, precisely in those contexts where a chunk of structure forces us into a separate derivational workspace and it can proceed no further as a separate unit (short of not encountering a viable PF expression).[29]

The two domains in (24) are compatible. (24a) is good at separating complements from non-complements, while (24b) determines exhaustive domains of grammaticality (without getting unnecessarily technical, the circled material in (25)). A priori this is interesting: having a complement as a designated element could serve as a stable, ordering point in a hierarchy; in turn having a limited domain specified could tell us what to expect with regards to the distinctions we can establish *within it*. In addition, while (24b) presupposes feature valuation – a context-sensitive procedure – (24a) is a context-free procedure. Inasmuch as context-free processes are more basic than corresponding context-sensitive ones (see

---

28 Observe this in detail, as follows:

(i)   a. The man saw a woman.

        b. {the, {the, man}}
            the ← ↑ → man

        c. {saw, {saw, {a, {a, woman}}}}
            saw ← ↑ → {a, {a, woman}}
                        a ← ↑ → woman

        d. saw, {{the, {the, man}}, {saw, {saw, {a, {a, woman}}}}}
            {the, {the, man}} ← ↑ → {saw, {saw, {a, {a, woman}}}}

There is no way to merge *the man* directly to *saw a woman*; we must assemble the former in a separate derivational work space (ib), and then assemble the results of working out the details of that workspace to those still active in (ic), as in (id). *Each derivational workspace defines a natural c-command domain.* This can be referred to as a 'command unit'.

29 See Hornstein *et al.* (in press) for related discussion involving extraction phenomena.

section 7.2 on this), then (24a) has to be taken to be more basic than (24b).[30] That way we have introduced a hierarchy into the derivational system – given independently needed derivational dynamics – and we could in principle assume as natural that the ordering point that (24a) establishes is presupposed in whatever is established in terms of (24b) – so we even have a solid base for our hierarchy (see, in this regard, the important formal considerations in fn. 30).

5.4.2   *Case dynamics*

Simply put, the Core Case arises in terms of a head/complement relation, thus *in the skeleton of a phrase-marker*. This is masked by the fact that the Core Case may involve pied-piping, and thus displacement to a site that is not a head/complement relation, and so is out of the main phrasal skeleton. However, the moment we conceive Case checking in terms of featural valuation through an Agreement process, the pied-piping is at least not necessary, and therefore one should surmise, also, not essential to the process. If so – much in the spirit of traditional grammar – the Core Case 'returns' to its basic geometric shape involving a complement. In contrast, all other structural Cases arise offline, as it were, with regards to phrasal components that relate to the phrasal skeleton by way of a *separate* CU. Note that this is the case even if Agree is the procedure for Case valuation: the goal of any non-Core probing for structural Case purposes is a fortiori a non-complement. The one exception to this is the passive situation, where the configuration for Core Case determination is effectively destroyed; that is, even in that instance the generalization obtains that *if* the appropriate configuration for the Core Case had obtained, then this sort of Case would be determined first.

We also need to distinguish among the non-Core Cases, in such a way that dative comes out lower than nominative/ergative. While the notion of CU is enough to separate two forms of case (basic vs. the rest), to make a finer-grained distinction we need to invoke the notion of phase. The idea is to associate the 'last' Case (nominative/ergative, 'beyond' which a new round of case valuation typically starts in further derivational cycles) to something

---

30 In fact (24a) is a second-order statement quantifying over (maximal) amounts of structure within a derivational work space, while (24b) is arguably an even higher order statement quantifying over (minimal) amounts of convergent derivational portions (each having whatever properties convergence encodes). This is not to say that the grammar couldn't encode (24a) or for that matter (24b) into some heuristic (e.g. 'a phase is defined by TP') of a lower order. Still, in terms of the systemic design, the difference in complexity should be obvious, regardless of what is the final coding mechanism.

special in a phase. If we got the bottom of the hierarchy from the CU, we ought to get its top from the phase. That is a promising prospect, for while CUs are bottom-up constructs, what is crucial for a phase, as shown graphically in (25), is a probing element in whose complement domain we seek some goal(s) for valuation purposes; thus these formal objects are determined from the top, and they may be good at determining, precisely, the top of the Case hierarchy. For that to happen, however, we must sharpen our understanding of phases.

Consider 'verb-based' phases, that is vP and CP. The latter includes part of the former, while the opposite is not the case. A CP is projected from a TP which must have a vP complement; in contrast, a vP may, but need not, have a CP dependent (directly or indirectly mediated through other categories). This reflects the fact that the vP phase is the locus of context-free theta relations of the configurational sort, while the CP phase involves context-dependent agreement relations (starting at the vP phase edge, the locus of accusative Case valuation via agreement with the v head itself). The only instance in which a vP may have a CP dependent is if the latter is an argument in an embedded clause, a special situation in which the CP as such plays no role in the vP specifications (it could have been any other phrase satisfying relevant theta-dependencies, for instance TP), and where we must have further substantive access to the lexical array from which we construct a derivation to continue with the computation. Note that the latter is never the case with a vP phase, as (27) shows.

(27)   [$_{v\text{P}}$ John [$_{v'}$ v [$_{\text{VP}}$ loves Mary]]]

When we mount a vP projection, we have all the substantive (theta role involved) material that we need to make a sentence. True, *John* in (27) cannot satisfy all its grammatical dependencies in the vP phase.[31] However, for the chunk of derivation to lead to a convergent result at the next phase, no further substantive structure has to be pulled out of the lexical array; all we need are T, C, perhaps a pleonastic in a language that licenses transitive expletives and so on. Further substantive lexical access won't take place until the next vP phase, if there is one. The point is, simply, that although both vP and CP are phases in Chomsky's system, CPs are 'final' in a way that vPs are not. We may thus define a final phase:

---

31 Luckily it is *at the phase-edge*, so no problem ensues, since it is not part of what gets evaluated by the system at this point of transfer, in the sense alluded to in chapter 4 via the TRANSFER condition in (49) there: the VP in the complement domain of v, where *Mary* gets its Case checked via agreement with v, with possible subsequent pied-piping to the phase edge.

(28)   A *phase* is *final* if it does not involve substantive lexical access.

With the notion of a final phase we can easily identify what we may think of as the Final Case in terms of its being the Case determined *by an inflectional element introduced at a given final phase*; for instance, nominative, determined through T, is the characteristic Case of the final CP phase. That said, we can think of dative as the *Elsewhere* Case, which is neither the Core Case nor the Final Case. That goes well with the fact that, although across languages we typically find one Core Case (accusative) and one Final Case (nominative), it is common to find more generosity with regards to dative case valuation, in particular for non-arguments (e.g. ethical datives) or elements for which not even event-involvement is necessary (e.g. illocutive datives). (29a) illustrates an ethical dative in Spanish and (29b) an illocutive dative in Galician. In (29a) the queen is not directly involved in Columbus's exploits; yet the event she sponsored benefits her, and thus she can be added as event participant. In (29b) the speaker decides to involve the addressee in the sentence, with a nominal akin to the colloquial expression 'you know'. In this instance there can be no event involvement on the side of the addressee, yet this element gains grammatical coding by way of a second-person pronominal clitic.

(29)   a. Colón le   descubrió América a Isabel de Castilla
            Colón her.DAT discovered América to Isabel of Castilla
            'Columbus discovered America on/for Isabella of Castille.'
         b. Colombo descubreu-che-lle
            Colombo discovered-you.know.DAT-to.her.DAT
            a   América á   Isabela de Castela.
            the America to-the Isabela of Castela.
            'Columbus, you know, discovered America on/for Isabella of Castille.'

Importantly, in both instances, relevant forms come out dative. Related to the Elsewhere nature of dative, also, is the fact that, while parameters exist for the valuation of Core (accusative vs. absolutive) or Final (nominative vs. ergative) Case systems,[32] *no such parameter exists for the one and only dative Elsewhere case valuation*. If this form truly arises in an Elsewhere or default situation, it is not clear what we could parameterize *when* to involve it, since

32 Ergative should not be identified with nominative and absolutive with accusative. In fact, as Legate (2006) argues, it is probably best to identify nominative with absolutive. If so, the parameter could be stated in terms of languages having or not access to the Core Case (Uriagereka in press). That leaves the question of what the resort to ergative is in languages without the Core Case. Etymologically ergative is associated to instrumental, an inherent Case – but it is hard to work this out.

the system is basically assuming *no specific conditions* for this particular Case valuation.

The Elsewhere case poses an ordering puzzle. We want the system to access it only after accessing the Core case. Structurally, however, the Final Case is higher than the Dative one, as is seen with triadic predicates like *give*. Nevertheless, when only two Cases are necessary in a sentence (setting aside more complex instances of quirky subjects)[33] typically the Elsewhere Case is not invoked. The latter suggests that it is truly an elsewhere, or default, sort of Case, and thus is accessed only when the conditions for the other two Cases are already met. At the same time, if that is how things work, why doesn't the grammar introduce it at the top of a (partial) derivation, *after* the Final case is determined? Note, however, that if that ordering took place, the grammar would violate the determination conditions for the Final Case, which by definition must be *final*. This suggests that we are on track when deriving the nature of the Case hierarchy from derivational *dynamics*, for it is in the subtleties of the latter that the present situation can emerge. If the Case hierarchy were purely configurational, it would make little sense to have an Elsewhere Case that is lower than two different hierarchically designated Cases. But the Case hierarchy as presently understood arises because we have an input stability point in terms of context-free CU conditions; a default strategy, *crucially within* CUs; and another output stability point in terms of context-sensitive final phase conditions.

From the present perspective, then, we find the following Case conditions:

(30)　　(i)　X is a *Core Case* if X is determined within a command unit (CU).
　　　　　　a. If X is determined through Merge in CU, X is inherent.
　　　　　　b. If X is determined through Agree in CU, X is structural.

　　　　(ii)　Where a CU is *complete* if structural Case has been established within it, X is an *Elsewhere Case* if determined depending on a complete CU.

　　　　(iii)　X is a *Final Case* if X is determined depending on the inflectional element Y that is introduced at a final phase (PhF).

The Core Case in (30i) is simple, its form depending on whether Agree is involved (inherent vs. structural Case at the verbal skeleton). The Elsewhere Case in (30ii) is straightforward in one sense: it is invoked only after a CU is complete (having involved the Core Case). But it is complex in another

---

33 The problem with instances where dative Case trumps nominative Case is compounded by the fact that it arises in predicates whose theta structure is misaligned vis-à-vis the corresponding surface structure, suggesting radical changes of the sort first analysed in Belletti and Rizzi (1988). This is now set aside, assuming it involves some form of nominative suppression, perhaps not unlike the accusative suppression witnessed in passives.

sense: if we have reached a key inflectional element determining a final phase, then the Final Case valuation in (30iii) trumps the Elsewhere Case. This, quite importantly, must mean that dative and nominative/ergative valuation take place in the same phase, or else there is no way that the grammar could establish the necessary Case 'competition'.

Thus observe (31), ignoring precise bracketing details in the verbal projections.

(31)

$$[\overparen{\ldots [_{vP} \text{John} [_{v'} v_{dat} [[_{v'} [\text{Mary}] v_{acc}}][_{VP} \text{gave presents}]]]]]]$$

The computational system must know – upon abandoning the complete CU where *presents* is associated to accusative Case – that although *Mary* is encountered before *John*, *precisely because of that* the Case that *Mary* gets is not the one that it would get if there were no *John* higher up. Saying that the Case *Mary* gets is 'simply' the one associated to an element like v_{dat}, aside from begging the question of why the present hierarchy exists, won't do, since then we would miss the fact that datives are default. But then the system must be able to evaluate the circled domain in (31), which is what a phase-based derivation predicts, coupled with the possibility of non-Markovian grammatical computation within those limited domains (see section 8.2.1).[34] This argues against an *entirely on line* system, where all computational decisions are established as binary relations advance in the derivation, of the sort argued for by Collins (1997), Frampton and Gutman (2002), or Epstein and Seely (2006) (see section 7.3.1).

5.4.3   *Case within nominals (with architectural implications)*
Let's evaluate now Case determination within nominals, specifically two situations that ought to be related in present terms: why nominals don't involve the Core case, and why they don't involve displacements of the ECM sort, whether it is using exceptional accusative, exceptional dative, or even the sort of (in a sense also exceptional) nominative/genitive that could have been possible in long-distance movement associated as pied-piping to Case valuation. The latter point is the most perplexing, since the issue was raised in Chomsky (1970). Compare:

(32)   a. * [Gertrude's seemingness [t to adore Picasso]] impresses everyone.
            (cf. '[That Gertrude seems [t to adore Picasso]] impresses everyone.')
        b. [Gertrude's portrait (by Picasso)] impresses everyone.
            (cf. '[That Gertrude was portrayed (by Picasso)] impresses everyone.')

---

34 This is of the sort argued for by Chomsky in 2001 for stylistic processes, as already discussed in section 4.3.

Passive is possible inside nominals, as (32b) shows, yet an a priori *comparable* long-distance raising is ungrammatical, as (32a) indicates. Incidentally, the matter has nothing to do with movement *per se*, as shown by the Spanish versions in (33), which exhibit mere agreement.

(33) a. * El parecer   adorar a Picasso de Gertrude impresiona a todos.
            the seemingness to-adore   Picasso of Gertrude impresses to everyone.
            (cf. [El que parezca adorar a Picasso Gertrude] impresiona a todos.')
            the that seems to-adore Picasso Gertrude impresses to everyone.
      b. El retrato de Gertrude (de Picasso) impresiona a todos.
            The portrait of Gertrude of Picasso impresses   everyone.
            (cf. '[El que fuese retratada Gertrude (por Picasso)] impresiona a todos.')
            the that be portrayed Gertrude by Picasso impresses everyone.

So the issue is simple: why should the implied long-distance agreement in (33a) be impossible, vis-à-vis the short-distance agreement in (33b)?

Consider the structure of dependents from the perspective of the integral system discussed in chapter 3. Abstractly:

(34)   D'
              / \
             D Agr'
                / \
              Agr SC
                   / \
            DEPENDENT NOMINAL

(34) successfully distinguishes (32a) and (33a) from (32b) and (33b), as follows:

(35)   a. D'   b.   D'
              / \   / \
             D Agr'   D Agr'
                / \   / \
              Agr SC   Agr SC
                   / \   / \
            Gertrude portrait   XP *seemingness*

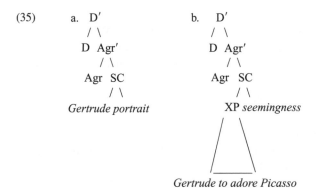

            Gertrude to adore Picasso

The key difference is that, from this perspective, the dependent argument of the nominal is the *subject* of a small clause. Probing this subject, as relevant in (35a), should be as good as probing the one implied in the movement in (36a). However, probing *into* the subject, as in (35b), should be as impossible as probing into the one implied in the movement in (36b).

(36)   a.   [This was considered [t impossible] until recently]
       b.   *[Water was considered [[(for) t to exist on Mars] impossible] until recently]
             (cf. '[[for water to exist on Mars] was considered [t impossible] until recently]')

Both in (36b) and (35b) (underlying (32a)/(33a)) we would violate some version of Huang's (1982) condition on extraction domains (CED), barring relations into non-complements.[35]

However, something drastic must then be said about verbal examples corresponding to the nominal ones above, all yielding grammatical agreement and corresponding pied-pipings. Our concern should be an analysis that now arises, *mutatis mutandis*, for *portray Gertrude* or *seem Gertrude to adore Picasso*, as in (37).

(37)

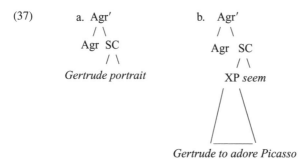

Of course, in these instances we do want to be able to probe into the small clause subject. Quite clearly, we need to provide a way to reanalyse the structures in (37) into a more conservative frame – albeit without extending that reanalysis to the instances that Castillo studied in (2001), where the structure, as he shows, has precisely the right opacity results.

5.4.4   Complement assumption
A reanalysis of the sort we require is arguably involved in the Spanish contrast between (38) and (39).

---

35 What Huang's condition follows from is an interesting matter that we return to in sections 6.4 and 6.5.

(38)   a. Juan considera [un retrato de Gertrude] brillante.
        Juan considers a   portrait of Gertrude brilliant.
      b. Juan considera brillante [un retrato de Gertrude].
        Juan considers brilliant [a portrait of Gertrude].

(39)   a. ?* De quién considera [un retrato t] brillante?
             of whom considers.he a portrait   brilliant?
           ('Of whom does he consider a portrait brilliant?')
      b. ? De quién considera   brillante [un retrato t]?
           of whom considers.he brilliant a   portrait?
           'Of whom does he consider brilliant a portrait?'

Wh-extraction out of the subject of a small clause is reported to sound better
as in (39b) than as in (39a) – that is, if the corresponding predicate has
associated to the verb. That would be a natural state of affairs if, upon
incorporation of the small clause predicate onto the verb, the remaining
subject is somehow reanalysed as a complement of the verbal complex; as a
complement, the dependent in question would not be subject to the CED.
Suppose, then, that the examples in (37) reanalyse as in (40b).

(40)   a. Agr′   b.   V-Agr′
            / \   / \
           Agr SC   V-Agr ...
           /\   / \
          V Agr ... t
          ▲_____/

Call this process *complement assumption*. Whatever complement assumption
ultimately is (see the notion 'reprojection' discussed in section 8.3), we
cannot allow it for nominal dependents.

The only obvious difference between the verbal and the nominal instance is that in
one case we want to involve, as per the assumptions in this chapter, an anti-nominal *v*
element, while in the other we want an anti-verbal *n* element. That is to say:[36]

(41)   a. Verbal instance: b. Nominal instance:
              v′   *n*′
             / \   / \
            v   SC   *n*   SC
               / \   / \
        DEPENDENT PREDICATE   DEPENDENT PREDICATE

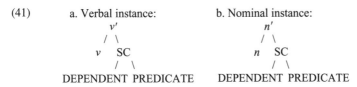

---

36 This substantively re-interprets the Agr in (40) the way Chomsky (1995, chapter 4) does more
   generally.

Recall also that, upon liberating a +N feature after category collision, the frame in (41a) is involved in Core Case determination, whereas the frame in (41b) liberates, instead, a +V feature that we took to be involved in Concord. Suppose this is the key. The liberated feature in (41a) in some sense *returns* to the complement domain of *v*, in the form of Case valuation after probing; in contrast, the liberated feature in (41b) never does. In effect, the emergent, uninterpretable, category in (41a) probes downwards into the already committed structure, whereas the equally emergent, yet interpretable category in (41b) projects upwards into new structural possibilities. Let's turn that into a defining condition for the reanalysis from (40a) to (40b), as follows:

(42)   A small clause [X [Y]] can reanalyse as a head-complement [Z X] if:

   (a) [X [Y]] is the complement of a head Z.
   (b) The predicate head Y of the small clause incorporates onto selecting head Z.
   (c) As a result of category collision between Z and Y, a feature W is released which valuates the remainder X (subject) of the small clause.

This is not a first-order statement: the conditions under which the transformational reanalysis can apply depend on a feature valuation on some arbitrary domain. In section 7.4.1 these sorts of conditions are discussed more broadly, showing that they pose no serious problem. Quite the opposite, the grammar exploits their second-order nature for central interpretive purposes.

Setting aside conceptual matters, we can put things more graphically and intuitively:

(43)

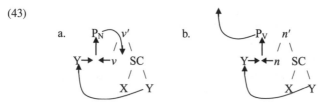

In (43a) we have a 'closed circuit', as the arrows indicate – that's what allows the reanalysis of the small clause into a complement. In (43b) the reanalysis is impossible because the liberated feature never returns to the structure we seek to reanalyse.

The gist of this proposal boils down to the intuition, forcefully pursued in Grimshaw (1991), that nominals do not have bona fide complements. That follows from the way their nominal nature gets determined by the system: the anti-category involved in the task liberates the sort of feature that does not 'feed back' (via Case) into the structure already assembled. In other words, the lack of Core Case determination correlates with the lack of complementation for nominals. But at that point any further processes involving displacement across dependents that do not enter a complement relation are doomed. That predicts the opacity of nominals for all sorts of purposes, except for those 'direct' dependents that independently manage to reach the genitive site, a possibility of the sort discussed in chapter 3.[37]

Lacking a complement, nominals will not be able to construct unified CUs in the way verbal elements can; missing such basic structures, they won't be able to determine the Core Case, a function of such CUs. In turn, if structural dative is an Elsewhere Case within CUs, it will also be absent from nominals. Inherent Cases, however, may be a possibility.

5.5   Residual Cases

Consider next a variety of wrinkles that need to be ironed out, including the matter just raised.

5.5.1   Null vs. inherent Case

In chapter 4 we saw various instances where it seemed profitable to postulate null Case. Most of those (the ones involving displacement to a specifier) will not affect our discussion. However, instances of null Case involving complements do seem to be relevant at this point. Curiously, nominals do not appear to assign null Case to their complement, and to the extent that they associate to elements that could potentially receive such a Case in the terms discussed in chapter 4, they resort to the pleonastic preposition *of*. This suggests that null Case is an eminently verbal phenomenon – perhaps extensible to prepositions more generally – in other words, the situation in (43a). This is consistent with the Case conditions in (30), especially if we identify null Case assigned to complements as in chapter 4 with inherent Case. From this perspective, those are just pre-theoretical labels to refer to the sort of Case that arises through Merge (as opposed to Agree) in a CU. It might seem as if, then, this particular instance of inherent Case (determined via complements within a CU) would be quite different from other forms of inherent Case (instrumental, ablative, locative and so on) assigned via lexical relations with various prepositions. But this isn't necessary. Each of those prepositions determines their own CU, and internal to it a particular Case

---

37 See Ticio (2003) for the source of this idea and much relevant discussion and references.

assigned through Merge would be unique to their lexical influence. Lexical/ inherent and (complement) null Case are simply Merge Cases, which the system establishes with various limitations – wherever sheer Merge is involved (complements), and, if section 4.2 is correct, also within conditions of Null Case Visibility and the intriguing interpretive consequences alluded to there.

Section 4.2.4 mentions that null Case-assigned-to-objects (Merge Case) 'competes' with, in particular, accusative Case. Why should this 'case uniqueness' obtain? In both instances we are involving v (recall (28) in chapter 4), and so the incompatibility would make sense if v carries a single Case feature (thus the Case Uniqueness Condition (CUC) in chapter 4). But why should *that* be? Why couldn't v have *two* Case features (or three, etc., a version of issue (1v) above – contra the CUC); or why couldn't there be two entirely different *sorts* of Case, one determined by V and one by v (which would satisfy the uniqueness demanded by the CUC)? In present terms, these questions make no sense: v *emerges* in the lexical combination between relevant elements, and it is interpreted by the system as a preposition because it couldn't survive as anything else – in that guise, it determines Case – a single case, as per thesis (4) above.

We should also ask why we have two forms of null Case (e.g. in terms of obeying Null Case Visibility conditions as in chapter 4), one obtaining via Merge, and another one through Agree. Surely Merge and Agree are two natural operations within the system, but why should each of these manifest Case determination in a full vs. partial flavor? Actually, for each and every one of the Case conditions examined in (30), a null-vs.-full opposition obtains, if the story in chapter 4 holds. In other words, up to Null Case Visibility considerations, the system in (30) has an essentially non-morphological variant. That is consistent with the system at large,[38] and moreover with the conjectures about Case visibility entertained in section 4.4: the phenomenon of Case may serve to distinguish D tokens via morphological marking, but if so, once in place nothing can prevent it from mechanically applying without useful morphological marking.

If these ideas are on track, we should see some of the interpretive conditions we discussed in section 4.2 for lexical/inherent Cases, in particular with

---

38 Since the times of the P&P model (Chomsky 1981, 1982) morphological vs. non-morphological paradigms have always been central, thereby the prediction of empty categories in general.

the matter of its incompatibility with personal marking. The prediction is clear in some instances.

(44)   a. Dirty Harry opened a window *with a man/??John* (cf. used John to open it).
        b. HAL ran *without an operator/??Dave* (cf. didn't need Dave as his operator).
        c. Phyllis the flea lived *in an armpit/??Clavero* (cf. used Clavero as her dwelling).

But not in others, where no particular restriction seems apparent:[39]

(45)   a. John gave a book to a woman/Mary.
        b. Mary received a book from a man/John.
        c. Mary threw the book at a man/John.
        d. John has a new present for a woman/Mary.

Of course nothing in the logic *per se* of Case assignment by prepositions demands that their associated Case be specifically lexical/inherent, so it may well be in (44) (where a personal effect arises) though not in (45). However, no systematic way exists yet of distinguishing those prepositions that necessarily associate to an impersonal effect (determine Merge Case) from those that may, but need not. Perhaps languages manifesting prepositional agreement (as is reported for Irish) may help in this respect; if this form of agreement involves Agree in the sense above, then we expect such agreement prepositions to co-occur only with personal forms (e.g. pronouns), not in-definites – a matter that won't be pursued now.

5.5.2   *Partitive Case*

One particular Case normally assigned to complements now gains new sig-nificance: partitive Case in the sense of Belletti (1988), who takes her core data from Finnish:

(46)   talossa   ei ole kirjaa.
        house-in-the not be book-a.
        'There is not a book in the house.'

This Case marking, aside from typical quantificational and polarity contexts, appears on direct objects when the verbal aspect is incomplete or the sen-tential mood is negative. This makes it tantalizingly similar to the so-called genitive-of-negation in Russian:

---

39 Although it is possible that familiar animacy restrictions on indirect objects are of the relevant sort.

(47)   V dome net ni odnoj   knigi
        in house no not one-Gen book-Gen
        'There is not a book in the house.'

In fact, once the 'genitive' issue is raised, we can also find something possibly related in Romance – where partitive manifests itself in genitive guise –
as in the French existential:

(48)   Il n'y   a pas de   livres dans la maison
        it no-there has not of-the books in the house
        'There are no books in the house.'

In all these instances the question is what the partitive/genitive (e.g. *de* 'of' in
Romance) is doing associated to the first Merge. The system discussed above
has room for it.

    Recall two basic structures we studied in chapter 3 (now using the *n* head in
place of the more neutral Agr head discussed at that point):

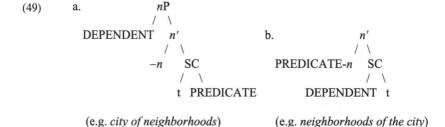

(49)   a.   *n*P
                               / \
              DEPENDENT   *n'*   b.   *n'*
                          / \   / \
                        –*n*   SC   PREDICATE-*n*   SC
                        / \   / \
                       t PREDICATE   DEPENDENT t

         (e.g. *city of neighborhoods*)   (e.g. *neighborhoods of the city*)

Here, too, pleonastic *of* placement is involved – across languages. Although
we did not justify this beyond the need imposed by an analysis in terms of
chain uniformity, we already had reasons to believe in section 3.6.3 that *of*
must head its own projection, which made the relevant structures as complex
as in (50), in present terms presupposing morphological fusion as in (50a).

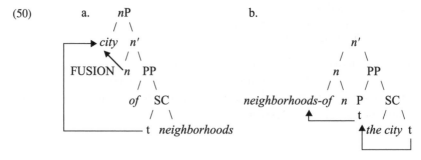

(50)   a.   *n*P   b.
                / \
          → *city* *n'*   *n'*
             \   / \   /   \
          FUSION ↖*n* PP   *n*   PP
                    / \   / \   / \
                  of SC   *neighborhoods-of* n P   SC
                       / \   ↑   t   / \
                     t *neighborhoods*   *the city* t

These two structures are obviously related, but how each is achieved is rather different. In (50a) the argument *city*, subject of the small clause, is displaced to the *n* specifier, thus making the intervening head *of* irrelevant.[40] In (50b), in contrast, the predicate *neighborhoods*, head of the small clause, is displaced via head movement, thus involving incorporation to the *of* head.[41]

If that structure is possible in nominals, verbal versions should exist too, with predicate incorporation as in (51b) (cf. (49b) and (50b)). This may be the source of partitive/genitive in direct object instances, a grammatical alternative to 'complement assumption'. That is, instead of a structure as in (51) (adapted from (40a)) yielding (51b) after complement assumption, everything remains unaffected, with the v-Agr head surfacing as *of* in these contexts (51b').[42]

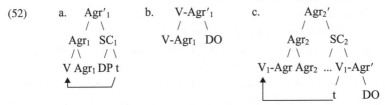

(51)   a. v' b.   V-v' b'. v'
                 / \   / \   / \
               v SC   V-v ... v SC
              /\   / \   [COMPLEMENT]   /\   / \
         PREDICATE v ... t   V v ... t
              ↑_____/   *of*

If so, we should see partitive/genitive only in circumstances where complement assumption is a grammatical alternative. To address that matter, consider n-adic predicates, in present terms involving small clause head incorporation, as in (43) in chapter 3 – a structure repeated as (52) – vis-à-vis the incorporations we saw in (38), and more generally the contrasts in (53).

(52)   a.   Agr$'_1$ b.   V-Agr$'_1$ c.   Agr$_2'$
             / \   / \   / \
           Agr$_1$ SC$_1$ V-Agr$_1$ DO   Agr$_2$ SC$_2$
          /\   / \   / \   / \
         V Agr$_1$ DP t   V$_1$-Agr Agr$_2$ ... V$_1$-Agr$'$
          ↑_____/   ↑   / \
                                                         |_____t DO

(53)   a. I saw injured many friends of mine.
        b. I saw many friends of mine carry several wounded people.
        c. *I saw carry several wounded people many friends of mine.
        d. *I saw carry many friends of mine several wounded people.

---

40 Subsequent morphological fusion is then implied between the head *n* and the lexical element that provides its referential conditions after moving to its specifier.
41 Here the morphological dependency with *n* is directly established, as well as the dependency with *of*.
42 Alternatively Agr would require the associated *of* element.

While predicate incorporation from the small clause to the selecting head can happen when the small clause is simplex (leaving behind a single dependent as in (53a)), comparable predicate incorporations from a complex small clause of the sort in (53b) are unviable, as in either (53c) or (53d). In English, this is arguably because there is not an extra (dative) source of Case for the second argument in the small clause. In a language like Spanish we find the possibility in (54).

(54)   Vi llevar muchos heridos a muchos amigos míos.
         saw.I carry many wounded to many friends mine
         'I saw carry-many-wounded many friend of mine.'

This has the import that ? *I saw go lion hunt many writers of novels* does in English, where incorporation of the direct object into *hunt* turns this verb into a complex one which can 'reserve' accusative Case for the agent of the small clause. But even in situations of this sort, the new argument doesn't behave as a direct object, as standard (e.g. extraction) tests show, indicating that there hasn't been any complement assumption here.

(55)   a.   ?*Esta es la mujer de quien vi llevar muchos heridos [a muchos amigos t].
              this is the woman of whom saw.I carry many wounded to many friends
         b.   ?*Romantic Safari is the kind of novel (which) I saw go lion hunt many
              writers of.

   The complement assumption conditions in (42) predict this fact, in particular the interaction between the demand in condition (42b) that the head of the small clause incorporate on the selecting head, and the requirement in (42c) that, after incorporation, the remainder of the small clause be crucially valuated by the newly formed object. The predicate head of a simplex small clause satisfies conditions on head-to-head incorporation, but in complex small clauses a tension arises. The entire complex predicate cannot incorporate, as only *part* of a projection would be moving. In addition, conditions on head incorporation would also be violated if more than a head incorporates. If on the other hand merely the head incorporates, the remainder of the small clause is no longer a subject that can be valuated by the newly created object; rather, it is a scattered object – the small clause subject *and* that portion of the complex predicate that has remained behind. This discontinuous constituent cannot be assumed as a complement. Now if partitive/genitive obtains in those domains where complement assumption is possible, we do not expect the former in any dependents other than direct objects – as is the case in practice.[43]

---

43 Only standard partitive/genitive associated to direct objects is being considered; the entire
   distribution of the relevant sort of case is more complex.

5.5.3 *A missing verbal structure*

Whereas a structure along the lines of (50b) above is plausibly used in verbal instances as well – almost identically in partitive cases, and with adjustments in cases involving complement assumption – there is reason to believe that (50a) is not viable in verbal guise, at least not in structures of the sort we are now exploring (though see the next section for an extension). Thus consider (56), which is designed to give a good semantic chance to the putative verb that would result from a structure of the appropriate sort.

(56)   a.   Bleed/skin/milk ... the creature/beast/goat ... !
        b.   *Creature/beast/goat ... the blood/skin/milk ... !

(56a) expresses, in verbal guise, an integral relation between some creature (beast, goat, etc.) and its blood (skin, milk, etc.), of the sort in *the noble blood of the creature, the creature's noble blood,* or *a creature of noble blood* (though not **the noble blood's creature*, as expected given the analysis in section 3.3). Presumably the expression has its source in a verbal version of (50b), as in (57b) with complement assumption. Then consider (50a)'s verbal version in (57a).

(57)

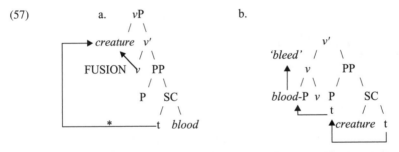

If the derivation in (57a) succeeds, we should be able to obtain the impossible verbs in (56b). The question is how to prevent this derivation in the verbal instance, when in fact we want it to be possible for nominal expressions like *creature of noble blood.*

A way to rule out (57a) is in terms of Case, if we take seriously the small clause dependency that integral relations express. In lexico-conceptual terms, *creature* in (57) is a dependent of *blood,* and if this sort of relationship needs to be Case-sanctioned, non-trivially, then this particular representation will be ill-formed. Note the minimal contrast with something like *(I saw) a beast of noble blood;* here *beast* is in a position to have its Case features determined simply because it will be heading a complex nominal expression that does so. Of course for the hypothetical sentence **there beasted of noble blood* (meaning 'a beast brought about noble blood') there just isn't a Case that would fall on (an expression headed by) *beast* – this is part of what it means to be a verb, as this chapter emphasizes. So a sentence of this sort would have the subject of its underlying small clause invisible for lexico-conceptual dependency. The situation is different when what attempts to be expressed as a verb is the small clause predicate, instead, as in *blood of the beast* and *you bleed the beast*. It is equally true in this instance that no Case will ever fall on (an expression headed by) *blood*; but it arguably need not, if this is the small clause *predicate*, and, unlike its corresponding subject, this sort of element (the one projecting in the small clause, thus not strictly a dependent) needs no Case.

5.5.4   *Denominal verbs redux*
Now we are ready to return to the so-called denominal verbs discussed in section 2.3, which as we saw can be of two sorts: like *saddle* (where the *locatum* nominal ends up gearing the derivation) or like *shelve* (where it is instead the *location* that does).

(58)   a.   *v*P   b.

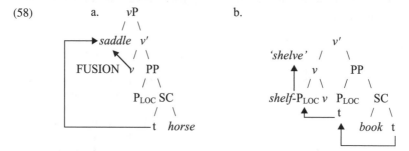

(58b) is so similar to (57b) that even the lexical adjustments in the incorporated small clause predicate can be observed in both instances: *blood* incorporated to P-*v* comes out as *bleed*, while *shelf* incorporated to P_{LOC}-*v* comes out as *shelve*. But comparing (58a) to (57a) results a major difference – strongly suggesting that there is nothing conceptually wrong even with that sort of structure *per se*. The question is: if Case conditions prevent (57a), why don't they in (58a)?

The key must be in the fact that the small clauses that introduced the locational preposition P_{LOC} in the examples in (58) are not integral. There certainly need not be a specifically integral relation between a saddle and its (easily interchangeable) horse, if it has one, and even more so a book and whichever shelf it happens to be shelved on, if any. Suppose that the Case need discussed in the previous section – the requirement to assign Case to a nominal element, although it will end up assuming different, verbal, categoricity, and one furthermore that, as such, requires no Case – affects only the subjects of *integral* small clauses, not regular small clause subjects. This must be an essential element behind the notion of integrality, involving what was called in chapter 3 a *space* and a *presentation* that operates on it. No such thing seems relevant for a regular small clause, where the subject is nothing like a mental space for the (in this instance) locational predicate to operate on. The blood/skin of a beast, the neighborhoods or skyscrapers of a city, even a portrait of whoever it represents, are conceptualized as a lexical dependency whereby the presentation affects the conceptualization of whatever mental space it represents (a blood-filled creature, a neighborhood-endowed city, a portrayed person). We must conclude that *only that* requires the lexico-conceptual Case marking that we alluded to in the previous section, an issue that is moot in (58a).

This suggestion predicts that denominal verbs should not have a lexicoconceptual origin in integral locations, such as that existing between a whole with obvious locational extension and its parts – even when such verbs would make sense. This seems correct, lending credence to Hornstein *et al.*'s analysis of these sorts of expressions in possessive terms, as opposed to merely locational ones, even when appearing in existential constructions of the sort in (59) (recall from section 3 above). Thus compare examples of that sort to those in (60).

(59)   a. There is/! happens to be ... blood in my veins.
         b. There is/! happens to be ... milk in those udders.
         c. There is/! happens to be ... (still) skin in/on that lamb.

(60)   a. There are/happen to be ... men in the shuttle.
         b. There is/happens to be ... a cork in the bottle.
         c. There is/happens to be ... a plant in the soil.

Although this may not be so obvious in English, integral expressions of the sort in (59) sound funny, ironical or professorial when the relation between *locatum* and location is hedged by way of a verb like *happen*; no such effect arises in (60), where the relevant relation is not integral.[44] Correspondingly, expressions of the integral sort only yield successful verbs as in (61), the point made in the previous section; in contrast, expressions of the purely locational sort yield verbs of two types, depending on whether what is the lexical base is the *locatum* or the location instead.

---

44 In other languages this is more obvious, expressions of the form in (59) appearing, unlike those in (60), in a variety of contexts which have been analysed as involving 'inalienability'.

(61)   a. Bleed my veins   vs.   a'. *Vein (back) my blood.
        b. Milk those udders   vs.   b'. *Udder (back) that milk.
        c. Skin that beast   vs.   c'. *Beast (back) that skin.

(62)   a. Man the shuttle   vs.   a'. Shuttle the men.
        b. Cork the bottle   vs.   b'. Bottle the cork.
        c. Plant that soil   vs.   c'. Soil that plant.

This is not to imply that the two sorts of expressions in (62) mean the same – when one corks a bottle one puts the cork on the bottle's mouth, whereas when one bottle's a cork, one puts the cork inside the bottle. But these are the lexical idiosyncrasies that emerge once the derived verb enters the realm of lexical dependency (see chapter 2). The only thing that should concern us now is that when integral expressions are involved, the logical possibility where the location projects the verb's lexical structure is not even an option, regardless of how the resulting meaning could have been narrowed down further.

5.6   Conclusions

The present chapter has given an account of the Case hierarchy that one can observe in the distribution of case values within derivational phases. It has been argued that (unlike the theta hierarchy), this one cannot be attributed to configurational conditions. That makes good conceptual sense, because whereas theta demands sanction configurational notions by way of their correspondence to appropriate interpretive demands (e.g. of the part/whole sort), Case demands are by their very nature uninterpretable. The key is, then, to justify the observable properties in the Case system in purely formal terms, instead of substantive interpretive conditions. Although we return in section 8.4 to the place of Case within a minimalist grammar, it is clear already that Case *values* are what they are because derivations exist, with cyclic architectural properties that define, in particular, *both* CUs and phases – the former being in a directly definable sense logically prior to the latter. The Table 5.1 chart summarizes the system.

The chapter also developed a dynamic system of feature release that distinguishes combinations of the nominal and the verbal sort, feeding complement assumption in the latter instance. Complement assumption is central in relating integral structures – the basis of theta structure – to more familiar representations of the head-complement sort, albeit ones that haven't lost internal hierarchical layers. The feature release that feeds this

Table 5.1 *A Case hierarchy emerging from derivational dynamics*

Case value	Domain of application	Conditions of application
Final Case (e.g. nominative)	CP/DP phase	Agreement with element projecting phase
Elsewhere Case (e.g. dative)	Command unit	After structural Case has been activated
Core Case (e.g. accusative)	Command unit	Through Merge (inherent) | Through Agree (structural)

process is also the main reason why structural Case cannot be activated through Agree within nominal expressions as a Core Case, unlike a corresponding inherent Case (activated through Merge). The anti-nominal v-feature determining complement assumption is responsible for structural Case-probing in the verbal instance; the anti-verbal n-feature involved in corresponding nominal dependencies establishes Concord relations without novel Case consequences.

The discussion in the last two sections supports the view advocated by Hale and Keyser in their seminal work on argumenthood. This proposal often meets with two criticisms, alluded to in chapter 2. One is that its syntax is not exactly what is customarily assumed, and can thus be reduced to something 'less syntactic' (e.g. mere compositionality conditions, see Fodor and Lepore [1998]); the other is that the notional structures they assume to correspond to their syntactic configurations are a bit wishful, mapping nominal and verbal categories to semantic primitives that may, but in the end need not, relate the way they suggest. Both of those concerns have been addressed. On one hand, the syntax used throughout the preceding chapters uses entirely principled components of the theory that have been argued for independently, in particular in terms of the Case/agreement system and conditions on transformations (the LRC, MLC, and CUC). On the other hand, we have begun to sketch – and will tie up in what follows – an overall correspondence between that syntax and the sort of semantics we find in natural language, in such a way that we capture the correlated layered structure of both, and we show how and why this correlation should indeed hold. As it turns out, the Case conditions discussed in this chapter will be central in making this desideratum true.

Inasmuch as the analysis of denominal and related structures sketched in the preceding chapters succeeds, we have an argument against strict atomism as reviewed in chapter 2. At the same time, the reader should bear in mind that a crucial atomist question remains: if things are as clean as implied, then why isn't the systematicity, productivity, and transparency of the system simply complete, as it is in 'normal' syntax? We come back to that in section 8.5, also in terms of complement assumption and the opacity it induces under certain circumstances.

6 *Iteration and related matters*

6.1   Introduction

This chapter is devoted, to start with, to a problem posed by iterative expressions, common in colloquial speech, of the sort in *I'm very very tired*. In a nutshell, as the second part of the chapter argues, the problem is that expressions of this sort work very similarly in all languages (invoking emphasis, but also a few, arguably related notions); this is an a priori puzzle for any theory that assumes the essential arbitrariness of the syntax/semantics mapping. A solution to this puzzle is proposed in the third section of the chapter; it implies treating the relevant expressions in finite-state fashion, following ideas already sketched in early works by Chomsky. If as is emphasized throughout this book, *all* levels of the Chomsky Hierarchy presupposed by the human language faculty are relevant to semantic interpretation(s), then the simplest among those levels too should enter the equation. Up to this point, we have only worried about phrasal (context-free) and transformational (context-sensitive) relations; now it's time to explore even more basic dependencies. In the fourth part of the chapter it is argued that finite-state syntax is both more common than it may seem, and crucial to mechanics argued for here. Section 5 raises some conjectures and speculations about adjunctal elements in general, and the chapter ends with a section summarizing the main conclusions for the project in the book.

6.2   The realm of iteration

We may organize the empirical discussion by sorting out the essential iterative data base.

6.2.1   *Iterative expressions that will and will not be relevant*
Apparent iterativity emerges in a variety of contexts, most of which will not be central to the discussion below. The examples of concern now are common

throughout the world's languages, particularly so in the colloquial speech of children. For instance, we find in Spanish:

(1)   a. Yo comí mucho mucho mucho...
             I   ate   much much much
             'I ate quite a lot.'
          b. Yo estoy muy muy muy cansada.
             I   am   very very very tired
             'I am really very tired.'
          c. Yo tuve que andar, andar, andar...hasta llegar.
             I   had to   walk walk walk   until arriving
             'I had to walk endlessly until arriving.'
          d. Mami   llega   hoy, hoy, hoy...!
             Mommy arrives today today today
             'The fact that it is today when Mommy arrives is exciting.'
          e. Yo, yo, yo...!
             me, me, me
             'Me, me, me...!'
          f. Papi,   Papi,   Papi...
             Daddy Daddy Daddy
             'I am talking to you, Daddy, and there's an issue with you.'
          g. Ay ay aaay...

The literature often refers to these sorts of expressions – all of which I owe to my daughters – as 'reduplicative'. This name is somewhat misleading, however.

To start with, genuine reduplications of the sort in (2) are well-attested across languages:[1]

(2)   Una belu-bela es una libélula chiquita
          a   belu-bela is a   dragon fly small
          'A belu-bela is a small dragonfly.'

My children coined such things as *belu-bela* using the same morphological process responsible for the Spanish reduplicate *tiquis-miquis* 'picky' or the English *fancy-schmancy*, expressions which can only be repeated twice, or *mirrored*. In contrast, we are using here expressions that can iterate several times. In addition, in morphological reduplication syllabic structure is often affected with truncations or epenthesis, whereas in iterations the basic pattern is iterated literally.

---

1 See for instance Lidz (1999) for a perspective on Kannada morphological reduplication, or Davies (2000) for extensive analysis of Madurese data, plus various references.

Consider also another sort of mirroring:

(3)   a. Luisa es una [[mujer] (muy) mujer].
        Luisa is a   woman very woman
        'Luisa is a real woman.'
    b. Luisa es mujer, mujer, mujer.
        Luisa is woman woman woman
        'Luisa is very feminine.'

(3a) is an instance of what Ghomeshi *et al.* (2004) call 'contrastive reduplication', essentially arising from combining a predicative expression with
itself. In those instances the intonation in Spanish – dropping between the first
and the second *mujer* 'woman' (with a slight pause in careful speech) –
reflects the bracketing structure in (3a). This contrasts sharply with (3b),
where the intonation is open ended; note also that the determiner introducing
mujer is missing.

The present book has little to say about those reduplicative, mirroring
instances. We will be concentrating instead on genuinely iterative expressions
that, based on a description by Pi (1995), Travis (2001) calls *syntactic
reduplication*. For example:

(4)   a. Taza tras taza (tras taza, etc.) de café
        cup after cup after cup   of coffee
    b. Taza de café tras taza de café   (tras taza de café, etc.)
        cup of coffee after cup of coffee after cup of coffee

These are more complex than those in (1), in that *entire phrases iterate*.
Nonetheless there is reason to believe that these constructions are related to
the simplest ones in (1).

6.2.2   *A puzzle for iteration*

The question for us to focus on is: how do iterative expressions get their
meaning? In the approach followed here, this is a consequence of the sort of
structure involved, which – to pursue an intuition mentioned in passing by
Travis (2001) – somehow 'creates copies' that thereby enter syntactic computation. Moreover, as Travis also observes, the domains for the application
of iteration are somewhat different from standard syntactic computations, and
in some sense simpler. This, together with the fact mentioned above that
iteration can repeat several times – which Travis also emphasizes – suggests
that we are dealing with a specific kind of operation.

Consider again (1a) or (1b), repeated now in a progressively more complex
guise in (5).

(5)   a. Yo comí mucho...   a'. Yo estoy muy cansada.
          I   ate   much   I   am   very tired
       b. Yo comí mucho mucho...   b'. Yo estoy muy muy cansada.
       c. Yo comí mucho mucho mucho... c'. Yo estoy muy muy muy cansada.

Descriptively, iteration along these lines somehow gets to mean 'more of the same', and further iterations vaguely increase on this. However, the output of functional application is not vague. If we were calculating the high degree of eating or tiredness in the various examples in, say, (5) in terms of some function of the lexical meaning of *very X* or *much X*, and that of the degree modifiers *muy* or *mucho*, we should be able to precisely distinguish the (b) and (c) examples, as we tell apart similar compounds. But speakers really can't do this. What's more, under those standardly phrasal conditions, one should be able to bracket these associations in various ways, for instance as in (6) (or any other such combination).

(6)   *Yo estoy [muy muy] [muy muy] cansada.
            I am very very very very tired

But these sorts of gimmicks, where phrasal intonations are imposed on the simple-minded iterative constructions, are very generally ungrammatical.

    To put things differently, our standard semantic composition, which as argued in chapter 2 directly reflects constituent structure, does not seem to be operative in these instances. Whatever these iterations mean, it just doesn't seem to be in strict correspondence with the meaning of the parts and the way they are combined – at least in customary, and perfectly reasonable, ways. Examples as in (7) ought to prove this beyond much doubt.

(7)   a. Ven,   ven,   ven!
          'Come, come, come!'
       b. Yo nunca nunca he visto   nada   igual.
          I   never never have seen nothing same
          'Never, never have I seen such a thing!'

(7a) doesn't normally mean that you should come three times, each denoted by a token use of the imperative *ven* 'come'. With the appropriate intonation (7a) could actually be used to command three different individuals, each, to come – or one individual to repeat the action three times. But this is clearly not the normal use of (7a) with its customary intense intonation: it just means 'do come!' Along these same lines, when Major Renault in the movie *Casablanca* claims to be 'shocked, shocked to find that gambling is going on' at Rick's café, he is not claiming to be shocked twice – he is just very shocked. Similarly, what (7b) means, with the iterative intonation, is that

I *really never* saw it, and not that it was never the case that it was never the case that I saw it (which would mean I did see it). Thus, for instance, when Churchill uttered his famous 'never give in – never, never, never...' he surely didn't mean his comment in customary compositional terms, or its validity would be cancelled by uttering any subsequent odd number of *never*s. Again that sort of reading *is* generally a possibility, but not with the iterative intonation. It more or less ironically arises thus:

(8)   Yo nunca...nunca lo vi. De hecho lo vi!
        I   never   never it saw.I In fact it saw.I
        'I never...never saw it. In fact I saw it!'

It is perhaps worth emphasizing that one could brute force a compositional meaning to the expressions in (7), involving empty operators denoting emphasis for (7a), factoring out a negative marker – and invoking negative Concord in the rest of the negatives – in (7b), or some such abstract move. One can always kill a sparrow with a bazooka. The issue, however, is not whether the relevant meaning *can* be computed that way, but rather whether it *is* so computed; we are, after all, cognitive psychologists, attempting to understand how meaning is achieved by humans, not just how it would be coded if all of semantics had to be compositional by fiat. In effect, this book is arguing that compositionality is a central mechanism of meaning that naturally corresponds to phrasal syntax. But there is syntax below and above phrasal relations, which if these ideas are on the right track correspond to less and also more nuanced semantic dependencies (see chapters 7 and 8 on this).

Not surprisingly, cognitive grammarians use the present puzzle as an argument against 'formalism', in the following guise:[2]

(9)   a. Iterative structures are productive in totally unrelated languages.
        b. They have common meanings cross-linguistically (emphasis, open-endedness, plurality...).
        c. These meanings are not obviously calculated from constituent structure.
        d. Therefore: the mapping between form and meaning *is* motivated.

Needless to say, (9d) goes against one of the formalists' most cherished conclusions.

Of course, cognitive grammarians allow themselves statements as in (10).

(10)   Semantic analysis can be sensitive to the *iconic effect* of syntactic accumulation.

---

2 Moravcsik (1978) presents the challenge, a view repeated in pieces like Attardo and Vivo (1997) or Regier (1998).

The cumulative interpretation in (1a), (1b) or (1c) is then allegedly read from surface syntax. Emphatic readings (1d) and (1e) are supposed to translate the cumulative semantic effect to emphasis. That relates to the 'excited' (1e) or the vocative (1f), both of which get associated to the interjective (1g) or grammaticalized animal calls. Other instances are seen as metaphorical.[3]

Linguists of a generative orientation do not accept any of this, but we must still address the puzzle (9) poses. We could start by questioning the standard reasoning just provided in terms of its own premises, by raising difficulties concerning impossible combinations. For example:

(11)   a. Yo   comí poco poco poco...
            I ate little little little
            'I ate quite a little.'

        b. *Yo comí un un un poco / un poco poco poco / un poco un poco un poco
               I   ate   a a a little   a little little little   a little a little a little
            ('I ate quite a little.')

        c. Eu estou facendo moitas (*moitas) cousas que ti non 'tas
            I   am   doing   many   many   things that you not are
            'I am doing many (*many) things that you're not.'

        d. *Yo no llegué,   no llegué,   no llegué.
             I not arrived-PERF not arrived-PERF not arrived-PERF
            ('I didn't arrive, didn't arrive, didn't arrive.')

        e. Yo no llegaba,   no llegaba,   no llegaba.
            I not arrived-IMP not arrived-IMP not arrived-IMP
            'I wouldn't arrive, wouldn't arrive, wouldn't arrive.'

        f. *Mami   llega, llega, llega hoy!
             Mommy arrives arrives arrives today
            ('The fact that it is to arrive that Mommy does today is exciting.')

        g. A mí, *(a) mí, *(a) mí ...!
            to me, to me, to me
            'To me, to me, to me ...!'

        h. *Tú, Tú, Tú ...
            You You You
            ('I am talking to you, you, and there's an issue with you.')

It is unclear in (11a) why the *accumulation* of a quantifier – of the sort cognitive grammarians allude to for their stab at an account – should yield *diminishing* returns. Granted, the quantifier in this instance means *little*, but an iconic accumulation ought to be an accumulation, regardless of the, after

---

3 See Lakoff and Johnson (1980) for the classic statement of 'sound symbolism' issues, and Abelin (1999) for a recent work along these lines.

all, perfectly *arbitrary*, meaning of the item accumulated.[4] Moreover, when we change the quantifier from *little* to *a little*, it is simply impossible to iterate it, in any imaginable combination, as we see in (11b). Observe also (11c). Quantifiers like *many* or *little* can have a proportional reading together with the cardinal one that we have been observing. That sort of reading is forced, for instance, in instances of antecedent-contained deletion (ACD, a structure allowed in various Western Iberian Romance variants, for instance Galician (11c)). Interestingly, iteration in these solidly quantificational conditions is entirely impossible. Observe also the contrast between (11d) and (11e): when the verb is presented in imperfective guise (11e), it can iterate, but not when it is presented in perfective guise (11d). Why should that be? And in (11f), why can't repetition of the verb turn its expression emphatic, if all that is at stake is something like 'iconic urge'? Or take (11g). Why can't we repeat the pronoun in *oblique* form, if such a notion is purely 'formalist'? Finally, note that in (11h) the iteration of a pronominal vocative is surprisingly barred. It is unclear why, if we are dealing with, say, mere extensions of animal calls, the most basic interjection involving our addressee cannot manifest itself in the desired format. Without attempting to provide an exhaustive explanation for the facts in (11), it is fair to say that those are the sorts of conditions that show the phenomenon is *formally* real; yet to make that argument convincing calls for a grammatical explanation.

6.3   Towards a grammatical explanation

The fact that these iterations have so few interpretations across languages (the key to the functionalist argument) would not be all that surprising if the formal mechanism employed to express them correlates with *a very limited expressive power*. Consider that possibility next.

6.3.1   *Finite-state properties of iterative structures*
Recall that Chomsky examined three progressively more complex models, as in (12), where (12c) presupposes structures as in (12b), which in turn presupposes structures as in (12a) (see chapter 7).

---

4 When one accumulates what is denoted as, say, *little cement*, one doesn't start having a *shrinking* amount of the stuff – the total is just a more modest accumulation. This is a fact about the denotata, but the issue cannot be dismissed in a theory seeking an iconic relation between sounds and meanings. Surely one can always claim that 'diminishing' operators exist in language – but that looks like a 'formalist' move.

(12)   a. Finite-state models generating regular languages (strings of symbols)
       b. Phrase structure grammars generating phrases (sets of strings of symbols)
       c. Transformational grammars generating transforms (sets of sets of strings of symbols)

Chomsky argued that English is at least a context-sensitive language. That does not entail (and Chomsky did not say) that English does not have fragments of a simpler sort. In fact, in 1955 he explicitly postulated the need for (at least) phrase structure analysis together with transformational (context-sensitive) analysis. In later works, this resulted in Deep and Surface Structure. In turn, as Howard Lasnik points out (personal communication), Chomsky (1961, p. 15 and 1963, p. 298) explicitly said that English may *also* have fragments of the finite-state sort.[5] More recently, concentrating their analysis on morphological reduplications, Raimy and Idsardi (1997) make again the point that finite-state operations are possible across languages.

Consider in that regard the examples in (13).

(13)   a. Anarquistas fueron arrestados muchos (muchos).
       anarchists   were   arrested   many many
       'Anarchists were arrested many.'
       b. Anarquistas fueron muchos (*muchos) arrestados.
       anarchists   were   arrested   many many
       'Anarchists were many arrested.'
       c. Muchos (muchos) anarquistas fueron arrestados.
       many   many   anarchists were   arrested
       'Many anarchists were arrested.'

(13c) is a simple passive sentence, while (13a) involves the 'floating' of the quantifier; iteration of this element is fine in both instances. But when the quantifier is floated to an intermediate site (subject of the participle) as in (13b), then iteration seems curiously disallowed. This can be explained if the iteration process is incompatible with a correlated transformation. In (13a) the quantifier is in its base-generated position, and it is the associated predicate *anarquistas* that has been displaced. In (13c) both quantifier and predicate are displaced, and thus the entire compositional structure has entered a transformation; that is compatible with the iteration process, arguably because the quantifier itself is not a term in any transformation. However, in (13b) the quantifier is neither in its base-generated position as in (13a) nor in a position

---

5 His argument is based on coordination, for which a flat structure is arguably desirable. See also Jackendoff (2002) for related ideas involving adjuncts.

that is part of a larger derived structure; rather, the floated quantifier itself is a term in the transformation, as per the analysis in Sportiche (1988). It is then that it cannot iterate.

Iteration processes never bleed transformational ones: there is no iterative structure that results from a transformational mechanism,[6] although such structures are logically imaginable. Thus, consider the English paradigm in (14) and the iterated structure in (15):

(14)　　a. Part of an auto
　　　　b. Auto-part __

(15)　　a. Many of many of them
　　　　b. *Many many __ of them

Whereas it is plausible to provide a transformational analysis for the compound in (14b), it is less so to extend this analysis to (15b). This is, first, because a grammatical version of the string of words in (15b) means something different from (15a); thus, (15a) can be read proportionally, but *many many of them* must not, which is easy to see by placing the expression in an ACD site.

(16)　　I met many (*many, many) of them that you did not.

Second, a compound like *auto-part*, regardless of whether it has the analysis in (14b), is generally not possible in Romance – but iterations exist rampantly in this language family.

The claim that the iteration process does not mingle with transformational terms is ultimately unremarkable: as we already saw in (8), the iteration is not well expressed in phrasal terms either, and transformations *presuppose* phrase structure. Now, having extended finite-state ideas from the realm of morphology to syntax, it remains to be understood why their interpretation should be so similar across languages. Although this will be discussed in section 8.2, it is easy to see already that structures generated by finite-state systems are simpler than context-free or context-sensitive ones: they only contain terminals, so they cannot express any category typing. The question is what expressive power this sort of system has, without types or anything presupposing them. Simply put, relevant objects are but strings of concatenated

---

6 We are departing here from the analysis in Travis (2001), which allows copies of the sort we are discussing to bleed transformational processes.

terminals, with at best some loop within them – which the iterations exploit. What *can* the interpretation of such loops be?

Presumably the only straightforward meaning one can associate to strings of terminals is that of a list, and that is reasonably happening in (17), corresponding to (18).

(17)   Speaker points: 'John, Mary, Bill, ...'

(18)   *John   Mary   Bill*
        $[1] \rightarrow [2] \rightarrow [3] \rightarrow ... \rightarrow [\text{HALT}]$

There is no interesting syntactic relation among *John*, *Mary*, etc., and correspondingly there can be no (non-holistic) semantic relation among relevant denotations either. That said, the issue is what added semantics (19) could obtain, after the application of a loop has a given item iterate:

(19)   John, John, John...

(20)

$... \rightarrow [\text{n}] \rightarrow ... \rightarrow [\text{HALT}]$

6.3.2   *The semantics of finite-state loops*

(20) may have very little meaning. In its simplest form, it could be used roughly the way a call presumably is, where the repetition codes mere urge or some such thing (an aspect of the analysis that this book has nothing to contribute to). Now since (20) has so little syntactic structure, it is not implausible to expect a slightly more complex meaning to be able to superimpose on it, as a result of the mere intonation that one discerns in examples of this sort.

(21)   a. My, my, my...
        b. Well, well, well...
        c. Hm, hm, hm...

In these instances the denotation of the repeated element carries no significance, meaning coming solely from the (falling) intonation. This is confirmed by the expression (22), crucially with the pitch contour in (21), which doesn't even involve separate elements, but a mere elongated *hum*.

(22)   Hum-mm-mm...

Facts along these lines obtain in many disparate languages, for instance Romance and Basque, and of course with the same import, suggesting that a very simple and basic mechanism is at stake. For instance:

(23)   a. Vaya, vaya, vaya...(Spanish)
         b. Benoooooo...(Basque)

It is now irrelevant why the tonal 'scales' in these examples carry the meaning(s) they do. What matters for present purposes is that it can be superimposed on a couple of different phonological spaces: (22), not surprisingly since this is just a long and neutral syllable; and those in (21), involving iteration, more interestingly for us. Apparently the unorganized list in these instances is treated by the prosodic mechanisms as a mere collection of repeated syllables. Presumably all that the repetition does is create a prosodic support for the tonal changes. That directly argues for the unstructured nature of the list and, associated to this, that its interpretation is really very trivial. The way to address, then, the puzzle posed by functionalists is simple. When there is little room for interpretive maneuvers, the very restricted possibilities left open – such as those provided by an added intonational layer, exploiting precisely the unstructured finite-state support of these symbols – should manifest themselves similarly across languages.

If we take that route, a class of more complex interpretations for iterative expressions follows. (1d) and (1e) plausibly have the same import as the enthusiastic locutions in (24).

(24)   a. Mami llega HOOOOY!
            Mommy arrives today
            'The fact that it is today when Mommy arrives is exciting.'
         b. YOOOO...!
            me
            'MEEEE...!'

Again, though surely an intriguing matter, it is unimportant now why emphasis shows up as phonological prominence. What is crucial is that the space where this feature manifests itself is either syllabic manipulation or an aggregate of syllables without much associated meaning that creates 'raw prosody' to sustain an elevated pitch.

In that respect (11f), repeated now, is interesting in its disallowing emphasis.

(25)   *Mami llega, llega, llega   hoy!
            Mommy arrives arrives arrives today
            ('The fact that it is to arrive that Mommy does today is exciting.')

The prosodic manipulations taking place in these iterations obviously have limits, plausibly of the sort explored by Zubizarreta (1998) in more general terms. Although we cannot go into the matter here, emphasis effects happen low (rightmost) within the phrase-marker, perhaps for the symmetry reasons discussed in Kahnemuyipour (2004). Be that as it may, these iterations are best at the end of a prosodic phrasing, a condition not obtaining in (25).

Next let's concentrate on iterations that do not carry an emphatic import. To explore their semantics, let's compare the examples in (26), which show how aspect is relevant. When the verb phrase has a telic character, as in (26b), the iteration is impossible. Otherwise it's fine, either because the iterated part is only denoting the action without a *telos*, as in (26a), or because the direct object is generic as in (26c), and thus again opens up the verbal action – this time towards denoting an unbounded class of house blowings (perhaps for reasons related to the discussion in Schmitt [1999], concerning Verkuyl's [1972] observations about verbal aspect).

(26)   a. Y   el lobo sopló, sopló la casa hasta que se derrumbó.
           and the wolf blew blew the house until that self fell down
           'And the wolf blew, blew the house until it fell down.'
        b. *Y el lobo sopló la casa, sopló la casa hasta que se derrumbó.
           and the wolf blew the house blew the house until that self fell down
           ('And the wolf blew the house, blew the house until it fell down.')
        c. Y el   lobo sopló casas, sopló casas hasta que se murió.
           and the wolf blew houses blew houses until that self died
           'And the wolf blew houses, blew houses until he died.'

One plausible interpretation of the correlation between iteration and imperfectivity comes from analysing examples as in (27), quite literally.

(27)   Yo tengo uno, uno, uno...
        I   have one one one
        'I have several.'

I recorded my own children, when they were actually younger than two, using this iterated direct object clearly to denote a plurality of objects. This is possibly significant because plurality is often expressed through morphological reduplication.[7] Although little can be said in present terms about morphological processes, the correlation cannot be ignored. We need not invoke iconic considerations to achieve it, or for that matter go into the

---

7 For a recent perspective and references, see Raimy (1999).

implicit quantifier postulated by Travis (2001) for the task.[8] All we have to do is interpret concatenated items conjunctively. That is, (27) means what it can mean when the listed items are aggregated.

Consider also the examples in (28).

(28)   a. Yo veía mar, mar, mar ... por todas partes
             I   saw sea sea sea   by every where
             'I saw (the vastness of) the sea everywhere.'
      b. Yo veía gaviotas, gaviotas, gaviotas ... por todas partes
             I   saw seagulls seagulls seagulls   by every where
             'I saw (a cloud of) seagulls everywhere.'

In this instance the iteration corresponds to an aggregation, not so much of individual items, as in (27), but of unstructured spaces, which mass terms (as in (28a)) or plurals (as in (28b)) are often taken to denote.[9] The resulting effect is the denotation of open, somewhat overwhelming, contexts.

Once this possibility arises for nominal predicates, as in the plurals and mass terms above, it should in principle be extensible to verbal predicates, to yield some of the variations we have seen already, for instance those in (29).

(29)   a. Yo tuve que andar, andar, andar ... hasta llegar.
             I   had to   walk walk walk   until arriving
             'I had to walk endlessly until arriving.'
      b. Yo no llegaba,   no llegaba,   no llegaba.
             I   not arrived-IMP not arrived-IMP not arrived-IMP
             'I wouldn't arrive, wouldn't arrive, wouldn't arrive.'

(29a) mimics (28a): the activity *andar* 'walk' can surely also be modeled in space-like terms (much as a corresponding mass term could), and therefore allow for unbounded expansions, in this instance of walking. (29b) is more interesting, since the accomplishment *llegar* 'arrive' carries an implicit *telos*. However, the verb in this context comes in imperfective guise, and that alone allows a treatment similar to the one just seen, albeit pertaining to that portion of the lexical space of the verb that corresponds to the *final stretch* towards the *telos*.[10] That is interesting in itself, and related to the fact that in Romance

---

8 One can always posit a hidden operator, but the issue is why it manifests itself precisely in these domains.

9 See Chierchia (1998) for much relevant discussion, although from a perspective different from the one taken here with regards to which of these – mass or plurals – is the most basic.

10 This is easier to see in an affirmative version of (29b), which could be used to denote those arduous final steps an athlete takes before crossing the finish line.

the relevant iterations are possible even with verbs that are high in the Vendler scale, for instance an accomplishment.[11]

(30)   Y   ella horneó, horneó, horneó el pastel hasta que se quemó.
             and she baked baked   baked the cake until that self burned
             'And she baked, baked, baked the cake until it burned.'

In (30) what is extended is that part of the baking event that precedes the accomplishment. This shows two things. On one hand, that the inner structure of accomplishments or achievements is visible enough to whatever mechanism is relevant here – contra any simple-minded atomistic analysis (see the discussion in chapter 2) – so that it can be appropriately modified by the iteration of the whole word. On the other, the mechanism itself can ignore the word as a whole (where it would not make sense) – which is yet another indication that the string of iterated words does not have much of a structure in itself.

6.3.3   More complex instances

So far we have concentrated on the iteration, through finite-state loops, of single words. But larger iterations are possible. Although the finite-state machinery allows for loops with any finite number of states, their existence raises an issue. Thus consider again (26c), now repeated.

(31)   Y   el lobo sopló casas,   sopló casas, hasta que se murió.
             and the wolf blew houses blew houses until that self died
             'And the wolf blew houses, blew houses, until he died.'

The verb and direct object clearly form a unit here, of a phrasal sort at least. So how can this unit be said to have finite-state properties?

That poses a question of precisely where the finite-state fragments lie within natural language. In principle, the question is no different from where phrase structure fragments lie within a language whose power we know to be transformational. The latter we have answered in the past in terms of levels of representation or corresponding (non-unified) components of the system, such as D-structure. But is there a level of representation, or corresponding (non-unified) component of the system, *where finite state loops can be coded*?

---

11 This sort of expression is possible in English only if the conjunction *and* is inserted in between the iterated items (*she baked and baked and baked the cake*) and then the expression can also denote a repeated accomplishment. It is worth considering whether the languages that demand this conjunctive marker are the ones that undergo conservative spell-out, in the sense in section 4.4.1 – while radical spell-out languages allow bare iteration.

One such component may be what Chomsky has called, since 1995, the *numeration* – an unordered collection of lexical tokens to be used up in the derivation. This sort of object is constructed from the lexicon (instantiating lexical types as token words) and, again, it is unstructured – good news for the iterative structures we are studying. Often numerations are taken to be, if anything, mere abstractions, but if we take them to be the component of the system where finite-state loops can be coded, they would have to be quite real, a conclusion that reinforces the assumption in section 4.2.1 regarding the minimal array condition (MAC), which aims at minimizing functional items within these multi-sets.

A problem with thinking of numerations as relevant to our discussion is the fact that iterative loops are sensitive to phrase structure, while numerations are not. Thus consider:

(32)   *Y él   sopló, él sopló, él sopló casas   hasta que se   murió.
          and he blew   he blew   he blew houses until that self died
          ('And he blew, he blew, he blew houses until he died.')

When items like *él* 'he' and *sopló* 'blew' are not co-constituents they cannot be iterated. But how can that be, if the relevant sub-numeration for (32) is the unordered multi-set in (33)?

(33)   {él, sopló, casas}

Consider the derivational fate of (34a), resulting in (34b).

(34)   a.   [to [leave John]]
          b.   *[John T [to leave]] (cf. John left.)

Theta relations as in (34a) are legitimate, but Case checking fails in (34b). For instances of this sort we assume the derivation must be perfect *in all its steps*, it being irrelevant whether it goes wrong initially or eventually, within some reasonable (cyclic) time span. With that perspective in mind, consider the derivation in (35), with finite-state (35a) and non-finite-state stages (35b).

(35)   *él* 'he'   *sopló* 'blew'
          a. [1] → [2]   → [3]
             ⤷_____⤴

          b. * [[él-sopló-él-sopló] casas]

Nothing prevents step (35a), if finite-state relations can be established in numerations. However, if they fail to meet phrase structure requirements in the next step, (35b), the derivation will terminate. Ruling out (35) in these terms induces no more computational blow-up than in the entirely analogous

(34). Moreover, in either instance the complexity of the problem is trivial if numerations are accessed cyclically, as is being assumed here.

Once this solution is devised for (32), we can extend it to instances of loops with various words involved. Two sub-cases come to mind. One is where a loop is created over chunks of an already-abandoned numeration. That case is simple, since the partial derivational output can be *compiled as a unit*, which thus iterates without complication. (36) illustrates this instance.

(36)   a. He said that he left, that he left, that he left . . . !
         b. He said [that he left]-[that he left]-[that he left]

Here the looped combination of *that-he-left* is finite state, but internally this element is complex, in customary phrasal and even transformational ways.

We should ponder that briefly, for this may seem incoherent from the traditional perspective of formal languages, which will be discussed more thoroughly in section 7.2. In classical terms, where language is considered a set of well-formed formulas, if a chunk of structure has reached, say, trans-formational complexity, then the corresponding language has that generative power. It is equally effective to propose an analysis as in (36b) within this language or to do things in more customary, phrasal, terms. The equivalence holds at the level of so-called weak generative capacity, the sorts of well-formed strings that a given system allows. Linguists, however, worry more about strong generative capacity, or the particular structure (equivalently, derivation) that underlies (carries the system to) a given output string like (36a). From that linguistic perspective, the loop implied in (36b) is both straightforward and meaningful, as it can be assigned the (here emphatic) meaning discussed above. Throughout what follows, we concentrate on strong generative capacity.

The more interesting example now is as in (31), the grammatical alterna-tive to the derivation in (35), which proceeds fine as in (37) (and see Raimy and Idsardi [1997] for similar instances).

(37)   *sopló* 'blew'   *casas* 'houses'
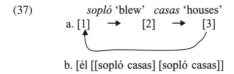

         b. [él [[sopló casas] [sopló casas]]]

Unlike what we saw for (35), this particular loop does find a grammatical counterpart in the representation in (37b) (and note the absence of hyphens inbetween the relevant words vis-à-vis (35b)) which satisfies theta theory in customary ways, upon phrasal reanalysis (and see section 8.3.3 on these reanalyses, via complement assumption).

6.3.4   *More iterative facts in the same direction*

This phenomenon is very pervasive in Spanish, extending throughout substantive items, as the following examples show.

(38)   a. ADJECTIVES:
               La pequeña (pequeña) hormiga
               the small   small ant
               La única (única) razón
               the only only reason
          b. LOCATIVE PREPOSITIONS:
               Debajo (debajo) de ti
               Detrás (detrás) de la casa
               under under of you
               behind behind of the house
          c. QUANTIFIERS:
               Mucho (mucho) parado
               Nada   (nada) de nada
               much much unemployed
               nothing nothing of nothing

Importantly, however, iteration is disallowed with pure functional items.

(39)   a. Infl: Juan ha (*ha) llegado.
               Juan has has   arrived
               (Intended meaning: 'Juan *has* indeed arrived.')
          b. Comp: Juan no sabe que (*que) la tierra es redonda.
               Juan not knows that that the earth is round
               Intended meaning: 'Juan doesn't know *that* the earth is round.')
          c. Det: Las (*las) brujas han escapado
               the the   witches have fled
               (Intended meaning: '*The* witches (not just *some* witches) have fled.')

Formal items typically involve checking features, which in turn presupposes deploying at least a context-free system – if not a context-sensitive one for instances involving Agree. Already in chapter 3 (54) we proposed a lexical projection thesis (LPT), whose effect for formal items is that they involve transformationally driven event-quantifications. That demand makes them incompatible with finite-state syntax, in much the same way that a quantifier floating as in (13) above is incompatible with iteration.

These ideas do not cover the entire phenomenology of iteration, or for that matter its obvious relations to processes of the mirroring sort, which we set aside. The main point underlying this brief study of iterative structures is simply to show that their analysis in context-free terms (let alone context-sensitive ones) is not plausible, and furthermore that there is no need to push things in that direction. Intuitively, the fact that a creature is shown to be able to run doesn't mean it cannot, then, walk or even crawl. There is no doubt that the human language faculty has context-sensitive capabilities, but that *per se* has no bearing on whether it also exploits presupposed context-free and finite-state processes. The present chapter extends ideas from morphology to syntax, to show evidence in favor of this view.

6.4   A finite-state syntax for small clauses

Now how far do such finite-state elements go? Moreover, can they address otherwise puzzling aspects of our basic structures in this book?

6.4.1   *The problem with small clauses*

The syntax of small clauses has never made much sense in more standard terms.[12] A small clause does look like a clause in having subject and predicate, but similarities end there. Thus, whereas typical clausal subjects reach their 'extended projection principle' site via movement, small clause subjects are generally taken to be base-generated. Curiously, despite this base-generation, small clauses do not take pleonastic subjects (*(I saw) (*there) a man tired/*tired a man*). This is inspite of the fact that only pleonastics can start their derivational life as base-generated clausal subjects. Also, small clauses are rarely composed of complex thematic arrays – they normally involve simple one-place predications like *(I consider) John smart* – and when they do get more complex, they must involve an extra (inherent) case-marker, like *of* in *(I consider) John proud *(of) his daughters*. In fact, small clauses arguably never have an internal source of Case assignment of their own, of the inflectional sort, and they instead rely on externally originating exceptional Case marking processes. Finally, projection-wise small clauses are bizarre: their subject/predicate relation cannot be seen as involving the small *v* and similar elements that are associated with standard theta structure, or they would start behaving contrary to fact in terms of (accusative) Case assignment and correlating thematic properties (Burzio's Generalization in section 2.3). Traditionally (since Stowell 1983), this was remedied by base-generating the subject as an adjunct to the predicate. This

---

12 Although specific details of these works won't be pursued, there are two original proposals that have influenced much of what follows: Déchaine *et al.* (1994), and Moro (2000).

may be the right general move to make (it was crucial in our invoking the condition on chain uniformity (CCU) in section 3.6.3), but it is not clear precisely what it means.

There are problems with taking small clause subjects as mere adjuncts. On the one hand, adjuncts are optional and stackable and small clause subjects are neither. Compare:

(40)   a. John's (phenomenal) (fast) dance (last night) (in his new play) (...) [was a success]
       b. John danced (last night) (in his new play) (...)

(41)   a. I declared [*(John) (*Mary) smart (in his new play)]
       b. I sensed [*(John) (Mary) feverish (last night)]

If we make the optionality and stackability of adjuncts a *consequence* of their adjunction syntax,[13] something else must guarantee the obligatoriness and uniqueness of small clause subjects. On the other hand, it is clear that the terms of the small clause interact heavily with the rest of the clause, in ways that adjuncts can't. Observe the contrasts below. The small clause dependents in (43) can raise to the matrix clause in ways that adjuncts certainly cannot (42).

(42)   a. ***For twenty four hours** seems [to have been raining cats and dogs **t**] (cf. 'It seems [to have been raining cats and dogs for twenty four hours]')
       b. *It seems **for twenty four hours** [to have been raining cats and dogs **t**]
       c. ***Behind a poster of his leader** though Jack died **t**, nobody took the thing away.
          (cf. Although Jack died behind a poster of his leader, nobody took the thing away.)

(43)   a. **Jack** was considered [**t** smart]
       b. I actually consider **rather smart** [that old fool Jack **t**]
       c. **Smart** though Jack was considered **t**, he never made it in politics.

Moreover, while extraction from inside small clausal dependents ranges from marginal to virtually perfect (45), comparable extractions from inside adjuncts are generally dismal (44).

(44)   ?* **Of whom** did Jack die [behind a poster **t**]

---

13 The intuition for this move is that adjunction dependencies do not change category type upon taking place, or that they occupy a 'different dimension'. The idea has been around, explicitly, since at least Goodall (1984), and it was exploited by both Lebeaux (1988) and Uriagereka (1988) to predict lack of connectivity into these items. For recent discussion of this matter, see Lasnik and Uriagereka (2005, chapter 7).

(45)   a. **Of whom** do you consider [Jack [proud **t**]]
        b. ? **Of whom** do you consider [[insulting] [several posters **t**]]

So, simply put, the subject and predicate of the small clause look like bona fide dependents that interact with the rest of the clause (they move, reanalyse, can be extracted from), in ways barred for adjuncts in their 'different dimension' (see fn. 13). One hopes that this lack of interaction relates to the adjunction mechanism – which then shouldn't extend to small clause dependents that do interact.

To sum up, we don't want small clause subjects to be like regular subjects in their thematic or Case properties, but we don't want them acting, either, like the archetypal elements that do not obey thematic or Case conditions, namely adjuncts. This is fine, but our bare phrase structures (BPS) don't leave room for maneuver: the system produces head/complement and head/specifier relations, and it can be twisted into yielding 'elsewhere' adjunctions in a 'different dimension'. But this is not enough to handle small clause subjects.

6.4.2   *Finite-state heads and the rest*

If, as was suggested in the preceding sections, finite-state mechanisms are real to the language faculty, it is worth exploring what new descriptive power – or restrictive apparatus – they provide, beyond the productive iterations studied thus far. Bear in mind, first of all, that small clauses can have complex dependents.

(46)   I consider [[the old capital's destruction by the military] [worthy of the worst murderers]]

This is comparable to the iteration in (37), involving complex loops. We already mentioned two ways of addressing this sort of phrasal complexity within a finite-state structure. One is to invoke a generalized transformation inserting essentially the output of an entire derivational cycle. Thus, it could be that the *old capital's destruction by the military* and *worthy of the worst murderers* in (46) are generated in separate derivational workspaces, and their results (in effect, the top label) are matched against identical labels in the finite-state object.

(47)

SUB-DERIVATION (a)
(finite-state component):   < <DP>, <AP> >

SUB-DERIVATION (b)   SUB-DERIVATION (c)
(phrasal component):   **(phrasal component):**
[$_{DP}$ *the old capital's destruction by the military*]$_{DP}$ [$_{AP}$ *worthy of the worst murderers*]$_{AP}$

SUB-DERIVATION (d)
(transformational component):   < <DP>, <AP> >

[SUBSTITUTION]
[$_{DP}$ *the old capital's destruction by the military*]$_{DP}$ [$_{AP}$ *worthy of the worst murderers*]$_{AP}$

In turn, if relevant component parts are small we can simply allow a direct finite-state analysis (as we did in our analysis of (37)); this will over-generate – though only slightly as very few elements are at play. When all relevant structures are sent to the phrasal component, only those that meet BPS specifications (and associated thematic, agreement, and similar considerations) will survive the derivation; others will be filtered out. This is all to say that, although not all small clauses are as trivial as *him tall*, that will not derail the finite-state analysis we're attempting.

It is worth emphasizing, again, the point raised at the end of section 6.3.3: we are dealing with strong generative capacity of a computational system, and therefore it is sound to ask which structurings proceed in finite-state fashion, which are phrasal, and so on – even if they all interact. The reminder is appropriate because, if that caveat is not kept in perspective, one might be tempted to ascribe to the automaton presupposed for the analysis in the previous paragraph the power needed to generate phrase structure dependencies or more. In particular, there are memory assumptions being made (what allows the system to store compiled bits of structure as they are assembled) that are quite non-trivial, and which do resemble the sort of memory needed to move upward in the Chomsky Hierarchy, as will be discussed in section 7.2. That said, the important thing to bear in mind now is that the linguistic automaton may indeed be ultimately more powerful than is implied in these finite-state structurings we're discussing, and this may even affect not just the way in which given structures (loops, phrases, chains, and so on) emerge, but even corresponding symbols of certain sorts (e.g. heads vs. non-heads). That doesn't mean, however, that the automaton in question, because of having said power, can directly generate all that this power allows, in formal-language fashion – because its mathematical properties allow such descriptions. That would disregard its inner workings and what triggers them, which is what contemporary generative grammar is about.

Logically, a BPS system in general should allow only three finite-state subcases of adjunction: <head, head>, <MaxP, MaxP>, and <head, MaxP>.[14] Notice that if these notions are to make sense in purely finite-state terms (without complex dominance paths or similar phrasal machinery, so extending the 'bareness' of 'phrase structure' to any form of syntactic dependency), we must define them accordingly. The notion head is as trivial

---

14 Linear order in the PF component is irrelevant, assuming a linearization procedure along the lines of some simplified version of Kayne's (1994) linear correspondence axiom; see Moro (2000) on this.

here as elsewhere in the grammar: a head is a lexical item, period[15] (LI). It would seem as if the notion of maximal projection is undefinable without complex brackets and non-terminal labels, but we can define it in finite-state terms as an elsewhere case: *whatever is not a head*.

As Pullum and Rogers (2007) show, several distinctions obtain within finite-state systems, an issue that we need not dwell on now. All that matters to us is that the simplest kinds of such systems involve mere symbols without complex structuring, so-called n-grams. Looping as such is already an added complexity, requiring a more powerful formal mechanism. This is intuitive. Whereas a regular list is generated by listing simple items, a loop emerges by manipulating a given item several times. The string *da-da* could be generated by taking two symbols which happen to be pronounced *da* or looping a single symbol *da*. In the former instance we can only generate *da-da* (if we want to generate *da-da-da* we need yet another symbol, and so on, which of course has the same formal complexity as *la-di-da*, say, using three different symbols). In the latter, instead, we can also generate *da-da-da, da-da-da-da, da-da-da-da-da* and so on, *ad infinitum*.

With that in mind, we can easily distinguish, if we so desire, heads from non-heads even in finite-state terms. We already said that heads are lexical items, single symbols from a lexicon, or LIs. What is 'the rest'? The answer is simple: any structure-to-be-interpreted that involves a loop, or a global finite-state mechanism of that overall complexity. Thus, we can conclude that in an expression like *very, very, very . . . tired*, the string *very, very, very . . .* is not a head, as it is not an LI (although of course the element *very*, used to generate the list, would be). But we may reach similar conclusions, also, for a more complex phrasal unit that happens to be iterated, of which we have seen several instances already. For instance, in *and he blew, and he blew, and he blew . . .* this method will dictate that the string emerging from iterating *and he blew* is not a head, even at a finite-state level, *because its structuring in iterated fashion demands a loop*. Finally, all of that said, we can also worry about structures-to-be-interpreted that have the same computational complexity as looped ones: those that the system can treat as wholes of some sort, or units of interpretation.

Implicit in the discussion in section 6.2 is that given looped structures can be conceived by the semantics as a phonological space of some sort; this is

---

15 Chomsky has moved from the term lexical item (LI) in his earlier work to member of the lexicon (ML) in more recent work, but the senses are interchangeable for consistency in this book, the term lexical item has been used throughout.

what, in the view presented here, gives them their characteristic open-endedness. That in turn presupposes that the finite-state component of the system can identify and transfer to the semantics the relevant units, to undergo interpretation. For that to happen, this particular chunk of finite-state structure must come to a halt, thus terminating that stage of the computation – it is, in effect, a complete finite-state cycle, however its size is determined. Now if this halting mechanism is used for interpreting loops, there is no reason why a similar transfer to the semantics shouldn't obtain more generally for other finite-state structures that *we want to treat as non-heads*. Note, incidentally, that even LIs can in principle be treated this way, if they manage to halt and transfer early. This is in the spirit of the BPS system, where given items can be both heads and maximal projections.

Again, although the ensuing computational system has more power than a mere finite-state system (we are allowing finite-state *collections*, the system generating which is weakly equivalent to one describing fully phrasal units), this doesn't affect the strong generative capacity considerations that matters to us here. Put another way, we have defined heads vs. non-heads by the latter resorting to abandoning the finite-state component. This is not all that surprising; we couldn't have conceived of a 'chunk' of structure in pure finite-state terms. But the definition works well enough to distinguish types of items already at the finite-state stage: heads will only be lexical items; everything else (including lexical items if transferred to interpretation) will be non-heads. Given that the finite-state component acts only locally, these distinctions will suffice for our purposes.

6.4.3   Combinatorial distinctions within a finite-state system
We thus obtain the sub-cases in (48) (again, PF order irrelevant, see fn. 14).

(48)   a. <head, head> = <LI, LI>
        b. <MaxP, MaxP> = <-LI, -LI>
        c. <head, MaxP> = <LI, -LI>

Sub-case (48a) corresponds to head-to-head movement, while (48b) must correspond to identificational small clauses, of the sort in *I declare Dr. Jeckyl Mr. Hyde*. Note that this sort of small clause must either involve a separate generalized transformation, or else complex finite-state structuring – unwanted combinations to be filtered out later on. In either instance, this 'elsewhere case' can be characterized as not involving just the simplest finite-state structuring that associates one LI to another. (48c) appears to be what we need for what were called integral small clauses in chapter 3. Notice that (48a) and (48b) are arguably simpler than (48c), in that their syntax is more trivial because it involves the combination of identical sorts of items (heads or non-heads). So those two sub-cases should fall into the Trivial Structure hypothesis in chapter 3 (37). This entails that, within the over-arching co-linearity thesis (CLT) defended throughout this book, elements combining as in (48a) or (48b) should have essentially identificational syntax – a point argued for in section 3.5.2. Sub-case (48c), however, should not be amenable to such a simple identification: it doesn't start with a totally trivial syntax.

Still within the overall CLT, in chapter 2 we also introduced the P/W^2 thesis to map complex phrasal elements into corresponding semantic representations, where keeping track of syntactic wholes and their syntactic parts matters for the appropriate thematic representation. It might seem as if situation (48c) should obey the P/W^2 thesis but, upon closer inspection, that result would be undesirable on two counts. Semantically, we want to distinguish integral small clauses from standard head/complement relations (e.g. those resulting from what was called complement assumption in chapter 5, or simply relations like the one obtaining between a formal item like T and its vP-VP substantive complement). Syntactically, it is not straightforward to get a small clause subject to be a proper part of a small clause, as we saw when considering uniformity factors in section 3.6.3 (which suggests that the small clause subject is not a standard subject, as reviewed in the previous section). Then perhaps objects of the form in (48c) obey a syntax/semantics mapping that is neither of the Trivial Structure nor the P/W^2 thesis sort.

The question ultimately boils down to the difference between a head/MaxP relation via the finite-state dependency (now defined for the head/non-head distinction) and via the context-free match, so that we can then address the matter of what sort of semantic mapping each of those should involve. A fact about derivational architecture can help us address that question.

In its context-free guise, a head/MaxP relation is a familiar head/ complement dependency. The intuition behind the notion of command unit, as discussed in section 5.4.1, is that successive head/complement relations within a BPS system do not ever necessitate (in themselves) the aid of a generalized transformation. Thus recall (24) in chapter 5, where we treated command units as the maximal amount of structure that can be assembled without abandoning a derivational workspace. As we saw above when considering complex small clauses, things are a fortiori different when finite-state syntax is involved: the only way to obtain complex structure, and still assemble it in finite-state fashion, is precisely if we *can* abandon a given derivational workspace (if we halt the finite-state procedure). Notice that, within the space of possibilities in (48), those combinations that involve -LI items (non-heads) will necessarily involve abandoning a derivational workspace, as that is the only way the system has, in its finite-state mode, to 'know' that something is not a head. The point is trivially true for instances involving complex-phrasal units treated in a finite-state way but must still obtain for items that come from the lexicon, but which *we want to treat as -LI elements for associative purposes* – e.g. to yield an integral small clause as in (48c).

Thus consider a simple small clause like the one which, in the terms discussed in chapter 3, obtains between a whole and its parts, for instance *city* and *neighborhood* in *city of neighborhoods*. These are obviously two LIs, since nothing gives *neighborhood* a privileged status over *city* within the lexicon, or vice versa. However, we want to treat *neighborhood* as a head (the small clause predicate, a presentation in present terminology), while treating *city* as a maximal projection (the corresponding small clause subject, a space in present terms). So at this level the only thing the system can do is send *city* into a separate derivational work space, as it would if it were the complex *city that I saw* – thus halting the finite-state procedure for that item. Nothing prevents that association, although others would be possible. Productive Spanish examples are used to illustrate.

(49)   a. <LI, LI>: [*ciudad barrio*] → *ciudad-barrio* 'a neighborhood-style-city'
       b. <-LI, -LI>: *(declaro)* [*ciudad* [*barrio*]] 'I hereby declare the city a/the neighborhood'
       c. <LI, -LI>: *(de)* [*ciudad* [*barrio*]] → *barrio (de) ciudad* 'a city neighborhood'

Though this is not systematic, one does find Spanish compounds as in (49a); in this instance what we see is what we get, a simple-minded combination of both terms as LIs, without doing anything to either one other than grabbing each from the lexicon. (Perhaps compounding more generally acts in this fashion.) (49b) is also a possibility in rhetorical speech of the sort that tends to drop determiners;[16] in this instance we have an identificational small clause, where neither term is taken as an LI, which means each is sent to a separate derivational workspace. Finally we have the more familiar possibility in (49c); here one term is sent to a separate derivational workspace (again,

16 This is common in slogans like *CONSTRUYE BARRIO Y CIUDAD* 'build neighborhood and city' or proverbial expressions of the sort of *barrios al poder, ciudad que prospera* 'neighborhoods to power, city that prospers'.

halting the finite-state procedure), but not the other – an asymmetry directly ensuing.

6.4.4   *Issues of interpretation*

What should concern us now is how the syntax/semantics mapping treats the particular asymmetry just alluded to. Suppose that *an item that goes into a separate derivational workspace is transferred to the PF and LF components.* That was the essence of the multiple spell-out (MSO) proposal in Uriagereka (1999), although it was concerned mostly with the mapping to the PF interface, spell-out proper.[17] At this point we are concentrating on the mapping to the semantics, referred to as Interpret. When some X is transferred by Interpret, two things can happen: (i) something else is in the 'interpretive buffer', or (ii) nothing else is. The situation distinguishes specifiers from the rest of structures (setting aside adjuncts for now) – 'the rest of structures' and not merely 'head/complement relations', since integral small clause subjects pattern with head/complement relations and not with specifiers. Simply put, a bottom-up derivation typically *starts* in a small clause, assembled by finite-state means. The logic of the present proposal for integral small clauses is that their subject is forced into a separate derivational work space. This constitutes a natural object to be sent by Interpret to the semantics. If this is the case, a natural syntax/semantic mapping would give us an interpretive clue in this instance, which will be called the cue thesis.

(50)   Cue Thesis (CT)
        The order of interpretation of [|X|] with respect to [|Y|] reflects the order of
        X's transfer with respect to Y's transfer.

This proposal is virtually a truism, if one assumes a derivational system and takes it earnestly. But it isn't vacuous: it forces the system to commit to the interpretation of some element that came in first, because it did.[18] Recall that, in lexico-conceptual terms, integral small clauses deploy a space and a presentation to affect that space. Now we can understand why things are not 'the other way around'. Given the CT, and provided that integral small clauses involve an X that goes into derivational transfer (unlike the other item Y that remains behind), it follows that X is interpreted first by the system, and Y comes in next. A natural way for the semantics to proceed in those terms is by

---

17 Although see Uriagereka (2002, chapter 8).
18 This is like the role that first impressions have on markets, as shown by the QWERTY keyboard, initially designed so as to slow typists down in order not to jam early type-writers, but which has long since taken over the market.

taking the item to be interpreted first as unstructured, while the item that comes in next is seen as structuring. Cognitive grammarians may find the idea congenial, as presentations are working out what they call a 'figure', while spaces are the 'ground' where those figures are established.[19] These sorts of issues are discussed in topological terms in section 7.4.

Relevant 'ground' elements are structure less with regards to the particular lexico-conceptual notions that their association with their presentation would introduce. That, however, doesn't imply that the element that reaches the lexico-conceptual interpretation first doesn't have any features. Obviously it does, or we wouldn't distinguish, say, a city from a beast, or any other thing, since all of these have parts and can enter into such dependencies as *neighborhood of a city* or *blood of a beast*. As in Uriagereka (2002, chapter 15), the system in question, while highly modular in the usual sense (Fodor 1982), also allows for a certain 'porous' modularity, this time in the spirit of Jackendoff's (1997) view – although without any connectionist implications. Thus relevant lexical representation can reach the visual, auditory, motor, or other systems to represent the differences among lexico-conceptual notions of the same 'dimensionality', in the sense discussed in chapter 2 (e.g. abstract terms of various sorts, mass terms of various sorts).[20]

Everything discussed for small clause subjects counts only when they are *not* identificational (one of the members of the small clause being the head). In identificational small clauses both such members are taken to be maximal projections, thus they associate in terms of a trivial syntax, and thus they are subject to the Trivial Structure Hypothesis, involving identificational semantics. Non-trivial small clauses, however, can, but need not, be of the integral sort; we also have simple individual-level expressions like *Jack smart* or stage-level expressions like *Jack drunk*. Rather than being lexico-conceptual, some of those distinctions correspond to grammatical differences outside of the small clause, as already suggested in Raposo and Uriagereka (1995). In the integral vs. predicational small clauses (to use the distinction in Hornstein *et al.* [1996]), the category of the predicate would appear to make a difference: adjectival and prepositional elements are not interpretable in integral guise. The matter however is more delicate with nominal predicates, which can be both.[21] One way to distinguish these is in terms of bare nominal

---

19 See, for instance, Talmy (1978), Langacker (1987), and Fauconnier (1997).
20 That such putative connections may happen across modules, but *within dimensions*, is what prevents this system from being merely connectionist: not all such imaginable relations take place.
21 The integral *Mary's man* vs. the predicational *Mary's a man*.

expressions (relevant in integral relations) vs. nominal expressions that come associated to some formal element, typically a determiner (relevant in more standard predicational relations). But does it have a bearing on the status of the small clause as such whether its predicate is a bare N or a more complex DP?

It may in one respect: a complex DP predicate can no longer be a *trivial* head, and thus forces us out of situation (48b) for standard predicational small clauses (and also forces us into precisely that situation for all integral small clauses, thus disallowing complex predicates, which we will come back to immediately). One potential problem with that emerges from such Romance expressions as *yo considero a María (un) chico* 'I consider Mary a boy', with an optionally bare noun where we find an indefinite in English. Evidently, we would have to impose some variant of the English analysis on these Romance instances, perhaps blaming it on the overt gender agreement status of the nominal (absent in English). The question is what to do then with the equally overt agreement marker in the integral version of these types of expressions, for instance *chico* (lit. 'boy.masc.sg.') in *el chico de María*? Interestingly, agreement seems to be pleonastic in this instance, at least in Spanish, as indicated by the contrasts with French in (51).

(51)   a. María es un/   *una chico.
            María is a.masc.sg. a.fem.sg boy.msc.sg
            'María is a boy.'
         b. María quiere a su   chico/chica.
            María loves to his/her/it.sg boy.msc.sg girl.fem.sg
            'María loves her boy/girl.'
         c. Marie aime son   garçon/sa fille.
            Marie loves his/her/it.masc.sg boy.msc.sg his/her/it.fem.sg girl.fem.sg
            'Marie loves her boy/her girl.'
         d. Marie est *(un) garçon.
            Marie is a   boy
            'Marie is a boy.'

Whereas *chico* 'boy' in the standard predicational example in (51a) agrees with its determiner *un* 'a' in gender and number, this is not the case in the integral case in (51b). Here *chico* agrees in number, but not in gender – there is no gender specification in this instance. Gender specification is necessary in a comparable French example (51c). Curiously, the French predicational instance in (51d) behaves as it would in English – the determiner is obligatory there. This does suggest that the peculiar determiner-dropping in Spanish predications somehow correlates with the gender agreement, this marker being pleonastic in the integral example.

More important to our concerns, the idea that integral small clauses are objects of the sort in (48c) – without any room for even a minimally complex predicate of the type that turns the relevant small clause into a standard predicational one – imposes an important constraint on what counts as 'integral'. In fact, it predicts a drastic difference between the shape of the subject and the predicate of the integral small clause, despite the fact that we want both elements to be 'objectual', at least in instances involving a whole (e.g. a city) and a part (e.g. a neighborhood). The fact that, in something like *a neighborhood of the city*, each of the integral elements associates with a determiner adds no particular problem, since we can take the definite article associated to *city* as part of the complex subject of the small clause, whereas the indefinite article associated to *neighborhood* can be analysed as the D that heads the entire expression – *neighborhood* starting its derivational life as a bare head. More problematic would be an instance where the syntax argued for in chapter 3 forces the presentation to be in situ, as in *city of neighborhoods*; that is, if such an in situ presentation comes associated to a determiner. The ungrammatical possibilities in (52) are good news, however.

(52)   a. This is a city (*of a/the/every neighborhood).
        b. This is a city (*of most/all neighborhoods).

The grammatical possibilities in (53) are bad news.

(53)   a. This is a city of (precisely) one neighborhood.
        b. This is a city of four/many/no neighborhoods.

Interestingly, the elements that appear in the presentation are what have been traditionally thought of as weak determiners, in the original sense of Milsark (1974); that is, essentially quantificational elements that can be explicit predicates elsewhere.

(54)   a. *God is a/the/every.
        b. *The evangelists were most/all.

(55)   a. God is (precisely) one.
        b. The evangelists were four/many.

That is a welcome result, if true quantificational elements require context-sensitive syntax to satisfy their semantic demands. The impossible instances in (52) follow if the elements in the presentation position (by hypothesis still a finite-state site) bring with them a demand for a complex syntax to be semantically coherent (more on this in section 8.2). At the same time, why are the examples in (53) possible, especially if we distinguish integral small clauses from predicational ones in terms of having the former involve a strict pattern along the lines of (48c)?

Within the confines of the present proposal, the only possible answer to that question is in terms of taking the determiner associated to the presentation as *a modifier*. For the purposes of heads, complements, specifiers – and now we would add small clause members – adjuncts 'should not count', in a sense to be explored further. The idea that weak determiners in general are modifiers has a respectable pedigree (starting in Milsark [1977]). But we need not commit to that specific position.[22] All we need to say is that weak determiners *start* their derivational life as modifiers, at least in instances where they associate to a presentation, in an integral small clause. If semantic demands and, more generally, derivational nuances carry them to some different position, that is consistent with the proposal. What is crucial is only that these adjunctal elements not affect the finite-state pattern in (48c) for integral small clauses, and thus their entry to the derivation must be treated as an adjunctal affair. The proposal is predicting an asymmetry between integral small clause subjects (spaces) and corresponding predicates (presentations), which need not be present in identificational small clauses (involving two maximal projections, hence abandoned finite-state syntax) or even in regular predicational small clauses, where a DP – instead of a bare noun – is expected in the predicate site (to be matched against subsequent context-free criteria).

In other words, we expect differences as follows:

(56)   a. *Identificational*
            I proclaim [[George's son] [the next President of the US]]
        b. *Predicative (IL)*
            I consider [[George's son] [the worst kind of fool]]
        c. *Predicative (SL)*
            I saw [[George's son] [drunk beyond recognition]]
        d. *Integral*
            [George's son] has [t [(a) talent (for convincing voters)]]

(56a) involves an identificational small clause, where two maximal projections, each capable of sustaining reference, are associated in terms of syntactic pattern (49b) and a corresponding identificational semantics. (56b) and (56c) present two varieties of predicative small clauses, whose component elements are associated in terms of syntactic pattern (49c), and whose predicate is of the DP sort and the AP or PP sort, respectively. These categorial differences are not even observable at the first finite-state pass on these objects, which entails that

---

22 See Herburger (2000) for arguments against the mainstream view.

the distinction between (56b) and (56c) is not established until relevantly generated objects are sent to the context-free stage in the derivation – here unwanted possibilities will be filtered out, and viable ones will obtain further nuances in interpretation by mechanisms that we will not go into here. Finally, (56d) involves an integral small clause, whose subject undergoes 'possessor-raising' to subject position of the main clause. In finite-state terms, this small clause is not distinguishable from (56b) or (56c), each involving syntactic pattern (49c) but again; the context-free component can be sensitive to the fact that, in this instance, a bare N (which can have extra optional adjuncts) is in predicative position, constituting a presentation. In all of these instances, there are no particular restrictions on the subject of the small clause, at least not in terms of the syntactic object. We have DPs that can denote individuals, but nothing else. As a consequence, as we saw in section 5.5.3, this sort of element – even when it will not end up sustaining reference – always requires Case.[23]

We must say a word, also, on the non-uniform displacements from small clause subject to a real clausal subject.[24] Syntactically, the way to avoid this problem was outlined in section 3.6.3. We must destroy non-uniform chains, turning them into antecedent/gap relations where uniformity is not an issue (as no chain is involved). We also saw at that point that the mechanics for this entail an intermediate step of movement involving an erasable trace. In general, this step will exist simply if the small clause subject displacing moves through the position involved in its Case determination or some other intermediate step.[25] Moreover, the erasure in question will, in effect, *sever the connection* between the displaced small clause subject (which typically moves to a position with intentional consequences in the LF component) and its lexico-conceptual origin inside the small clause. This will be important in section 8.5, when we discuss the opacity of lexical specifications.

A predicate is customarily seen as a collection of individuals, in standard semantic theories. That view cannot be taken here, for three reasons. First, integral predicates are not individuals in any trivial sense,[26] thus these

---

23 Recall that the element remains a conceptual space throughout the derivation, into the interpretive components.

24 As in (56a); similar examples can be constructed, involving passive predicates, with all the other examples in (56).

25 For instance a preposition like *of*, or a participle site in a passive instance like *he was t considered t a fool*.

26 They are *parts* of individuals, and in instances we have not gone into, also *measures* of masses of the sort analysed in Castillo (2001), and possibly even more bizarre notions, as sketched in Uriagereka (2002, chapter 15).

predicates cannot be individual collections, nor for that matter collections of any obvious entities. Second, in the system defended here, and as argued for by Muromatsu (1998) and Castillo (2001), individuals themselves are very complex notions that involve, in their representation, precisely the sort of integral syntax we are now analysing. If the syntactic representation of individuals involves integral predication, the predication cannot, in its turn, be an individual collection. Third, the system presented here is meant to extend to verbal predicates, as the basis for a nuanced articulation of the sort explored by Mori (2005), capable of syntactically coding both Vendler-style verbal dimensions and corresponding lexical entailments. It seems unintuitive to take as individual collections the various predications involved in the several layers of something as complex as, say, *Jack built himself a house in the Alps.*[27] As a whole, *built himself a house in the Alps* holds of a collection of individuals including Jack; but what we cannot do in this system – as semantics does customarily – is treat that fact as a primitive, and furthermore one that speaks to the ontological status of *build*. Things bottom out in non-intentional terms. This point is defended by Hinzen (2006), where integral predication is shown to hold even in the relation between propositions and their putative truth, the very foundation – he argues – of linguistic judgements.

In the present view the lexico-conceptual predicates that constitute the head of a small clause are *primitive operations on mental spaces*. Space is a mathematical notion, which needs no further justification here – though see Hinzen and Uriagereka (2006) for a philosophical grounding of the idea. It would be fair to raise similar questions for the other sorts of primitives customarily assumed in semantics, namely individual and truth. What's interesting is that these notions can be manipulated mentally, in terms of what is being called a presentation in this book. That, in effect, is the closest notion to a predication in the present approach. Given a space of some dimensionality n and an operation on it, its dimensionality may be boosted in one degree.[28] In turn, and presumably up to some cognitive limit, that newly 'warped' space of $n+1$ dimensionality can be presented (thus 'warped') again, and so on. That way one obtains (access to)[29] abstract, mass, objectual,

---

27 Involving predications for integral relations between a house and a certain process, *that* predication and a certain location, *that* new predication and a certain beneficiary, *that* further predication and an agent and so on.

28 As in the observably 3D origami bird that one can make by cleverly folding a 2D piece of paper.

29 It is an open question for the present system whether the categories have some sort of Platonic reality of their own or they are rather constructed by the system as warps proceed.

animate objects in nominal spaces, or formally comparable states, activities, achievements and accomplishments in verbal spaces, a matter to be further discussed in section 7.4.4. There are individuals here, surely, but they are the result of some classificatory operation (Muromatsu 1998); they have a status comparable to that of bounded events like achievements. In either instance a mental operation does the appropriate delimiting, and *that* is a lexico-conceptual predication.

6.5   A brief note on adjuncts

If lexico-conceptual syntax is articulated as just suggested, a first cut for (some) adjunct dependencies is already in place, particularly if adjuncts are predicates of corresponding sub-events within a complex predicate, as in the Neo-Davidsonian project.[30] If so, (pure) adjuncts are, in effect, 'just there', in the dimensional cuts that lexico-conceptual syntax provides.

Recall our syntactic possibilities in (48). We got the most mileage out of (48c), given its asymmetry and the fact that we took the non-head (small clause subject) to go into interpretation first, thereby setting its own lexico-conceptual import as the semantic fate for the derivation. But now suppose that, given the sort of syntactic object in (48c), something has already gone to interpretation. One such scenario is presupposed in the multiple 'warpings' alluded to above for complex nominal or verbal spaces. Those all involve repetitions of a schema along the lines in (48).[31] The lexico-conceptual fate of the structure in (57), no matter how complex it gets (how many 'warps' we introduce via available presentations), is sealed off in terms of the denotation associated to $SPACE_1$; symbols '#' and '|' denote heads and maximal projections, respectively.

(57)
$$SC_2$$
$$\diagup \quad \diagdown$$
$$|SPACE_2| \quad \#PRESENTATION_2\#$$
$$\cdots$$
$$SC_1$$
$$\diagup \quad \diagdown$$
$$|SPACE_1| \quad \#PRESENTATION_1\#$$

---

30 For instance, Parsons' (1990) sub-events correspond to each of the 'warps' in the text, the ideas being compatible in the terms advocated by Pietroski (2005).

31 Although Case conditions will arguably demand this, it is now immaterial whether there is further structure between the stacking small clauses.

In that instance, the internal make-up of $SPACE_2$ gets complicated, as the latter is a convoluted version of $SPACE_1$. But the SPACE/PRESENTATION relation remains abstractly constant, in both instances. Compare that with the situation in (58).

(58)

$$
\begin{array}{c}
SC_2 \\
/\quad\backslash \\
|...|\quad |XP| \\
SC_1 \\
/\quad\backslash \\
|SPACE_1|\ \#PRESENTATION_1\#
\end{array}
$$

So far, (58) is just an identificational small clause, falling into sub-case (48b). The finite-state system itself cannot produce the (non-terminal) layers in the structure, but that can be achieved in two different ways, already explored: if the system generates a flat structure that gets filtered out upon reaching context-free syntax if it falls into an inappropriate combination, or if the non-terminal cuts in (58) correspond to derivational cycles. Now suppose we associate another YP, to add yet another layer, this time as in (59).

(59)

$$
\begin{array}{c}
SC_2 \\
/\quad\backslash \\
|...|\quad |XP| \\
/\quad\backslash \\
SC_1\quad |YP| \\
/\quad\backslash \\
|SPACE_1|\ \#PRESENTATION_1\#
\end{array}
$$

The issue is what the $(SC_1, |YP|)$ relation is. The situation is different from any of those sketched in (48). It may seem identical to (48b), but there is a significant difference: whereas the structure in (48b) is intended to associate two maximal projections, here a maximal projection, namely $|YP|$, associates to something that manages to be *neither* a head nor a maximal projection.

The finite-state system only allows for heads from the lexicon vs. 'the rest' – so it won't compute the subtlety in (59). But suppose that at the point of finite-state association, the relevant structuring is as in (60).

(60) $< |SC_1|, |YP| >$

This is a legitimate instance of (48b). The key, though, is not to send this to interpretation in the fashion of an identificational small clause, but to *continue with the structure active*, associating it further to $|XP|$ to yield (59). For that association to count as valid, we have to treat (60) as a unit – the $|...|$ in (59) – and the only way for that to happen is to go into the context-free syntax. Granted, if we forge ahead into that level of syntax with *both* dependents of $|\ldots|$, we will not be able to avoid an identificational relation between SC_1 and $|YP|$ – something we don't want. So we must send $|YP|$ to interpretation *without doing anything with SC_1 at this point*. That implies having a derivational memory buffer just for $|YP|$, since we will not be able to do anything with this element vis-à-vis SC_1, and thus its component elements, which the sentence will be articulated around. A simple way for the system to signal the fact that $|YP|$ is not 'skeletal' to the clause is by matching $|YP|$'s semantic transfer with its phonetic spell-out.

That matching will never occur in skeletal head/complement and similar dependencies. This is because skeletal dependencies enter into a command unit (CU), and a CU does not need to undergo early, and separate, spell-out in order to meet Kayne-style linearization demands: the very command relations map to linear phonetic ordering (what Uriagereka 1999 calls the linear correspondence theorem or LCT). As a consequence, the spell-out of a skeletal CU can happen much later than the sorts of semantic transfers that have been considered above, which the system introduces in order to come up with the various modes of association in (48). In contrast, non-skeletal dependencies create their own separate CUs, facing unique spell-out conditions. These come in two guises. On one hand, specifiers spell-out even when they have not transferred semantically;[32] in fact, given their characteristic role in theta and scope relations, it is fundamental that spelled-out specifiers should gear their semantic transfer in ways that are independent from their phonetic transfer – the phenomenon of 'reconstruction' introduced in section 1.5.1. On the other, in true adjuncts Spell-out and Interpret do go hand in hand, thus, for instance, predicting lack of 'reconstruction' effects in these sorts of categories (as argued by Freidin [1986] and Lebeaux [1988]). Later on, SC_1 in (59) will continue associating to other elements, in terms of whatever committed structure already existed in the CU part of the interpretation – that is, irrespective of $|YP|$'s fate, which is thus left to dwell in a 'different dimension'. $|YP|$ won't be wildly associated, however, because the system can keep track of the fact that it enters the derivation associated to the CU of SC_1, indeed sandwiched in between the transfer of SC_1's component elements and whatever comes in next associated to SC_2 in (59).

Similar issues arise for a simpler kind of modification obtaining for those adjectives whose semantic import is akin to that of compounds, one of whose

32 This was used as an argument, at the beginning of section 6.4.4, that Spell-out is different from Interpret.

possible sources is the dependency in (48a). Just as in structures of the form in (48b) – also involving trivial syntax – there is the possibility of storing a transferred element in a separate memory buffer, to treat it adjunctally when the syntax in (48a) is at issue; that should be behind direct head modifications, including the weak determiners mentioned in the previous section.

Modifiers manage to be interpreted as predicates, not on the ultimate reference of whatever they are predicated on, but rather *of its conceptual space*. For instance, suppose we are considering a structure as in (61a). Given everything said about argument-taking in chapter 3, and the further precisions raised in the preceding sections, the present approach is committed to a structure along the lines in (61b) (see Mori 2005 for much relevant discussion).

(61)   a. Send flowers rapidly to Mary.

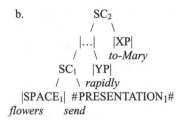

Several corners are being cut here, in terms of Case and agreement issues, complement assumption, and so forth. But the point is this: the structure in (61) ends up denoting (in a complete sentential structure) an event of flower-sending where Mary is the goal. Under the reading that interests us, that whole event need not be modified by *rapidly*, although surely the adverb is a syntactic modifier of the verb *send* or its projection;[33] the reading of concern now emerges in the modification *of the motion path* that the flowers must take, an activity whose *telos* will be Mary. The specific structural array in (61b) has the desired effect, as *rapidly* modifies only SC_1.[34] Modifiers of this sort always proceed in this way, being associated to lexico-conceptual structure of the sort introduced by a small clause, and not the ultimate intentional details that are brought about by quantificational structure

---

33 That is, we are setting aside at this point a putative reading whereby what has to be rapid is the entire state of affairs, from the onset of the sending order to Mary's reception of the flowers.

34 An alternative reading could arise with higher modification of SC_2, and so on, depending on structural details. See both Mori (2005) and Muromatsu (1998) for detailed discussions of this point with regard to adverbs and adjectives respectively, and Castillo (2001) for many related qualifications.

associated to higher formal heads. That directly means that their mode of semantic association cannot be regulated by the version of the Trivial Structure hypothesis discussed in chapter 3,[35] nor for that matter the P/W^2 thesis.[36] In fact, not even (strict) compositionality strictures hold for them, as the notion 'sister' makes little sense in finite-state terms. Intuitively, we want this type of modifier to be of the same sort as the simple individual predicate, holding of an individual event, that we witness in the paraphrase:

(62)   The (carrying) activity within the event of flower sending **was rapid**.

But as we saw above, in the present system individual predication turns out to be an elaborate notion. Perhaps one way to go about this matter is in terms of having, in this instance, an identification not of the predicates associated to their intentional fate,[37] but rather of the predicates *themselves*, as lexico-conceptual notions.[38]

6.6   Conclusions

This chapter has suggested that even the simplest, finite-state, scale in the Chomsky Hierarchy has a place in grammar, feeding the phrasal component which in turn feeds the transformational component. Moreover, having interpretation read finite-state structures seems desirable.

This was proposed, first, as a solution to the puzzle posed by cognitive grammarians with regards to the interpretive uniformity of iterative interpretation. This chapter reminded us that there is not much to interpret in these instances, and so different languages come up with similarly flat results. But that presupposes the interpretive legitimacy of finite-state representations. That said we may exploit these representations to solve other puzzles, especially those posed by small clauses and adjuncts more broadly. This is worth bearing in mind at a time when – perhaps too hastily – we take grammar to be

---

35 They also don't involve totally trivial syntax, at least not as trivial as identificational matchings.
36 These elements are added to the system at the finite-state level, where parts and wholes don't mean anything.
37 This results in intentional identification of the sort explored for identificational small clauses.
38 There are other adjectival dependencies that must be much more complex, for instance the comparative instances studied by Fults (2006). The existence of those does not challenge anything said so far, although it does pose very serious questions regarding the syntax needed to account for them; indeed, even non-restrictive relative clauses raise relatively similar issues, perhaps with less convoluted dependencies.

merely a pairing of sound and meaning. It might be impossible to *pair* those two sorts of representations, if meaning is an affair dealing, at one end, with context-sensitivity, and with finite-states at the other, then presupposing the context-free layer in between.

Finally, the fact that the suggested system must deploy articulated memory buffers, for offline storage of representations, doesn't automatically make the architectural organization proposed here identical to those that are weakly equivalent, in computational terms. In fact, strong generative capacity distinctions are what presumably results in various elements being interpreted in terms of different semantic modes, precisely because of the way in which the syntax articulates them. This is in the spirit of the co-linearity thesis, whether it is interpreted radically (these very syntactic nuances *construct* the relevant semantics) or conservatively (the semantics are made to *correspond*, in as natural a fashion as viable, to the articulated structures that the complex derivation yields).

7 (Re)Interpreting the Chomsky Hierarchy

7.1 Introduction

Having presented a broad empirical base, and a variety of mechanisms needed to deal with the distribution of meaning throughout the derivation, this chapter is devoted to clarifying the specific role that the Chomsky Hierarchy (CH) plays in the distributed interpretation thesis. After the classical CH is reviewed in section 7.2.1, section 7.2.2 suggests ways to revamp the hierarchy in more current terms. Section 7.3 discusses the relevance of the CH to the derivational theory of complexity, which becomes important again within the Minimalist Program. Section 7.3.1 shows how considerations of formal complexity in roughly the CH sense are often raised when it comes to the actual procedural workings of the grammar, and whether it is purely linear or somewhat parallel, and if so to what extent. Section 7.3.2 discusses some sophisticated experimental observations suggesting that the DTC is not only relevant to current theorizing, but possibly also a way to help us focus the broad program of syntax, where different theoretical alternatives are often reasonably entertained. This is seen in more detail in a case study on island conditions briefly sketched in section 7.3.3. Section 7.4.1 returns to the central concern of this book – how paradigmatic notions relate to complexity in syntax – and in section 7.4.2 the DIT is explicitly proposed. In order to find a way to relate syntactic and semantic structures naturally through the DIT, the project of 'naturalizing meaning' (more fully discussed in chapter 8), in section 7.4.3 the formal concept of a 'manifold' is introduced. Finally, section 7.4.4 deploys these manifolds to provide a scaffolding for Aktionsart, which is taken as the model story to be pursued in the last chapter. A brief set of conclusions is presented in section 7.5. These ideas have a formal, if still tentative, nature to them, and some readers may be more interested in jumping directly to the architectural consequences they have for the system at large, the topic of the last chapter.

7.2   The Chomsky Hierarchy redux

The CH is the only linguistic concept known in scientific circles outside the field. This can be misleading, as the hierarchy was originally stated by Chomsky (1956, 1958) in terms of *formal languages*, a notion (E-language) that Chomsky later abandoned (1986) in favor of the notion of a *generative procedure* (I-language). Let's first address this concern.[1]

7.2.1   *The classical CH*

In its classical formulation the CH classifies progressively less inclusive formal languages – that is, enumerated collections of linear expressions – and thus corresponding grammars (in italics).

(1)   a. Recursively enumerable languages (objects of any computational complexity) – *unrestricted grammars.*
       b. Context-sensitive languages (sets of symbol string sets) – *context-sensitive grammars.*
       c. Context-free languages (sets of symbol strings) – *context-free grammars.*
       d. Regular languages (strings of symbols) – *regular grammars.*

An expression is a structured object. In that sense, the CH as in (1) is of relatively little interest to the working linguist, as it pertains to the mere string formulas – the structure-less sequence of terminal items in the expression. Describing this is referred to as 'weak generation', but linguists are more interested in 'strong generation': the hierarchy, interrelations, implications and so on that articulate linguistic expressions. While 'weak generation' has no meaning in linguistics, 'strong generation' is taken, at least by some linguists, as a psychological or even biological phenomenon.

So the CH must be focused from a perspective that is sensitive to our strong generation concerns, for instance by considering another aspect of this hierarchy: the automata that generate the structures in (1). As such, those objects are mere mathematical constructs; however, it is useful to consider the devices that implement them computationally. Relevant automata have the same basic architecture, originally conceived by Alan Turing: *a logical processor* and *an unlimited memory tape*, these components interacting until the system halts. With that architecture in mind, it is important to evaluate the memory resources that algorithms implementing each of the grammars in (1)

---

1 Thanks to Bob Berwick, Tim Hunter, Howard Lasnik, Phil Resnik, Ed Stabler, and Mark Steedman for helpful discussion in clarifying these matters. Phil and I taught a seminar along these lines in the fall of 2007, where we address in more detail some of the concerns that are only sketched in the pages that follow.

require (how they access the memory tape). As alluded to in the introduction to this book, such memory limitations play a key role *in linguistic competence* (see Drury 2005).

Automata corresponding to the categories in (1) differ in their memory deployment. Finite-state automata (FSA) corresponding to regular grammars (1d) have no separate access to the memory tape. Pushdown automata (PDA) corresponding to context-free grammars (1c) can be seen as defining a stack within the tape, with a corresponding 'stack alphabet' (an inventory of symbols that go on the tape, e.g. non-terminals in familiar grammars). Moreover this *stack memory* has a storage/retrieval regime to it: it permits access only to the most recently stored symbol(s) in making decisions about what state to go to next. This isn't arbitrary: it reflects the idea that information is stored *over previously stored information*, and that there is a *current state* in the derivation; so the last material stored in the stack is used first because, in effect, it is the most accessible to this mode of storage. In contrast a linear bounded automaton (LBA), corresponding to context-sensitive grammars (1b), allows symbol manipulation through a less restricted regime: the automaton can probe *anywhere in the memory stack*, to an extent that is a linear function of the initial input's length; this means that an automaton of this sort is not directly restricted by limitations of its current state. Finally a Turing machine corresponding to an unrestricted grammar (1a) has no memory limitation: any manipulation of the memory tape is permissible. In sum, there are significant memory differences in terms of *how much more than just the mere states of the processor* the relevant devices are deploying (from nothing to indefinitely much, through some linear function of the input) and the *specific details of the access regime* (whether it is restricted in last-in-first-out fashion).

Such systemic memory differences have architectural consequences, affecting the strong generative capacity of the grammar each system supports. The difference between 'no' and 'some' memory access is what distinguishes *true recursion* (embedding anywhere in the structure) from so-called *head/ tail recursion* (embedding solely on either the beginning or the end of the structure, which is replaceable by mere iteration without significant information loss) – and distinguishes fully hierarchical representations in the general case. In turn having the 'last-in-first-out' restriction is what permits a symbol representing a phrasal constituent on the stack to include simultaneously information from outside and inside the constituent, thus allowing 'probing' into inner properties of the latter (context sensitivity). Moreover, the size of the memory alone takes us towards a structuring of any imaginable

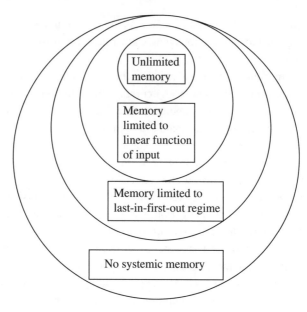

Figure 7.1. *Classes of structures generable with automata varying in memory resources*

(computable) complexity. So memory distinctions organize generative procedures as in (2), here presented in derivational fashion for concreteness.

(2)   a. A Turing machine presupposes unlimited memory, allowing all computable tasks.
       b. LBAs presuppose a derivational memory, allowing internal manipulations.
       c. PDAs presuppose a stack memory, allowing true recursion.
       d. Independent memory is orthogonal to FSAs, allowing only head/tail recursion.

Clearly, structures generated by these procedures imply one another. Structural properties described by more intricate devices presuppose those generated by lesser devices (Figure 7.1).

Chomsky demonstrated that natural languages are definitely context-free, and arguably context-sensitive, systems – of a restricted kind, according to later results. This demonstration was made using E-languages, but it can be adapted to I-languages. The adaptation may not have the force of a proof, but elements integrating I-language have to be high in the (revamped) CH. This is because the entire concept is built around the notion of (linguistic) 'structure', which implies true (not just mere head/tail) recursion, and thus some significant use of the memory tape – or some other memory encoding. Moreover structured objects (whatever that means beyond familiar territories) do not 'stop' there. According to results established by Gödel (1931), mathematics must certainly conceive of entities (e.g. the real numbers) that fall outside the classifications above, and thus are provably non-computable; it is anybody's guess whether I-language somehow includes such bizarre entities, at least in some of its fragments.[2]

7.2.2 Towards a revamped Chomsky Hierarchy

Work in linguistics in the 1960s spelled out these intricacies (in E-language terms) and attempted to show how the devices then proposed to deal with linguistic complexities were too unrestricted. This is worrisome if grammars have to be both placed in realistically limited human brains and moreover be non-inductively acquired. Thus many researchers in the computational literature, following the lead of Joshi (1985), limit grammars to those that are *mildly* context sensitive. Although mild context-sensitivity (MCS) does not have a precise mathematical definition, it involves characteristics that seem relevant to understanding the workings of the language faculty.[3] The MCS project has two active and ultimately different camps working on its specifics and/or extensions. The UPenn group starts with the PDA architecture and enriches the stack memory in various ways.[4] Instead of assuming the stack memory regime, the UCLA group focuses directly on Joshi's intuition that the grammar only needs a small number of elements 'waiting assembly' – and the issue is, then, how to determine that bound.[5] A third group of researchers,

---

2 See Langendoen and Postal (1984) on this topic and Uriagereka (2005) for a reconstruction of their argument restricted to a class of adjuncts in infinite regress situations involved in ellipsis.

3 A grammar is mildly context-sensitive if it involves, at least: (a) polynomial parsing complexity, (b) constant growth, and (c) limited crossing dependencies (see Stabler [2003] for a useful presentation).

4 For example, one particular implementation is the Linear Indexed Grammars (LIG) (Weir 1988). These grammars' automaton is the embedded or extended PDA, whose stack allows stacked-valued Fs, as opposed to finite bundles of features (atomic categories) as in the regular PDA (it is, in effect, a stack of stacks). LIGs are members of an infinite hierarchy of linear context-free rewriting systems (LCFRS), all of which are MCS. However, as Mark Steedman points out (personal communication), it is not clear that all MCS systems are LCFRS. Moreover, LIGs are only 'weakly adequate' for many standard constructions in language (i.e. they do not yield the usual structure). While this may mean that linguists need to rethink those structures (see Steedman [2007]), another possibility is that these are ultimately not the grammars that the field is after.

5 A recent example of this approach is outlined in Kobele (2006), which formalizes some aspects of the Minimalist Program and studies in detail the mechanics of copying, and what sort of memory

working at MIT with Robert Berwick, is not committed to an MCS architecture, but otherwise shares the same goals. For our purposes, it is not central
to decide which of these approaches is correct, if any, or whether a synthesis
is possible. What matters is that, in the end, a PDA for merely context-free
systems is 'too little', while an LBA for fully context-sensitive systems is 'too
much'. Within this still traditional perspective, we may call the sought-after
grammar the proverbial (still hypothetical) 'just right' system, and its
automaton a PDA+ (see fns. 4 and 5 for possibilities). The point is that a
PDA+ is an entity concrete enough for us to know that it involves more
systemic memory than a PDA, but less than an LBA. We see below and in
chapter 8 that this is a powerful assumption to make.

Some theoretical linguists moved in the direction of abstract systems to
describe generative procedures, rather than their formal outputs, by way of
analyzing and constraining rule schemata (see Boeckx and Uriagereka [2007]
for a summary). Much of the work going on within syntax can be described as
exploring *how local* context-sensitive dependencies are, or whether they are
subject to *last-resort* or *uniformity* conditions forcing transformations to be
motivated or conservative. This approach crystallized in the P&P (eventually
MP) approach, seen throughout this book, within which the classical CH
seemed irrelevant.

But considerations about the CH have formal force, and thus stand
regardless of whether one particular scientific discipline uses them. It is
possible that the notion 'grammatical sentence' does not correspond neatly to
the notion 'well-formed formula' of any (known) computational system.
Nonetheless, if talk about 'the computational system' in MP is meant non-
metaphorically, surely the relevant system will have well-formed formulas of
some sort. This is the case even for systems of the type explored here, where
simple algorithms can implement, say, feature checking, and produce a
legitimate 'well-formed formula'. Although this is perhaps not the same as a
sentence, understood as an object with psychological reality – a separate, and
difficult, issue. Now strictly speaking the entire CH has to be restated for
Merge procedures, as these are not based on concatenative mechanisms
yielding strings (recall the discussion in section 1.2.2). There is, however, no
clear reason to doubt that a formalization of the Merge-based system would

buffer this requires (recall the discussion in sections 6.4.2 and 6.4.3). The group is still working on
an automaton to implement these, in effect, extended MCS grammars. When specifically asked
about this question, Ed Stabler (personal communication) suggests that perhaps some version of
Villemonte de la Clergerie's (2002) thread automaton is the way to go.

fall outside the broad outline in figure 7.1, with versions of those automata designed to yield organized sets of sets, instead of sets of strings, but otherwise involving progressively more complex memory limitations as more nuanced manipulations of the structures become necessary.

It is hard to know how much the classical Turing architecture will ultimately have to be finessed to yield non-concatenative procedures as the base of the formal system. One possibility is to give up the idea of the memory repository as a tape, and think of it, instead, as *an organized set*, on analogy with the number plane. Chomsky (2006, p. 6) seems to imply as much:

> Suppos[ing] that a language has the simplest possible lexicon: just one LI [lexical item], call it 'one'. Application of Merge to the LI yields {one}, call it 'two'. Application of Merge to {one} yields {{one}}, call it 'three'. Etc. In effect, Merge applied in this manner yields the successor function. It is straightforward to define addition in terms of Merge (X, Y), and in familiar ways, the rest of arithmetic.

If that is the right base for the system, the issue is how to 'write on a memory tape' the results.[6] The question applies more generally for numbering computations: how are they mentally stored? Nobody knows, but it is certainly possible to imagine a sound storage in non-linear terms.[7] There may be a temptation to think that mere time, real time – which the computation occupies as the physical procedure that it is, and as we have seen affects its 'current state' – already forces linearity. However, that begs a question that, strictly, is prior: whether mental computations in the brain are in some sense

---

6 Keep in mind that, strictly, the results of standard arithmetic cannot all be written on a line. In particular, the roots of negative numbers a fortiori fall outside the number line, and 'rooting' is one of the inverse operations of squaring (which in turn is an extended form of multiplication, itself an extended form of addition), while negative numbers themselves arise by way of a direct inverse of addition.

7 As a matter of fact, for complex numbers (emerging via the procedures alluded to in the previous note) to be (systematically) mentally manipulated and stored, non-linear representations would be required. That, however, raises arcane issues regarding the mental representation of non-computable structures, of the sort alluded to in fn. 2. All that matters now is that memory representation in linear terms is merely assumed, and of course describes the way a standard calculator works – no more, no less. It is known that computational power doesn't change even if non-linear representation for memory is assumed, so long as computational rule application is strictly sequential. Similarly, computational power doesn't increase with (even massively) parallel computation, if the memory representation remains linear. The question is what happens when computation is allowed to run in parallel *and* memory representation is allowed to be non-linear. The resulting device is still a computer and more powerful than the usual one. But this brings us into matters of so-called hyper-computation that we cannot go into.

parallel, even massively so, resulting in a sort of memory that, for lack of a better image, constitutes some kind of *slate*, as opposed to a mere linear tape. Be that as it may, if 'Merge-memory' is more multi-dimensional than the linear metaphor would lead us to believe, it is reasonable to expect the revamped CH to be implementing memory limitations that are based on weaker set-relations instead, which arguably moves us in the direction of topology, as discussed below.

It may seem as if the finite-state procedures discussed in chapter 6 a fortiori fall outside a Merge-based CH – but this need not be the case, and exploring the matter gives us a hint as to how the revamped CH ought to be conceived. All we have to do, to integrate those structures into the current system, is to consider them (label-less) *sets* instead of strings, disregarding linear ordering among the structured elements. This will yield no structuring among the collected elements other than being 'in the same set'. But that's what we expect, first, of items in a Numeration – and recall that plausibly the Numeration is where we want to assume the finite-state component to be.

In addition, we have discussed three other arguably attested finite-state procedures: looped materials, small clauses and modification. The last two are straightforward inasmuch as, as we saw in chapter 6, they involve binary dependencies, either of a symmetrical or an asymmetrical sort. If the former, their trivial syntax will correspond to an equally trivial semantics (see section 8.2.1); importantly, ordering among the relevant items will not be decidable, leading to characteristic 'reversibility' of the sort Higgins (1979) observed for such constructions as 'James Bond, 007', which is equivalent to '007, James Bond'. Strictly, in situations of this sort the issue would not be obtaining one structure from the other, as there is no structuring the system can assume as 'more basic', and both linearizations surface with roughly equal probability, i.e. randomly.[8] In turn, for asymmetrical constructions of the modificational or small clausal sort, precisely that asymmetry – which as we saw in sections 6.4 and 6.5 is achieved only upon halting finite-state computation – is what determines the appropriate articulation for the expression. Finally, in looped structures a set vs. string status won't make a difference for single-symbol loops (the dotted loop represents the generation of an unordered set).

---

8 A recent count in Google shows 'James Bond, 007' 1,940,000 times and '007, James Bond' 580,000 times. Granted, that will include many unwanted combinations with these expressions, but these should average out in both instances. The important point is that these are not overwhelming numbers for either expression, and the tilt for one order over the other seems more pragmatic than syntactic.

(3)   a.

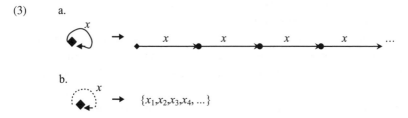

b.

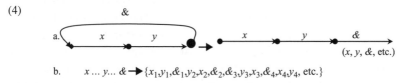

Differences will emerge, however, for multiple symbol-loops, as (4a) and (4b) show.

(4)

a.

b. $x \dots y \dots \& \rightarrow \{x_1, y_1, \&_1, y_2, x_2, \&_2, \&_3, y_3, x_3, \&_4, x_4, y_4,$ etc.$\}$

Plainly, the multiple symbols within the loop will not be ordered in a Merge-based system that disregards strict concatenation. That, however, is not a problem if the ensuing structure will have to be filtered out by the phrase-structure component, as discussed in section 6.4.2. First, the demands of linearization, to be reviewed in sections 7.3.2 and 7.4, will require that all tokens of the looped material be consistently ordered. Moreover, relevant parameters in the language, stated at the phrasal component, will determine which of the possible orders obtain.

These are subtle matters, to be addressed elsewhere, but one thing is certain: The ensuing formal system will yield restricted structures, although the restrictions will come from slightly different directions vis-à-vis the traditional system. For example, in the classical theory the order of rule application – assumed by fiat – will yield certain articulations already. Now, it is not that there is no ordering in the new, Merge-based, system. First, the application of the operation itself will entail a given structure, which will be different depending on what particular associations obtain (intuitively, *the man saw Mary* does not have the same shape as *Mary saw the man*). Moreover, systemic cyclicity will also impose a characteristic ordering crucially so, to define given stable objects (e.g. 'non-heads' of a finite-state sort, as we saw in section 6.5, but also domains of Case specification, as we saw in chapter 5 and will review again shortly, and surely other complex long-distance dependencies of the 'subjacent' sort). That said, how exactly this ordering works, how much parallel computation it leads to, and precisely how the ensuing representations are stored in some memory space, are anybody's guesses.

Appropriately abstract versions of the CH should probably be neutral as to what particular formulation of phrase structure and related details is assumed. The traditional construct was observed in terms of concatenation algebras, in particular the rewrite and transformational grammars formulated in Chomsky (1955) and subsequent work (e.g. Lasnik and Kupin 1977). The discussion in the preceding paragraphs, instead, assumes set-theoretic objects of the sort Merge deploys, basically suggesting that a set of categories without any further specifications ought to be treated in finite-state fashion, for constructions of the relevant sort (loops, adjuncts and so on). If, in turn, we code a certain asymmetry into the Merge operation, having one structure 'project' (keeping its type for further computation, as a label in the system), then we would be facing an instance of 'external' Merge (EM), intuitively a context-free process inasmuch as it creates, in the current state of a grammar, a set with any elements A and B selected for phrasal association. That operation demands a memory stack of some kind, as is clear when it involves the association of two complex operands (the equivalent of 'true embedding', (5)). Each of the operands will bear whatever formal complexity it already brings to the subsequent association, and that has to be represented somewhere in the computation, particularly because it affects how the subsequent association ensues – that is, what projects.[9]

(5)   External Merge (EM) (with projection of A)

$$\{A\{A, B\}\}$$

A ←⌐→ B
[independently   [independently
merged]   merged]

'Internal' Merge, IM, can in contrast be shown to be an (arguably mild) context-sensitive process. This may not be obvious, since in this kind of Merge the elements A, B that enter into a set are such that B is contained within some sister element C. But that's the key: A must *search* within C to

---

9 This view is not the one taken in Chomsky (2004) and related papers, for which (following Collins [2002]) Merge is taken not to invoke labeling/typing, but mere set-theoretic association between syntactic objects (see section 7.3.1). Hornstein *et al.* (in press) question that view, following Chametzky (2000) and Uriagereka (1998, 2002) in taking only adjuncts to bear no labels. Hinzen (in press) suggests that the recursive, set-theoretic, system just discussed, without label/types, is best suited for adjunct description. In what follows the notation in Chomsky (1995, chapter 4) will be used (as discussed in Uriagereka [1998]), with representation in projected structures of both the constituents of the relation and the label that projects – when this happens. It will be assumed, in contrast, that pure adjuncts *do not involve either labels or projection*.

find B, which is nowadays typically executed (e.g. Chomsky 2004) through an Agree mechanism, involving a Probe with unvalued features that must match a Goal in an appropriately local configuration with the necessary values. That process requires access to the inner components of a derivational memory stack, or something in that league (and see fns. 4 and 5).

(6)   Internal Merge (IM) (with projection of B)

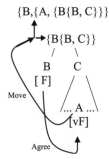

Of course, not having precisely characterized the ('spatial'?) memory tape in Merge systems, it is unclear exactly what it is that is being manipulated in instances of this sort. But it is obvious that, whatever it is, it must peek into material that is 'within the previously merged structure', and in that sense it forces the system an access to the online computation, beyond its current state, that EM doesn't demand. To put it in terms of an arithmetic metaphor, this sort of operation is analogous to, say, complex addition. One can directly add two small numbers, but to add two large numbers we typically proceed by recording partial additions (of the units, the tens, etc.), and 'carrying them through' to the next step in the computation. That requires an extra step of memory that, at least for arithmetic, demands explicit writing from most of us. What extra machinery is demanded for syntactic computations is hard to ascertain at this point of our research, but it is logically presupposed in the computation. Be that as it may, note also that, because of the intricate operations in (6), the resulting object is strictly not a phrase marker, but a more elaborate entity with the category A distributed over two separate derivational contexts (one associated to C and one to B).[10] We return to this in section 7.4.

10 This is true regardless of which notation is used, whether it is transformations as is being assumed here or some form of information transfer, of the sort implied in other generative systems. The phenomenon of 'discontinuous constituency' is just factual, and it presupposes the extra memory resources now being discussed.

Bear in mind that the discussion of the automata in (2) is theoretical: these are not concrete algorithms, but *limitations on how to conceive relevant structuring in a computational fashion*. Many actual machines can be devised within the limits seen here, which adds more nuances to present consider- ations – if ultimately the goal is to *embody* some such device within human brains. What neuro/psychological implementation may the abstract memory regimes just alluded to have? What is a 'current state' of a derivation for a brain, and what does it mean to manipulate *prior states* thereof? It is possible that, for example, what psychologists call 'procedural' memory is involved in what is being referred to as 'derivational' memory.[11]

In sum, a revamped presentation of the hierarchy as in Figure 7.1 should be useful, if abstractly compatible with the classical formulation, but not involving the specific objects (formal languages) that look questionable as models of human language. Seen from the perspective of the generative procedure or the automaton supporting it, the CH (or a modified version in terms of Merge) is just a nice way to characterize the sorts of mechanisms involved in entangling linguistic structures. If it is not stipulated that the outputs of the computation – formal languages in their own right – are human languages,[12] it seems both innocuous and profitable not to give up the structural insight we obtain as a result of the exercise. At the very least, proceeding this way – taking formal assumptions seriously – will allow us to disregard hypotheses that look too unconstrained, or reduce results whose equivalence can be demonstrated, particularly at the level of strong generative capacity (e.g. the grammar/automata correspondences above).

7.3   The derivational theory of complexity redux

The hypothesis that the number of operations the grammar uses to generate a sentence should correlate with appropriate psycholinguistic measures was once known as the derivational theory of complexity (DTC). Famously, it

---

11 Ullman and Pierpont (2005) characterize *procedural memory* as both inaccessible to consciousness and concerned with the operational workings of rules, whereas *declarative memory* is somewhat accessible to consciousness and concerned with lexical retrieval in general.

12 In retrospect, this was a bizarre assumption to make: that the outputs of machines conceived by Turing and formally refined by Chomsky, via the work of other logicians, when manipulating words from a lexicon should precisely coincide with the psychologically real notion of a sentence in a language. It's possible, but it would be as extraordinary as if something like that happened for, say, stable compounds in chemistry.

was attacked by Fodor *et al.* (1974), which summarized current psycho-linguistic results (during the historical time of both the turmoil surrounding the Chomsky Hierarchy, presented above, and also the aftermath of the Linguistic Wars, reviewed in chapter 2) and argued that they were 'not explicable within the constructs manipulated by formal linguistics' [p. 369]. Needless to say, there are lots of presuppositions in the old DTC that do not hold any longer. To start with, the transformational grammar that Fodor *et al.* discuss is considerably more cumbersome, and removed from psychological and biological plausibility, than one would want to think the present system is. It should be emphasized, then, that what is about to be reviewed is quite neutral with respect to which particular implementation, at least within the broad span of minimalism, turns out to be preferable. The notions of what is an 'individual computational step', and how much 'computational action' it involves vis-à-vis alternative ones, and whether any of this depends on the 'representational weight' involved, and moreover whether partial results add up to further 'computational complexity', are surely delicate matters – particularly so when one intends to think of them in terms of how an organism embodies them in its brain. But it is clear where the logic of the proposal is taking us, and it should thus be explored, no matter how tentatively.

7.3.1   *Conditions on rule application and derivational complexity*
Considerations about formal complexity, while dismissed for theorizing about grammatical structures, tacitly remained within linguistics throughout the decades, albeit at a higher level of abstraction – in terms of whether or not the grammar 'is Markovian'. Technically, if probabilities are added to transitional stages in a finite-state automaton, Markovian sources ensue (although probabilistic issues will not be important here). The consideration of whether a generative device is Markovian does not involve the outputs of the grammar, but rule application itself.

Aside from the paradigms reviewed already in section 1.5.2, one other instance involving non-Markovian conditions in grammar, entirely central to the proposals in this book, was shown in chapter 5. We saw how (verbal) Case hierarchies separate a *first* (accusative) and the *rest* of Case values, and how among the latter, there is a designated *last* Case (nominative) and a *default* Case (dative, which appears on several types of nominals). First and last Cases are such *within derivational cycles*. Although Case valuation has configurational consequences, it cannot be defined in any non-circular way, bottom-up in a phrase marker: the 'second Case up' may be dative or nominative depending on what other Case values have taken place within a given cycle. The first/last 'Case points' within cycles are subject to value parameterization, unlike undefined default valuations. So Case valuation has to be *causally correlated to cyclicity*, which entails that the grammar responsible for it must have at least enough memory, and of the relevant sort, to contemplate an active cycle and make comparative decisions within it. The determination of grammatical conditions via such 'open cycles' was also used in section 6.5 to determine architectural specifications for adjuncts.

Those are all considerations about I-language, not E-language; what is at stake is the *procedure* responsible for generating linguistic observables, not the observables themselves. Here, too, we see that (some) layers of the CH are relevant, and furthermore that language is nothing like a simple list, in this instance of rule applications. At times rules, procedures or representations are considered in parallel, a hallmark of non-Markovian/finite-state processes requiring systemic memory. Nobody knows whether the best way of representing *the workings of a grammar* – say, whether it obeys Chomsky's (1955), one-at-a-time, Traffic Convention on rule application – is specifically in terms of a formal language, or rather, for instance, in the terms alluded to above for a Merge grammar. It is not even obvious that the ultimate issue should be to *represent* these notions, the way symbols can be said to be represented in a computer. Present science cannot specify what relation exists between the notions the mind operates with (words like *book* or processes like anaphoric binding) and the brain that supports them. We do not even have a good idea as to how presupposed forms of memory obtain in brains, as Gallistel (2008) reminds us. However, that limitation doesn't make the relevant notions (symbol, process, (kinds of) memory, and so on) any less real, psychologically, biologically or physically, nor would a clever formalization make them more so. This is all to say that the sense of 'hierarchy' we are now implying when discussing the CH has a deliberate vagueness to it. One wants to capitalize on the formal results of the past, so that implicit entailments can be said to have mathematical force, from which ultimately provable consequences can be extracted. Then again, the moment we move in the direction of I-language, unfortunately, we lose track of the rigor that came together with E-language notions. Such is life.

Marantz (2005) pointedly observes that an expected, yet regrettable, result of the dialogue between classical generative grammar and the psycholinguistics developed at the time is the rejection of the DTC. That rejection must be rethought if minimalist presuppositions are embraced. As Marantz puts it, 'in every psycholinguistic experiment, the mechanisms of the computational system should be evident' [p. 439] and in fact:

> linguists really have no choice but to embrace the [DTC] since it's essentially just a name for standard methodology in cognitive science and cognitive neuroscience. All other things being equal, the more complex a representation – the longer and more complex the linguistic computations necessary to generate the representation – the longer it should take for a subject to perform any task involving the representation and the more activity should be observed in the subject's brain in areas associated with creating or accessing the representation and with performing the task.

This is essentially because, given minimalist assumptions, the only cognitive procedure that the language faculty uses is syntax; the rest is really interpretive (whether it exists independently and the syntax has to interface it, or it is actually a direct reflection of the syntax itself). That said, the considerations posed above about Merge systems and the sort(s) of memory they presuppose become all the more real. The DTC forces us to track complexity – computational complexity that is – on the basis of syntactic steps. But what is the measuring stick?

We cannot assume by fiat that it is the wonderful architecture Alan Turing assumed 70 years ago, at least in all its details regarding its memory tape and the output of concrete computations, simply because it may affect the relevant calculation. Relations between symbols organized in a very long list may be quite different – and more or less costly – than relations among symbols organized in some other array of dependencies, in some set-theoretic shape, particularly if multiple manipulations of those symbols can run in parallel (see fn. 7). We just don't know, not yet. Granted, exploring alternatives, and in particular forms of computational memory of a more topological sort – whatever that means (and see below) – will require tough formal analysis which may take a generation to obtain. But we cannot blindly place ourselves in the position of, as it were, looking for the keys only where the light shines.

7.3.2   Experimental examples

A couple of examples may make these ideas concrete. Phillips and Wagers (2007) review psycholinguistic evidence on the status of gaps, which the theory situates at the base of syntactic procedures of familiar sorts, yielding displacement. Standard evidence consists of information about the timing of such long-distance dependencies, which happens in rapid, active, top-down, fashion – without the human parser waiting for unambiguous evidence of the gap's position. (Instead of waiting, the parser posits a gap at the first position compatible with the lexico-semantic conditions of an identified antecedent.) This allows experimenters to test relevant structures by providing actual 'filler' in predicted gap sites, which typically creates a parsing disruption, or 'filled-gap effect', measured through a variety of techniques. The timing of long-distance dependency formation provides indirect evidence of how such relations are grammatically encoded. Interestingly, event-related potential (ERP) brain studies show how processing of the verb that successfully allows completion of, in particular, a Wh-dependency elicits a posterior positivity vis-à-vis control instances (involving the same verb unrelated to one such dependency). This takes place roughly 600 milliseconds after the relevant measuring point, a marker which is typically associated with syntactic reanalysis. Phillips *et al.* (2005) interpret the timing in these results to mean that long-distance dependencies are formed as soon as an appropriate verb (which theta-selects the appropriate gap) is encountered.

That is consistent with the theoretical matters examined here. Positing a gap is more costly (for a parser) than not. But as Phillips and Wagers observe, this evidence is inconclusive for the purposes of the kind of complexity we're interested in, as it might be due to specific parsing considerations, as opposed to the complexity of the relevant structures themselves. An interesting twist to this discussion is added by the results in Pablos *et al.* (2005), which show effects similar to the ones just mentioned emerging in relations of the clitic left-dislocation sort – that is, between a topic element in the left-periphery of the clause and a clitic element. In other words, it would appear that the effect in question emerges regardless of whether the resolution of the long-distance dependency is specifically a gap, or is instead a feature bundle.

A more controversial study gives us a finer gauge for the structural model sketched above. In the previous section we examined external and internal Merge, suggesting they obtain at different levels of the (revamped) CH, the latter presupposing the architecture of the former. If so, all other things being equal, parsing calculations involving IM should be more costly than calculations involving EM, again assuming that parsing complexity does track grammatical complexity. The results in Saddy and beim Graben (2002) can be interpreted precisely along these lines. These involve the processing of minimally different German sentences containing Case-ambiguous initial noun phrases, whose format is Nominative or Accusative.

(8) a. *Number condition*
        Welche Frau **besuchten** die Richter?
        which woman[sng] (amb) visit[pl] the judges[pl] (amb)
        'Which woman did the judges visit?'
     b. *Case condition*
        Welche Frau besuchte **der Richter**?
        which woman[sng] (amb) visited[sng] the judge[sng] (nom)
        'Which woman did the judge visit?'

Note that the plural verb disambiguates the sentence in (8a) ('the number condition'), whereas in (8b) the last NP in the nominative format does ('the case condition'). Although these stimuli involve displaced phrases (*welche Frau*, 'which woman'), and thus a complexity of the sort relevant to 'filler-gap' effects, what is important in determining the appropriate structuring is different. First, these are ambiguous structures, which arise because morphological conditions in German allow for multiple readings, and because in fact the sentences involve displacement, thus destroying the possibility of directly assigning phrasal dependencies based on word order. That said, the gap is not what matters for this experiment, but some other ingredient in an ambiguity resolution that depends on one of the possible morphological specifications in the sentence. As it turns out, the grammatical dependency that this extra ingredient carries (whether Number concord or Case agreement) is very relevant to the experimental measurements. Table 7.1 below summarizes evoked brain responses, measured *at the disambiguating point*, for both the Number and the Case conditions. The measure referred to as 'voltage average' is the standard in ERP analysis, indicating voltage increments over a base line; the

Table 7.1 *Different measures of ambiguity resolution effects*

Post-stimulus time windows	200 ms Cylinder entropy	Voltage average	400 ms Cylinder entropy	Voltage average	600 ms Cylinder entropy	Voltage average
Number condition	Increase	No effect	Increase	No effect	Decrease	Positivity
Case condition	Decrease	No effect	Increase	No effect	Increase	No effect

time-windows of 200, 400, and 600 ms. refer to post-stimulus so-called peak-latencies, which have been independently determined to provide grammatical markers linked to particular brain activity. The measure called 'cylinder entropy' is more interesting, and new to this study. Without getting technical, this non-linear technique measures signal coherence at any given point, and this is inversely proportional to signal complexity. Beim Graben and Saddy show, first, that this method is sensitive to the usual markers; but also that more sensitive measurements are possible. Observe how, although voltage average effects obtain in Table 7.1 in the Number condition, as expected, 600 ms after the measuring point (this being the canonical 'syntactic reanalysis' marker), surprisingly no such circumstance can be observed for the Case condition, with that standard technique. In contrast, calculation of the more elaborate cylinder entropies finds effects for *both* conditions in the three time windows identified in ERP research. The pattern of responses for the two conditions is nearly complementary: early entropy increase and late entropy decrease in the Number condition vs. the opposite for the Case condition.

Such are the facts as reported. What can we make of them? Competence-wise, in terms of Chomsky's Probe/Goal analysis presupposed in the Agree dependency (the prerequisite for internal merge), T is centrally involved in the resolution of both ambiguities in (8) (bear in mind that in German T is displaced to the C head, the 'verb second' effect). This is obvious in (8a), where the agreement head signals the mismatch with the first noun phrase in the sentence. But even in (8b), where the mismatch is discovered only when hitting the nominative noun phrase, the T head is fundamental, as it determines the checking of this sort of Case – in a roundabout fashion.

(9)   a. *Number condition*
       'Which woman did the judges visit?'

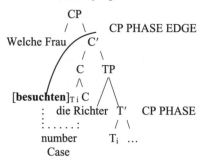

b. *Case condition*

'Which woman did the judge visit?'

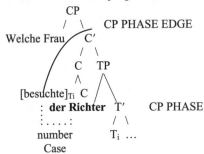

So it seems that the system senses upon hitting *besuchten* in (8a), that it is dealing with an agreement relation that does not involve the already parsed *Welche Frau*. This is not true in (8b): only when the lower, nominatively marked, *der Richter* is parsed does the system detect that agreement on *besuchte* is to be with this element. In other words, in the first of these instances Case/agreement matters are resolved *as the edge of the CP phase is parsed*, whereas these matters are not resolved in the second instance *until processing of the core of the CP phase* takes place.

Those differences in phase parsing seem to have a result in the system's 'action': there is patently more in the Case condition than in the Number condition. In (8b) all relevant Probe/Goal parsing decisions involving Case and agreement can be taken at the upper, first-parsed, CP phase edge. The system will expect a Goal to match the appropriate features expressed in the displace Probe *besuchten*, which is inconsistent with the already parsed *welche Frau*; this expectation is directly met when *die Rechter* is found at the core of the CP phase. In contrast in (8b) similar decisions have to both involve that very CP edge phase (where the Probe for the relations is, this time, *besuchte* – which is compatible with the already parsed *Welche Frau*) and wait until parsing of the lower core CP phase starts; there the disambiguating Goal for the relation, namely the nominatively marked *der Richter*, will force the parser to reconsider a putative association between *Welche Frau* and *besuchte*. Now could this systemic 'action' correlate with the quantity that Saddy and beim Graben were measuring? The observed entropy-modulation changes in the signal happen in grammatically significant contexts – indeed within the time frames of previously observed ERP markers. Surely the data, even if significant, could turn out to be as intrinsically neutral as the very polarity of 'peak latency' is in other evoked brain responses (in short, neurolinguists do not know why they find, say, specifically negativity at 400 milliseconds or specifically positivity at 600). But increases in signal entropy could also be correlating with pre-resolution activity, and posterior decreases in this quantity with 'pattern establishment', in a significant syntactic sense.

A skeptic might say that we could merely be witnessing a refined, yet perfectly standard, information-entropy effect (in roughly the sense this term gets in information studies, that advancing in a signal normally clarifies its contents, reducing its entropy – see Cover and Thomas (2006). However, if mere information-entropy were at stake, it is unclear why we should have the *asymmetries* in (8). For the Number condition, the shape of the entropy curve does make some sense in traditional information-theoretic terms: after hitting the key for resolving the ambiguity, entropy increases, and then decreases. The problem is that, information-entropy-wise, why should the Case condition exhibit *an inverse entropy curve*, if here too the matter involves ambiguity resolution, and thus sheer 'information clarification'? What's more, something, apparently against the logic of information-entropy, happens already at 200 milliseconds, with *entropy dropping* there – almost as if the system were preparing itself for some action, to be executed in the ensuing few milliseconds. Patterns of this sort cannot be easily explained away, and suggest a very intricate system in action, of roughly the sort presupposed here: *more complexity within the CH appears to yield more systemic action.*

The analysis of the previous case study has the advantage that it involves fairly well-studied syntactic systems, although it does present the disadvantage that the experimental results are based on a class of analytical techniques for brain signals that is not yet widely applied in psycholinguistic research. So, in short, more classical studies, of the sort reviewed before in this section, are arguably too vague to prove the point of interest here, and cutting-edge research is in need of serious replication before it can be used as decisive evidence. But this ought to give readers a flavor of what awaits us if we take seriously some appropriate version of the DTC, coupled together with some appropriately revamped version of the CH. These two projects should probably feed off one another, as Phillips and Wagers (2007) reasonably suggest. One last example easily makes this point, and deserves a separate section.

7.3.3   Integrating island constraints

Discontinuous dependencies do not happen between arbitrarily distant antecedent/gap relations. Concretely, aside from 'minimality' considerations of the sort reviewed in section 3.3, so-called 'islands' of the sort first analysed by Ross (1968) also prevent said dependencies. The question is what this follows from, and two broad traditions have been developed: one blames islands on computational efficiency concerns; the other on interactions between the syntactic computational machinery and the systems it interfaces with. Indeed, Hornstein *et al.* (2007) suggest that the phenomenon is so intricate that both perspectives may well be right for different sorts of islands.

This is not the place to address such concerns, but it is worth emphasizing that, once again, new experimental evidence, as well as cleaned-up assumptions about computational architecture, may help us focus that important sub-field, in the process grounding various nuances of the underlying representations. For instance, Phillips (2006) shows that the parser treats a sub-class of subject islands as non-islands, despite judgements confirming that speakers interpret subject islands as unacceptable. Phillips connects the fact that the parser ignores these subject islands with the fact that they may contain a so-called parasitic gap under certain circumstances.

(10)   a. *What did the attempt to repair __ ultimately damage the car?
        b. What did the attempt to repair the car ultimately damage __?
        c. What did the attempt to repair __ ultimately damage __?

As its well-formedness relies upon the presence of another gap, the first gap in (10c) is considered 'parasitic' on the second, or 'real gap' (cf. the grammatical (10b) and the ungrammatical (10a), when the 'real gap' has been filled). Examples like (10c) are interesting for real-time processing, because they are key to showing how a sentence parse that goes all the way up to *what did the attempt to repair* cannot, there and then, assume a grammaticality decision as to the fate of the rest of the sentence – it may end up being grammatical, as in (10c), but then again it may not, as in (10a). So if, from the point of view of the parser, the subject fragment of (10a) cannot be summarily declared ungrammatical, the ultimate ungrammaticality of the sentence cannot be just a matter of on line computation. More generally, then, the source of unacceptability for all islands cannot be parsing failures alone, and some formal account is necessary.

Facts like (10a) were first systematically observed in Huang (1982), and have been given minimalist explanations in various pieces reviewed by Stepanov (2007). Curiously, whatever the source of this sort of island is, it cannot extend to dependencies as in the left-dislocated *this damn car, the attempt to repair it ultimately damaged the entire garage*, which of course involves a structure relevantly similar to that in (10a). Why is an antecedent/ gap dependency disallowed across an island, while a corresponding binding relation is fine? Cases of standard left-dislocation (as opposed to clitic left-dislocation, mentioned in the previous section) might be explained away suggesting that, perhaps, they do not even involve a grammatical dependency, relevant co-reference (between the antecedent and the gap) then ensuing pragmatically. This, however, is dubious, given the fact that quantifiers bind into variables inside subjects, as in *no linguist wants that criticisms of his or her work should appear in print*. The relation between *his or her* and *no linguist* is quite nuanced, distributive in standard terms. Then again, the mere fact that the variable can be *his or her* – which involves complex lexical relations and possibly an intricate phrasal structure – directly suggests that whatever dependency is going on here is not of the standard context-sensitive (e.g. transformational) sort, and its intricacies for some reason do not invoke familiar locality restrictions of the island sort.[13]

Uriagereka (1999) accounts for that difference in terms of taking chain-formation relations to be standardly cyclic, while approaching bound-variable binding as a post-cyclic phenomenon that does not involve articulated syntactic terms in a phrase marker, but mere free range terms within a structure to be interpreted. This is based on an idea of cyclicity alluded to in sections 4.4.1 and 5.4.1, which works with 'command units' of the sort emerging when Merge is allowed to proceed as the derivation unfolds. Basically, every time the system must halt the 'spinal' derivation (mounted through monotonic applications of Merge without ever invoking new phrasal structures, proceeding instead with mere head selection), a new command unit emerges. In turn, said units cannot undergo standard linearization into the PF component, and the system must treat them, effectively, as compounds of sorts, which results in their islandhood as their phrasal scaffolding is destroyed by the process of Spell-out. Importantly, though, while the inner structural guts are thus destroyed, the basic building blocks remain, as perfectly definable syntactic terms.[14] So although a relation that requires all those structural specifications – typically, a context-sensitive one in need of precisely

---

13 Although the dependency is still subject to one form of locality. It only holds under c-command conditions:

(i)　　　　*[no linguist] mother wants that his or her work (the linguist's) be criticized in print.

14 Given Chomsky's 'bare' phrase structure assumptions (1995, chapter 4), a root-syntactic object is a term and, inductively, a term is also a member of a member of a term – while a mere member of a term is a label. When linearizing a set-theoretic syntactic object $\{a, \{ a, \beta \}\}$ into a sequence $<a, \beta>$, formally equivalent to $\{\{a\}, \{a, \beta\}\}$, the labels disappear, but a and β are still identified as terms – even though the new, linearized, object is not defined as a phrase marker any longer.

identifying derivational contexts – will not survive the 'flattening' of the complex structure, a looser dependency will pose no particular difficulties if it must merely ascertain that a given term exists within a surviving structure (here, a pronoun to be the object of binding within a given domain).

But precisely how is that dependency expressed within the system? Does the language faculty, in instances of binding, merely record the fact that a given domain contains an unstructured 'term soup', one of whose loose chunks can be made to correspond to an antecedent that must semantically distribute over its meaning as a variable? Is that enough? And what sort of memory records things that way, without carefully listing them? Recall in this regard how it was suggested in section 7.2.2 above that 'Merge memory' may well be quite different from what Turing tapes would lead us to expect, neatly arranging items in an endless sequence (see fn. 7). If that avenue is pursued, then perhaps the intuition in Uriagereka (1999) is actually backwards. Possibly Merge itself simply arranges relevant terms set-theoretically, and it is only their transfer to PF that lists them in concatenative fashion. If so the unstructured 'term soup' may only emerge in morpho-phonemic terms, but things remain articulated in their way to LF, and the binding mechanism can take place in that pristine space, disregarding structural decisions taken because of PF motivations. That would be quite consistent with Huang's (1982) contention that islands rarely emerge in the LF component,[15] although it would suggest that derivational transfer to PF and to LF are entirely different processes, with different motivations and perhaps even different timings. So deciding on the actual form of the derivational memory – whether it is a list of some sort or a set-theoretic object dispersed in a less obvious space – has very direct consequences for what the precise architecture of the system is, and how it contributes to the emergence of such intricate road blocks as islands for (some) long-distance dependencies.

In what follows, it will be taken for granted that the CH is a way of understanding different, implicationally more complex, modelings that one can attempt of (natural) computational phenomena. Having acknowledged the

---

A non-formal way of understanding this is that, although the Merge-dependencies have been flattened into a sequence, the objects that entered into the Merge remain as identifiable entities.

15 Although see Hornstein and Uriagereka (1999, 2002) for an analysis that crucially deploys islands (different from the ones above) emerging in the LF component, which Hornstein *et al.* (in press) discuss in roughly the terms presented here.

limitations that classical analyses impose, it will nonetheless be assumed that some version of the hierarchy obtains in some appropriately revamped form, hopefully within relevantly similar presuppositions about formal complexity as structures become more entangled. One could be posing these same questions in chemistry, immunology or molecular biology, concerning how given interactions take place. Whatever the answer in each instance – whatever the 'processor' and the 'memory' is for each sort of system studied, as well as substantively specific dependencies in each instance – the concern is sensible if meant as asking what sorts of computations (e.g. Merge or other associations) or how much or what sort of memory – whatever that means in each system – specific systemic interactions demand.

7.4   The problem of paradigmaticity

The next question is whether the CH, as revamped as needed, helps us analyse the main puzzle this book is concerned with: how to capture the systematicity of paradigmatic relations. In this section a thesis is proposed to deal with the matter, once certain assumptions about lexical concepts are made, after borrowing some notions from topology. Such a move will give us a grounding for spatial notions that seem central to this overall program.

7.4.1   *Paradigmatic relations and orders of complexity in syntax*

Theories have always worried both about syntagmatic (horizontal) combinations together with paradigmatic (vertical) regularities among words. These 'parts of speech' are certainly very constrained, as we have seen throughout. As a consequence, we can factually assert that:

(i)   speakers have intuitions about relevant paradigmatic entailments, even when these may make little sense reference-wise. (If the irresistible force moves the unmovable object, then the unmovable object must move; for Jack to square the circle, the circle must square; if it's true he sprozed me, well then I must have sprozed, whatever that is!)

(ii)   selectional restrictions can be stated over various layers in the assumed hierarchies ('an indirect object must be animate', hence *I sent the wall a ball* vs. *I sent a ball towards the wall*; 'a generalized quantifier cannot quantify over a mass or abstract term', hence *most accelerations/* acceleration impress(*es) me*).

(iii)   if a grammatical morpheme is associated to specifications of the implied sort, then morphemic complexity correlates with paradigmatic complexity (we may not know what *skurp* is, but we know that if *skurps* (plural) also exist, then *skurp* can be relevantly classified into count units, and then we can quantify over it; we may not know what *slurching* is, but we know that if *John can slurch himself a gadget in his new place*, *slurch* must denote some accomplishment, whereas if it is not even the case that **John is slurching* – he can only *slurch* – this must denote a state).

And so on. The problem is how to capture these subtleties, if syntax is only to take care of syntagmatic conditions, for reasons reviewed in chapter 2. This leaves us at an impasse: paradigmatic conditions won't go away because of not being *standardly* syntactic.

To break the stalemate, we can start by considering an observation of Chomsky's, which directly follows the quote presented in the previous section:

> The emergence of the arithmetical capacity has been puzzling ever since Alfred Russell Wallace [...] observed that the 'gigantic development of the mathematical capacity is wholly unexplained by the theory of natural selection, and must be due to some altogether distinct cause,' if only because it remained unused. It may, then, have been a side product of some other evolved capacity (not Wallace's conclusion), and *it has often been speculated that it [i.e. the mathematical capacity] may be abstracted from FL by reducing the latter to its bare minimum*. Reduction to a single-membered lexicon is a simple way to yield this consequence. [Chomsky (2006, p. 6), italics added.]

Wallace's evolutionary point and Chomsky's technical correlation between language and math (in terms of the successor function) seem straightforward. However, if math can be abstracted from FL, how much of math is FL actually using to begin with, or vice versa?

To address that, we can build on an intuition expressed in Uriagereka (2002, chapter 15), which is ultimately based on Group Theory. Compact implications in algebraic structures are easy to see when considering the following simple facts: (i) the number line is included in the number plane; (ii) the number plane is included in the number hyper-plane; (iii) the number hyper-plane is included in ... Comparing the number line, to represent real numbers, and the number plane, where complex numbers are represented, it is clear that the complex are defined on the reals, so the former imply the latter. The inclusive hierarchy doesn't stop there: the number plane is the basis for the space needed to represent hyper-complex numbers. These are easy to visualize by thinking, first, of a complex number as a vector. The arrow head is at the coordinates (x, y) expressed by the real (x) and imaginary (y) parameters, its tail ranging from those coordinates to zero in (11a). Then we introduce a further axis (z) to represent coordinates (x, y, z) for a new vector head existing in the three dimensions of Euclidean space, as in (11b).

(11)   a.   b.

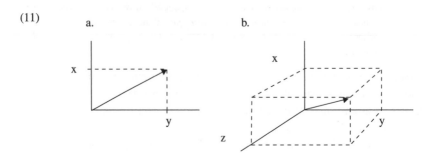

The number represented that way is hyper-complex, its definitional characteristics implying those of a complex number. And hyper-complex numbers
can be more cumbersome, involving more dimensions to them, although still
preserving relevant implicational characteristics.

Hinzen and Uriagereka (2006) observe that what gives its implicational
structure to the number analysis instance is not the associative conditions that
recursively generate number sets, but *inverse functions*, whose output is
outside the set where they are first defined, which forces the system to expand
on those sets. For instance, attempting to invert a squaring into a root function
an impossibility arises for the number line (i, denoting the square root of
minus one) – a formal object represented in the number plane. The point is
this: the successor function that Chomsky used for the purposes of getting
recursion off the ground will not suffice to lay the foundations of mathematics. Technically, this will only generate a *semi-group*, which is certainly
part of the system, but not the entire system, in any sense. The *inverse
function(s)* organize(s) numerical spaces in dimensional ways, an architectural base as central as the one introduced by numerical expansion. Again,
technically this is how we get from semi-groups to *groups*. And Hinzen and
Uriagereka ask: 'Could there be a reflex of this in FL, and in particular its
implicational, paradigmatic structures? Moreover ... could this aspect of
the number theory have been *abstracted* from FL?' [p.85]

Hinzen and Uriagereka then construct an argument that can be schematized
as follows (for FL the faculty of language): (i) there are obvious implicational
paradigms in FL; (ii) linguists do not know how to account for such implications; (iii) mathematical knowledge also involves obvious implicational paradigms; (iv) FL tightly correlates with mathematics, formally and in evolution;
and (v) the linguistic implications could be characterized as the mathematical
implications if, in some relevant respect, linguistic spaces *are* numerical
spaces. Mathematics could not be abstracted from FL if this system were just

syntagmatic in familiar ways – at best that would give us the 'expansion side' of the numerical coin (as in successors and other such associative functions). Arithmetic also needs some way of boosting its categorial domains, to avail itself of its full array of formal objects (line, plane, hyper-plane and so on).[16]

Now, even if one does admit this argument, a question remains. How is the implicational structure present in the number system to even *translate* to that in the language faculty? It is one thing to say that the 'bracketing' system implied by succession corresponds to syntactic constituency, and a very different thing to claim that the implicational layers that the inverse function generates show up as paradigmatic in grammar. For that to be even possible, as noted in section 2.4, we must have a syntax presenting various orders of complexity, or there won't be a way of anchoring the desired correspondence – short of stipulating it. Interestingly, the issue of higher orders of complexity within syntax is quite old, if examined thoroughly.

As noted in passing in section 2.4.3, if relevant context-sensitive rules allow quantificational and Boolean statements to specify their contexts, and can be both obligatory and optional, partially (extrinsically) ordered, and full of implicit variables between arbitrary terms, a learnability paradox ensues (Lasnik 2000, p. 107ff.). The solution to this puzzle has been to take out of the learning space of possibilities anything creating such complexities (recoding it in some universal 'filtering' way). But this has a consequence: *it implies a second-order logic* – recall the discussion in section 2.3. The ensuing theory will rely not only on first-order objects (items from the lexicon) and their manipulations, but also on quantifications over those manipulations.

To see that concretely, recall the Case conditions in chapter 5:

(12)   (i)   X is a *Core Case* if X is determined within a command unit (CU).

            a. If X is determined through Merge in CU, X is inherent.
            b. If X is determined through Agree in CU, X is structural.

    (ii)   Where a CU is *complete* if structural Case has been established within it, X is an *Elsewhere Case* if determined depending on a complete CU.

    (iii) X is a *Final Case* if X is determined depending on the inflectional element Y that is introduced at a final phase (PhF).

Much of this is second-order talk. We are examining the shape that X, an uninterpretable feature, will take in various contexts. X cannot be an item

---

16 As was mentioned in fn. 6, not even classical arithmetic can be performed without going into the number plane. That said, it is difficult to determine whether the 'inverse' functions to be discussed below come as naturally to human beings as 'successor' functions do.

from the lexicon; it is, instead, a morphological unit that must be eliminated, on pain of violating Full Interpretation. Moreover, the statements in (12) all have quantificational force. This is obvious for the 'if' clauses, which have the definitional status of 'whenever' statements. If such definitional propositions could be abstracted away as an overall property of grammar, re-coded as predicates of some sort, then they would not need to count as quantificational statements. But the conditions under which the features turn out to be inherent or structural, elsewhere or final, are *contextual*: they depend on specific arrangements in given phrase markers, whether they involve phases or command units (CU), and whether the latter are complete. Completion of a CU can only be determined in a given derivation, so a quantification over that sort of condition is second-order.

Many other instances in standard theorizing can also be shown to involve second-order properties – and there is nothing wrong with that.[17] Of relevance now, though, is whether those conditions on syntactic representations can be made to correspond to domains where we know semantics must also 'go higher-order': the dimensional shifts that we hope give us implicational layers of the paradigmatic sort. In this respect it is important to see the role played by *complement assumption*, which we know corresponds, precisely, to those domains where we expect there to be dimensional shifts in verbal representations. To recall (42) in chapter 5:

(13)   A small clause [X [Y]] can reanalyse as a head-complement [Z X] if:

      (a) [X [Y]] is the complement of a head Z.
      (b) The predicate head Y of the small clause incorporates onto selecting head Z.
      (c) As a result of category collision between Z and Y, a feature W is released which valuates the remainder X (subject) of the small clause.

Here, too, the conditions under which the transformational reanalysis can apply depend on a feature valuation on some arbitrary domain. Moreover, the valuation in question is of the sort in (12), which as we saw implies a higher-order system.

It is good that the syntax should be higher-order when complement assumption is invoked: we want the process to signal those instances where lexical implications must be live. This is, first, to address the puzzles posed by philosophers concerning the claim that, in effect, syntax is arbitrary with

---

17 See Rogers (1999), Cornell and Rogers (2000), and Stabler (2003) on this and related matters.

regards to the semantics it carries, and so any semantic representation for that syntax is as valid as any other.[18] If the present approach is correct, *human syntax is not entirely arbitrary* vis-à-vis the sorts of conceptual semantics it sanctions. As Hinzen and Uriagereka (2006) note, the problem with the philosophical argument is that it assumes a first-order syntax, but this turns out to be the wrong assumption for human language. Moreover, if syntax is higher-order *because* it uses the mathematical tools that Chomsky (following Wallace) thinks ought to construct syntax, then in addition we can gain an understanding of the implicational complexities that arithmetic gives us when we explore it in its own right, hoping to address what structures lexical entailment.

Readers unfamiliar with the 'indeterminacies of translation' (see fn. 18) might find the little space-craft thought experiment sketched in section 2.4 helpful. We wanted our alien friends – who do not share our human language – to understand something like (14), for a syntactic expression like *humans created this* (attached to a space craft).

(14) $\exists e \{$ Agent(e, *Humans*) & $\exists f$ [Terminater (e, f) & $\exists s <$ Change(f, s) & Exist(s) & [Theme (s, *this*)]$>$]$\}$

Recall also that we left pending how to code the transitivity of the expression, assuming the aliens share some form of the P/W^2 thesis. The question was how to express (14) for it to reflect the fact that whatever structure corresponds to the denotation of 'become existent' is a proper part of whatever structure corresponds to the denotation of the entire expression.

If the aliens' intelligence presupposes some form of mathematics, we could communicate to them the intricacies of our P/W^2 assumptions by doing something formally interesting, based on *different orders of formal complexity*.[19] We could assume, in particular, two orders of complexity: one for the syntax corresponding to the part, another for that of the whole. For example, we could use real numbers to represent first-order functions (the part) and complex ones to represent second-order functions (the whole). Suppose x stands for a real number, and the pair (y, z) for a complex number. The syntactic expression in (15) could be recognized as having two different

---

18 The 'indeterminacies of translation' thesis is postulated in Quine (1960), when considering the 'methods' available to the linguist. Such worries become moot within generative grammar, under the assumption that the linguist's own language and the studied one are identical in their logical form. That, though, cannot be presupposed for the alien scenario in the thought experiment immediately below.

19 Let's pretend for the sake of presentation – non-trivially, as will become apparent shortly – that the aliens make the underlying distinction between numerical concepts and their digital representation.

orders of complexity, the function involving *this* being a proper part, in an obvious way if one knows the relevant math, of the function involving *Humans* (we are assuming the aliens have access to the denotation of both *humans* and *this*).

(15)   (y, z) (*Humans*, x (*this*))

Now there is some realistic hope of knowing how to map (15) to something like (14) – at least we have the right stuff to do so, having 'naturalized' (relevant parts of) its meaning.

Returning to language, the problem one human being faces with respect to another, in language acquisition and its use, is not that different. This is particularly so if the issue is conceived from the point of view of the evolution of the system, at a stage where we cannot beg the question by assuming the species already has some appropriate – at this point, possibly arbitrary – mapping between syntax and semantics. How did that system emerge? If our ancestors had the sort of brain we are willing to grant the hypothetical aliens, they would have been able to come up with some form of (15). This is obviously not true in terms of the formal nuances of these systems, which took millennia to perfect. But such a magnificent formal edifice would be unnecessary – for our ancestors or the aliens. It would be enough to invoke *the sort of brain* that allows for an understanding of the 'expansion' and 'inverse' operations that determine the number system – to comprehend groups, in the mathematical sense.

7.4.2   *The distributed interpretation thesis*

The conclusion reached in the previous paragraph still leaves us with a serious question. If, from a minimalist perspective, the language faculty is an *optimal* computational solution to interface conditions, how does that computational procedure interface whatever it does? The analytical foundations we have begun to lay presuppose two sorts of interfaces: those that emerge from standard syntagmatic dependencies, and those that should emerge from what-ever is involved in the paradigmatic arrays we have attempted to characterize. To reduce one to the other would be either to fall into generative semantics again – if everything in the language faculty is taken to be syntagmatic – or to have to deny the paradigmatic facts. But how are we supposed to get (at least) two points of interface, if language 'merely' pairs sound and meaning?

Recall that the CH is a formal characterization of computational systems, and furthermore one that is relevant to I-language as well. We can then propose the following thesis.

(16)   *Distributed Interpretation Thesis (DIT)*
        Interpretation interfaces any maximal stable object within the CH.

This asserts that immediately after a 'maximal stable' object in the CH sense is discernible by an interpretable system, it is indeed interpreted, regardless of whether the syntactic computation is actually finished. Stable objects should presumably be (finite-state) sets, (context-free) phrases, and ((mildly) context-sensitive) chains (at least). We need to determine what we mean by one such *maximal* object, but we will return to that in section 8.3.3 – after discussing whether there is any plausibility to the general assumptions being made at this juncture.

For the phonetic interface, the issue seems straightforward. Phenomena like *liaison*, happening across adjacent words, could be stated in finite-state terms, and we already mentioned in section 6.3.1 that Raimy and Idsardi (1997) present a finite-state analysis of reduplicative structures. Phrasal stress determination or considerations about prosodic phrasing are arguably context-free processes. But phonetic context-sensitive processes exist as well. One is the decision to pronounce only one of several copies generated in movement (e.g. each occurrence of *John* in *John was arrested John*, only the upper one being pronounced), as discussed by Nunes (2004);[20] for a decision of this sort, the grammar must have phonological access to non-contiguous constituents. Similar considerations arise for elliptical objects, especially so in their de-accented version (*the cow kicked the bucket, and so did the farmer* kick the bucket too). A PF deciding to de-accent a site must have had access to a non-contiguous antecedent, and thus the interpretive process must involve phonetic access to a stable context-sensitive object.[21]

Similar considerations about semantics are harder to establish. Almost everyone agrees that semantics interprets context-sensitive objects, or we would not be able to express non-surface scopal relations. Nonetheless, a serious disagreement exists as to whether phrases are also meaningful to interpretation. That they are has been proposed by Hale and Keyser (1993, 2002). Their argument rests on the empirical claim that certain lexico-conceptual relations (theta-roles) are of a hierarchical sort, and this can be captured in terms of

---

20 Nunes' (2004) deduction of why only one among multiple occurrences in a chain is pronounced is based on Kayne's (1994) linear correspondence axiom. Multiple occurrences in different hierarchical sites within a phrase marker cannot linearize with regards to their context, so only one such occurrence survives, to be treated as any other token with a singular occurrence. Last resort considerations normally entail keeping the highest occurrence in detriment of the others.

21 See Murguia (2004) on these and related matters from a minimalist perspective.

context-free phrase-structure. This intuitive idea, however, hasn't been proven, and is thus generally stipulated. Defenders of the 'output' interface approach, in contrast, view theta-roles as mere features (see e.g. Hornstein 2001). While the most natural situation for them to expect, given this architecture, is one where features are unordered, they could also stipulate some ordering among these, blaming it on extra-linguistic notions.[22] One stipulation is as good as any.

For the DIT approach to be semantically convincing, it should ideally show that:

(17)   a. Thematic relations are real and ordered.
        b. It is natural to capture the thematic ordering in CH terms.

(17a) is an empirical question, bearing on whether there is a thematic hierarchy demanding, for instance, that agents be syntactically mapped in a configurational position higher than that of themes. (17b) is partly a formal matter and partly an issue of what counts as 'natural'.

Much discussion has emerged over the precise nature of thematic hierarchies. (Several have been proposed.) While that is important, it is even more so to reflect on what *could* be the nature of the correct hierarchy, why it obtains and how this is represented in the system. Recall in this respect the hierarchical numerical relations discussed above which Group Theory predicts:

(18)   real > complex > hypercomplex ...

No such *direct* implicational relation, in contrast, has ever been proposed for paradigmatic structurings along the lines of (17a), which are typically asserted on the basis of empirical observations. Let's call an inclusive implicational hierarchy as in (18) a *deduction*, while reserving the term (mere) *hierarchy* for a weaker ordering without natural implicational conditions. With that in mind, let's return to thematic ordering, which, as the facts at the beginning of section 7.4.1 remind us, ought to constitute bona fide deductive, not merely hierarchical, arrays. We should be specifically interested in something like the ordering in (19).[23]

(19)   achievement > activity > state

This should also follow, at least in its basic structure or 'scaffolding' (i.e. disregarding lexical nuances), as some sort of deduction. As a mere

---

22 The proposal, for instance, in Motomura (2004). Here it is, on the one hand, admitted that hierarchical conditions of the thematic sort are crucial but, on the other, the system is based on theta-roles as mere features to be checked as the derivation unfolds. Motomura is thus forced to blame the hierarchy on something pragmatic that she does not specify.

23 See Mori (2005) for discussion of these sorts of issues, and many refinements.

hierarchy it can obviously be stipulated in various ways, and it ultimately poses too many problems to be of much architectural interest.

7.4.3 Manifolds

To proceed further, it is now useful to introduce some intuitive mathematical notions, in particular a concept from topology: the 'manifold'. This allows us to speak, in the same terms, of spaces and objects, and to study how each (type of manifold) relates to the other in terms of their dimensionality (and other formal properties, although only dimensionality will matter here). The 'dimension' of a manifold is, basically, the number of variables (also called 'parameters') that are needed to specify a point in that manifold. Prototypically, an n-dimensional Euclidean space is a manifold (n parameters needed to specify a point within it). Intuitively, n dimensions in a manifold entail n *degrees of freedom* for that formal entity. Manifolds of one dimension involve collections of points that can all be unambiguously specified by a single real number – the number line is a 1D manifold, but so are many curves. 2D manifolds are surfaces, and all their points require two coordinates – the number plane counts as a 2D manifold, and also many 'cuts' to spheres, cylinders, ellipsoids. Things get hard to visualize with 3D manifolds, beyond the entire, open-ended, Euclidean space – more so with higher dimensional manifolds.[24] Luckily this will be mostly irrelevant to us here.

Of particular interest to us is how a manifold of dimensionality n relates to one of dimensionality $n+1$; we need not concern ourselves beyond the simple instances that we will require to articulate our particular deduction. To address this matter we need to understand three ideas: first, that a 'submanifold' X is a subset of a manifold Y with a smaller dimensionality than Y; (for example, the equator is a sub-manifold of earth's manifold); second, that a manifold can be *open* if it has no boundary to it, or *closed* if it does; and third, that we can, in principle, *identify* the boundaries of a closed manifold in such a way that its dimensionality is boosted in the process. Let's call a 'super-manifold' X that entity which, while still being a closed manifold, is obtained from a lower dimensional manifold Y by identifying Y's edges. We may call the operation of projecting a manifold into a super-manifold a 'warp'. This is a central operation, for it would appear that human cognition

---

24 See for instance Armstrong (1983), Kinsey (1993), Willard (1970), and Lee (2000). The ensuing discussion will remind some readers of cognitive work by René Thom (see e.g. Aubin [2004]), but the connection is tenuous. The notions below are meant as specifically linguistic, not just part of an overall theory of cognition.

can perform warps with manifolds of low dimensionality at least, and that they articulate numerical and lexical concepts.[25]

An obvious warp is obtained by taking a cut in the number line – e.g. that going from 0 to 12 as in (20a) – and identifying the edges of the resulting segment, as in (20b).

(20)   a.   b.

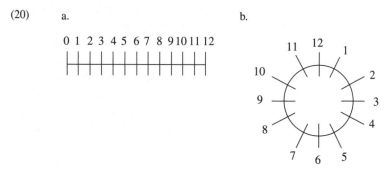

Similarly, we could warp a cut in any plane – as in (21a) – into the entity in (21b), by identifying the relevant edges (in this instance, we identify all vertices into a single point and the edges into themselves half way through, in a mirror-image fashion).

(21)   a.   b.   c.

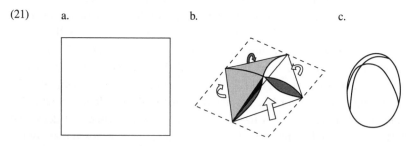

What is important for our purposes is that the tetrahedron in (21b) (or more curved versions of this object for an elastic space, a bubble in the limit (21c)) is, in some sense, still a 2D manifold, the very same one in (21a), but having

---

25 One of the emerging areas in mathematical research, arithmetic topology, relates low-dimensional topology and number theory. The field is too new and advanced to present a summary beyond noting that mathematicians have long known that knots are similar to prime numbers and 3D manifolds to number fields.

undergone some foldings. In this super-manifold of (21a), parallel lines that would never meet in a surface like (22a) clearly meet afterwards.

(22)   a.   b.

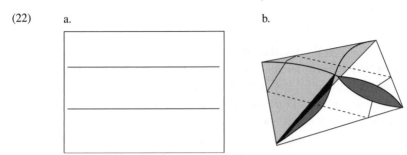

But parallel lines *not* meeting in a given space is the defining characteristic of a Euclidean space, so *the super-manifold that we obtain via warping is not Euclidean*. In fact, if we were to represent that super-manifold in Euclidean space we'd need three dimensions. (Incidentally, actual bubbles can be formed in pretty much this warping way, for a viscous enough fluid.)

In sum, by warping an n-dimensional (Euclidean) space we obtain an $n+1$-dimensional (non-Euclidean) space that, in some instances at least, behaves as an 'object' – at least within low dimensions.[26] Notice two more important things about these warps. First, the folding procedures in (20b) and (21b), from a sheer computational perspective, are arguably context-sensitive: precisely what the boundaries do in (20a) and (21a) is *define relevant such contexts*, which the identification process then brings together into a unit. If we were to program a computational device to perform the appropriate warps, it would need enough derivational memory to isolate and identify distinct token edges in the space we are operating on. Second, it is clear that steps (20a) and (21a) are *presupposed by the warping procedure*. A little reflection shows that whereas the (b) entities can univocally be traced back to the featureless (a) entities, the converse is not true. As noted, for instance, (21a) can map (21b), but also (21c) and other homomorphic objects that can be 'chartered' as 2D manifolds – so the relation between (21a) and relevant warped objects is one-to-many, though the converse is one-to-one. Another way of saying this is that in the warping construction of (21b/c) we must pass through (21a), but we could obtain (21a) in a variety of ways, from

---

26 What happens at higher dimensions, though possibly consistent with this conjecture, is anybody's guess.

various other homomorphic manifolds. So (21b) or (21c) presuppose (21a), but not conversely. The relation between the two elements, thus, constitutes a deduction.

7.4.4   *Towards a deduction of the Aktionsart scaffolding*

To turn (19) into a deduction we may consider each *Aktionsart denotation as a manifold*, so that a given VP-layer is, at its core, an n D super-manifold warped from an (n-1) D manifold. If this is the case, the fact that any n D super-manifold relates to the (n-1) D manifold it is warped from is what becomes responsible for the ensuing deduction in the Aktionsart instance; the entailment is not peculiar to lexical structure. This is not how the entailment is run in the literature, if it's even acknowledged as internal to linguistics. But the proposal advocated for here is faced with a non-trivial task: to identify the dimensionality of each linguistic (here Aktionsart) manifold, and moreover to give some indication as to why a dimensionality of that particular sort is made to correspond intentionally to familiar linguistic notions.

The good news is that verbal space comes out in ways that are consistent with the picture just presented. For example, linguistic arguments show that states or activities are open-ended, in a way that achievements or accomplishments are not, the latter being bounded. This kind of talk (open-endedness, telicity) is what manifolds are good at, as the warped manifolds are *necessarily* bounded out of the open ones. At the same time, it is less clear what happens to a state for it to be warped into an activity, or to an achievement for it to be warped into an accomplishment. We obviously need more than mere warps along the lines just indicated.

Mori (2005) suggests that matters are cumbersome only because the Aktionsart hierarchy should be thought as in (23), rather than as in (19) above:

(23)   accomplishment > activity > achievement > state

McClure (1995) Mori takes an activity to be a collection of achievements. Moreover, she takes the Aktionsart field to be divided in two cuts, as follows:

(24)

$$\begin{array}{c|c}
 & | \\
\text{accomplishment} > \text{activity} > & \text{achievement} > \text{state} \\
\text{biclausal } (vP+CP) & | \quad \text{monoclausal (VP)}
\end{array}$$

If this is correct, within each of the fields in (24) the warp dynamics work well, for after all the lowest elements in each constitute the atelic spaces that simple manifolds intuitively correspond to, while the highest constitute the telic spaces that super-manifolds are apt to model. Then the question is what relation exists between the lower and upper Aktionsart fields, so that one warps a state into an achievement while the other warps an activity into an accomplishment, specifically. What, to start with, is the relation between achievements and activities – or what does it mean to obtain a *collection* of the former to define the latter?

The suggestive answer Mori provides is consistent with the topological intuitions just introduced. Topologically, a 'space' is a *collection of points connected to one another*. The warp mechanism produces a kind of point:[27] a bounded manifold. A collection of such created points is itself an open manifold if it constitutes a connected set, a sort of hyper-space constructed with objects of a lower dimensionality. The procedure is no different from the standard way in which natural numbers are created by adding brackets to the empty set (Peano's associative system, discussed in Chomsky's quote in section 7.2.2) – or for that matter how a foam space emerges from aggregating point-like bubbles in an optimal way (see Figure 7.2). Call this space-creating mechanism an *expansion*. Evidently, under the right circumstances the newly expanded foam can itself be warped into a super-bubble, which in turn could be taken, in point-fashion, as the unit for a super-foam and so on. This is again the characteristic association/inversion found in mathematical groups.

In Mori's sense, then, the following deduction holds:

(25)

warp	*warp*
4D-super-hyper-manifold < 3D hyper-manifold	< 2D super-manifold < 1D manifold
two syntactic cyles	one syntactic cycle

The sequence *surface > bubble > foam* is perfectly straightforward and easy to observe in natural fluids. It is a fact that our universe uses both expansion (largely aggregative) and warping (strangely folding) mechanisms,

---

27 An object can be seen as a point whose internal dimensionality is ignored. For instance, a sphere is an atom in a higher space for which it counts as a 0D element, its internal dimensions not interacting with the ones outside.

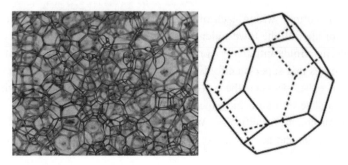

Figure 7.2. *Bubble foam and the Weaire–Phelan structure*

at all observable levels – it would be a miracle if this didn't reduce to some, as of yet not well understood, constraint on how low-dimensional manifolds relate to one another. This is at least food for thought, formal details aside.

Considerably more worrisome from the perspective of this book, and internal to linguistics, are questions of the following sort.

(i)   How do the biclausal units end up reduced to a single verbal projection?
(ii)   Characterizing an activity as a hyper-spatial collection of achievements, why does the ensuing manifold, when warped into a bounded super-hyper-manifold, invite resultative inferences?
(iii)   How does all of this relate to argument taking and a variety of verbal morphemes and auxiliaries witnessed in the world's languages? Although these questions won't be answered here, they seem reasonable and worth posing.

A further question to ask with regards to the deduction in (25) is whether the 1D manifold there is itself derived from something else. Given the fact that verbs are constructed from arguments and, in particular, as Mori (2005) emphasizes, they always deploy an 'event space' arranged around a theme, the natural thing to say is that the simplest verbal manifold is some construct involving, precisely, a theme manifold. Muromatsu (1998) has already showed a way in which, effectively, nominal spaces can be seen as manifolds, deducing the customary hierarchy in (26a) from warps starting with abstract spaces (26b).[28]

---

28 Muromatsu (1998) studies nominal categories in terms of the topological notions discussed here, thus organizing nominal space in terms of the manifolds in (i), which progressively increase in dimensionality.

(i)   abstract > mass > object > animate

Since viable quantifications start at mass terms, these can be analogized to the 1D number

(26)   a. animate > count > mass > abstract
           b. 4D manifold > 3D manifold > 2D manifold > 1D manifold

On the basis of manifold themes corresponding to (26), of various dimensionalities, a verbal manifold can be constructed by 'chartering' it from the theme space. This is essentially how 'internal aspect' relations are deployed, based on the theme space. Drinking a beer can be seen as a dynamic function over whatever amount is in the mug, which changes over a period of time until it's gone – the event thus sadly ending. This structuring for verbal events isn't logically necessary, but it appears factually true (recall the discussion in section 2.4).

One direct way of making the fact formally entailed is by assuming that:

(27)   A verbal manifold is a derivative over time of a theme manifold.

(27) is tantamount to saying that a verbal state manifold is not primitive – *it requires a theme manifold* to monitor over time. The theme manifold itself can have any of the degrees of complexity in Muromatsu's (26), and then depending on how warped the dynamic function involving the theme turns out to be, we will obtain the various degrees of verbal complexity in Mori's (25) (or a related deduction). For example, we want the 'state' derivative over some theme to be a flat line (no change in time), while we want the 'achievement' derivative over some theme to be some curve with a characteristic limit. Similarly for the 'bi-clausal' hyper-spaces: the 'activity' derivative ought to be quite linear, unlike the 'accomplishment' one, whose telos again indicates some sort of limit in the curve.[29]

It is worth emphasizing that, if the deductions just alluded to do hold in some form, their arrangements are not contingent on any reality external to their formal apparatus. For instance, there is no way of expressing a relation of the sort just discussed excluding themes from the picture, any more than one could make a non-trivial generalization about, say, complex numbers that

---

line. Objects would naturally be 2D manifolds, animate entities 3D topologies and abstract terms 0D spaces without an extension, their specific conceptual properties being orthogonal to this system. Muromatsu correlates (i) with morphemes: measures for the 1D space, classifiers for 2D space, animacy markers for 3D space.

29 A situation worth studying in this respect is the emergence of phase transitions in thermodynamics. The paradigmatic accomplishment – baking a cake – denotes a thermodynamic event, and many other such verbs that seem prototypical – e.g. of the building sort – denote complexly dynamic eventualities. Those are observations about the denotatum, but the denotation too may make use of the sorts of complex-dynamic topologies that seem necessary to describe the dynamics of what is being referred to scientifically.

isn't also a generalization about the real numbers the former are constructed from. This is no small achievement. Going this abstract forces us into daring analytical moves of the sort Muromatsu (1998), Castillo (2001), and Mori (2005) have attempted – all of which may be wrong. But the *sort* of theory implied in this view of things, while elegant, seems also quite predictive.

7.5   Conclusions

This chapter was necessary to ground the formal basis of the distributed interpretation thesis, the Chomsky Hierarchy. This construct is no longer fashionable within linguistics, which doesn't mean that it isn't true in some form. For it to be of any use, however, the hierarchy has to be revamped in terms that are sensitive to correct linguistic concerns, namely the strong generative capacity of computational systems. The ideas discussed above can be seen as suggestions in this regard; they are not conclusive, but if the Minimalist Program is even remotely right, the precise formalization will not differ too much from what has been discussed here.

Perhaps most importantly for a natural science, the fact that psycholinguistic results begin to back it up suggests that things are indeed on track, and we are not too far from meeting the demands of some present-day derivational theory of complexity. Be that as it may, either the Chomsky Hierarchy is right in some sense, or else the thesis discussed in this book, for dynamic semantic interpretation, ultimately makes little sense as stated. In the previous section we took the first step, within all these formal assumptions, towards 'naturalizing meaning', using the scaffolding of Aktionsart organization as a test case. A hierarchy such as this flies in the face of minimalist assumptions, with all its emphasis on eliminating stipulative representations and having conditions follow either from internal coherence (economy of design) or natural interactions (interface properties). The attempt sketched here should be seen as just that – an attempt, within the overall assumptions of this project. If better stories emerge we should compare them to this account.

The picture is at least consistent with the adjustment of the Chomsky Hierarchy discussed above, in ways that make it sensitive to Merge operations. Note in that regard that a Merge-memory was alluded to that is intended – within a non-Markovian computational device running derivational histories 'in parallel' – as a substitute for the standard Turing tape, whose set-theoretic properties were likened to that of the number system. If that idea is taken seriously, the 'slate' for human linguistic memory wouldn't be blank, it would bear the pathways of whatever constitutes mathematics – perhaps minus the relations we can find among distant points within it. Who knows how articulated that space is, at least in the case of 'naïve' linguistic memory?

Then again, the fact that children succeed so rapidly – and so much better than adults – in acquiring nuanced lexical concepts, whose scaffolding this theory presupposes, may be an indication that the fabric with which they weave their organized thoughts constitutes no adjustment over a preexisting 'cognitive space/time'. It *is* that very cognitive space/time. Just as it makes no sense to ask what space/time existed prior to the Big Bang, it may not be sensible to ask what articulated cognitive space/time exists prior to the emergence of the syntactic mind. Ultimately the same mathematical tools that enter into the characterization of syntactic operations build the very computational memory space where the outputs of those operations rest – perhaps as dynamic a rest as that of any physical body over the fabric of space/time.

8 *Naturalizing meaning*

8.1   Introduction

In the previous chapter we began to outline how the relation between
paradigmatic and syntagmatic structures can be soundly expressed in a
minimalist grammar. In this last chapter we ought to further that idea,
explicitly stated as desideratum (19) in chapter 7, as part of what can be
thought of as the 'naturalization' of purely structural aspects of meaning –
either because they are directly so (the radical version of the present
program) or because they somehow reflect the relevant syntax (the conservative version). Along these lines, and assuming deductive relations as
expressed in chapter 7, section 8.2 attempts to anchor semantics on syntactic
nuances of the Chomsky Hierarchy (CH) sort. Possible interpretations of the
various layers of this hierarchy are explored first (for finite-state relations in
section 8.2.1, context-free relations in section 8.2.2, and context-sensitive
ones in section 8.2.3). Section 8.3 examines the syntactic tool of 'reprojection',
by first analysing syntactic limits on the expression of quantificational scope
(in section 8.3.1), going next into matters of focalization (in section 8.3.2),
which bears on how sub-events in a clause can be organized around binary
event quantifiers, and finally section 8.3.3 discusses why binary quantificational
relations could not be turned around, with the scope of the quantifier being
mapped from a syntactically lower position than its restriction. Section 8.4
wraps up various ideas, dealing with mental spaces, lexical features, feature
valuation as a Markovian process, Case as a tokenization mechanism, the
idea that reprojected entanglements may yield paradigms, and finally how
context-sensitivity may relate to the notion 'context' in a pragmatic sense.
Although technical, this section is also meant to lay the groundwork to
address one of the main concerns of this book – the problem underlying
the Linguistic Wars, concerning the nature of lexical structure, which is
explicitly taken up in section 8.5. Finally, section 8.6 presents some broad
conclusions.

8.2   Possible semantics for syntactic layers of the CH

While formal *deduction*s of the sort in (26) in chapter 7 (the scaffolding of Aktionsart) a priori seem (lexical) semantic in nature, the CH itself is a computational, entirely formal and thus purely syntactic, generalization. Intuitively, the CH can be used to characterize automata, whether they underlie language, biology, chemistry or nothing whatsoever, while of course intuitions about Aktionsart, or other linguistic hierarchies, feel meaningful to humans, in some sense to be understood. The difficult question, then, is what sort of relation exists – perhaps *naturally* exists – between the syntax of natural language and its observed semantics, what we have been calling the Mapping Problem. Let's analyse the matter, first, in abstract terms.

8.2.1   Interpreting finite-state relations

An elementary finite-state syntax cannot express symbol types and associated groupings, other than those indirectly emerging via *looping* and sheer *adjacency*.[1] That radically restricts corresponding interpretive possibilities, for n elements associated via that sort of syntax, to: (a) interpreting each n on its own; (b) making looped elements the focus of some semantic process compatible with unbounded iterative symbolism; and (c) channeling some minimal associative interpretation through adjacency processes. (c) arguably sub-divides into (ci) pure adjacent dependency (reduced to binary relations in linear conditions demanded by speech) and (cii) global associative dependency expressed through adjacency.

(1)   a. Condition on Full Interpretation (FI)
           All and only syntactic symbols that make it to the semantic interface are interpreted.
       b. Condition on Iterative Interpretation
           Elements that enter a finite-state loop generate a syntactic space for appropriate 'open-ended' interpretation.
       c. Conditions on Adjacent Interpretation
           i. Locally adjacent interpretations express predications.
           ii. Globally adjacent interpretations express coordinations.

These logical possibilities that such a simple-minded syntax allows seem to be exhaustively used by UG, in terms of what was called in chapter 3 the Trivial Structure hypothesis. Let's consider each of these conditions, as

---

1 As Pullum and Rogers (2007) show, these sorts of intuitive cuts (adjacency, loops, and others) actually determine finer cuts within finite-state automata, a matter that will not be pursued here.

specifications of how a trivial (finite-state) syntax can anchor trivial (isolated, identificational, coordinative) semantics.

The condition on full interpretation (FI, originally stated in Chomsky [1986]) is intended to rule out holistic interpretations such as: 'The cat is on the mat' *is true if and only if* I have cramp in my left foot. Although that would be a legitimate process of decoding in a variety of semiotic contexts – and is surely involved in the interpretation of both (arbitrary aspects of) words and idiomatic expressions – it plays no role in the syntax of natural language. If in a sentence like the one just quoted, barring arbitrary idiomatic projections, we must interpret each and every one of the words, a fortiori the interpreted message must somehow be about cats, mats, and so on. Note in this regard that in particular (1a) is most naturally a finite-state condition, as higher syntactic combinations are essentially combinatorial – while condition (1a) is not.

The iterative expressions that (1b) alludes to were discussed in chapter 6. But after talking about manifolds and space-creating expansions, in section 7.4.3, it should be easy to see that a loop is the ultimate 'space-expander'. In fact, a finite-state loop can model the generation of the series *one*, {*one*}, {{*one*}}, and so on, alluded to in section 7.2.2 – without the system having to resort to *hierarchical* bracketing.[2] So it may not be unreasonable to associate this *expanding* mechanism to the finite-state machinery in the grammar.[3] That is arguably a pervasive machinery, quite aside from the iterative processes studied in chapter 6 or even the Aktionsart situations that Mori (2005) associated to a space expansion, as discussed in section 7.4.4. We just have to think of those situations where we want multiple 'copies', as in reconstruction effects of the sort discussed in section 1.5.1, which are customarily assumed by fiat. What is responsible for the copying mechanism, if entities in a system don't just spontaneously replicate? We may pack this stipulation into the very definition of context-sensitive operation of the Movement sort, just as we may not.[4] But the copying mechanism need not be, in itself, a context-sensitive

2 Although this generating fashion wouldn't allow the system to capture relations among the numbers thus generated. In 1889, Peano (translated in van Heijenoort [1967]) had a separate axiom to stipulate that distinction.
3 All that we care about at this elementary level is to 'create space', whether it is organized sequentially or in any other way.
4 Historically, movement first entailed copying, then it was taken to leave skeletal traces of what moved, only to return to full copies a decade ago – with suggestions that in some instances it doesn't even leave a trace. In other words, no necessary connection exists between the movement operation and the copying mechanism.

procedure, or even a context-free one.[5] The simplest way of creating copies are finite-state loops, designed solely for that purpose. Proceeding this way has one advantage.

Consider the puzzle posed by reconstruction effects that we alluded to in section 1.5.1, now in a slightly different version which highlights further difficulties.

(2)   a.   Which picture of themselves did John and Mary say Bill and Sue sold?
       b.   Which picture of John and Mary did John and Mary say Bill and Sue sold? [interpretation]
       c.   Which picture of Bill and Sue did John and Mary say Bill and Sue sold? [interpretation]
       d.   *Which picture of John and Bill (and Mary and Sue) did John and Mary say Bill and Sue sold? [interpretation]
       e.   Which picture of themselves did John tell Mary that I sold?

(2a) can be interpreted as (2b) or as (2c) – we assume this is because the moved Wh-phrase can 'reconstruct' in the theta position (taking as antecedent *Bill and Sue*) or in the intermediate complementizer position (taking as antecedent *John and Mary*). But the Wh-phrase cannot reconstruct in *both* positions, as in (2d), or it would be able to take antecedents from either the matrix or the embedded clause (just as *themselves* within the 'picture' nominal in (2e) can take 'split' antecedents).[6] The question is why reconstruction is, in some sense, unique – a matter that cannot be trivially presupposed or summarily stipulated. The operator (Wh-element here) must make it to the scope position, the variable (a Wh-trace in this instance) must remain in the theta position, and the operator restriction (where the anaphor is contained) has as many interpretive possibilities as sites this material has moved through. But if so, why can't *all* of those sites contribute to interpretation, particularly if anaphoric licensing legitimizes convergence at those sites? Why must the system ignore all such movement sites *except one*? In terms of the Copy Theory of Movement this is puzzling, and the reason Hornstein (1995) adds his Uniqueness qualification in the LF component stipulating the fact just described.

---

5 As this book is in its final stages, Kobele (2006) addresses this very question. For practical reasons of both time and space, this interesting approach will not be discussed now.

6 This version of the puzzle cannot obviously be solved with the idea mentioned in section 1.5.1 – namely, to minimize the number of deletions in comparable derivations. This is because each of the reconstruction sites in this instance would seem to be legitimately licensed by a separate anaphoric dependency, leading to a convergent derivation. Technically, comparison with another convergent derivation involving anaphoric reconstruction at a different site is incommensurable, as it involves a different derivational horizon.

If copies are generated by the looping process, their interpretive uniqueness, to use Hornstein's term, directly follows. A finite-state loop can only allow unique interpretations, because it cannot anchor any compositional mechanism. Hornstein (1999) compares the workings of his Uniqueness qualification to the uniqueness effect that emerges in the PF component when Kayne-style conditions of linearization are imposed on chains, as shown by Nunes (2004). But this is not obvious. The fact that linearization conditions impose uniqueness is naturally interpretable as a 'compression' problem, of the sort first systematically discussed in Higginbotham (1985): the grammar's task is to flatten an (at least) 2D phrasal representation into the 1D channel of speech. This translates, in the case of chains including several identical occurrences of given tokens, as relevant elements surfacing only once per token – Nunes' point. However, just what interface condition is to have a comparable effect in the LF component? What reason do we have to think that the compression problem arises there too, forcing the system to go from higher to lower dimensionalities (of interpretation)? If the only way the grammar has of creating copies is through loops, this matter is moot – indeed both for LF and PF. The chain interpretive collapse at given positions would be the result of its not being able to support *any* form of non-trivial interpretation, internal to its expansion via copies.

The only other interpretive condition that a trivial finite-state syntax is compatible with turns out to be (1c). Syntactically, non-loop strings can only anchor either adjacent interpretations or global ones, if there is a way to isolate a given, relevant, finite-state chunk. On the one hand this corresponds to various predicational dependencies, through what was called in section 6.4.4 the cue thesis; on the other, it arguably corresponds, also, to various open-ended coordinate associations.

Finally, the most direct way to capture *adjacency* conditions is, again, in finite-state terms. This was alluded to when studying Concord in section 5.2.4, in conditions emerging after a feature release in nominal contexts. To the extent that the relevant concord involves total semantic collapse (identification) between the related terms, it seems reasonable to conclude that this follows from the corresponding trivial syntax.

8.2.2   *Interpreting context-free relations*
Next, consider a context-free phrase-structure syntax. Inasmuch as those sorts of relations presuppose finite-state ones, none of the interpretive anchors alluded to in the previous section – from mere interpretation of isolated symbols to finite-state dependency, including looping, identification or coordination – need to be disregarded when moving up in the CH. The only

thing we need is an active domain (e.g. the Numeration or parallel dimensions within the derivation) where the more basic interpretation can happen prior to the relevant structure being obliterated by further computational assembly. That said we customarily assume far more for phrase structure.

(3)   Principle of Strong Compositionality (PSC)
        R is a possible semantic rule for a human natural language only if R is strictly local and purely interpretive.

(3) could not hold of a finite-state syntax: there could be no groupings there (within it 'strictly local' can only mean adjacent). However, in a phrase-structure syntax where groupings emerge, a statement with this force has a significant consequence, as discussed in section 2.4. A 'strictly local' R cannot look down deeper than the immediate constituents of a given category X to interpret it. In turn 'purely interpretive' entails that R cannot create structure – it only interprets the one given by the syntax. More semantic structure is possible once we allow for symbolic groupings, but if the principle of strong compositionality (PSC) in (3) holds, only that extension is allowed that tracks *the immediate groupings down to the original symbols that constitute them.*

Neither full interpretation nor strong compositionality are logically necessary, but they are customarily seen as natural mappings between syntax and semantics: they ensure that we take seriously those unit symbols that are being syntactically manipulated and, as per Larson and Segal's (1995) perspective, that semantic interpretation piggy-backs on syntactic structuring alone. Moreover, in section 2.4 an argument, adapted from Larson and Segal's work, was provided to the effect that overall mappings along these lines are central in the acquisition of lexical notions. But is this all there is to say about the form of the syntax/semantics anchoring?

A further puzzle emerges if the following syntactic condition holds.

(4)   Binary Branching Condition (BBC)
        Syntactic relations in natural language are binary.

Kayne first proposed this condition in the early 1980s, eventually deducing it from deeper principles in *The Antisymmetry of Syntax* (1994). It eliminates the possibility of representing two-place semantic relations in the 'flat' terms in (5a), forcing either (5b) or (5c) instead.[7]

---

7 It might seem as if any formalism that likens phrasal merger to function application entails binary branching – one branch for the functor and one for the argument. But this is not necessary. The argument of a function could be any n-tuple, so then only mono-argumental functions would count – a fact we need to explain.

(5)   a.   X P
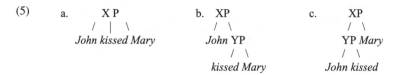

Importantly, in (5b) relevant semantic relations between *kissed* and its arguments *Mary* and *John* are locally determined. That is, *kissed* syntactically combines with *Mary* – which can have a semantic interpretation in satisfaction of both FI and SC – and then the resulting combination *kissed-Mary* syntactically combines with *John*, which again has a semantic interpretation in FI and SC satisfaction. The same formal fact is true about (5c), so that doesn't decide between the structures. The tilting factor is provided by a lexico-semantic hierarchy along the lines of (26) and specifically the definition of a verb in (28) in that section. Then (5b) is preferred by the system over (5c). In the former the theme *Mary* combines with the verb to yield a state from which to build the expression; in contrast in (5c) the relevant expression would have to be built around the agent/experiencer *John*, in direct violation of (28).

But that highlights situations when matters are not so straightforward. Consider this:

(6)   John kissed most girls.

In a scenario of this nature we want a determiner like *most* to be a two-place relation holding of the denotation of *girls* and the entities that John kissed. Arguably, this shouldn't be much more complicated than what we saw in (5) if it were expressed as in (7).

(7)   Mostly girls John kissed.

Perhaps one could argue that the syntax for (7) is roughly as in (8).

(8)
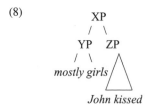

In (8) *mostly* takes *girls* as its first syntactic dependent, which could be mapped as its restriction or first argument, and it takes *John kissed* as its second syntactic dependent, which (with some help, as we see in section 8.3)

could be mapped as the matrix of *most*, or its second argument. However, on the face of it, (6) isn't remotely close to the sort of syntax in (8). This is quasi-paradoxical. On the one hand *most* and similar determiners can be shown to be two-place relations. That is not surprising: several verbs are too. However, unlike what we see for verbs, in this instance one of the arguments is not, in any trivial syntactic sense, related to the determiner. Then something's got to give. The stringent semantic-mapping conditions (concretely the FI and the PSC) coupled with BBC considerations in syntax yield an impossibility – two-place relations involving long-distance dependents (in (6), for instance, *most* and 'what John kissed') – so long as we stay within context-free grammars.

What must give is either syntactic or semantic. If one insists on a context-free *syntax*, one has to give up the specific version of the SC thesis proposed in (3). For example, if one allows the semantics to be generative too, enriching the system to allow for semantic type-lifting, then it is possible to emend the situation above by treating *most girls* as a new sort of object, which is semantically dual: it represents an entity, but also a predicate that can take the rest of the expression as its argument. All of this, the determination of a designated element as dual and the procedure by which it decides on what to take as its argument once its type has been lifted, are generative procedures in the semantic component. If, in contrast, one assumes a *purely interpretive* semantics, whereby any structural modification required to resolve the paradox must be effected by the syntax, then one's syntax must move to the realm of context-sensitivity.

8.2.3   *Interpreting (mildly) context-sensitive relations*

The modeling capabilities of unconstrained context-sensitive relations are equivalent to those of a Turing machine,[8] which, in a sense to be immediately qualified, is not saying much about any system. The problem can be focused, to start with, from a certain language acquisition perspective. A human child, with access to hypothesis-forming capabilities stated in terms of classical context-sensitive relations, could be searching anywhere rational for data analyses, thus arguably falling into dramatic learnability traps. Now, things are really not that bad if the language learner is not a hypothesis tester, but

---

8 Peters and Ritchie (1973) showed how the standard transformational theory in Chomsky (1965) can generate all recursively enumerable formal languages, making the corresponding grammars in this respect equivalent to Turing machines. Again, those results hold only for E-languages. That said, it is possible (though hard to prove) that essentially the same result obtains in a modified version of the CH for I-languages, of the sort assumed here.

rather a more abstract 'acquirer' who somehow fixes parametric settings directly within linguistic structures of the sort studied here, caring about the strong generative capacity of the overall system, at least in theory.[9] In any case, the generative enterprise during the last three decades can be largely seen as an attempt to frame the question of how context-sensitive relations in grammar can be constrained so that only a handful become possible. Whether or not the learner is a dull hypothesis tester, a constrained system would help the acquisition. Although certainly not a finished project, some appropriate version of this has been assumed throughout this book, as problems such as those outlined at the end of the previous section clearly exist, theory-neutrally, and a solution that doesn't complicate the syntax will have to complicate other components of grammar. For concreteness, let's say that the appropriate syntax is *mildly* context-sensitive, albeit with the caveats and suggested lines of research already outlined in section 7.2.

That said, a question to explore here is what semantics mild context-sensitivity can anchor. Already in chapter 2 the need became clear for thesis (9).

(9)   *Part/Whole-to-Part/Whole Thesis* (P/W^2)
        If X is a proper part of Y in the syntactic object, and only then, the denotation [|X|] of X is a proper part of the denotation [|Y|] of Y assigned by interpretive axioms in the system.

For this P/W^2 thesis to hold, there has to be a way of determining what a part is with respect to a whole. It is then important to consider *deductions* as in section 7.4.2, for *the deduction is an integral whole to the premises within it.* The solution suggested in 7.4.1 to the space-craft riddle introduced in chapter 2 was precisely in those terms: if the aliens want to understand that one means X as a whole to Y, let's denote X in a numerical way that a fortiori is whole to Y. But at that point our syntactic object cannot just be a 2D context-free syntax, where nothing is obviously a part to any whole. (Of course we could *define* relevant such parts, but that would be extrinsically to the relevant syntax, thus not addressing our worries.) Precisely how, then, a more complex, or topologically 'warped', formal object is (a) to represent syntactic relations and (b) to anchor corresponding Part/Whole semantics becomes an interesting exercise.

9 Postulating an 'acquirer' of that sort is easier said than done, though, since then questions emerge as to what sorts of cues the learner can actually use – beyond first order data – and how this predicts not just successful language acquisition, but also language change. See Uriagereka (2007) for perspective and some references.

Some of the tools we need to succeed in the formal aspect of that intriguing mapping ought to come from the process by which a quantification as in (6) is coded. Unfortunately there is no worked-out model of these matters to summarize in a T-shirt-style thesis like the FI or the PSC. The statements in (10), however, are agreed-upon facts about these sorts of relations. It is because of empirically determined conditions like these that we take linguistic relations to be only of the *mildly* context-sensitive sort – these conditions would be irrelevant in a more powerful system.

(10)   (Determiner) Quantificational Relations are ...

a.   ... bounded.
b.   ... unary or binary, but generally not more complex.
c.   ... restricted to a configurational dependent.
d.   ... scoped to an inclusive, non-configurational dependent.

Suppose that, as suggested by the DIT as stated in (16) in chapter 7, in principle both context-free and mildly context-sensitive syntactic conditions are relevant to semantic interpretation. Then perhaps fact (10b) is just a reflection of the fact that a mapping from a context-free to a context-sensitive formal object a fortiori involves two points of stability: one at the input and one at the output. Fact (10a) is also consistent, if locality is seen in familiar transformational terms involving derivational memory: a connection between an input and an output condition is easier to establish, in systemic memory terms alone (of the sort discussed in section 7.2), the shorter the derivational time is that the connection has to remain unresolved. That said the interpretive procedure must choose how to map input and output representations associated to quantifiers: which to the restriction, which to the scope. (10c) and (10d) provide the answer; the question is why *that* answer. Linguists think of the combined action of (10c) and (10d) as the Conservativity Thesis.[10]

8.3   Reprojection

In what follows some speculations are offered as to why conservativity holds for natural language determiners, and what this may tell us about the P/W^2 thesis.

---

10 A determiner δ is conservative if for any sets/pluralities B and A that are its arguments the semantic value of 'δ (B)(A)' is the same as the semantic value of 'δ (B)(A∩B)'. This is trivial for unary determiners, but not so for binary determiners involving both a restriction and a scope, which must be logically ordered. It is thought that all natural language determiners are conservative.

8.3.1   *Syntactic limits on quantificational scope*

Given its lexical content, a sentence like (11a) could in principle (and contra the conservativity thesis) have meant that most disappearances are data.[11]

(11)   a. Most data disappear.
        b. [Most data's disappearance] depresses me.
        c. [That most data disappear] depresses me.

Of course, aside from mapping the quantifier restriction as its scope and vice versa to obtain the 'inverted' reading, we must ignore the fact that *disappear* is a verb and assume that *data* can be the main predicate introduced by *are* in the bizarre interpretation. To prevent these extra considerations, we could attempt to construct the quantification internal to a nominalized expression (so that swapping the arguments would not require changes in syntactic category). But then something intriguing happens: (11b) *cannot mean what* (11c) *asserts*. It roughly means that the intersection of the things that depress me and the data disappearances is proportionally large. Why shouldn't there be a reading of (11b) whereby what depresses me is a disappearing event whose subject is most data? Descriptively, the scope of a quantifier cannot be of a nominal sort – it must be verbal. That demands an explanation. Hopefully, whatever is behind the account relates also to the impossibility of a 'non-conservative' reading for (11a).

Now compare the structure where a determiner can gain a relevant scope (12a) with a structure where this is not possible, (12b).

(12)

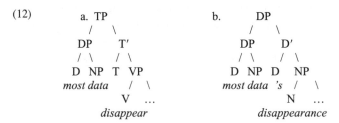

The issue is why *most* cannot take *data* as its restriction and *disappearance* as its scope in (12b), as it can in (12a). One syntactic difference between these two examples is that in the grammatical (12a) *most data* is a sister to a

---

11 So that the example involves reasonably close verbal and nominal counterparts that don't force uniqueness for pragmatic reasons, data (dis)appearances are taken to be relative to theoretical interpretation, thus potentially multiple – X can emerge as data for a given theory, disappear as data for the next theory, and so on.

T projection, while in the ungrammatical (12b) *most data* is a sister to a D projection; *most data* is itself a D projection. This could be important.

Hornstein and Uriagereka (1999, 2002) argue that binary quantifiers like *most* take their scope through a *reprojection*. They assume standard quantificational scope conditions, by way of whatever process is responsible for this context-sensitive dependency in the mapping to LF. But in addition to that, the argument is advanced that after a quantifier raises to its scope position, bringing with it its first argument or restriction, its structure must 'reproject', so as to take the remainder syntactic structure as its second argument. In other words, the structure we have in (12) is incomplete.[12] This is then interesting, given the two different conditions there. For while it's obvious what it would mean for the displaced DP to reproject in (12a) (the dominating TP would need to be reconsidered as a DP), it is less clear how the displaced DP could reproject in (12b). The dominating DP – the projection of a different D head (not the displaced determiner with quantificational force) – would have to be reconsidered as *another* DP, this time the DP projected by the quantifier. If we assume a *bare* phrase structure, along the lines of Chomsky (1994), it is unclear how such a reprojection could obtain, as it would require indexing the two Ds that enter into the combinatorial process, and re-indexing the result as a consequence. If such subtle distinctions are grammatically unavailable, we have modeled the impossibility of a quantificational reading for (12b). This directly argues for the reprojection process, as no other explanation is known for the contrast associated to the structures in (12).

Reprojections bear also on a deduction of the conservativity thesis above. If we were to reverse the order of the two arguments of a quantifier, so that the restriction becomes the scope and vice versa, then we would have to *reproject the relation involving the restriction*, not the scope. Then a mismatch would occur between the syntax and the semantics for the quantifier. Logically, we want the quantifier restriction to be a sort of internal argument of the quantifier, the expression where the quantifier 'lives on', to use the terminology

---

12 The example in (i) illustrates the mechanics of reprojection:

   (i)   a. John likes every book.
             b. $[_{\text{IP}}$ John$_i$ I^0 $[_{\text{VP}}$ $[_{\text{DP}}$ every book$]_j$ $[_{\text{VP}}$ t_i likes $t_j]]]$
             c. $[_{\text{IP}}$ John$_i$ I^0 $[_{\text{DP}}$ $[_{\text{D}'}$ every book$]_j$ $[_{\text{VP}}$ t_i likes $t_j]]]$

   Hornstein and Uriagereka covertly re-label the phrase-marker in (ib) as in (ic), where the scope of *every* occupies the reprojected specifier of this category. The proposal associates the projection/reprojection dynamics to Beck's Quantifier Induced Islands in the LF component (Beck 1996). Basically, the reprojected structure becomes an opaque domain for syntactic relations, in a manner discussed in Hornstein *et al.* (2007).

from Barwise and Cooper (1981). The scope is a kind of external argument of the quantifier, computed with regards to the previously computed quantifier-restriction relation. If the restriction stands in a context-free relation with the quantifier (as its complement) and the scope in a context-sensitive relation with regards to the quantifier, the implicit ordering corresponds to a syntactic alignment given to us by the CH: context-free relations are logically prior to context-sensitive ones. We need not stipulate any further mapping between the relevant syntax and semantics; all we have to do is assume a simple (co-linear) correlation between the two. However if the restriction were to reproject we would need an explicit, cumbersome, mapping between that sort of formally complex syntax and a correspondingly simpler semantics. This is, of course, doable, but certainly not elegant.

That result bears also on how we plan to relate the process of 'complement assumption' to Aktionsart *deductions*. It was noted above that the syntax in point is higher order, but that is too broad a conclusion. We require something nar-rower: that at the point we want the semantic hierarchy to obtain there is exactly *one* identifiable syntactic hierarchy to match it with. The general conclusion about the order of complexity in the syntax is consistent with this desideratum, but can we pin down the syntactic 'warp' *to the corresponding semantic deduction*? We may if we apply the moral of reprojection to those instances as well. All this process does is code the fact that a relevant structure X is attuned, first, to a context-free status, and next to a context-sensitive extension in the course of the derivation – the very same structure X. Moreover, according to the arguments given above, the context-sensitive extension, in instances of 'complement assumption', is second-order in its formal properties. That structure X has reprojected in those terms means that it involves two hierarch-ically *ordered* aspects, in a serious sense of the term ordering. Then, as per the DIT, this ordered syntax should correspond to a comparably ordered semantics.

8.3.2   *Focal mappings*

In order to flesh out the desideratum just discussed, we need first to present the sort of issues that emerge in focal mappings, which we will adapt as a tool for deducing Aktionsart hierarchies as presented above. Bear in mind that we will be working with a semantic structure like (13b) for (13a), which pre-supposes one like (14b) for (14a).

(13)   a. Jack grew beans.
       b. $\exists e'$ CAUSE (e') [[$\exists e$ grow (e)] Agent (Jack, e') & Theme (e, e') & Theme (beans, e)]

(14)   a. Beans grew.
       b. $\exists$e grow (e) Theme (beans, e)

The general issue is whether such an implication can be naturally and generally coded in reprojection terms, thus turning it into a *deduction*.

Herburger (2000) has argued that event quantification is restricted, on the basis of considerations about the semantics of focus. Compare the focalized (15) to (14).

(15)   a. BEANS grew.
       b. [$\exists$e: Grew (e)] Grew (e) & Theme (beans, e)

(15a) asserts that what grew are beans, unlike (14), which merely asserts the (neutral) growth of beans. Herburger captures that difference by treating the existential event operator as a binary quantifier, which takes as its restriction the entire lexical content in the sentence *except for the focused element*, and as its scope the lexical content of the sentence. Such a 'repetition' of lexical material (e.g. *grew* in (15b)) is something we return to. This general view of things is possible within the Neo-Davidsonian approach assumed here, whereby predicates are generally decomposed in the manner in (15). This allows Herburger to withhold thematic information from the restriction (the focalized *beans*), which results in a clean logical form for focused sentences. Assuming this approach in its most general form (whereby restricted quantification is invoked *in all the Aktionsart layers* that involve sub-event quantification), by the previous reasoning about restricted quantification, event quantification in general will need systematic reprojection.

Consider how a binary event existential quantifier as in (15b), encoded on a T or similar head, can result in an LF from which a semantics of that sort is readable. One can stipulate the relevant mapping (including the duplication of non-focused material) the way Herburger (2000) does, but this doesn't come out as naturally as in (12) above. However recall the mapping introduced in section 3.7. The key there was that a standard verb/complement structure as in (15) above is obtained by way of a derivational process along the lines in (16), whereby each new argument is introduced as the subject of a small clause (16a) (cf. (57) in section 3.7). Moreover, in section 5.4.4 it was argued that the predicate of a small clause as in (16a) incorporates to a verbalizing head, as in (16b); the resulting object is a bona fide verb, and the remainder structure is reanalysed as its nominal complement (16c). This is the process of *complement assumption*, notated here with an agreement subscript.

(16)   a.   *v*-Agr′
            / \
         v-Agr SC
               / \
            DP PRED
            beans grew

        b.   *v*-Agr′
            /   \
         v-Agr   SC
            / \   / \
          V *v*-Agr *beans* t
          grew   /
              ↑_____/

        c.   V_{Agr′}
            /   \
         V_{Agr} *beans*
         grew

Observe that complement assumption as in (16c) involves the reprojection of *v*-Agr′ in (16b) as V′. Moreover, just as in the instances of reprojections in Hornstein and Uriagereka, here too a context-free structure like (16a) is derivationally organized vis-à-vis a context-sensitive structure like (16b). In addition, the derivational process takes us from (16a) to (16c), after all the nuances in chapter 5 are integrated (this is not expressed in the diagrams). We need all of this to run a deduction.

A mapping relevant to focal concerns, just alluded to, is viable in the terms presented here because *the relevant lexical information is present twice* – in the terms where all the lexical presuppositions are cashed out through small clauses, and then in the guise that emerges after such processes as complement assumption (for themes) or appropriate head incorporations (the more familiar, customary, Hale/Kayser-style format). Moreover, the initial representation is simpler in terms of the CH. The small clauses are finite-state and their association to whatever determines their reference (D-*n* for nominal versions, T-*v* for verbal ones) is merely context-free; context-sensitive dependencies emerge only after relevant incorporations ensue. This signals a pre-lexical/post-lexical divide. The first half marks those lexico-conceptual dependencies that join the event-operator restriction, whereas the second establishes logico-intentional associations that delineate the event-operator scope, according to the ordering conditions studied above for the Conservativity scenario – extended from regular determiner operators to event operators.

Consider a detailed analysis of the focalized (15), albeit with the machinery in (16).

(17)   a. *v*-Agr′
            / \
         v-Agr SC
               / \
            DP PRED
            BEANS grew

        b.   *v*-Agr′
            /   \
         v-Agr   SC
            / \   / \
          V *v*-Agr *BEANS* t
          grew   /
              ↑_____/

        c. V_{Agr′}
            / \
         V_{Agr} *BEANS*
         grew

The issue, to start with, is why focalization involves phonetic prominence, a matter that has never been explained. It is interesting to observe that focalization resembles, in that respect, the sort of phonetic prominence we saw associated to emphasis in section 6.3. In that instance we associated this fact to the creation of raw phonological space, which is doable through either looping mechanisms or extension procedures that elongate either phonological nuclei or their pitch/stress. In focus, too, this is typical, focalized elements across languages being iterated, or their nuclei elongated in some fashion.[13] This cannot be an accident. Suppose it tells us that, in some respects, focal structure has a finite-state component to it.

(18)   Any portion of syntactic material that is designated as 'raw-phonological-space' via any form of finite-state-expansion is interpreted in merely finite-state terms.

By 'finite-state terms' for interpretation one can only mean conditions along the lines in (1) above. To see the effect this has on the interpretation of (17), let's observe first what happens when given structures are *not* designated as 'raw-phonological-space' through the customary PF-mechanisms of emphasis and the like.

Undesignated occurrences of given lexical tokens deployed in the derivation as in (17) are seen by the interpretive components twice: in their pre-lexical, 'decomposed' fashion in (17a), and in the post-lexical, 'atomic' fashion in (17c). This is good, for Herburger's analysis requires that given occurrences of relevant lexical information be interpreted *twice*. Although she does not give us a way in which this can be achieved – she just shows that it is semantically necessary – the present system deduces that duality. In effect we have presupposed material cashed out from whatever occurrences of interpretable items decompositionalists decompose, and asserted material read from whatever, corresponding, occurrences of those very interpretable items even atomists admit make it to the 'real' syntax. This is a virtue of the present way of seeing things, as it makes it unnecessary, in order to ensure Herburger's results, to resort to copying (the other way of obtaining multiple occurrences of given tokens, as in the 'reconstruction' instances studied

---

13 Focus is intonational in English, while in Indonesian dialects it involves syllabic lengthening. But focus can also be positional, as in Basque or Hungarian, and then involves displacement of the focalized material. It can be accompanied by explicit focalizing particles, which may show up in the focal material (in Chickasaw or Wolof) or as 'associative' elements like the English *only* (e.g. in Bantu languages). And it can show up as reduplication, e.g. as in 'a PARTY party'. Importantly, focus seems to always involve some sort of overt cue, thereby differing from standard quantifiers (which behave in most instances without any such cues).

above). That said, we need to understand what role the phonetic prominence is playing *for the focused material*.

If designated as finite-state, *relevant occurrences cannot be separated by the interpretive component as different interpretable items*. By the overarching DIT, finite-state structuring is too unsophisticated to support such a duality. In a sense, this is the same fact we discussed in the 'reconstruction' analysis. The chain occurrences cannot reconstruct multiply: their finite-state origin doesn't allow the system to tap into the memory resources that would be necessary to hold one occurrence in derivational memory while the other occurrence goes about its derivational life until hitting some appropriate place for interpretation. A limitation of this sort, we saw, prevents wild anaphorical dependencies. In this instance it has the effect of forcing the system to interpret occurrences of focal material once, not twice as needed for all other (unfocused) material.

But then which occurrence is to be interpreted, the one entering the derivation or the one exiting it (e.g. *BEANS* as in (17a) or *BEANS* as in (17c))? Herburger (2000) shows, empirically, that the last copy survives. Why this should be is no different from the situation emerging with chain occurrences studied by Nunes (2004): there, too, setting aside alternative conditions, the default interpretation for sets of occurrences involves the last derivational survivor. The occurrences (whether integrated into a chain or as restriction-scope pairs) go about their derivational life as long as appropriate derivational forces carry them forward. At the last relevant point for interpretation this process takes place, *maximizing the scope* of the object thus far achieved; it would have been pointless to go on in the derivational flow for the interpretive components and then to ignore the occurrence that made it 'thus far', as expected in a minimalist syntax. The architecture predicts, also, that there shouldn't be 'reverse focus', with scopal nuances being informationally poorer than presupposed ones: that would go against the derivational flow.[14]

---

14 Expressions like this would also be uninformative. Conversations can be uninformative ('Oh, men are men') yet fully grammatical. Not even in redundant circumstances do we find expressions like 'BEANS grew (in my backyard)' asserting that, as for the beans that grew (in my backyard), something or other grew (in my backyard). It is also worth pointing out that an expression without any sort of focus would be rare. This is because the material to join the event quantifier restriction is always there, but in the absence of any focus it would be interpreted twice, without qualifications. Perhaps expressions like *that you will eat them, you will eat them* are of the relevant sort, although it isn't clear why the simpler *you will eat them* doesn't obtain that interpretation unless the context is loaded (e.g. the parent looks at the child having said 'you will eat them'). As for situations where nothing is presupposed, while in the system proposed the information will be available twice, we can assume that the entire

One more thing, which has always been mysterious, is worth emphasizing.

(19)   a. I hate snow-MEN, only.
       b. Don't tell me 'Sorry I arrived late'; you're arriv-ING late as we speak!
       c. Dear, you should definitely *RE*-consider, not just reconsider.
       d. Well, she's not just trendy; I'd say she is actually trendi-ER every minute.
       e. He's child-LIKE – not child-ISH.
       f. He's really tire-SOME – not just tir-ING!

As Jackendoff (1972) shows, one can focalize chunks of lexical items. The examples in (19) get more problematic as we go down the list, from compounds to more or less standard instances of derivational affixes. The latter ought to trouble the atomist the most, as they are the less syntactic – and yet focusing as in, say, (19f) doesn't seem particularly bad.[15] From the perspective presented, the analysis of even these sorts of examples becomes straightforward, so long as they are 'decomposable' in some pre-lexical sense. The relevant information is there in the pre-lexical structure, thus it can be signaled for focalization by the finite-state mechanisms, thereby disappearing from the restrictive clause in the manner just explored.

8.3.3   Consequences for Aktionsart

By the same logic in (16), and now ignoring focal matters, the way we introduce a syntactic argument beyond the theme (say *Jack*) should be as in (20) – as the 'subject' of a new small clause. Notice that the entire structure in (16c) (including a given derivational history, literally) is taken as the predicate of the small clause, which undergoes the computations below. The complex verbal structure in (20b) has a warped syntax, in the technical sense introduced in section 7.4.3. The upper layer of structure, associated via T to the CAUSE sub-event, is obvious.

(20)   a. *v*-Agr′   b.   *v*-Agr′
            / \   /   \
        v-Agr SC   *v*-Agr   SC
            / \   / \   / \
          DP PRED   V_Agr *v*-Agr *Jack* PRED
        Jack / \   *grow*   /   \
            V_Agr *beans*   ↑_____t   *beans*
            grow

sentence is focused, and thus the material that would go into the event operator restriction is not interpreted. Then the sentence is fully assertive in all its contents.

15 Although it is impossible to focus information that doesn't make it into PF in any shape (and recall fn. 13).

But more importantly, within this structure we have a V_{Agr} element telling us that, internal to the verbal expression, there exists a whole derivational history with phrasal and transformational import, just as (20a) has phrasal import whereas (20b) is the result of a transformational process. As noted in section 5.5.2, however, *Jack* in (20b) does not meet the structural conditions for being assumed as a complement.[16] Nevertheless (20b) still feeds a reprojection as in (21), with aspectual consequences of the sort explored by Schmitt (1995).[17]

(21)

$$V_{AgrO\text{-}AgrS'}$$
```
            V_AgrO-AgrS'
           /          \
    V_AgrO-AgrS       SC
       grow          /  \
                  Jack  PRED
                       /    \
                      t    beans
```

Given a step along the lines of (21), we need not stipulate the ordering relevant to convey the proper semantic deduction in Aktionsart. The way the syntax has proceeded, (16) is logically ordered prior to (20a), and that in turn prior to (21). The CH, encoded through the Agr subscripts, provides us with the ordering tool we need to map the semantics.[18] These could be focally complex, many elements (*Jack, grew, beans*) being focalizable; such foci will simply not make it to interpretation as part of the restrictive semantics read off (20a). In turn, all of (21), the syntactic object after reprojection, will make it to the semantics as what determines the scope of the event operator, thus constituting the bulk of what's asserted.

The whole analysis is built on the premise that binary quantifiers reproject, in the sense used by Hornstein and Uriagereka, and this is what it means for them to be conservative: a quantifier's restriction is determined first in the derivation, and its scope last. Conservativity is the result of a concrete derivational flow, which entangles structures as it goes along. Scope, the ultimate logico-intentional notion, is the archetypical 'end of derivation' process, a context-sensitive one inasmuch as elements that 'gain scope' must

---

16 Basically, complement assumption works when the contents of the small clause divide evenly: the predicate incorporates up and the subject is the only remainder. These conditions are only met for the lowest subject of a small clause, which ends up being the Theme or first, articulating, argument.

17 Schmitt calculates aspect in the dynamic terms first discussed by Verkuyl (1972), that is, as a relation between the verb and, mainly, its theme (see the previous footnote). She executes this in terms of AgrO projections, which are translatable in terms of the devices in the text.

18 Following Pietroski (2003), we can surmise that this is the role theta roles play, constructing lexico-semantic representations from progressively more complex syntactic objects.

also 'remember' what they are gaining their complex scope *for* – the restriction they 'live on'. By that very reasoning the process presupposes the more primitive lexico-conceptual notion of the restriction. In instances of standard quantification there is no more to say. Language presents this duality, period, which the DIT expresses in terms of semantics being opportunistic in interpreting matters, early and late – or more radically, in *that* being the essence of structural semantics. Interestingly, however, if Herbuger is right and the architecture of sentences is also *binarily* quantificational, assuming these event quantifiers also obey Conservativity, this gives us two consequences. One is an elegant syntax for focus, if the semantic input/output duality is taken seriously and the considerations about finite-state syntax alluded to above suspend the interpretation of unwanted repeated occurrences. The second result is the ability to deduce the Aktionsart implicational hierarchy.

To wrap up that deduction, a structure like (21) has to be taken seriously, in particular the agreement sub-indices alluding to prior stages in the derivation. Those prior stages are entanglements of the relevant syntactic object, involving (at least) two reprojections. They are as radical as adding an axis to the number line to yield the number plane, or yet another axis to the latter to yield a number space. Just as manifolds on a 3D (Euclidean) space can be 'chartered' as a 2D (non-Euclidean) manifold, so too a complex accomplishment like Jack's growing of beans can be 'chartered' as something emergent through some sort of folding of an open-ended activity of bean growing. The formal support for that denotation is a phrasal formal object of a significantly warped complexity ((21) with all the subscripts deployed as derivational processes) 'chartered' as (16a) with *Jack* (eventually) 'added'. In this syntactic warp the appropriate denotation cannot be other than what it is, short of violating minimalist desiderata. In the formal object whatever boundary on the phrasal space is imposed by the inclusion of *Jack* (which carries the expression 'up one notch') anchors the relevent semantics. That emergent formal boundary can map to a semantic boundary – distinguishing, in this instance, an activity like the intransitive *grow* from the corresponding transitive accomplishment. If such a correspondence holds, the syntax/semantics mapping becomes natural, indeed relatively trivial (completely so in the radical version of this project). If, on the other hand, we choose to ignore the formal boundary the syntax gives us, should we need to express a formal boundary in our semantics we would have to signal that in arbitrary ways. That poses the indeterminacy-of-translation puzzle mentioned for the space-craft scenario, and so, as Einstein would quip about such matters, 'God may not have had a choice!'

8.3.4   Why not 'The other way around'?

The title in this section amounts to asking, for instance, why the abstract CAUSE could not compose *before* the lexical *grow*, which depends on the LPT in section 3.6.4.[19]

(22)   *Lexical Projection Thesis (LPT)*

    (a) Formal items involve transformationally driven event-quantification semantics.

    (b) Substantive items involve configurationally expressed predicative semantics.

This thesis – which will not be deduced here from anything more basic – should eventually allow us to provide explanations for at least the following additional questions.

(23)   a. Why are there only a few formal items?

       b. Why do they generally involve 'checking', unlike substantive items?

       c. Why are they morphologically special (weak/null, uninterpretable)?

       d. Why are they semantically special (not 'thematic' or 'modificational')?

The answer to (23a) might follow from (23b), if the latter implies a complex context-sensitive syntax (thus a more costly, so comparably scarce, sort of formal object). Chomsky (1995) also suggests that (23c) correlates with (23b), inconclusively (see Chomsky [2000]). Some aspects of (23d), if it involves binary quantification, correlate with (23b) and the fact that context-sensitive structures start their derivational life as context-free ones (the phenomenon of reprojection when these two facts are interpretably correlated).

Functional items are interspersed with lexical ones, which suggests they are *grammatical codings of 'maximally stable' syntactic chunks* established in CH terms. Identification of a type of structure involves distinguishing it from a different type. By scanning up a syntactic object, the interpretive interfaces could identify an nth order entity in the CH by hitting upon an entity of order $n+1$. (We use this sort of reasoning in identifying dynamic events: water is boiling when bubbles start emerging from the fluid, signaling a phase transition – we don't need a thermometer to measure this.) That maximally isolates an nth order chunk, 'stabilizing' it. Interpretation can have access to that, and hold the interpretive results in derivational memory until some later

---

19 As stated, this predicts that the lexical dependencies in a small clause (involving adjunction) are neither substantive nor formal. This is consistent with the finite-state treatment of small clauses in chapter 6, suggesting that such elements (and associated compounding perhaps) are more elementary than substantive or formal.

stage – the logic behind reprojection. Functional structure can *signal* this process through a grammatical formative. Such a formative is thus different from more ordinary substantive items expressing lexico-conceptual notions. Matters could not be turned around arguably any more than the higher-order complex numbers could have been organized differently with regards to the lower-order reals: they each would cease being what they are. If in grammar, too, functional structure is logically ordered (in the strong terms explored here) with regards to lexical structure, no reversibility is possible if these two layers of structure are to keep their identity. We could not change the way functional structure is 'chartered', in the topological sense, as some high-order manifold over a more basic manifold deploying lexico-conceptual relations.

We assume, non-trivially as we saw, that first-order combinations in human language are interpretable (Full Interpretation). This (ultimately finite-state) assumption is so powerful that if the grammar hits a non-interpretable element it must be eliminated before reaching the interfaces. Feature erasure, in turn, results in a higher-order syntax. In a sense, then, the uninterpretable elements can be soundly *defined* as second-order functions over first-order objects. For instance, a case feature signals to the system how to relate two distant contexts in a phrase marker, after Agree has relevantly obtained. If this machinery is central to ('structure preserving') context-free relations, it is only when this sort of second-order syntax is involved (establishing uninterpretability) that the system is even allowed to go into significant transformational dependencies. It remains to be seen whether other context-sensitive operations are less drastic, and if so whether they count as truly context-sensitive dependencies or, instead, the very notion of context dependency comes out as second-order.

Not all functional categories or features are unintepretable. For instance, there is an obvious difference between T, C or D, and Case or similar features. Why does this duality hold? There probably is a tight connection between those functional categories that have an interpretation and those that do not.[20] Indeed, if Last Resort is generally the way to go about ('structure preserving') transformations, things could not have been otherwise. Second-order, interpretable, functional stuff demands context-sensitive dependencies (cf. Herburger's [2000] claim for event quantification being binary). If the syntactic machinery that gives us context dependency has to be geared by

---

20 See among others Pesetsky and Torrego (2004), Chomsky (2006), Boeckx (in press), Gallego (2007).

Last Resort (uninterpretable) demands, *without relevant uninterpretable elements* to set the system in motion *there won't be any entanglement* in structure to attain appropriate context-dependency.

The points raised in the last two paragraphs are directly related, and they should ultimately tell us something about how functional items associate to one another – why C is higher than T and so on. We are beginning to have a map, à la Cinque (2002), but the next step ought to be asking why it has the properties it does. The suggestion being entertained is that, just as the present approach deduces nominal or Aktionsart hierarchies, so too an appropriate extension ought to have similar consequences for other, higher-order, cartographies.

8.4   Arguments and Case

The mechanisms we have been led to throughout this book help us pose many new questions. Whenever possible, they will be framed as evolutionary concerns, probably their natural locus (see Epilogue).

8.4.1   *Basic mental spaces?*

Lexico-conceptual structuring has been grounded on relational terms; the manifolds discussed in chapter 7 are essential spaces, which get 'chartered' as lower-dimensional manifolds, all the way down to 'ur' concepts. Such foundational concepts, as it were, 'have in them' more complex forms, much as Carrara marble 'had' Michelangelo's David – and vice versa, the complex forms 'have' the stuff that makes them, the way David 'has' marble. It is hard to understand how these relations work, beyond saying that they ought to do so, the way basic numerical spaces relate to more convoluted ones, something that human beings grasp – mysteriously.

The syntax suggested for bottom-line concepts is eminently finite-state, in some appropriate sense. It is natural to assume that such a 'proto-syntax' *obtains in the Numeration*, a bona fide component of the system. If numerations are real, the minimal array condition (MAC) from chapter 4 – which aims at minimizing functional items in this domain – is an expected and desired economy specification. While genuine syntactic access to numerations is probably very limited, we saw it above in instances of focalization, and in section 6.3.2 in terms of looping of what, semantically at least, amounts to a sub-lexical notion.

A finite-state syntax, we saw in section 6.4.2, can still distinguish combinations as in (24), for 'heads' being defined as lexical items (LI) and

'MaxPs' as an elsewhere situation, that is items with *some* derivational life to them (−LI).

(24)   a. $\langle\text{head, head}\rangle = \langle\text{LI, LI}\rangle$
        b. $\langle\text{MaxP, MaxP}\rangle = \langle-\text{LI}, -\text{LI}\rangle$
        c. $\langle\text{head, MaxP}\rangle = \langle\text{LI}, -\text{LI}\rangle$

(24a) and (24b), combining identical sorts of items, involve 'trivial structure'; thus, by the CLT their semantics is identificational, and irrelevant to what were called, in chapter 3, 'integral' dependencies of the part/whole sort, and similar, more general, associations. By the same reasoning (24c) is more interesting. It is not, as shown in section 6.4.2, a head/complement relation, as would be the case for a head-MaxP combination in a context-free incarnation. But inasmuch as the MaxP, in the finite-state instance, can involve *abandoning the derivational workspace* to signal the non-head, an integral small clause dependency can be achieved. Thus cyclicity is at the core of this form of dependency, in a characteristically dynamic fashion.

(25) $\langle[\text{city}_{-\text{LI}}], \text{neighborhood}_{\text{LI}}\rangle$

                 INTERPRET

In section 6.4.3 interpreting a −LI like *city* in (25) in terms of the cue thesis was suggested, making the denotation of *city* the space which the denotation of *neighborhood* operates on; in the warp terms presented above, *neighborhood* is a space operator. Manifolds can generate further manifolds, so a given space that has been operated on can result in *a higher dimensional space*, which again can in principle be operated on. This is central in supporting a semantic deduction.

8.4.2   *Relativistic intentional relations?*

What has just been described could be entirely solipsistic, and so how such structured thoughts can be shared with other mind-endowed creatures poses 'translation' problems. If you want to tap into my conceptual system it is not enough for us to think alike: we have to find a way (barring telepathy) of sharing our thoughts, which means translating them into observables. Then we are at risk of losing the very structure of our thoughts in the translation process, to the point that they become unrecognizable upon being reconstructed in someone else's mind. Here is where the foundational Distributed Interpretation and Co-Linearity theses help. If I manage to associate (some of) the complex nuances of my thoughts uniquely to comparably complex nuances of a neutral formal system we share, our chances at communicating increase. What is that common language? In some form, mathematical groups. Except that is still, in a sense, semantics: the warp sequence itself that yields structured thought. How can that be made public?

Syntax allows us to reconstruct topologies, of the sort just alluded to, from a phonological support that isolates symbolic units like words.[21] But inasmuch as the phonological channel is unidimensional, that sort of support will at best allow us to carry through essentially Markovian messages. This might describe what Bickerton (1990) refers to as proto-language. If we need to express more, in particular any usable recursion (whereby symbolic use of any X is repeated down the derivational stream), then we need some sort of *tokenization mechanism in the system,* whereby one X can be told apart from another. Without having evolved such tokenization processes, proto-language could have been internally complex, a real 'language of thought' in all respects – albeit an incommunicable one beyond trivialities: 'me & you, Buddy', 'you idiot' and the like.

If all communicable syntactic structuring at this point – with Markovian formal complexity – is essentially lumping symbols together, it is unclear what parsers could do to distinguish token X from another token X. It is tempting to attempt: (i) evolving derivational cycles, as alluded to in the previous section, so that one X goes in one cycle and the next X in a different one; or (ii) marking each X for distinctness through some mechanism. But (i) begs the question: what does it mean to have cycles in a finite-state system, where only before and after (plus loops) exist? Brackets don't mean a thing at this CH level, as they involve non-terminal symbolic representation; more technically the system lacks the memory resources to code any of these nuances, as discussed in section 7.2. (Note: the solution proposed in section 6.4.2 presupposed that the entire architecture is in place, with a phrasal component that actually sanctions, entirely a posteriori, that certain finite-state combinations are valid, vis-à-vis other flat alternatives; presupposing that much is what begs the question from an evolutionary perspective: how did *that* more complex system come about?) (ii) is even more hopeless. It requires stepping out of the 'normal' system that interprets, say, grunts as symbolic, to now code a given grunt as uninterpretable, with the sole purpose of separating some different grunt X from yet another grunt X of the same type, yet separately tokenized. That seems, in some sense, 'going

---

21 It may be much to grant. How exactly humans process even word units out of the speech mess is a difficult problem; see Hickok and Poeppel (2000) for perspective.

higher-order' although not obviously how. It is not clear, to start with, how meaningfully to relate each X without, again, begging the question, if the Xs are not already part of the same structure, indeed one that is complex enough to now host the extra 'tokenizing' grunt, with no interpretive value of its own. But how does a finite-state system express all of this?

Suppose some brain reorganization takes place that gives access to the Case system studied here, plus the derivational memory to parse it.[22] Tokenization, then, in a sense becomes a triviality: a case-marked grunt is different from a differently case-marked grunt – even grunts of the same type – because each case mark is a pointer to the computational system, so that in due time (when context-sensitivity is meaningfully deployed, appropriate contexts being derivationally constructed) sheer phrasal context separates one grunt from the other. That sort of system is obviously richer, and it can go into the quantificational complexities that have been outlined above, in sections 8.2.3 and 8.3. Those, in turn, can presumably anchor intentionality, assuming that these processes – the determination of reference or the judgement of truth – are essentially quantificational.[23] Another way of saying this is that, prior to this extra step, strictly *proto-language wasn't (publicly) symbolic.* It may have used 'symbols' of some sort to carry through mental computations, but in much the same way we could say that the immune system or protein folding involve 'computations'. The system would not have achieved the sense of symbolic we now give it until it achieved quantificational status.[24]

If that is how intentionality (somehow, see fn. 23) comes into the picture, the standard philosophical approach to these matters is wrong, as Hinzen (2006, 2007) observes. Intentionality (a public affair) cannot be presupposed in the language faculty. It is a mechanism that the system achieved, in evolution, apparently after it managed to deploy context-sensitive syntax. If so, also, the fact that referentiality should be, as argued in chapter 3, a relativistic notion – relative to a given derivation in a given speaker's mind – is in fact not a quirk, but a design specification in the system, thus a virtual conceptual necessity.

---

22 These two may go together, as argued in Piattelli-Palmarini and Uriagereka (2005). If Ullman and Pierpont (2005) are correct, the recently isolated gene FOXP2 may be involved precisely in this task.

23 Although how that happens also remains mysterious, and this book has had little to say about it.

24 This is consistent with the idea in Hauser *et al.* (2002) that the last great evolutionary event had to do with recursion, or more precisely *usable* recursion (Piattelli-Palmarini and Uriagereka 2005).

In a system of these characteristics, *cyclicity can now emerge*, as Drury (2005) shows. Within these tokenization strictures, if two, say, Cs fail to be distinguished as different C tokens, the derivation can be salvaged by the parser pushing the first C encountered out of on line computation. This would be through the Cue strategy, albeit instead of creating a raw mental space for the next item in computation to modify, it would create whatever 'cashed out' intentional structure the system with the enriched characteristics can muster. Cyclicity in turn would be the basis for articulated complex concepts, albeit now in principle communicable ones. That's the underlying assumption behind thematic or Aktionsart hierarchies, and similar paradigmatic dependencies that the enriched system directly allows.

8.4.3   Opposing lexical features?

The evolutionary brain reorganization alluded to above may have had something to do with what was called 'category collision' in section 5.2. For a distinction based on the substantive/formal divide that the LPT introduces, so that $+/-N$ and $+/-V$ parameters correspond to that essential distinction, four logical possibilities emerge.

(26)   a. $[-N, -V]$ elements (P) are neither substantive nor formal.
           b. $[+N, +V]$ elements (A) are both substantive and formal.
           c. $[-N, +V]$ elements (V) are not substantive but formal.
           d. $[+N, -V]$ elements (N) are substantive but not formal.

Now suppose some 'predicational' distinction existed *prior* to the evolutionary leap forward that gave us case-tokenization, say in terms of a distinction for the 'permanent' (Pe) vs. the 'transient' (Tr).[25] If so, though, how did this distinction, natural for a finite-state system with little interpretive capabilities, get pushed forward in the new stage – arguably precipitating it?

Feature release resulting from category collision determines the emergence of 'free floating prepositions' whose presence is signaled in the system as the Case phenomenon. Category collision itself arises because it was assumed in section 5.2.3 that all lexical roots are listed in the lexicon *in their most marked/specific guise*, thus as $[+N, +V]$ categories. So from this point on, when combining *any* two lexical categories a feature clash emerges. This may not have been an issue in proto-language.[26] In turn, listing lexical items in its maximally marked form is natural, at least on learnability grounds. Sub-case

---

25 See Neale (1990) for ideas on descriptions and names along these lines.
26 Either because such a rich set of distinctions didn't exist in it, or, if it did in some form, because the system didn't have mechanisms to 'look inside' categories to start with.

conditions on learning under 'poverty of the stimulus' force learners to posit the most marked forms as their first hypothesis, the familiar Sub-case situation – if one has a real lexicon to learn to start with, that is.

Nowak *et al.* (2001) argue, on the basis of a computational analysis, that the size of a lexicon has to pass a certain (small) threshold for non-trivial combinatorial (i.e. at least context-free) syntactic communication to be advantageous. Suppose the Markovian lexicon was stable at a couple of dozen items, most of which denoted permanent (Pe) notions and perhaps a handful denoting transient properties (Tr).[27] Call that distinction the Pe/Tr parameter. The idea is that more such items wouldn't have been learnable unless combinatorial syntax were accessible to the relevant hominids. The question is then how such a syntax arose. Intriguingly, if the Pe/Tr opposition just alluded to becomes entrenched, so that *every* item is for some reason assumed to participate in it (every item is assumed to be *both* permanent and transient), then whether the Pe side of the equation wins, or the Tr side does instead, is in the end a matter of contextualization, in a broad sense of this term (and see section 8.4.7 below).

Perhaps originally that even correlated with pronunciation order. Thus imagine two elements, *bat* and *large*, normally used to denote elongated wood-chunks and notions that involve size, respectively. In the original proto-language form *bat* would be a Pe element and *large*, instead, of the Tr sort. In the 'improved' version, though, both of these elements would be +Pe, +Tr (capable of) sustaining permanence and transience conceptualization *at the same time*. However, combinatorial context would highlight one or the other combination. We might imagine that the first element spoken in the proto-combination is seen – by assumptions of the cue thesis sort – to denote a space that the second element somehow modifies. Of course, the opposite order, whereby the last element heard becomes the first element interpreted, also does the trick at this pre-syntactic stage. The point is merely that combinations like *bat large* vs. *large bat* would contextually make each 'word' gain meanings.

More importantly, suppose that the meanings that 'go away' in the combinatorial process – the transient aspect of 'bat' if it is meant permanently, or vice versa – are recovered by the system, albeit *without an interpretation.*

---

27 This is not very different in size from the sort of 'lexicon' psychologists report for the very early stages of language acquisition, and as Baker (in press) points out, it is close, also, to what the 'atomic base' appears to be in languages with very productive agglutinative processes to generate complex words.

At that point the issue is what to do with these 'free ranging' elements that the derivation creates, under the assumptions mentioned. The obvious possibility in present terms is that the elimination of such 'extra' features is what triggers a cascade of systemic reactions with remarkable consequences. What started with a simple extension of opposing properties, to be conceived as being present in all elements-to-be-combined, ended up creating, in the end, the possibility for intentionality.[28]

That hides a huge assumption: that features cannot 'freely float' in derivational space, they must integrate into categories. Why is it that we would be willing to assign, say, permanence and transience *notions* to whatever we denote, but once one of these properties themselves gets 'kicked out' of the system by the assumed dynamics, we cannot let it denote in itself? What is it about these mysterious notions that allows us to use them as properties of what we conceive of, but *not as mental objects in their own right*? This takes us right into the toughest question: what sort of entities are the features that the system is based on?

8.4.4   *Feature valuations are Markovian?*

The context-free Merge operation, in its standard conception, requires non-terminal categories – feature matrices – to be stated. A feature is not a feature matrix, any more than an object can be a set including that object, according to the Foundation Axiom of Set Theory.[29] Therefore operations involving features cannot be of the Merge sort, they have to be simpler. In terms of the CH, they have to be Markovian. In most instances this is true, e.g. by way of Concord processes of the sort studied in section 5.2.4, which take place under adjacency as expected for Markovian mechanisms. But what happens when the valuation between a feature attribute and whatever other feature that holds the crucial specification of this attribute *happens not to be adjacent* – the Agree situation?

Even in those circumstances the mechanism of feature valuation itself *should be Markovian*. But then the grammar must be managing to ignore intervening material between the two crucial features, Probe and Goal. From this perspective, the syntax needs to create a 'warp' in syntactic space, so that

---

28 This recalls the 'virus' idea in Piattelli-Palmarini and Uriagereka (2005), itself consistent with the proposal in Chomsky (2006) that the trigger for the last mutation in the language faculty was 'peripheral features'.

29 This axiom (also called the Axiom of Regularity) makes it impossible for a set-theoretic object to be equivalent to the set formed by this formal object. Note that if, for instance, the empty set were identical to the set including the empty set, zero would be identical to one.

two far apart points in this syntactic fabric end up being adjacent at some higher dimension, for valuation to proceed.[30] The phenomenon of context-sensitivity is, then, a kind of booster of systemic resources so that the features that 'seek one another' end up being in a hyper-space of their own, where Markovian conditions hold. For this warp to be meant seriously the objects that emerge in the CH must themselves be manifolds, where such formal specifications are possible. Although it is hard to prove this, the conditions linguists have found on context-sensitivity, locality, and uniformity at least, are what one expects of viable topological mechanisms that preserve some homomorphism.[31] In other words, a viable syntactic transformation may be *a viable (low-dimensional) topological transformation*. If so, conditions on transformations follow from virtual conceptual necessity, instead of interface interactions.

Given the foundational assumption that a feature cannot Merge, one that gets expelled upon category collision must either be absorbed into a new category or turned into a category by itself. We saw in section 5.2 how these two fates lead to the spread of Concord or the phenomenon of Case. In the integrative solution *syntactic space is expanded*.

(27)

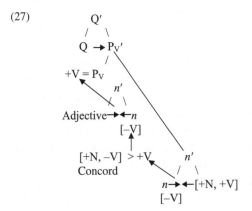

30 The connection is made explicitly in Uriagereka (1996, 2002) and Piattelli-Palmarini and Uriagereka (2005). If syntactic representations in general are manifolds, it is worth asking whether variations among languages emerge in terms of mathematical parameters in the manifolds, within the dimensions needed to describe them.

31 Much of topology is devoted to studying what makes different objects homomorphic (e.g. a doughnut and a coffee cup, by stretching the latter into the former). That presupposes locality and uniformity in the stretch, so that the spatial stuff doesn't tear apart. Curiously syntactic transformations also obey locality/uniformity demands, as do other complex dynamic systems (see Saddy and Uriagereka [2004] on this matter).

The feature released in the collision with an *n* anti-category is +V, and it opens up a separate source of syntactic projection – a syntactic 'expansion'. Via Concord, then, the polarity of the released +V feature is reversed, and upon collision with an adjectival element this produces a further +V element; that new release can further enter the Concord process, and so on.[32] Morphological fusion associates concord features to their resting PF destination.

In contrast, the solution involving 'reading' the released feature as a category is more radical. First the released featured is interpreted as the only category it can survive as.

(28)

$$\begin{array}{c} \text{Case}' \\ / \ \backslash \\ +\text{N} = \text{P}_\text{N} \ v' \\ \ \ \ \ \ \ / \ \backslash \\ v \to \leftarrow [+\text{N}, +\text{V}] \\ [-\text{N}] \end{array}$$

The featureless P element determines Case properties, and through this feature, via valuation mechanisms, Agree is executed with a relevant, distant, element. To represent this process we really need a three-dimensional graph – for a VP like *arrest most people* with Case valuation at *v*.[33] In the warped object in (29b), first of all, the emergent Case projection in (29a) (as in the structure in (28)) is eliminated via reprojection: the Case′ becomes a *v*P. But it leaves an imprint on the next derivational stage, having created an uninterpretable P_N feature that the system has to eliminate. This is done by way of the D features in the DP valuating the featureless P_N as a DP, thereby creating a DP chain with agreement on *v*. The tight connection between *v* (T and other elements involved in Case valuation) and the Case phenomenon is expected. The uninterpretable Case feature results from the category collision between some predicate (here *arrest* ...) and the appropriate anticategory (here *v*), and it gets eliminated by relating *v* to the distant DP.[34]

---

32 The adjectival space is an option, only. Still, a +V feature is released even if the adjective is absent, upon the collision of *n* with the nominal predicate. The feature is necessary for theta binding, in present terms.

33 The object in point is meant as protruding from the page of this book, in a third dimension. See Drury (2005) and his references on these and similar 'remerges', and Guimaraes (2004) for even more complex objects.

34 Although, as we saw in chapter 4, instances also emerge where Case marking applies mechanically, without useful morphological marking (Null Case), with a variety of consequences for transformations.

(29)

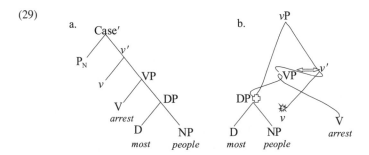

Although the relation between the (person) features in *v* and DP is Markovian and possible only in the warped object in (29b), for the categorial elements in this object a new, context-sensitive, dependency has become possible. Topologically, the Case arrangement has opened up *a new type of entangled space*, one capable of sustaining new semantic dependencies, given the co-linearity thesis. In effect, then, semantics has co-evolved with syntax.

8.4.5   *Case as tokenization?*

Case can be seen as a morphological mechanism that associates to context-sensitive syntax. It does so by marking a given D domain with an uninter-pretable feature whose elimination from the system is geared towards another domain. This is, as was noted, a second-order mechanism, which makes use of first-order objects but in a dynamic way that depends on contextual considerations, appropriately quantified. This contextualization results in the appropriate tokenization of the D-related elements that enter into Case dependencies. Whether that tokenization is itself the cause or the consequence of the process is up for grabs.

That proposal can be made concrete if the numeration is a finite-state component of the derivation. Drury (2005) argues that cyclically-accessed numerations (phases) are sets of token categories where convergence can be achieved, thus we have in each set one C, one T and so on. We couldn't have two unless we had a way of coding that. Apparently the grammar has evolved a way of achieving multiple tokenization for Case-dependent systems, that is D. That issue has always been resolved by a trick: one T is expressed as T_1 whereas two Ds is expressed as D_2, and so on. But that's our problem, not its solution.[35] In the present system *each D is marked for distinctness* as D-nom,

---

35 Adding this index to the lexical type is either non-inclusive or non-recoverable. This violates what Lasnik *et al.* (2005) call the First Conservation Law of derivations.

D-acc and so on. As Mori (2005, chapter 6) argues, this is why we don't find more than two layers of Aktionsart dependents, as in (24) above.[36]

8.4.6   *Reprojected entanglements yield paradigms?*

We have gone from a finite-state numeration to a context-sensitive dependency, of the sort Case specifications require. In evolutionary terms this is interesting, because under the scenario being considered what triggered such a move was, in the end, the capacity to separate a featural notion from a *set* somehow integrating such notions, in opposing terms under learnability assumptions that lead to category collision and the release – when anti-categories are involved – of free-range uninterpretable features. It is unclear what came first, the anti-category or the ability to separate a notion from a set.[37] What seems reasonable is that once the system went, possibly in one burst, from Markovian proto-language to the warped context-sensitive objects that sanction quantification, if in addition it evolved *a way to compile* said convoluted notions into idioms or, in the end, words, then a modern lexicon would have emerged within it.

This is the logic of reprojection-via-complement-assumption discussed above, or more generally the sort of reprojection that arises, also, even when nothing as drastic is viable – this being the distinction between foundational theme dependents and those assumed for all other arguments, including nominal dependents. When not enough Case options ensue to differentiate relevant D dependents,[38] dependencies have to reduce. Syntactic identification of the sort studied in section 3.4, involving head-to-head adjunction, seems to be the mechanism achieving the 'valence reduction' purpose. To

---

36 Mori takes Case marking to be a second-order mechanism of a binary sort, allowing a two-way distinction. As her system allows for a biclausal division between subjacent domains, this adds one more opposition, hence a total of four distinctive layers. To have yet another distinction would require going into third-order markings.

37 This poses a 'chicken-and-egg' puzzle, which Piattelli-Palmarini and Uriagereka (2005) refer to as the 'Morphology First' vs. '(Derivational) Memory First' evolutionary scenarios. Was it the case that some trivial, in a sense 'viral', morphological glitch in the system 'liberated' the machinery necessary to entertain the great quantificational organization that defines human thought; or that the 'pressure' of quantificational organization in the (derivational memory) demands that the human brain had, as it evolved, were so great that it had to co-opt a morphological glitch to allow the system into the entanglements it needed to express that elevated thought?

38 In Uriagereka (1997) this distinctness was cued to the phenomenon of (local) obviation, given the precursor of the CLT in this volume. If two Ds have to be marked for syntactic distinctness it is natural to interpret them as semantically distinct (see Lasnik *et al.* [2005, chapter 7] for discussion).

recall that instance, we have multiple dependencies both in relational nouns – in a certain sense, most in the lexicon – and in corresponding verbs – say, for instance, *construction* and *construct*. The conceptual base is relational in both instances, the constructed entity (say, a city) being the subject/space of an integral small clause, and the constructing notion somehow instantiating a topological warp on that space, thus presenting it in some guise. What requires an explanation, on the one hand, is why: (a) in the nominal instance, grammatical combinations include *recent construction of the city, city's recent construction*, or *a city of recent construction*, while (b) in the verbal instance *construct the city* or *the city (was) constructed* are possible, but not **(to) city the construction* (meaning something like 'to shape the construction as a city'). On the other hand, one should also seek to understand why in the verbal instance we can quantify separately over the cities and their constructions, and in fact also any other dependent that we associate to the articulated ensuing event (*few builders always construct most cities*), whereas in the nominal instance we can only quantify over the event that arranges everything into a conceptual unit, and either the underlying space or the articulating presentation – not both. The reason for this, it was argued in section 3.6, is Case theoretic. Because of the nuances of Case diversity in verbal instances – themselves the consequence of the sort of category collision holding there, with results in emergent P elements – each quantificational element binding each dependent can surface as a separately identified token of the same type. In contrast, in the nominal instances there are fewer token identification resources, and as a result only identification of one of the dependents with the main event is viable. The reasons evaluated in section 5.5.3 for why **city the construction* and the like do not emerge verbally are also Case Theoretic: in lexical terms *city* is the argument of *construction*, but if it gets identified as the head of a verbal projection it will never be in a position to obtain a Case tokenization and the same is not true for nominal heads. This suggests that Case tokenization is not just a way of distinguishing arguments, but moreover that once the Case system holds, the system makes Case distinctions a *sine qua non* for argumenthood – the Visibility Hypothesis.

That said, if matters proceed as indicated a still unresolved issue is why many DP that displace associating to *v*, T or C projections, don't result in the same sort of identificational collapse that we see in relational terms when displacements take place internal to D projections. The sort of identification we witness in the DP instances holds because of the syntactic relation involved (adjunction) and also because the target and the source of the adjunction are both D elements, which in the absence of tokenization *for each* results in the entire formal collapse of both into one single element. A D displaced to *v*, T or C is not the same as any of these target categories, so the conditions for collapse would, in the end, not be met in those instances, appropriately.[39]

Now, regardless of those various differences, determined by the way in which Case conditions are deployed, in either the nominal or the verbal instance, paradigmatic dependencies are constructed by basically pushing forward the CH specifications, until at a given level of complexity we again 'push down' matters in cyclic fashion. Making some assumptions about the psychological nature of memory, that 'push down' can be achieved in two ways, one apparently more permanent than the other. If information is stored into the more static *declarative* memory (see fn. 11 in chapter 7), then the relevant storage is of the *lexico-paradigmatic* sort, and thus is normally inaccessible to further regular computation. If, on the other hand, information is stored merely into the more dynamic *operational* memory (again see fn. 11, chapter 7), then the relevant storage will be more or less accessible *throughout a derivation*, depending on a variety of nuances of the sort explored in Hornstein *et al.* (2007). Presumably, and quite regardless of the actual shape of linguistic memory (a tape, a set, or something else), this is the main divide between the lexicon and syntax – how the articulated information is stored, which may entail entirely different neuro-molecular locations for each form of memory.[40]

8.4.7   Contexts and 'contexts'?

The Case system just reviewed makes the notion 'syntactic context' – the history of a given derivational process committed to derivational memory – usable to some extent. Given the CLT, a natural question is what the semantic consequences of that syntactic context are. In part we have already seen how they have a bearing on intentionality by way of providing the machinery for quantifiers to relate to arguments: one based, in effect, in specifications of the lexico-conceptual sort, and another one emerging in the course of a derivation. Is there more? Given that this system is heavily dynamic, with various

---

39 An interesting issue arises in terms of (some) relative clauses, where arguably we do want the relevant collapse – as discussed in Chomsky (2006b), following ideas in Donati (2006).

40 This is meant literally, and is currently being explored in work in progress with Massimo Piattelli-Palmarini.

'push down' processes of the cyclic sort, can't the opportunistic interpretive components *also* exploit that very dynamism?

From what we saw in section 4.2.4, the answer relates to the Person Generalization.

(30)   *The Person Generalization*
       Full (vs. weak) generalized Infl ⟷ Person (vs. only number) features in
       inflections.

It is fully inflectional elements that deploy the context-sensitive system of Case just reviewed. Interestingly, person specifications expressed in those very inflectional elements grammatically code pragmatic context – the grounding of quantifications on cues that relate to the speaker/addressee. In other words, syntactic specificity (*complexity* resulting from the transformational component) corresponds to information specificity (a contextually rich presentational array of a referring expression). In section 4.4 it was suggested that this situation emerges due to learnability considerations.

Learners take the most specific option first, again following the Sub-case Principle. In the case of 'surface syntax', the issue is whether there are different ways to deploy in PF a syntactic object with unified conceptual specifications – and, if the optionality emerges, whether each possibility correlates with one interpretation. The optionality is language-specific, depending on whether a language assumes the radical spell-out of non-skeletal branches as in (31a) or not as in (31b), the former being derivationally preferred, although it depends on explicit marks to relate both structural chunks, which makes this option subject to morphologically driven linguistic change.

(31)   a. Radical spell-out of specifiers:

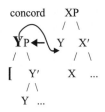

concord   XP

Construal of YP in Y in performance
through *concord addressing*
(system only sees label **Y** and border [ )

b. Conservative spell-out of
   specifiers:

```
        XP
       /  \
     YP    X'
[...-Y-...] /  \
          X  ...
```

Interpretation of flattened
YP in place

A language of the sort in (31b) allows more lee way with regards to reconstruction effects; a language of the sort in (31a) presents the possibility of surface-semantic nuances, given:

(32)   *The Pragmatic Assumption*
        Context effects arise wherever there is a quantification Q that needs context confinement, which is syntactically coded in Q's specifier.

Basically put, (syntactically correlated) pragmatic effects emerge anywhere that the intentional mechanisms allow a quantifier – thus DPs, TPs, and *v*Ps for event quantifiers, CPs for propositional or force quantifiers and so on. In languages where it is a possibility, 'surface syntax' relates to any of this because in (31a) phase borders are identifiable domains that the system can then align with interpretation, in the opportunistic ways that the CLT encourages. This opportunity does not emerge for languages of the sort in (31b).

It is arguably because of these cross-linguistic differences that we cannot give a unified evolutionary solution as part of the language faculty. In this instance matters go in the same minimalistic direction seen throughout, but *they haven't been coded into a universal syntactic mode.* That said the developmental dynamics of the system, if they too are subject to the overarching distributed interpretation and co-linearity theses, still provide the desired results. In languages where this is an option, a syntactically context-sensitive relation between X and Y – which triggers the radical spell out in (31a) – will be taken by learners as a domain of specificity where a given semantic interpretation is open. By the CLT, learners assign to this designated domain the most context-sensitive among the semantic interpretations available. Personal relations systematize that sensitivity to context, fixating it to the speaker/addressee axis. The fact that the overall dynamics are present in development lends plausibility to the hypothesized evolutionary scenario. At the same time it suggests that the way syntax relates to semantics is radically different from the way it relates to pragmatics. The former link appears to be fixed in our evolutionary history, whereas the latter is not. Thus pragmatics is certainly consistent with the language faculty, yielding in fact more than one way for it to manifest itself in populations; but strictly pragmatics is not part of the language faculty, which is an evolutionary phenomenon.

8.5   Why is the lexicon different from the grammar? – and why one should care

So what's the difference between *presupposing* (at any rate, some form of) syntax to structure one's concepts and *deploying* syntax to organize one's thoughts? That is a very tough question, and one of the reasons we should probably leave open the interpretation of the present project, in terms of following a radical, eliminative route, or staying instead within more conservative assumptions that retain semantics as a syntactically correlated, yet independent entity (see Introduction). On one hand, it is good for the overall system, assuming it has a complex enough syntax, to *compile* regular bits of information into frozen units of the idiomatic sort. That makes sense for the same reason it does to automatize a sequence of repeated movements (brushing one's teeth) or a set of familiar visual cues (the sight of one's house). That said, the compiled formal entities – atomic after compilation – were 'once' decomposed, or they would not have been acquired in full detail, to start with.

It is a subtle judgement however, whether 'once', in this sense, presupposes using the full-blown syntactic system or, instead, some more abstract mathematical scaffolding that underlies both syntax and lexical semantics, and perhaps more generally our abilities for exact numerosity. Among other things the issue bears on what one makes of mathematics (and concretely Group Theory) itself, whether it is constructed by a human mind or somehow lies outside its confines, in ways mysterious to present understanding, not just in the cognitive sciences. This book has little to say about such a huge question, and can only signal a follow-up concern: how does the decomposition presupposed in the previous paragraph bottom out?

Interestingly, once things are expressed in terms of the sorts of manifolds raised in chapter 7, nothing prevents 'intra-dimensional' communication between manifolds of a very different 'modular' origin (language, vision, the motor system and so on), which clearly boosts the possibilities of the system to analyse the phenomenology of the world without going merely 'connectionist' – what can be thought of as 'porous modularity'. This would constitute a 'decompositional' phase of the acquisition process, where idioms cannot (yet) be idiomatic or words entirely arbitrary. It may seem as if that alone predisposes the architectural answer to the great puzzle we face in a 'constructivist' direction. But in truth this isn't so: that aspect of the acquisition process may well be irrelevant to the language faculty as such. Ultimately, the scaffolding studied in section 7.4.4 may be the linguistic core of this system, the one irreducible to intra-modular connections of any sort. And there it is really anybody's guess, again, whether access to the 'ur' structure is mediated through syntax or, rather, drives directly from a deeper mathematical form. Be that as it may, at some other phase the system becomes 'atomic', fixing given combinations that hold within local cycles, meaning they are stored into something like declarative memory – more or less radically, depending on what it means to enter the morphological component.

Whatever their ultimate nature, those two systemic phases do not generally 'talk to one another'. The 'phase transition' in the system, as it is acquired, is *the compilation of complex structures into frozen lexical units*, at that point deemed essentially atomic. Children obviously take some time to get to that stage, struggling with idioms until puberty. Similarly, their creative capabilities – they 'un-turn-around' their clothes, and so on – can last pristinely until roughly that age. In any case, as the quote this book starts with reminds us, even five year olds can ask us how come the words they (know to) make up sound weird, while others they pick up from the environment don't.[41] Maybe poets and comedians extend their pre-puberty creativity into old age. All of this suggests that both systems are present at the same time, the transition from one to the other being perhaps regulated by endocrinal conditions, which may for some reason emphasize the role of one system to the detriment of the other.[42] What seems clear is that the adult lexicon stabilizes into something largely atomic, at that point mostly opaque to syntax. Does this have to do with different forms of memory storage, one declarative and one procedural or operational? Do those forms of memory have different underlying topologies? Do they have physical loci, either in time or in place, including possibly occupying different orders of biological expression?

Regardless of how we answer those questions, that still leaves yet a further one concerning why things 'freeze' in this way only at around puberty – at the time our ability to learn new languages decreases – and the issue still remains as to precisely why we don't have better access to pre-lexical structure, if it's there. The procedure we discussed in section 3.6, to get a successful referential object when the subject of the sub-lexical small clause displaces 'to the syntactic realm', is consistent with this fact. Because of chain uniformity considerations, this mechanism implies a trace erasure that all but severs the direct syntactic connection between a lexical item displaced to a referential site and the lexico-conceptual 'inner variable' it starts from.[43] As a consequence, the relation between the theta-identification site with referential

---

41 My daughter Isabel told me she assumed that words are made up by someone, normally other than herself.

42 Related to the idea in fn. 27, this idea is also being pursued in the same work in progress with Massimo Piattelli-Palmarini, adapting original ideas by Michael Ullman.

43 Otherwise the chain thus obtained would not be uniform. The relationship between word-external binders and word-internal variables is merely presupposed, even in foundational pieces like Higginbotham (1985).

import and the integral site with conceptual import is one of mere binding, even if it originates through movement. This is important, given the distinctions raised in section 7.3.3 between chain-like and binding relations – for which psycho-linguistic evidence exists, and which the formal system captures quite distinctly. However, when, rather than the small clause subject, it is the corresponding predicate that displaces to determine reference, the displacement is different. The predicate can move as a head entering into a head/head relation, for which uniformity considerations become immaterial upon entering the Word Interpretation realm of heads.[44] So this is a radical distinction between representations that may have originated via transformational processes, but which end up having quite distinct output properties, centering around a real dependency vis-à-vis a 'mere' binding. Now note that already presupposes the divide we're trying to understand – between a Word Interpretation realm and the rest.

One intriguing approach to the opacity of compiled words comes from exploiting the fact that they arise *after reprojection processes have assembled them*. Hornstein and Uriagereka associate islands induced by quantifiers at LF (Beck 1996) to the reprojection mechanism in this component. Hornstein *et al.* (in press) argue that this is because intervening labels have to be reconsidered upon reprojection, and this entails a derivational 'overwrite' in these sense of Uriagereka (1998) (Chomsky [2000] calls it 'tampering'). Both the reprojected label, and all dominating formal objects containing it, must change. That has immediate consequences for posterior context-sensitive dependencies, if these are constrained in terms of the following:

(33)   Conservation Condition (CC)
          Context-sensitive dependencies must be unambiguous throughout their
          derivation.

A context-sensitive dependency is unformulable across a reprojection, given (33). If the reprojection takes place late, at LF, this will result in a covert island. But if it takes place as early as we have assumed, feeding the D-structure component of the system, it will prevent *any* context-sensitive dependency that needs to use material inside the reprojected structure. That entails radical opacity, arguably what we want as discussed in section 2.2.1.

---

44 Chomsky (1995) needs to stipulate that heads incorporating to other heads via adjunction
   pose no uniformity issues, or elements that start their derivational life as heads would end up
   as maximal projections (upon adjunction, as they do not project). He stipulates that WI has its
   own rules, thus disregarding uniformity considerations. Part of what we seek to explain is
   what it means for WI to have its own specific rules.

Isn't that too strong, however, preventing even the simple binding alluded to immediately above, into a variable inside a lexical item with relational properties (e.g. a simple verb)? Not if *binding is not a context-sensitive process*, which is all that (33) cares about. We know this independently, for as shown in section 7.3.3, binding processes are fine across any island, unlike corresponding chain-formation processes. How about the sorts of finite-state mechanics that we saw associated to focal mapping, which must reach into presuppositional specifications internal to words? Again, (33) is irrelevant to those, as they are not context-sensitive. Indeed, even certain more complex processes should be able to happen, relating, in context-free terms, word-peripheral morphemes to neighboring syntactic elements under conditions that sustain context-freeness, for the same reason. Clitic (re)placement phenomena could well be of this sort.[45]

A proposal along these lines – assuming reprojections in these early derivational stages and the combined action of the Conservation Condition – has the net effect of forcing the system into storing a structure as a word, presumably in declarative memory, translating into *mere featural specifications* every bit of information associated to the compiled element. With features involving only finite-state dependencies, our capacity to operate word-internally, both from the outside of words and also internal to words themselves, is drastically limited.[46] It might seem that this destroys the articulated structure of presupposed lexical information that we have worked so hard to obtain, which must have all the syntactic layers discussed above. But that is not a problem in a cyclic system. At some derivational point, prior to the standard syntactic association via Merge, all the presupposed information is fully in place. At this stage we cannot interact with it 'from the outside' simply because there is no 'outside' yet. Next, the compilation takes place with Word Interpretation entering the picture, and the bits of information are interpreted from that point on as merely featural, thus unordered, having served their hierarchical purposes. At this point, when other symbols are merged that could interact with sublexical information, features can only act in Markovian fashion and the remaining mechanisms looking inside words (e.g. reaching into theta roles) must be of the binding sort. In sum, when the relevant information is usable, there is nothing outside the word

---

45 This need not affect the Pablos *et al.* (2005) results reported in section 7.3.2, which show essentially 'filler-gap' effects for clitic-left dislocation relations. Those connect a clitic to its left-peripheral antecedent. The suggestion in the text refers to the placement of the (special) clitic itself, which is at right angles to its relation to an antecedent.

46 Context-sensitive processes are not normally assumed to take place word-internally.

domain to use it with. When something comes along that could combine with the information, it becomes useless for real combination. The observed opacity then ensues.

The gist of what is being said is that *children are decompositionalists and adults are atomists*, the growth process involving a phase transition in the system (arguably of the reprojection sort) that correlates with endocrinal changes associated to puberty. In other words, both decompositionalists and atomists are right in some sense – but about different systemic phases. Now doesn't *that* decide the issue of the ultimate interpretation of this overall system? Isn't what we have just said a direct indication that the early machinery in the system is purely syntactic and only masked after compilation drives us into the adult world? Well, not quite.

True, this view of things presupposes a clear, early, scaffolding that later on becomes virtually unusable – except for a few situations of the focal sort, general presuppositions, and perhaps instances of poetic uses that may or may not work depending on individual abilities. And, moreover, the form of that scaffolding is really quite similar to that which syntax builds, particularly when we consider elementary syntactic dependencies like those involved in small clauses. But, to insist, we may be witnessing sheer mathematics at work here, not necessarily the syntactic engine. In other words, it may be – we just don't know – that what we call (productive) syntax is already the more complex system, made that way through a variety of externalization factors. The 'inner' stuff may be there articulating thought, perhaps, and for all we know may even be shared by other species, at least to some extent. This is very hard to decide.

In the radical interpretation of this project one would be led to eliminate semantics as a primitive field. What is not syntactic in it, in this view, is just a complex mess of intra-modular relations, and perhaps even personal perspectives. Note that this view is, in the end, fairly close to generative semantics, except going in the exact opposite direction. Just as generative semanticists denied the existence of a syntactic system – as what looked at the time like a semantic engine seemed to be enough – so, too, the new eliminativist thesis gets rid of one of these two components, again blaming the decision on the fact that we only need one engine (in this view, syntax). That, indeed, a single engine is sufficient is probably true, if the Minimalist Program is right. But making that move at the expense of eliminating semantics has the effect of, again, eliminating the distinction between the lexicon and the grammar, supposing that what is systemic in the former is a construct of the latter: if it's not syntactic, it's just a mess. That may be, but an alternative is, it would seem, equally plausible. The basic conceptual articulation that we have been considering is, as such, independent of the engine we call syntax. It is also independent of the sorts of constructs that get customarily called semantics, which presuppose easy answers to most of the difficult conceptual questions we are dealing with.[47] That said, it is possible that this ultimately innate mathematical edifice relates to syntax and semantics in different, though related, ways, which in turn may find their physical locus in quite distinct domains: procedural or operational memory for syntactic nuances and declarative memory for semantic ones.

To syntax, the more basic edifice would relate in essentially developmental terms, which go through deploying the subsequent, more dynamic, system via steps that involve making thought public, with all the consequences that has for linearization, tokenization, memory resources, reprojections, featural dependencies and more. Strictly, nothing of that sort exists in the mind of a fetus, other than *in potentia*. It is only through the interaction of the elementary, totally innate, early system *and input data* that syntax is genuinely deployed. Such data doesn't just include arbitrary pairings of external forms and internal concepts; in those pairings lies, also, a set of cues to let the syntactic apparatus be deployed as more or less configurational, with more or less phonetically realized features, earlier or later timings in dynamic processes, and so on – the stuff of parametric syntax. In rigor, *that* cannot deploy conceptual relations that hide in (sound, meaning) pairs because those presuppose the former. Of course, bootstrapping can be partial, perhaps avoiding an exhaustive setting of all the parametric settings hidden in lexical combinations. But that's a dangerous exercise, given present understanding of parameters. A more natural thing to do would be to grant certain structuring to concepts prior to the full acquisition of syntax, in which case 'all' the learner would have to do is 'just' find arbitrary pairings, which is complex enough when realizing that those come in the middle of the noisy speech stream. But then the basis of the conceptual structuring has to be prior to full syntax, even if the two are, in rather non-trivial senses, surely related.

The broad topological array we studied for concepts would relate to semantics in indirect ways as well, if by semantics we mean something like

47 For example, packing relevant lexical presuppositions into 'meaning postulates', assuming intentionality as some simple, indeed trivial, representational stance (in the classical philosophical sense), treating predicates as mere sets, and otherwise assuming models for corresponding first-order syntactic systems – as higher order systems have no known corresponding model – despite the fact that learnable syntax has been shown to be higher order.

what we're using right now to understand these sentences, with full blown intentionality and not just skeletal conceptual nuances to it. First, as noted, such an intricate array involves more than scaffoldings: all sorts of relations are added to those, or one couldn't speak about the world around, or inside, us. In this sense, connectionism has to be obviously right, in the 'connective' part that held of classical associationism as well. Elaborate links exist among myriad different ideas, and they probably grow every second in any given mind. But in another sense that doctrine has to be, also, obviously wrong: the associations themselves are far from random, they fall into a pre-existing space that cannot possibly be carved by the concepts themselves. Second, that elaborate, articulated, set of expansions and inversions, which yields (group-based) scaffoldings that would seem to work both for nominal and verbal concepts – the latter being derived on the former, over some time representation that makes them denotationally dynamic – still has to be put to use to refer, with more or less accuracy, to events 'out there'. That mechanism, whatever it is, is definitely not foolproof, or there wouldn't be wars and divorces. But it works well enough to have allowed us to construct civilizations of unbelievable cultural stability. Is that a system, in the sense syntax probably is? Who knows, but if it is, it seems reasonably well paired with the syntactic system, which is the main motivation behind what is now being called 'co-linearity'.

Co-linearity is obvious for the eliminative thesis: there is nothing more co-linear than having two structures reduce to one another. But why should co-linearity hold in the conservative view that doesn't attempt to eliminate semantics in favor of syntax? In part, it is because both of those aspects of language ultimately come, more or less indirectly, from the same topological base. Of course, in this view of things, so does exact numerocity more generally, and perhaps even our musical and dancing abilities, and others. Why aren't those domains co-linear with syntax? Probably because evolution did not need to pair them. Then again, how evolution succeeded in pairing syntax and semantics is, to be sure, yet another great question. But, in that, science is probably not in a different boat from the one occupied by several other co-linearities out there: for example, that between areas in the cerebral cortex and corresponding sensory arrays in the body, or that between genomic expression and corresponding organ deployment in phenotypes. Surprising? No doubt – but surely possible, indeed common. In any case, co-linearities like these apparently yield successful body plans, stable sensory systems, and – so it appears – the useful linguistic system with which we are presently exchanging ideas. Hopefully.

8.6   Conclusions

This chapter showed ways in which the various levels of the Chomsky Hierarchy, due to the sorts of formal limitations they involve, naturally correspond to various levels of semantic complexity, each presupposing the previous in terms of the systemic memory resources it needs to deploy. Things get interestingly complex, for both syntax and semantics, once we go beyond immediate constituency, for which strict compositionality works nicely – although it is binary quantificational relations that exhibit new prospects. The idea explored here is that those types of relations, whose basis is so-called conservativity, involve a kind of organized semantics presupposing syntactic mechanisms that do not give up on previously processed information. Their full interpretation emerges only when conditions interpreted at the point of first Merge are coupled with others that arise later in the derivation, as ensuing representations are overwritten in intricate ways (the essence of 'reprojections'). Needless to say, the fact that one needs a characteristic context-sensitivity to achieve binary quantification relations doesn't, in itself, mean that this has to be coded in the syntax. One can pack context-sensitivity, for instance, in terms of functions that allow a given determiner to 'reach out' to a distant syntactic domain to turn it into its scope. But the question is not whether one can do that, but rather what else it explains. The particular mechanism proposed here (a derivation involving reprojection) has consequences for a variety of observables: from mental spaces and the notions 'feature' and 'paradigm' to why Case is present in the system.

At some level of abstraction, both syntax and semantics are mathematical entities, of the sort presumably constraining the waves and knots that make our universe cohere the way it does. That organising power apparently forces the behavior of light in various ways, matter in various others, organisms in yet others, and so on, all the way up – or down – to mind. This, in the physical instance, is 'merely' the group-based logical structure of the numbering system, in some appropriate sense, which is routinely taken to determine some central aspects of, at least, the realm of particle physics, and cosmology more generally. Now both Wallace and Chomsky thought that human beings had somehow evolved access to the structure of that edifice, and that belief is at the core of their linguistic system and its recursive syntax. Differently put, the connection between language and mathematics, at least in the form of exact numerosity, probably ought not to be in dispute. In a sense, all that the discussion in chapter 7 did, as more precisely explained in this chapter, is extend the connection to paradigmatic syntax. Technically, the idea was to emphasize inverse relations in mathematics just as one obviously needs expansion relations. In rigor, arithmetic doesn't exist without both of those, and then if language and math are indeed connected, one has to ponder whether this is only through expansion procedures, or also inverse procedures play a decisive role. Intuitively, the latter are at the core of such natural human activities as knotting and weaving more generally, or backwards games and origami, or any other structuring involving groups in the technical sense. The only question is whether language, too, uses such inversions, together with the expansions it deploys through Merge mechanisms. If it does, we may be able to address otherwise puzzling aspects of lexical pre-suppositions, which we want to somehow be there, yet not use the customary syntactic machinery – or we fall into generative semantics.

The present approach, then, provides a foundational step on possible semantics, which will be *co-linear with syntactic architecture.* Whether that co-linearity is an isomorphic reflection, or some lesser, homo-morphic, relation, is an interesting matter to explore on empirical grounds – either way, meaning ends up being appropriately 'naturalized'. In any case, if we accept the duality of semantics (or its *triple* nature, including pre-compositional manifestations) then something richer is needed than the customary minim-alist dictum about an 'optimal system interfacing sound and meaning'. The interfaces have to be distributed enough to yield, precisely, double or triple points of meaning shades (perhaps more, if pragmatic interfaces are signifi-cant as well, even if in a less systemic fashion). Many agree that theta semantics is phrasal, while scopal semantics is that and more – context-sensitive within familiar limits. That this should be purely arbitrary seems unacceptable, as it makes no sense to turn things around, given the observed facts of language. Once we see that pre-compositional semantics also play an important role in the system, and that these are naturally characterized in finite-state terms, then the full Chomsky Hierarchy, as revamped as it may be (and up to where we can use it, perhaps given our cognitive limitations as a species) seems entirely in place. All that the linguist has to do is show how syntax partially determines – more neutrally, anchors – the semantic inter-faces, or how it supports the distributed interpretation thesis.

Epilogue: Evo-Devo-Perfo

This book started by reflecting on the relation between expression and meaning, in both words and sentences. Philosophers customarily take this to be a matter of representation, a relation between a subject and a theory of a formal language, an 'intentional' stance correlating a 'symbol' and 'what it stands for'. It should now be clear that this must be heavily qualified.

First, formal languages, as chapter 7 discusses, are only very remotely related to natural language. The real issue in linguistics is not so much describing something like a well-formed formula of sequentially arranged words; at best a construct like that constitutes the *phonetic support* of what we're interested in. As important, though, is the nuanced hierarchical array that carries meaning – which, if this book is on track, is an extremely dynamic affair.

Second, when it comes to intentionality in the intuitive sense that we can take 'book' to refer to what the reader is holding (so *'the reader is holding a book'* is true if and only if the reader is holding a book), present understanding tells us little as to how that wonderful act succeeds. This book has been, in part, about that relation; but one has to be both honest and humble here. All that has been definitively claimed is that the relation in point is mediated by an elaborate syntax (which chapter 3 introduced), and that its 'scaffolding' utilizes more basic topological notions (as discussed in the last two chapters).

So if that's where we stand when it comes to standard reference, what can one really say about the putative representational relation between, 'feature F', 'phrase P', 'chain CH' or similar syntactic notions and whatever feature F, phrase P, or chain CH ultimately do or signify for the system? That's the third point to admit. One can still say relatively little, so far anyway. At most we know that different forms of computational memory drastically affect meaningful possibilities, so that in effect more memory allows for more computational complexity, and of a more complex sort, which naturally affects the semantic import of each construct.

If the syntax/semantic mapping were *totally* arbitrary, there would be no reason not to code, say, emphasis via entangled chains of dependencies and quantificational expressions somehow into single, all-purpose, features – the opposite of what we actually observe in the world's languages. One could do that, but at the expense of having a hopelessly opaque system, which would arguably be unlearnable by a human child, at least – a matter first raised in section 2.4. The fact remains that the language faculty has hit on what seems like a more natural correlation between form and meaning: structured sense utilizes, to its expressive advantage, various formal details of the structure carrying the meaning. In a way, this is not surprising.

Structured sense also utilizes even very basic *signal* properties – like its fundamental frequency or amplitude – to carry a variety of 'surface' meaning expressions, for instance those based on pitch, stress, and the like. Importantly, such systemic properties don't just allow the coding of holistic clues about the speaker's attitude (of attention, anger, interest, sympathy and so on). More relevantly to this book's concerns, they also serve to signal such fundamental processes as focalization, as discussed in section 8.3.2, which probably means that sense finds its way out of speakers' minds in just about any reasonable way, given obvious limitations of what humans are (as higher apes) and what the external medium is (air waves).

Then again, things get more interesting when we move from signal to structure, however it is that this is done. Such is the realm of syntax, which we saw throughout is a convoluted affair, with various layers of complexity emerging in successive orders, yielding a 'dimensional' structure of sorts. Those very cuts in structuring appear also to be utilized by the system to carry essential semantic nuances, notably the compositional organization of arguments and predicates, and even the 'conservative' timing of quantificational restrictions vis-à-vis derivationally achieved quantificational scopes. Logically matters could have been otherwise, but the system that happened to evolve works rather nicely, streamlining core aspects of meaning into the very stuff that somehow carries this meaning on its structural back bone.

We can call that 'representational' – in the sense that philosophers use this word, as a way to denote the correspondence between a (hypothetical) cognitive entity and reality – but the match-up remains largely mysterious beyond the factual correlation itself, and its reliance on degrees of formal complexity. Matters are somewhat tangible for phonetic features, whose brain-correlate is being unearthed as we speak, and the hope remains strong to extend such findings to the categorial or agreement features studied in chapters 4 or 5 here (though less so for basic semantic ones, of the sort organized via the topologies of conceptual dimensions examined in the last two chapters). But it isn't obvious that insisting on all of that being 'representational' adds much to the equation. Through complex electrical currents, protein interactions, and surely much more, something like +*voice* makes it as a complex mental event, involving such motor milestones as the onset of voicing from the vocal folds. But does it really help us understand how voicing does get activated to say that the feature +*voice* is 'represented' in the neo-cortex?

If the question seems somewhat odd for whatever complex array of (motor, auditive, visual) commands are involved in phonetic consonants, is the fact that all other features are even less understood supposed to make the claim more solid, for syntax or semantics? How is the representational claim going to help us clarify what c-command or binding are, what constitutes a phrase as opposed to a set thereof (the basis for a chain), or how all of that ultimately relates to events in the world, so that one can claim that the reader is holding a book, or this very book?

That question is not meant as critical of the Computational Theory of Mind, at least not in the sense of 'computational' that this word is given in computational biology, the field that approaches biology by applying familiar computational techniques. These days we even have a computational chemistry and computational physics, all of them deploying related methods to tackle tricky problems in a variety of sub-disciplines. In none of these would it make much sense to extend the computational metaphor to the extent that particles, compounds, organisms, or whatever relevant units the system takes as its vocabulary for computational purposes, literally *represent* anything. In those fields such a correlation serves no purpose, and is simply not made. If we leave matters at that in the cognitive sciences, there's nothing more to be said. Expecting that there is an extra representational step in the latter seems as unjustified here as elsewhere, even if computers were originally conceived by logicians as representational devices.

Obviously, also, the fact that one may not see how a representational stance may help to clarify what amounts to a tricky dependency (the relation between an expression and what it is taken to mean in some sense) doesn't entail that one is skeptical about the dependency holding. One may be cynical about arranging the marriage, only. The approach pursued here, as a consequence, has been to take that classical view as a convenient fiction or *desideratum*. One may be willing to grant that humans do succeed in referring, judging, and all the behaviors associated to intentionality. However, being dogmatic about what the appropriate relations then ought to be between expression and meaning, or simply adapting them from a logical tradition that was never particularly worried about biology or even cognition, seems at least uncritical.

So the first overall conclusion of this book is that *structuring semantics* is as genuine a quest as that of structuring pragmatics, phonetics, or whatever else we think is relevant. It would be sad to think that semanticists consider such a project finished. This, of course, is not to say that the present theory is right – that will have to be examined by comparing it to others, in customary fashion. But it does mean that this, or similar theories, have the right to be right or wrong, and their postulation itself shouldn't be dismissed because it pushes the envelope.

In that regard, minimalists at least probably ought to examine the arguments discussed in chapter 1, concerning whether the interface between syntax and semantics is distributed, and whether their rhetoric in this regard squares with their daily assumptions. The facts discussed in chapter 6 are probably also relevant. There just seem to exist chunks of natural language that are flatter than customarily assumed. Moreover, far from being restricted to conjunctions and iterations, these may well be the sorts of structures that the system bottoms out as, in the form of both adjuncts and small clauses.

Once a compositional machinery is assumed to deal with more complex structurings, it could also be used to analyse the simpler ones. But that kind of reasoning, while standard if dealing with formal languages, is not very sound for natural objects. For example, one may have discovered cells in an organism that fire into one another, in the process transporting electro-magnetic currents that carry information. But that discovery doesn't entail that all cells in relevant organisms are of that particular sort, nor that the way other, simpler, cells communicate is through the very same (electro-chemical) signaling processes. Maybe they do and maybe they don't (compare neuronal, immune, and endocrine signaling). It's hard to see how this biological analogy doesn't apply to whether patently simpler syntactic structures get their meaning associations resolved via compositionality, if that too is ultimately a biological phenomenon.

Within that general spirit, it is probably time to go back to the fascinating debate that took place in the 1960s, and was summarized in chapter 2. That's where it all starts in generative grammar when it comes to the Mapping Problem and, more generally, whether we should have a principled distinction between the lexicon and the grammar – a divide as old as the field of linguistics at large. This book has taken a position on this, suggesting that actually both camps involved, reconstructing history a bit, were probably right. This is not just being eclectic.

If something has been learnt from contemporary biology, and more concretely the Evo-Devo paradigm, this is that organisms are extremely subtle, dynamic, processes, which, via a set of remarkable transitions, carry life from strands of DNA, through different larval stages, all the way up to phenotypically distinct adults. This is so in the case of organic morphology, and there's every reason to believe it should be, also, in behavioral structure. From this perspective, why shouldn't the language organ, if it is really an organ as linguists often claim, go through a 'decompositionalist' stage preceding an 'atomist' one?

It's hardly worth mentioning that the processes studied here can be viewed as proposals regarding a purely abstract formal system. But they make more sense, as chapter 8 attempts to emphasize, as mechanisms that resulted from evolution, precisely as understood in the Evo-Devo paradigm. Granted, we're still far from understanding the forces that gear evolution, and new surprises emerge monthly. But at the level of abstraction that mechanisms were discussed here – involving notions ranging from memory characterizations to the nature of symbols understood as topological spaces – we already know enough to reach tentative conclusions.

We know, for instance: about ever-present co-linearity in development (and we have shown a characteristic co-linearity between syntax and semantics); about complex loops in growth processes being packed into forms of systemic memory, not to mention the Adaptive Immune System (and we find that levels of memory limitation articulate linguistic structuring); about foldings in the realm of proteins, and we appear to find abstract foldings in linguistic topologies – in both of those instances, the structural shape determining systemic properties. We even know that certain accidents in nucleic acid arrays, for instance of the viral sort, can surprisingly get integrated into new organic systems (such as, again, adaptive immunity), and we find that uninterpretable features – a linguistic noise – surprisingly gear transformations.

One can make much or little of all that, this being largely a matter of taste. The question, in the end, boils down to whether the ensuing system, proposed and examined under this light, really makes any progress. If our goal is to, some day, unify competence and performance, to begin to grasp the mystery of how thought emerges in matter, or how all this breathtaking mess could have evolved, are we better off with notions like the ones just reviewed, or insisting on language being representational, as simple logic would dictate?

There is one more respect in which the present book may be topical for biolinguistic studies of the Evo-Devo sort. Such a paradigm attempts to demonstrate, in effect, how the problem of evolution is rooted in the problem of development, at bio-molecular levels. We may envision an 'Evo-Devo-Perfo' field, whereby some aspects of performance are added as a third leg of a triangle for which, in all likelihood, not just inter-cellular (e.g. cerebral) networks count in constraining structural behavior nuances, but intra-cellular ones do too.

If we take the reality of syntactic derivations at face value, we are virtually forced to explore this avenue.

For we should say this very clearly: this book has argued, over and over, that it is deeply correct to understand syntactic derivations as proceeding in a (radically) bottom-up fashion. If syntactic information does flow that way, the fact that it must obviously be parsed left-to-right (and for all we know it may also be planned that way) poses a prima facie puzzle. If one chooses not to ignore it (as is customary), there are two ways to face it: (i) we can go representational on the theory, disregarding its bottom-up-derivational aspects and, at best, coding them somehow (what psycholinguists customarily assume without argument); or (ii) we can bite the bullet and assume that the left-to-right performance event is no more real than the Evo-Devo event it works with, as we speak. Their scale is different, but that is all. And an Evo-Devo-Perfo discipline would seek to explore how structural conditions in the relevant domains narrow down, in more or less co-linear fashion, from an evolutionary, to a developmental, to a behavioral timescale.

For that putative field, such concepts as compression of multidimensional inner thoughts into unidimensional public expression, and the systemic memory requirements that a relevant solution demands, should be central avenues of research. Empirically finding that, say, hormonal regulation effects a transition, from a fully syntactic device to an atomistic one based on pattern recognition, will only mean that the language faculty is subtle and complex. From this angle it should not be surprising to find language undergoing, in short, a *metamorphosis* in the course of development, so much so that the blind scientists studying it may have reasonably observed it both as a worm and as a flower. Taking this perspective, it is, rather, like a caterpillar eating lots of information as it fattens into a butterfly. Not being moved by this, as it were, *endocrinal* aspect of language seems to plainly ignore a sizable chunk of the data.

I develop these and related ideas in work with Massimo Piattelli-Palmarini (2004, 2005, in press), which basically attempts to ground minimalist concepts in current biological notions of the sort just alluded to. The prospects don't seem hopeless, if nothing else because relevant genes are being isolated, as well as brain circuitry that goes beyond traditional distinctions (of the sort of 'syntax' vs. 'semantics'). In the new biolinguistics generation we will probably be hearing more about notions like 'operational memory', 'linearization', 'tokenization', or 'mental space' than customary ones like 'representation' or even 'symbol'. At least that's what I'm betting on.

References

Abelin, A. 1999. Phonesthemes in Swedish. In *Proceedings of XIV International Conference of Phonetic Sciences 99*. Berkeley, CA: University of California.

Abney, S. 1987. *The English noun phrase in its sentential aspect*. Ph.D. Thesis, MIT.

Alexiadou, A. and E. Anagnostopoulou. 1998. "Parametrizing AGR: Word Order, V-movement and EPP-checking," *Natural Language and Linguistic Theory* 16 (3): 491–539.

Aoun, Joseph. 1979. On Government, Case-marking, and Clitic Placement. Ms. MIT, Cambridge, Mass.

Armstrong, M. 1983 *Basic topology: undergraduate texts in Mathematics*. Berlin: Springer Verlag.

Attardo, S. and G. Vivo. 1997. "The semantics of reduplication in Sicilian," *Romance Languages Annual* 9: 153–159.

Aubin, D. 2004. Forms of explanations in the catastrophe theory of René Thom: topology, morphogenesis, and structuralism. In M.N. Wise (ed.) *Growing explanations: historical perspective on the sciences of complexity*. Durham, NC: Duke University Press, pp. 95–130.

Baker, M. C. 1988. *Incorporation: a theory of grammatical function changing*. University of Chicago Press.

2003. *Lexical categories: verbs, nouns and adjectives*. Cambridge University Press.

In press. *The lego of sentence structure*. Blackwell/Maryland Lectures in Language and Cognition at the University of Maryland. Malden, MA: Blackwell Publishing, pp. 541–574.

Baltin, M. 2005. "Is Grammar Markovian?" Lecture at the Korean Association of English Language and Linguistics, Seoul. Available at www.nyu.edu (accessed November 2007).

Banfield, A. 1973. "Narrative style and the grammar of direct and indirect speech," *Foundations of Language* 10:1–39.

Barlow, M. and C. Fergusson (eds.) 1988. *Agreement in natural language: approaches, theory, description*. Stanford, CA: CSLI Publications.

Barsky, R. F. 1997. *Noam Chomsky: a life of dissent*. Cambridge, MA: MIT Press.

Barwise, J. and R. Cooper. 1981. "Generalized quantifiers and natural language," *Linguistics and Philosophy* 4:159–219.

Beck, S. 1996. "Quantified structures as barriers for LF movement," *Natural Language Semantics* 4:1–56.

Belletti, A. 1988. "The case of unaccusatives," *Linguistic Inquiry* 19: 1–34.

2004. *The cartography of syntactic structures*. Oxford University Press.

Belletti, A. and L. Rizzi. 1988. "Psych-verbs and theta theory," *Natural Language and Linguistic Theory* 6: 291–352.

Benveniste, E. 1971. *Problems in general linguistics*. Coral Gables, FL: University of Miami Press.

Bickerton, D. 1990. *Species and language*. University of Chicago Press.

Bierman, D. J. 2003. "Does consciousness collapse the wave-packet?" *Mind and Matter* 1: 45–57.

Bittner, M. and K. Hale. 1996. "The structural determination of case and agreement," *Linguistic Inquiry* 27: 1–68.

Bloomfield, L. 1933. *Language*. London: Allen and Unwin.

Bobaljik, J. 1995. *Morphosyntax: the syntax of verbal inflection*. Ph.D. Thesis, MIT.
  2001. The implications of rich agreement: why morphology does not drive syntax. In K. Megerdoomian and L. A. Bar-el (eds.) *Proceedings of the 20th West Coast Conference on Formal Linguistics*. Somerville, MA: Cascadilla Press.

Boeckx, C. In press. *Bare syntax*. Oxford University Press.

Boeckx, C. and J. Uriagereka. 2007. Minimalism. In G. Ramchand and C. Reiss (eds.) *Handbook of Linguistic Interfaces*. Oxford University Press.

Borer, H. 2004. *Structuring sense: in name only*, Volume 1. Oxford University Press.
  2005. *Structuring sense: the normal course of events*, Volume 2. Oxford University Press.

Boskovic, Z. 1997. *The syntax of nonfinite complementation: an economy approach*. Cambridge, MA: MIT Press.
  2002. "A-movement and the EPP," *Syntax* 5: 167–218.

Bostrom, N. 2005. "Understanding Quine's Thesis of Indeterminacy," *Linguistic and Philosophical Investigations* 4: 60–96.

Bresnan, J. 1971. "Sentence stress and syntactic transformation," *Language* 47: 257–281.

Bresnan, J. and R. Kaplan. 1982. Lexical-functional grammar: a formal system for grammatical representation. In J. Bresnan (ed.) *The mental representation of grammatical relations*. Cambridge, MA: MIT Press, pp. 173–281.

Brody, M. 1995. *Lexico-logical form: a radically minimalist theory*. Cambridge, MA: MIT Press.

Browning, M. 1987. *Null operator constructions*. Ph.D. Thesis, MIT.

Burzio, L. 1986. *Italian syntax*. Dordrecht: Reidel.

Cardinaletti, A. and M. Starke. 1999. The typology of structural deficiency: a case study of the three classes of pronouns. In H. van Riemsdijk (ed.) *Clitics in the languages of Europe*. Berlin: Mouton de Gruyter, pp. 145–233.

Carstens, V. 2005. "Agree and EPP in Bantu," *Natural language & linguistic theory* 23(2): 219–279.

Castillo, J. C. 2001. *Thematic relations between nouns*. Ph.D. Thesis, University of Maryland.

Castillo, J. C., J. Drury, and K. K. Grohmann. 1999. Merge over Move and the Extended Projection Principle. In S. Aoshima, J. Drury, and T. Neuovonen (eds.) *University of Maryland Working Papers in Linguistics* 8: 63–103.

Chametzky, R. 2000. *Phrase structure: from GB to minimalism*. Oxford: Blackwell.

Chierchia, G. 1998. Plurality of mass nouns and the notion of "semantic parameter". In S. Rothstein (ed.) *Events and grammar*. Dordrecht: Kluwer.

Chomsky, N. 1955. *The logical structure of linguistic theory*. Ms., Harvard University. (Published in part in (1975) *The logical structure of linguistic theory*. New York: Plenum Press.)

1956. "Three models for the description of language," *IRE Transactions on Information Theory* 2: 113–124.

1957. *Syntactic structures*. Paris: Mouton.

1958. "Finite state languages," *Information and control* 1: 91–112.

1961. On the notion rule of grammar. In *Structure of language and its mathematical aspects*. Proceedings of the Symposia on Applied Mathematics XII. Providence, RI: American Mathematical Society, pp. 6–24.

1963. Formal properties of grammars. In R. D. Luce, R. B. Bush and E. Galanter (eds.) *Handbook of mathematical psychology*, Volume 1. New York: John Wiley, pp. 323–418.

1965. *Aspects of the theory of syntax*. Cambridge, MA: MIT Press.

1970. Remarks on nominalization. In R. A. Jacob and P. S. Rosenbaum (eds.) *Readings in English transformational grammar*. Waltham, MA: Ginn, pp. 184–221.

1972. *Studies on semantics in generative grammar*. The Hague: Mouton.

1977. On wh-movement. In P. Culicover, T. Wasow and A. Akmajian (eds.) *Formal syntax*. New York: Academic Press, pp. 71–132.

1981. *Lectures on government and binding*. Dordrecht: Foris.

1982. *Some concepts and consequences of the theory of government and binding*. Cambridge: MIT Press.

1986. *Barriers*. Cambridge, MA: MIT Press.

1994. Bare phrase structure. In H. Campos and P. Kempchinsky (eds.) *Evolution and revolution in linguistic theory: studies in honor of C.P. Otero*, pp. 51–109.

1995. *The Minimalist Program*. Cambridge, MA: MIT Press.

2000. Minimalist inquiries: the framework. In H. Lasnik, R. Martin, D. Michaels and J. Uriagereka (eds.) *Step by step: essays on minimalist syntax in honor of Howard Lasnik*. Cambridge, MA: MIT Press, pp. 89–156.

2001. Derivation by phase. In M. Kenstowicz (ed.) *Ken Hale: a life in language*. Cambridge, MA: MIT Press, pp. 1–52.

2004. Beyond explanatory adequacy. In A. Belletti (ed.) *Structures and beyond*. New York: Oxford University Press, pp. 104–131.

2006. *On phases*. Ms., MIT.

Chomsky, N. and H. Lasnik. 1977. "Filters and control," *Linguistic inquiry* 8: 425–504.

1993. The theory of principles and parameters. In J. Jacobs, A. von Stechow, W. Sternefeld and T. Vennemann (eds.) *Syntax: an international handbook of contemporary research*. Berlin: Walter de Gruyter, pp. 506–569.

Cinque, G. 1990. *Types of A′-dependencies*. Cambridge, MA: MIT Press.

1999. *Adverbs and functional heads: a cross-linguistic perspective*. Oxford University Press.

(ed.) 2002. *Functional structure in DP and IP: the cartography of syntactic structures*, Volume 1. Oxford University Press.

Collins, C. 1997. *Local Economy*. Cambridge, MA: MIT Press.

2002. Eliminating labels. In S. Epstein and D. Seely (eds.) *Derivation and explanation in the Minimalist Program*. London: Blackwell, pp. 42–64.

Cornell, T. and J. Rogers. 2000. Model theoretic syntax. In L. L.-S. Cheng and R. Sybesma (eds.) *The Glot International state-of-the-article book*. Berlin: Walter de Gruyter, pp. 171–198.

Cover, T. M. and J. A. Thomas. 2006. *Elements of information theory*. 2nd edn. New York: Wiley Interscience.

Davies, W. D. 2000. "Events in Madurese reciprocals," *Oceanic linguistics* 39(1): 123–143.

Déchaine, R., T. Hoekstra and J. Rooryk. 1994. Augmented and non-augmented HAVE. In L. Nahs and G. Tsoulas (eds.) *Proceedings of langues et grammaire I*, Université Paris VIII, pp. 85–101.

de Hoop, H. 1992. *Case configuration and noun phrase interpretation*. Ph.D. Thesis, University of Groningen.

de la Clergerie, E. V. 2002. Parsing mildly context-sensitive languages with thread automata. In *COLING 2002: Proceedings of the 19th International Conference on Computational Linguistics*. San Francisco: Morgan Kaufmann, pp. 1–7.

den Dikken, M. 1997. "The syntax of possession and the verb 'have'," *Lingua* 101: 129–150.

Donati, C. 2003. Merge copy. In K. Schewave and S. Winkler (eds.) *Interfaces: Deriving and interpreting omitted structure*. Amsterdam: John Benjamins, pp. 155–175.

2006. "On wh-head movement." In L. Cheng and N. Corver (eds.) *Wh-movement: moving on*. Cambridge: MIT Press, pp. 21–46.

Dowty, D. R., R. E. Wall and S. Peters. 1981. *Introduction to Montague Semantics*. Dordrecht: Reidel.

Drury, J. 2005. *Alternative directions for minimalist inquiry: expanding and contracting phases of derivation*. Ph.D. Thesis, University of Maryland.

Emonds, J. E. 1976. *A transformational approach to English syntax*. New York: Academic Press.

1985. *A unified theory of syntactic categories*. Dordrecht: Foris.

Epstein, S. D. and T. D. Seely. 2006. *Derivations in minimalism*. Cambridge University Press.

Etxepare, R. 1997. *On the grammatical representation of speech events*. Ph.D. Thesis, University of Maryland.

Fauconnier, G. 1997. *Mappings in thought and language*. Cambridge University Press.

Fillmore, C. J. 1968. The case for case. In E. W. Bach and R. T. Harms (eds.) *Universals in linguistic theory*. New York: Holt, Rinehart and Winston, pp. 1–88.

Fodor, J. 1970. "Three reasons for not deriving 'kill' from 'cause to die'," *Linguistic inquiry* 1: 429–438.

1976. *The language of thought*. Hassocks, UK: Harvester Press.

1982. *The modularity of mind*. Cambridge, MA: MIT Press.

Fodor, J., T. G. Bever and M. Garrett. 1974. *The psychology of language*. New York: McGraw Hill.

Fodor, J. A. and E. Lepore. 1998. "The emptiness of the lexicon: reflections on James Pustejovsky's 'The Generative Lexicon'," *Linguistic inquiry* 29: 269–288.

Fox, D. 2000. *Economy and semantic interpretation.* Cambridge, MA: MIT Press.

Frampton, J. and S. Gutman. 2002. Crash-proof syntax. In S. D. Epstein and T. D. Seely (eds.) *Derivation and explanation in the Minimalist Program.* Oxford: Blackwell Publishing, pp. 90–105.

Freeze, R. 1992. "Existentials and other locatives," *Language* 68: 553–595.

Freidin, R. 1986. Fundamental issues in the theory of binding. In B. Lust (ed.) *Studies in the acquisition of anaphora.* Dordrecht: Reidel, pp. 151–188.

Fults, S. 2006. *The structure of comparison.* Ph.D. Thesis, University of Maryland.

Gallego, A. 2007. *Phase theory and parametric variation.* Ph.D. Thesis, Autonomous University of Barcelona.

Gallistel, C. R. 2008. *The nature of learning.* Blackwell/Maryland Lectures in Language and Cognition.

Gazdar, G., E. H. Klein, G. K. Pullum and I. A. Sag. 1985. *Generalized phrase structure grammar.* Cambridge, MA: Harvard University Press.

George, L. M. 1980. *Analogical Generalization in Natural Language Syntax.* Ph.D. Thesis, MIT.

Ghomeshi, J., R. Jackendoff, N. Rosen and K. Russell. 2004. "Contrastive focus reduplication in English (the salad-salad paper)," *Natural language and linguistic theory* 22: 307–357.

Gleitman, L. 1990. "The structural sources of verb meanings," *Language acquisition* 1: 3–55.

Gödel, K. 1931(1962). *On formally undecidable propositions of principia mathematica and related systems.* New York: Basic Books. (Translation of "Über formal unentscheidbare Sätze der Principia Mathematica und verwandter Systeme," *Monatshefte füer Mathematik und Physik* 38: 173–198.)

Goodall, G. 1984. *Parallel structures in syntax.* Ph.D. Thesis, University of California.

Grimshaw, J. 1991. *Argument structure.* Cambridge, MA: MIT Press.

Guimaraes, M. 2004. *Derivation and representation of syntactic amalgams.* Ph.D. Thesis, University of Maryland.

Hale, K. and S. J. Keyser. 1993. On argument structure and the lexical expression of syntactic relations. In K. Hale and S. J. Keyser (eds.) *The view from building 20: essays in linguistics in honor of Sylvain Bromberger.* Cambridge, MA: MIT Press, pp. 51–109.

Hale, K. and J. Keyser. 1997. On the complex nature of simple predicators. In A. Alsina, J. Bresnan and P. Sells (eds.) *Complex predicates,* Stanford, CA: CSLI Publications, pp. 29–65.

Hale, K. and S. J. Keyser. 2002. *Prolegomenon to a theory of argument structure.* Cambridge, MA: MIT Press.

Halle, M. and A. Marantz. 1993. Distributed morphology and the pieces of inflection. In K. Hale and S. J. Keyser (eds.) *The view from building 20: essays in linguistics in honor of Sylvain Bromberger.* Cambridge, MA: MIT Press, pp. 111–176.

Harris. R. A. 1993. *The linguistics wars.* Oxford University Press.

Hauser, M. D., N. Chomsky and W. T. Fitch. 2002. "The faculty of language: what is it, who has it, and how did it evolve?" *Science* 298: 1569–1579.

Henderson, B. 2006. Multiple agreement, concord and case checking in Bantu. In O. F. Arasanyin and M. A. Pemberton (eds.) *Selected proceedings of the 36th Annual Conference on African Linguistics.* Somerville, MA: Cascadilla Press, pp. 60–65.

Herburger, E. 2000. *What counts: focus and quantification.* Cambridge, MA: MIT Press.

Hickok, G. and D. Poeppel. 2000. "Towards a functional neuroanatomy of speech perception," *Trends in cognitive sciences* 4: 131–138.

Higginbotham, J. 1985. A note on phrase markers. *MIT Working Papers in Linguistics* 6: 87–101.

Higginbotham J. 1988. Contexts, models and meanings: a note on the data of semantics. In R. Kempson (ed.) *Mental representations: the interface between language and reality.* Cambridge University Press, pp. 29–48.

  2000a. On events in linguistic semantics. In J. Higginbotham, F. Pianesi and A. Varzi (eds.) *Speaking of events.* New York: Oxford University Press, pp. 49–79.

  2000b. Accomplishments. In *Proceedings of Glow in Asia II.* Nagoya, Japan: Nanzan University, pp. 72–82.

Higgins, R. 1979. *The pseudo-cleft construction in English.* Ph.D. Thesis, MIT.

Hinzen, W. 2003. "Truth's fabric," *Mind and language* 18: 194–219.

  2006. *Mind design and minimal syntax.* Oxford University Press.

  2007. *An essay on naming and truth.* Oxford University Press.

  In press. Hierarchy, merge and truth. In M. Piattelli-Palmarini *et al.* (in press).

Hinzen, W. and J. Uriagereka. 2006. "On the metaphysics of linguistics," In Hinzen, W. (ed.) *Prospects for dualism: interdisciplinary perspectives,* special issue of *Erkenntnis* 65: 71–96.

Hiraiwa, K. 2005. *Dimensions of symmetry in syntax: agreement and clausal architecture.* PhD. Thesis, MIT.

Hjelmslev, L. 1935. *La catégorie des cas: étude de grammaire générale I.* Copenhagen: Munksgaard.

  1937. *La catégorie des cas: étude de grammaire générale II.* Copenhagen: Munksgaard.

Hoffman, J. 1996. *Syntactic and paratactic word order.* Ph.D. Thesis, University of Maryland.

Horn, L. 1989. *A natural history of negation.* Chicago University Press.

Hornstein, N. 1995. *Logical form: from GB to Minimalism.* Oxford: Blackwell.

  1999. "Movement and control," *Linguistic inquiry* 30: 69–96.

  2001. *Move! A minimalist theory of construal.* Oxford: Blackwell.

Hornstein, N., H. Lasnik and J. Uriagereka. 2007. "Islands and linearization," Proposal for NSF grant BCS-0722648. University of Maryland.

Hornstein, N., J. Nunes and K. Grohmann. 2005. *Understanding minimalism.* Cambridge University Press.

Hornstein, N., J. Nunes and P. Pietroski. In press. "Some thoughts on adjunction," *Biolinguistics* 1(1).

Hornstein, N., S. Rosen and J. Uriagereka. 1994. "Integrals," *University of Maryland working papers in linguistics* 2: 70–90.

1996. Integral predication. In J. Camacho, L. Choueiri and M. Watanabe (eds.) *Proceedings of WCCFL 14*, Stanford: CSLI, pp. 169–184.

Hornstein, N. and J. Uriagereka. 1999. "Labels and projections: a note on the syntax of quantifiers," *University of Maryland working papers in linguistics* 8: 249–270.

2002. Reprojections. In S. Epstein and D. Seely (eds.) *Derivation and explanation in the Minimalist Program*. London: Blackwell, pp. 107–132.

Hornstein, N. and A. Weinberg. 1981. "Case theory and preposition stranding," *Linguistic inquiry* 12: 55–91.

Huang, C.-T.J. 1982. *Logical relations in Chinese and the theory of grammar*. PhD. Thesis, MIT.

1984. "On the distribution and reference of empty pronouns," *Linguistic inquiry* 15: 531–574.

Huck, G.J. and J.A. Goldsmith. 1995. *Ideology and linguistic theory: Noam Chomsky and the deep structure debates*. London: Routledge.

Jackendoff, R. 1972. *Semantic interpretation in generative grammar*. Cambridge, MA: MIT Press.

1990. *Semantic Structures*. Cambridge, MA: MIT Press.

1977. *X-bar syntax: a study of phrase structure*. Cambridge, MA: MIT Press.

1997. *The architecture of the language faculty*. Cambridge, MA: MIT Press.

2002. *Foundations of language: brain, meaning, grammar, evolution*. New York: Oxford University Press.

Jakobson, R. 1941(1968). *Child language, aphasia, and phonological universals*. The Hague: Mouton. (Translation of R. Jakobson (1941) *Kindersprache, aphasie und allgemeine Lautgesetze*. Uppsala: Almqvist & Wilsells.)

Jeong, Y. 2006. *The landscape of applications*. Ph.D. Thesis, University of Maryland.

Joshi, A.K. 1985. How much context-sensitivity is necessary for characterizing structural descriptions? Tree adjoining grammars. In D. Dowty, L. Karttunen and A. Zwicky (eds.) *Natural language processing: theoretical, computational and psychological perspective*. Cambridge University Press, pp. 206–250.

Kahnemuyipour, A. 2004. *The syntax of sentential stress*. Ph.D. Thesis, University of Toronto.

Kaplan, R. and J. Bresnan. 1982. Lexical functional grammar: a formal system for grammatical representation. In J. Bresnan (ed.) *The mental representation of grammatical relations*. Cambridge, MA: MIT Press, pp. 173–281.

Kayne, R.S. 1984. *Connectedness and binary branching*. Dordrecht: Foris.

1987. Facets of romance past participle agreement. In P. Benincà (ed.) *Dialect variation and the theory of grammar*. Dordrecht: Foris, pp. 55–84.

1991. "Romance clitics, verb movement and PRO," *Linguistic inquiry* 22: 647–686.

1994. *The antisymmetry of syntax*. Cambridge, MA: MIT Press.

1999. "Prepositional complementizers as attractors," *Probus* 11: 39–73.

Keenan, E.L. 1987. A semantic definition of "Indefinite NP". In E.J. Reuland and A.G.B. ter Meulen (eds.) *The representation of (in)definiteness*. Cambridge, MA: MIT Press, pp. 286–317.

Kinsey, C. 1993. *Topology of surfaces*. Berlin: Springer Verlag.

Kobele, G. 2006. *Generating copies: an investigation into structural identity in language and grammar*. Ph.D. Thesis, UCLA.

Kratzer, A. In press. *The event argument and the semantics of voice*. Cambridge, MA: MIT Press.

Kuroda, S-Y. 1972. "The categorical and the thetic judgment: evidence from Japanese syntax," *Foundations of language* 9: 153–185.

Laka, I. 2006. Deriving split ergativity in the progressive: the case of Basque. In A. Johns, D. Massam and J. Ndayiragije (eds.) *Ergativity: emerging issues*. Dordrecht: Springer, pp. 173–196.

Lakoff, G. 1971. On generative semantics. In D. Steinberg and L. Jakobovits (eds.) *Semantics: an interdisciplinary reader*. Cambridge University Press, pp. 232–296.

Lakoff, G. 1974. Syntactic amalgams. In R. F. M. LaGaly and A. Bruck (eds.) *Papers from the 10th Annual Regional Meeting of the Chicago Linguistic Society*. Chicago Linguistic Society, pp. 421–434.

    1986. Frame semantic control of the coordinate structure constraint. In A. Farley, P. Farley and K.-E. McCullough (eds.) *Papers from the 22nd Annual Regional Meeting of the Chicago Linguistic Society*. Chicago Linguistic Society, pp. 152–167.

Lakoff, G. and M. Johnson. 1980. *Metaphors we live by*. University of Chicago Press.

Lakoff, G. and J. Ross. 1976. Is deep structure necessary? In J. McCawley (ed.) *Notes from the linguistic underground*. Syntax and Semantics 7. New York: Academic Press, pp. 159–164.

Lambova, M. 2003. *On information structure and clausal architecture: evidence from Bulgarian*. Ph.D. Thesis, University of Connecticut.

Langacker, R. W. 1987. *Foundations of cognitive grammar: theoretical perspectives*, Volume 1. Stanford University Press.

    1997. "Constituency, dependency, and conceptual grouping," *Cognitive Linguistics* 8: 1–32.

Langendoen, D. T. and P. M. Postal. 1984. *The vastness of natural languages*. Oxford: Blackwell.

Lappin, S., R. D. Levine and D. E. Johnson. 2000. "Topic . . . comment," *Natural language and linguistic theory* 18: 665–671.

Larson, R. 1988. "On the double object construction," *Linguistic inquiry* 19: 335–391.

Larson, R. and G. Segal. 1995. *Knowledge of meaning*. Cambridge, MA: MIT Press.

Lasnik, H. 1972. *Analyses of negation in English*. Ph.D. Thesis, MIT.

    1981. Restricting the theory of transformations: a case study. In N. Hornstein and D. Lightfoot (eds.) *Explanations in Linguistics*. London: Longman, pp. 152–173.

    1990. *Essays on restrictiveness and learnability*. Dordrecht: Kluwer.

    2000. *Syntactic structures revisited*. Cambridge, MA: MIT Press.

    2001. *Minimalist analysis*. Oxford: Blackwell.

    2003. *Minimalist investigations in linguistic theory*. London: Routledge.

Lasnik, H. and R. Freidin. 1981. Core grammar, case theory, and markedness. In A. Belletti, L. Brandi and L. Rizzi (eds.) *Theory of markedness in generative grammar*. Pisa: Scuola Normale Superiore, pp. 407–421.

Lasnik, H. and J. Kupin. 1977. "A restrictive theory of transformational grammar," *Theoretical Linguistics* 4(3): 73–196.

Lasnik, H. and J. Uriagereka with C. Boeckx. 2005. *A course in minimalist syntax.* Oxford: Blackwell.

Lebeaux, D. 1988. *Language acquisition and the form of grammar.* Ph.D. Thesis, University of Massachusetts.

Lee, J. 2000. *Introduction to topological manifolds.* Berlin: Springer Verlag.

Legate, J. 2006. *Morphological and abstract case.* Ms., University of Delaware.

Lewis, D. 1991. *Parts of classes.* Oxford: Blackwell.

Lidz, J. 1999. The morphosemantics of object case in Kannada. In S. Bird, A. Carnie, J. D. Haugen and P. Norquest (eds.) *Proceedings of the 18th West Coast Conference on Formal Linguistics.* Somerville, MA: Cascadilla Press, pp. 325–336.

McCawley, J. D. 1968. The role of semantics in a grammar. In E. Bach and R. T. Harms (eds.) *Universals in linguistic theory.* New York: Holt, Rinehart and Winston, pp. 125–170.

McClure, W. 1995. *Syntactic projection of the semantics of aspect.* Tokyo: Hitsuzi-Syoboo.

Manzini, R. and K. Wexler. 1987. "Parameters, binding and learning theory," *Linguistic inquiry* 18: 413–444.

Marantz, A. 2005. "Generative linguistics within the cognitive neuroscience of language," *The linguistic review* 22: 429–445.

Martin, R. 1996. *A minimalist theory of PRO and control.* Ph.D. Thesis, University of Connecticut.

1999. Case, the Extended Projection Principle, and minimalism. In S. Epstein and N. Hornstein (eds.) *Working minimalism.* Cambridge, MA: MIT Press, pp. 1–25.

Mendelson, E. 1997. *Introduction to mathematical logic.* New York: CRC Press.

Milsark, G. 1974. *Existential sentences in English.* Ph.D. Thesis, MIT.

1977. "Towards an explanation of certain peculiarities of the existential construction in English," *Linguistic Analysis* 3(1): 1–29.

Moravcsik, E. 1978. Reduplicative constructions. In J. Greenberg (ed.) *Universals of human language.* Stanford University Press, pp. 297–334.

Moravcsik, J. 1995. What makes reality intelligible? Reflections on Aristotle's Theory of Aitia. In L. Judson (ed.) *Aristotle's physics: a collection of essays.* Oxford Unversity Press, pp. 31–48.

Mori, N. 2005. *A syntactic structure of lexical verbs.* Ph.D. Thesis, University of Maryland.

Moro, A. 2000. *Dynamic antisymmetry.* Cambridge, MA: MIT Press.

Motomura, M. 2004. *Thematically driven movement in Japanese: a study of psych verb constructions.* Ph.D. Thesis, University of Maryland.

Mourelatos, A. P. D. 1978. "Events, processes, and states," *Linguistics and philosophy* 2: 415–434.

Murguia, E. 2004. *Syntactic identity and locality restrictions on verbal ellipsis.* Ph.D. Thesis, University of Maryland.

Muromatsu, K. 1998. *On the syntax of classifiers*. Ph.D. Thesis, University of Maryland.

Neale, S. 1990. *Descriptions*. Cambridge, MA: MIT Press.

Newmeyer, F. J. 1980. *Linguistic theory in America*. New York: Academic Press.

1996. *Generative linguistics: a historical perspective*. London: Routledge.

Newmeyer, F. 2002. "Optimality and functionality: a critique of functionally-based optimality-theoretic syntax," *Natural language and linguistic theory* 20: 43–80.

Nowak, M. A., N. L. Komarova and P. Niyogi. 2001. "Evolution of universal grammar," *Science* 291: 114–118.

Nunes, J. 2004. *Linearization of chains and sideward movement*. Cambridge, MA: MIT Press.

Ormazabal, J. 2000. A conspiracy theory of case and agreement. In R. Martin, D. Michaels and J. Uriagereka (eds.) *Step by step: essays on minimalist syntax in honor of Howard Lasnik*. Cambridge, MA: MIT Press, pp. 235–260.

Ortega-Santos, I. 2006. On postverbal subjects, PF and the copy theory: the Spanish case. In N. Sagarra and A. J. Toribio (eds.) *Selected proceedings of the 9th Hispanic Linguistics Symposium*. Somerville, MA: Cascadilla Press, pp. 56–66.

Ortiz de Urbina, J. and J. I. Hualde. 1987. "Restructuring with ARI," *Anuario del Seminario Julio de Urquijo* 21(2): 425–452.

Pablos, L., C. Phillips and J. Uriagereka. 2005. "Active search for clitic pronouns in Galician long-distance dependencies." Paper presented to the 11th Annual Conference on Architectures and Mechanisms for Language Processing, Ghent University.

Parsons, T. 1990. *Events in the semantics of English*. Cambridge, MA: MIT Press.

Pereira, F. 2000. "Formal grammar and information theory: together again?" *Philosophical transactions of the Royal Society* 358: 1239–1253.

Perlmutter, D. M. 1983. *Studies in relational grammar I*. University of Chicago Press.

Pesetsky, D. and E. Torrego. 2004. Tense, case, and the nature of syntactic categories. In J. Gueron and J. Lecarme (eds.) *The syntax of time*. Cambridge, MA: MIT Press, pp. 495–539.

Peters, P. S. and R. W. Ritchie. 1973. "Context-sensitive immediate constituent analysis: context-free languages revisited," *Mathematical systems theory* 6: 324–333.

Phillips, C. 2006. "The real-time status of island phenomena," *Language* 82: 795–823.

Phillips, C. and M. Wagers. 2007. Relating structure and time in linguistics and psycholinguistics. In M. G. Gaskell (ed.) *Oxford Handbook of Psycholinguistics*. Oxford University Press, pp. 739–756.

Phillips, C., N. Kazanina, and S. Abada. 2005. "ERP effects of the processing of syntactic long-distance dependencies," *Cognitive brain research* 22: 407–428.

Pi, T. 1995. The syntax of English iteratives. In P. Koskinen (ed.) *Proceedings of the 1995 Annual Conference of the Canadian Linguistic Association*. University of Toronto Working Papers in Linguistics.

Piattelli-Palmarini, M. 1989. "Evolution, selection and cognition: from 'learning' to parameter setting in biology and in the study of language," *Cognition* 31: 1–44.

Piattelli-Palmarini, M. and J. Uriagereka. 2004. The immune syntax: the evolution of the language virus. In L. Jenkins (ed.) *Variation and universals in biolinguistics.* Oxford: Elsevier, pp. 341–377.

    2005. "The evolution of the narrow faculty of language: the skeptical view and a reasonable conjecture," *Lingue e linguaggio* 4(1): 27–79.

    In press. The case of FOXP2 revisited. In A-M. Di Sciullo and C. Boeckx (eds.) *Studies in the evolution of language.* Oxford University Press.

Piattelli-Palmarini, M., P. Salaburu and J. Uriagereka (eds.) In press. *Of minds and language.* Oxford University Press.

Pietroski, P. 2000. *Causing actions.* Oxford University Press.

    2003. The character of natural language semantics. In A. Barber (ed.) *Epistemology of language.* Oxford University Press, pp. 217–256.

    2005. *Events and semantic architecture.* Oxford University Press.

Pietroski, P. and J. Uriagereka. 2001. "Dimensions of natural language," *University of Maryland Working Papers in Linguistics* 11: 112–219.

Pinker, S. 1994. *The language instinct.* New York: W. Morrow.

Plann, S. 1986. "On case-marking clauses in Spanish: evidence against the Case Resistance Principle," *Linguistic inquiry* 17: 336–345.

Poeppel, D., J. Idsardi and V. van Wassenhove. In press. "Speech perception at the interface of neurobiology and linguistics," *Philosophical Transactions of the Royal Society B (Biological Sciences).*

Postal, P. M. 1972. "On some rules that are not successive cyclic," *Linguistic inquiry* 3: 211–222.

Prasada, S. 2003. "Conceptual representation of animacy and its perceptual and linguistic reflections," *Developmental science* 6: 18–19.

    2005. Being near the ceramic, but not the mug: on the role of construal in spatial language. In L. A. Carlson and E. van der Zee (eds.) *Functional features in language and space: insights from perception, categorization and development.* Oxford University Press, pp. 205–234.

Pullum, G. and J. Rogers. 2007. *Animal pattern-learning experiments: some mathematical background.* Ms., Radcliffe Institute for Advanced Study, Harvard University.

Pustejovsky, J. 1995. *The generative lexicon.* Cambridge, MA: MIT Press.

Putnam, H. 1970. Is semantics possible? In H. E. Kiefer and M. K. Munitz (eds.) *Language, belief, and metaphysics.* New York: State University of New York Press, pp. 50–63.

Quine, W. V. O. 1960. *Word and object.* Cambridge, MA: MIT Press.

Raimy, E. 1999. *Representing reduplication.* Ph.D. Thesis, University of Delaware.

Raimy, E. and W. Idsardi. 1997. A minimalist approach to reduplication in Optimality Theory. In K. Kusomoto (ed.) *Proceedings of NELS 27.* Amherst, MA: Graduate Linguistic Student Association, University of Massachusetts, pp. 369–382.

Raposo, E. 1987. "Case theory and infl-to-comp: the inflected infinitive in European Portuguese," *Linguistic inquiry* 18: 85–109.

    2000. Clitic positions and verb movement. In J. Costa (ed.) *Portuguese syntax: new comparative studies.* Oxford University Press, pp. 266–297.

Raposo, E. and J. Uriagereka. 1990. Long-distance Case assignment. *Linguistic inquiry* 21: 505–538.

2005. Clitic placement in Western Iberian: a minimalist view. In C. Cinque and R. Kayne (eds.) *Handbook of comparative syntax*. Oxford University Press, pp. 639–697.

Regier, T. 1998. Reduplication and the arbitrariness of the sign. In M. Gernsbacher and S. Derry (eds.) *Proceedings of the 20th Annual Conference of the Cognitive Science Society*. Mahwah, NJ: Lawrence Erlbaum Associates, pp. 887–892.

Richards, M. 2004. *Object shift and scrambling in North and West Germanic: a case study in symmetrical syntax*. Ph.D. Thesis, University of Cambridge.

Rivero, M. L. and D. Geber. 2003. "Quirky subjects and person restrictions in Romance: Rumanian and Spanish," *Cahiers Linguistiques d'Ottawa* 31: 20–53.

2004. *Raising in Romanian: move and agree*. Paper presented to the Linguistic Symposium on Romance Languages (LSRL) 34, Salt Lake City, UT.

Rizzi, L. 1982. *Issues in Italian syntax*. Dordrecht: Foris.

Rizzi, L. 1997. The fine structure of the left periphery. In L. Haegeman (ed.) *Elements of grammar: handbook in generative syntax*. Dordrecht: Kluwer, pp. 281–337.

(ed.) 2004. *The structure of CP and IP: the cartography of syntactic structures*, Volume 2. New York: Oxford University Press.

Rogers, J. 1999. *A descriptive approach to language-theoretic complexity*. Cambridge University Press.

Rosenbloom, P. 1950. *Introduction to logic*. New York: Dover.

Ross, J. R. 1968. *Constraints on variables in syntax*. Ph.D. Thesis, MIT.

Saddy, J. D. and beim Graben, P. 2002. Measuring the neural dynamics of language comprehension processes. In E. Witruk, A. D. Friederici and T. Lachmann (eds.) *Basic functions of language, reading and reading disorder*. Boston: Kluwer Academic Press, pp. 41–60.

Saddy, D. and J. Uriagereka. 2004. "Language and complexity: a tutorial," *International journal of bifurcation and chaos* 14(2): 383–404.

Safir, K. 1985. *Syntactic chains*. Cambridge University Press.

San Martin, I. 2004. *On subordination and the distribution of PRO*. PhD. Thesis, University of Maryland.

Schmitt, C. 1996. *Aspect and the syntax of noun phrases*. Ph.D. Thesis, University of Maryland.

Searls, D. B. 2002. "The language of genes," *Nature* 420: 211–217.

Seuren, P. A. M. 2004. *Chomsky's minimalism*. Oxford University Press.

Snyder, W. 1995. *Language acquisition and language variation: the role of morphology*. Ph.D. Thesis, MIT.

Soltan, U. 2007. *On mechanisms of formal features licensing in a minimalist syntax: investigations in the morphosyntax of Arabic dialects*. Ph.D. Thesis, University of Maryland.

Sportiche, D. 1988. A theory of floating quantifiers and its corollaries for constituent structure. *Linguistic inquiry* 19: 425–450.

Stabler, E. 2003. *Notes on computational linguistics*. Ms., UCLA. Available at www.linguistics.ucla.edu (accessed November 2007).

Steedman, M. 2007. On "the computation". In G. Ramchand and C. Reiss (eds.) *Oxford handbook of linguistic interfaces*. Oxford University Press, pp. 575–611.

Stepanov, A. 2007. "The end of CED? Minimalism and extraction domains," *Syntax* 10: 80–126.

Stowell, T. 1981. *Origins of phrase structure*. PhD. Thesis, MIT.

1983. "Subjects across categories," *The linguistic review* 2: 285–312.

Szabolcsi, A. 1983. "The possessor that ran away from home," *The linguistic review* 3: 89–102.

Talmy, L. 1978. Figure and ground in complex sentences. In J. Greenberg (ed.) *Universals of human language*. Stanford University Press, pp. 625–649.

Tenny, C. 1994. *Aspectual roles and the syntax–semantics interface*. Dordrecht: Kluwer.

Ticio, M. E. 2003. *On the structure of DPs*. Ph.D. Thesis, University of Connecticut.

Tomalin, M. (ed.) 2006. *Linguistics and the formal sciences*. Cambridge University Press.

Torrego, E. 1998. *The dependencies of objects*. Cambridge, MA: MIT Press.

Torrego, E. and J. Uriagereka. 2002. Parataxis. In J. Uriagereka (ed.) *Derivations: exploring the dynamics of syntax*. London: Routledge, pp. 253–265.

Travis, L. 2001. The syntax of reduplication. In M. Kim and U. Strauss (eds.) *Proceedings of NELS 31*. Amherst, MA: Graduate Linguistic Student Association, University of Massachusetts, pp. 455–469.

Trubetzkoy, N. S. 1969. *Principles of phonology*. Berkeley and Los Angeles: University of California Press.

Ullman, M. and E. Pierpont. 2005. "Specific language impairment is not specific to language," *Cortex* 41: 399–433.

Ura, H. 1994. Varieties of raising and the feature-based Bare Phrase Structure theory. *MIT occasional papers in linguistics* 7.

Uriagereka, J. 1988. *On government*. Ph.D. Thesis, University of Connecticut.

1992. An F position in Western Romance. In K.É. Kiss (ed.) *Discourse configurational languages*. Oxford University Press, pp. 153–175.

1995. Aspects of the syntax of clitic placement in Western Romance. *Linguistic inquiry* 26: 79–123.

1996. "Warps," *University of Maryland working papers in linguistics* 3: 256–308.

1997. Formal and substantive elegance in the Minimalist Program. In C. Wilder, H.-M. Gärtner and M. Bierwisch (eds.) *The role of economy principles in linguistic theory*. Berlin: Akademie Verlag, pp. 170–204.

1998. *Rhyme and reason*. Cambridge, MA: MIT Press.

1999. Multiple spell-out. In S. D. Epstein and N. Hornstein (eds.) *Working minimalism*. Cambridge, MA: MIT Press, pp. 251–282.

2001. Doubling and possession. In B. Gerlach and J. Grijzenhout (eds.) *Clitics in phonology, morphology and syntax*. Amsterdam: John Benjamins, pp. 401–431.

2002. *Derivations: exploring the dynamics of syntax*. London: Routledge.

2003. Evidentiality contexts. In J. Gueron and L. Tasmowsky (eds.) *Time and point of view*. Université Paris X.

2005. On the syntax of doubling. In L. Heggie and F. Ordonez (eds.) *Clitic and affix combinations (theoretical perspectives)*. Amsterdam: John Benjamins, pp. 343–374.

2006. Complete and partial Infl. In C. Boeckx (ed.) *Agreement systems*. Amsterdam: John Benjamins, pp. 267–298.

2007. "Clarifying the notion parameter," *Biolinguistics* 1: 99–113.

In press. Uninterpretable features in syntactic evolution. In M. Piattelli-Palamarini, P. Salaburu and J. Uriagereka (eds.) *Of minds and language*. Oxford University Press.

van Heijenoort, J. (ed.) 1967. *From Frege to Goedel: a sourcebook in mathematical logic, 1879–1931*. Cambridge, MA: Harvard University Press.

Vendler, Z. 1967. Verbs and times. In Z. Vendler *Linguistics in Philosophy*. Ithaca, NY: Cornell University Press, pp. 97–121.

Verkuyl, H. J. 1972. *On the compositional nature of the aspects*. Dordrecht: Reidel.

Watanabe, A. 1993. *Agr-based case theory and its interaction with the A-bar system*. Ph.D. Thesis, MIT.

Weir, D. 1988. *Characterizing mildly context-sensitive grammar formalisms*. Ph.D. Thesis, University of Pennsylvania.

Willard, S. 1970. *General topology*. London: Addison-Wesley.

Williams, E. 1994. *Thematic structure in syntax*. Cambridge, MA: MIT Press.

Xu, J. 1993. *An I-parameter and its consequences*. PhD. Thesis, University of Maryland.

Zhang, N. 2002. *Counting and classifying eventualities in Chinese*. Ms., ZAS, Berlin. Available at www.usc.edu (accessed November 2007).

Zubizarreta, M. L. 1998. *Prosody, focus, and word order*. Cambridge, MA: MIT Press.

Index